A HISTORY OF CIVILISATION IN ANCIENT INDIA

A HISTORY OF CIVILISATION IN ANCIENT INDIA

BASED ON SANSKRIT LITERATURE

By
ROMESH CHANDER DUTT

SET IN TWO VOLUMES
VOLUME 1 -B.C. 2000 to 320

COSMO PUBLICATIONS
New Delhi

A History of Civilisation in Ancient India

This COSMO Print 2025

ISBN: 81-7020-964-1 (Set)
81-7020-965-x (Volume 1)

Published by
MRS. RANI KAPOOR
for COSMO PUBLICATIONS Div. of
GENESIS PUBLISHING PVT. LTD.
24-B, Ansari Road, Darya Ganj,
New Delhi-110 002, INDIA
Ph.: 4365 6579, 4678 3359
Fax : 2324 1200

TO

MY GENTLE AND LOVING DAUGHTERS,

KAMALĀ AND BIMALĀ,

WHO HAVE CHEERED MY LABOURS AND BLESSED MY LIFE

WITH THEIR AFFECTION,

I DEDICATE THIS WORK

WITH A FATHER'S LOVE.

PREFACE.

"If I were asked," says Professor Max Müller, "what I consider the most important discovery which has been made during the Nineteenth Century with respect to the ancient history of mankind, I should answer by the following short line:—

"Sanscrit, Dyaush Pitar = Greek, *ΖΕΥΣΠΑΤΗΡ* (Zeus Pater) = Latin, Jupiter = Old Norse, Tyr."

And certainly, the discoveries which have been made by European scholars within the last hundred years, with the help of the old Aryan language preserved in India, form one of the most brilliant chapters in the history of the advancement of human knowledge. It is not my intention to give a sketch of that history here; but a few facts which relate specially to Indian Antiquities may be considered interesting.

It is about a century since Sir William Jones startled the scholars of Europe by his translation of Sakuntalâ, "one of the greatest curiosities," as he said in his preface, "that the literature of Asia has yet brought to light," and one of the tenderest and most beautiful creations of human imagination produced in any age or country. The attention of European literary men was roused to the value and beauty of Sanscrit literature; and the greatest literary genius of the modern age has recorded his appreciation of the Hindu dramatic piece in lines which have been often quoted, in original and in translation :—

> "Wouldst thou the life's young blossoms and the fruits of its decline,
> And all by which the soul is pleased, enraptured, feasted, fed,—
> Wouldst thou the earth and heaven itself in one sweet name combine?
> I name thee, O Sakuntalâ, and all at once is said."—GŎETHE.

Sir William Jones translated Manu, founded the Asiatic Society of Bengal, and lived to continue his researches into the store-house of Sanscrit literature, and achieved valuable results; but he did not live to find what he sought,—a clue to India's "ancient history without any mixture of fable." For his enthusiastic labours were mostly confined to the later Sanscrit literature,—the literature of the Post-Buddhist Era; and he paid little heed to the mine of wealth that lay beyond.

Colebrooke followed in the footsteps of Sir William Jones. He was a mathematician, and was the most careful and accurate Sanscrit scholar that England has ever produced. Ancient Sanscrit literature concealed nothing from his eyes. He gave a careful and accurate account of Hindu Philosophy, wrote on Hindu Algebra and Mathematics, and, in 1805, he first made Europeans acquainted with the oldest work of the Hindu and of the Aryan world, viz., the Vedas. Colebrooke, however, failed to grasp the importance of the discovery he had made, and declared that the study of the Vedas "would hardly reward the labour of the reader, much less that of the translator."

Dr. H. H. Wilson followed in the footsteps of Colebrooke; and although he translated the Rig Veda Sanhitâ into English, his labours were mostly confined to later

Sanscrit literature. He translated into elegant English the best dramatic works in Sanscrit, as well as the beautiful poem of Kâlidâsa, called "Meghadûta." He also translated the Vishnu Purâna, and laboured to adjust the history of the later Hindu period, and settled many points on a satisfactory basis.

In the meantime, a great genius had arisen in France. The history of Oriental scholarship contains no brighter name than that of Burnouf. He traced the connection between the Zend and the Vedic Sanscrit, and framed a Comparative Grammar for his own use before German scholars had written on Comparative Grammar. By such means he deciphered the Zend language and scriptures, elucidated the Rig Veda, and showed its true position in the history of Aryan nations. Versatile as he was profound, he also deciphered the Cuneiform inscriptions of Assyria, and thus earned for himself an undying fame in Europe. And further, in his Introduction to Buddhism, he gave the first philosophical and intelligible account of that great religion. His lessons created a deep sensation in Europe during nearly a quarter of a century (1829–1852), and left a lasting impression on the minds of admiring and enthusiastic pupils in Paris, some of whom, like Roth and Max Müller, have lived to be the profoundest Vedic scholars of our age.

German scholars, in the meantime, had commenced their labours; and when once they began work in this line, they soon excelled and even ousted all other labourers in the field of Indian Antiquities! Rosen, the contemporary and friend of Raja Ram Mohan Roy, published the first Ashtaka of the Rig Veda, with a Latin translation, but his untimely death prevented the further progress of the work.

But the most eminent German scholars of the day set before themselves a higher task; and the industry, perseverance, and genius of men like Bopp, Grimm, and Humboldt, soon achieved a result which ranks as one of the noblest and most brilliant discoveries of the century. They marked and traced the connection among all the Indo-European languages,—the Sanscrit, the Zend, the Greek, the Latin, the Slav, the Tuton, and the Celtic,—they demonstrated all these languages to be the offshoots of the same original stock, and they even discovered the laws under which words were transformed in passing from one language to another. Classical scholars of the day, who believed that all civilisation and culture began with the Greek and the Latin, at first smiled and ridiculed, then stood aghast, and ultimately gave way with considerable chagrin and anger to the irresistible march of Truth!

The desire to elucidate ancient Hindu literature and history deepened among scholars as they became more thoroughly alive to the value of Sanscrit. Roth, one of the profoundest Vedic scholars of the century, produced his edition of Yâska with his most valuable notes, and later on he published, with Whitney, an edition of the Atharva Veda, and completed, with Böehtlingk, the most accurate and comprehensive Sanscrit Dictionary yet written. Lassen published his profound work, Indische Alterthumskunde, displaying a deep learning and accurate scholarship which has seldom been excelled. Weber published the White Yajur Veda with its Brâhmana and Sûtras, elucidated many obscure points of Ancient Hindu History in his Indische Studien, and gave the first clear and comprehensive account of Sanscrit literature in his History of Indian Literature. Benfey published a most valuable edition of the Sâma Veda, of which an edition, with translation, had been published by Stevenson and Wilson before. And Muir collected the most suggestive and historically-valuable texts from Sanscrit literature, in five volumes, which are a monument of his industry and learning.

And lastly, Professor Max Müller mapped out the whole of the ancient Sanscrit literature chronologically in 1859.

More valuable to Hindus than this great work—more valuable than the learned Professor's numerous works and contributions on Language, Religion, and Mythology, is his magnificent edition of the Rig Veda Sanhitâ, with Sâyana's Commentary. The work was hailed in India with gratitude and joy; it opened to Hindu students generally the great and ancient volume, which had hitherto remained sealed with seven seals to all but a very few scholars; and it awakened in them a historical interest in the past,—a desire to inquire into their ancient history and ancient faith from original sources.

Jones and Colebrooke and Wilson had worthy successors in India, but none more distinguished than James Prinsep. The inscriptions of Asoka on pillars and rocks all over India had remained unintelligible for over a thousand years, and had defied the skill of Sir William Jones and his successors. James Prinsep, then Secretary to the Asiatic Society, deciphered these inscriptions, and a flood of light was thus thrown on Buddhist antiquities and post-Buddhist history. Prinsep was also the first to deal in a scholar-like way with the coins of the post-Buddhist kings found all over Western India. He has been followed by able scholars. Dr. Haug edited and translated the Aitareya Brâhmana, and elucidated the history of the Parsis; Dr. Burnell wrote on South Indian Paleography; Dr. Bühler has ably dealt with the ancient legal literature; and Dr. Thibaut has, in late years, discovered Ancient Hindu Geometry.

Among my countrymen, the great reformers, Raja Ram Mohan Roy and Dayanand Sarasvatî, turned their attention to ancient Sanscrit literature. The first translated a number of Upanishads into English, and the latter published a translation of the Rig Veda Sanhitá in Hindi. Sir Raja Radha Kanta Dev cultivated Sanscrit learning, and published a comprehensive and excellent dictionary entitled the Sabdakalpadruma. Dr. Bhao Daji and Professor Bhandarkar, Dr. K. M. Banerjea and Dr. Rajendra Lala Mitra have, by their varied and valuable contributions, taken their fair share of work in the field of antiquities. My esteemed friend, Pandit Satyavrata Sâmasramin has published an excellent edition of the Sâma Veda with Sâyana's Commentary, and an edition of the White Yajur Veda with Mahîdhara's Commentary, and is now engaged in a learned edition of Yâska's Nirukta. And lastly, my learned friend, Mr. Anand Ram Borooah,* of the Bengal Civil Service, has published a handy and excellent English-Sanscrit Dictionary, and is now engaged in a Sanscrit Grammar of formidable size and erudition!

General Cunningham's labours in archæology and in the elucidation of ancient Indian Geography are invaluable; and Burgess and Fergusson have treated on Indian

* Since the above lines were written, the author has received the sad intelligence of the death of the talented scholar. His untimely death is a loss to Sanscrit scholarship in this country, which will not be easily remedied. To the present writer, the sorrow is of a personal nature, as he enjoyed the friendship of the deceased for twenty years and more,—since the old College days in this country and in England.

Architecture. Fergusson's work on the subject is accepted as the standard work.

In Europe, Dr. Fausböll may be said to be the founder of Pâli scholarship, and edited the Dhammapada so far back as 1855, and has since edited the Jâtaka Tales. Dr. Oldenberg has edited the Vinaya texts; and these scholars, as well as Rhys Davids and Max Müller, have now given us an English translation of the most important portions of the Buddhist Scriptures in the invaluable series of Sacred Books of the East.

I wish to say a word about this series, because I am in a special degree indebted to it. Professor Max Müller, who has, by his life-long labours, done more than any living scholar to elucidate ancient Hindu literature and history, has now conceived the noble idea of enabling English readers to go to the fountain-source, and consult Oriental works in a series of faithful translations. More than thirty volumes, translated from the Sanscrit, Chinese, Zend, Pahlavi, Pâli, Arabic, &c., have already been published, and more volumes are expected. I take this opportunity to own my great indebtedness to the volumes of this series which relate to Indian History. I have freely quoted from them,—allowing myself the liberty of a verbal alteration here and there; and I have seldom thought it necessary to consult those original Sanscrit works which have been translated in this faithful and valuable series.

And this brings me to the subject of the present work, about which I wish to say a few words. I have often asked myself: Is it possible, with the help that is now available, to write, in a handy work, a clear, historical account of the civilisation of Ancient India, based on ancient Sanscrit literature, and written in a sufficiently popular manner to be acceptable to the general reader? I never doubted the possibility of such a work; but I have often wished—even when engaged in this task—that it had been undertaken by an abler scholar, and by one who could devote his attention and time more exclusively to it than I could possibly do.

Scholars who have devoted their lifetime to the study of Indian Antiquities, and who have brought out rich ores from that inexhaustible mine, seem however to have little time or little inclination to coin the metal for the every-day use of the general public. That unambitious task must, therefore, devolve on humbler labourers.

That there is need for such a popular work will not be denied. The Hindu student's knowledge of Indian History practically begins with the date of the Mahommedan Conquest,—the Hindu period is almost a blank to him. The school-boy who knows all about the twelve invasions of Mahmud, knows little of the first invasions and wars of the Aryans, who conquered and settled in the Punjab three thousand years before the Sultan of Ghazni. He has read of Shahab-ud-din Muhammad Ghori's conquest of Delhi and Kanouj, but has scarcely any historical knowledge of the ancient kingdoms of the Kurus and the Panchâlas in the same tract of country. He knows what emperor reigned in Delhi when Sivaji lived and fought, but scarcely knows of the king who ruled in Magadha when Gautama Buddha lived and preached. He is familiar with the history of Ahmadnagar, Bijapur, and Golkonda, but has scarcely heard of the Andhras, the Guptas, and the Chalukyas. He knows exactly the date of Nadir Shah's invasion of India, but scarcely knows, within five centuries, the date when the Sakas invaded India, and were repelled by

Vikramâditya the Great. He knows more of the dates of Ferdusi and Ferishta than of Âryabhatta or Bhavabhûti, and can tell who built the Taj Mahal without having the faintest notion when the topes of Sanchi, the caves of Karli and Ajanta, the temples of Ellora, Bhuvanesvara, and Jagannâtha were built.

And yet, such things should not be. For the Hindu student the history of the Hindu Period should not be a blank, nor a confused jumble of historic and legendary names, religious parables, and Epic and Puranic myths. No study has so potent an influence in forming a nation's mind and a nation's character as a critical and careful study of its past history. And it is by such study alone that an unreasoning and superstitious worship of the past is replaced by a legitimate and manly admiration.

It almost seems an irony of fate that the past should be considered a blank in a country where ancient sages have handed down traditions and elaborate compositions through thousands of years, and where, generation after generation, they have preserved the heritage by a feat of memory which is considered a miracle in modern days! In vain must the thousands of ancient Hindu students and scholars have toiled to preserve these works, if the works give us no clue to a general outline History of Ancient India. And in vain, too, must eminent European scholars and antiquarians have worked during the last hundred years, if it be still impossible to put together the results of their learned researches in the shape of a connected history which will be intelligible to the general reader and the ordinary student.

Happily this is no longer impossible. And although many portions of Indian History are still obscure, although many questions of detail are still subjects of controversy, to construct a general history of the Hindu Period is no longer a hopeless task. And, however unfit I feel myself to accomplish this task, I, nevertheless, venture to make a commencement, in the hope that abler scholars will pardon my shortcomings, rectify my inevitable errors, and perform skilfully and well what I may do clumsily or leave undone.

In undertaking this great work, I must, once for all, disclaim any intention to make any new discoveries, or to extend in any way the limits of Oriental scholarship and research. My limited knowledge of the subject precludes the possibility of such a pretension being advanced, and the limits of the present work make it impossible that any such results should be achieved. I have simply tried to string together, in a methodical order, the results of the labours of abler scholars, in order to produce a readable work for the general reader. If, in the fulfilment of this design, I have been sometimes betrayed into conjectures and suppositions, I can only ask my readers to accept them as such,—not as historical discoveries.

Ten years ago I collected and arranged the materials then available to me, with a view to write a little school-book in my own vernacular; and the little work has since been accepted as a text-book in many schools in Bengal. Since that time I have continued my work in this line, as far as my time permitted; and when, three years ago, I was enabled by the generosity of the Government of Bengal to place a complete Bengali translation of the Rig Veda Sanhitâ before my countrymen, I felt more than ever impelled to rearrange the historical materials furnished by our ancient literature in a permanent form. In pursuance of this object, I published some papers, from time to time, in the *Calcutta Review;* and these papers, together with all other materials which I have collected, have been embodied and arranged in the present work.

The method on which this work has been written is very simple. My principal object has been to furnish the general reader with a practical and handy work on the Ancient History of India,—not to compose an elaborate work of discussions on Indian Antiquities. To study clearness and conciseness on a subject like this was not, however, an easy task. Every chapter in the present work deals with matters about which long researches have been made, and various opinions have been recorded. It would have afforded some satisfaction to me to have given the reader the history of every controversy, the account of every antiquarian discovery, and the *pros* and *cons* of every opinion advanced. But I could not yield to this temptation without increasing the work to three or four times its present humble size, and thus sacrificing the very object with which it is written. To carry out my primary object, I have avoided every needless controversy and discussion, and I have tried to explain as clearly, concisely, and distinctly as I was able, each succeeding phase of Hindu civilisation and Hindu life in ancient times.

But, while conciseness has been the main object of the present work, I have also endeavoured to tell my story so that it may leave some distinct memories on my readers after they have closed the work. For this reason, I have avoided details as far as possible, and tried to develop, fully and clearly, the leading facts and features of each succeeding age. Repetition has not been avoided, where such repetition seemed necessary to impress on my readers the cardinal facts—the salient features of the story of Hindu civilisation.

The very copious extracts which I have given (in translation) from the Sanscrit works may, at first sight, seem to be inconsistent with my desire for conciseness. Such extracts, however, have been advisedly given. In the first place, on a subject where there is so much room for difference in opinion, it is of the highest importance to furnish the reader with the text on which my conclusions are based, to enable him to form his own judgment, and to rectify my mistakes if my conclusions are erroneous. In the second place, it is a gain in the cause of historical knowledge to familiarize the reader with the texts of our ancient authors. It is scarcely to be hoped that the busy student will spend much of his time in reading the ancient and abstruse works in the original or even in learned translations, and the historian who seeks to familiarize his readers with some portions at least of these ancient works, adds in so far to the accurate knowledge of his readers on this subject. And lastly, it has been well said, that thought is language, and language is thought. And if it be the intention of the historian to convey an idea of ancient thought,—of what the ancient Hindus felt and believed,—he cannot do this better than by quoting the words by which that ancient people expressed themselves. Such brief extracts very often give the modern reader a far more realistic and intimate knowledge of ancient Hindu society and manners and ways of thinking than any account that I could give at twice the length. And it is because I have desired the modern reader to enter into the spirit and the inner life of the ancient Hindus, that I have tried to bring the old composers of hymns and sûtras face to face with the reader, and allowed them to speak for themselves. Such an intimate grasp of the inner life and feelings of the ancients is the very kernel of true historical knowledge, and I have felt it a hopeless task to impart this knowledge more accurately or more concisely than in the words of the ancients. It is for this reason mainly, and consistently with my anxiety to be concise, that I have quoted copiously from ancient works.

In conclusion, I have to crave the indulgence of the reader for the many deficiencies which he will, no doubt, find in the present work, written in moments stolen from official work, and in places where a decent library was never available. Such claim to indulgence is seldom admitted, and the reader very pertinently inquires why a writer should ever undertake a work for which he was not in every way fully equipped. Nevertheless, I mention these circumstances, as they may explain, if they cannot justify, the shortcomings of the work. The time of the present writer is not his own, and the charge of a Bengal District with an area of over six thousand square miles and a population of over three millions, leaves little leisure for other work. To arrange my materials, under these circumstances, has been an arduous work, and I can only ask the indulgent consideration of my readers for any errors and defects which may have crept into this work.

R. C. DUTT.

MYMENSING DISTRICT, BENGAL,
13th August 1888.

CONTENTS OF VOL. I.

BOOK III.

RATIONALISTIC PERIOD, B.C. 1000 TO 320.

CIVILISATION IN ANCIENT INDIA.

INTRODUCTION.

EPOCHS AND DATES.

THE History of Ancient India is a history of thirty centuries of human culture and progress. It divides itself into several distinct periods, each of which, for length of years, will compare with the entire history of many a modern people.

Other nations claim an equal or even a higher antiquity than the Hindus. Egyptian scholars have claimed a date over four thousand years B.C. for the foundation of the first Egyptian dynasty of kings. Assyrian scholars have claimed a date over three thousand years B.C. for Saragon I., who united Sumir and Accad under the Semetic rule; and they claim a still earlier date for the native Turanian civilisation of Accad which preceded the Semetic conquest of Chaldea. The Chinese claim to have an authentic history of dynasties and facts from about 2400 B.C. For India, modern scholars have not claimed an earlier date than 2000 B.C. for the hymns of the Rig Veda, although Hindu civilisation must have been centuries or thousands of years old when these hymns were composed.

But there is a difference between the records of the Hindus and the records of other nations. The hieroglyphic records of the ancient Egyptians yield little information beyond the names of kings and pyramid-builders, and accounts of dynasties and wars. The cuneiform inscriptions of Assyria and Babylon tell us much the same story. And even ancient Chinese records shed little light on the gradual progress of human culture and civilisation.

Ancient Hindu works are of a different character. If they are defective in some respects, as they undoubtedly are, they are defective as accounts of dynasties, of wars, of so-called historical incidents. On the other hand, they give us a full, connected, and clear account of the advancement of civilisation, of the progress of the human mind, such as we shall seek for in vain among the records of any other equally ancient nation. The literature of each period is a perfect picture—a photograph, if we may so call it—of the Hindu civilisation of that period. And the works of successive periods form a complete history of ancient Hindu civilisation for three thousand years, so full, so clear, that he who runs may read.

Inscriptions on stone and tablets, and writings on papyri are recorded with a design to commemorate passing events. The songs and hymns and religious effusions of a people are an unconscious and true reflection of its civilisation and its thought. The earliest effusions of the Hindus were not recorded in writing,—they are, therefore, full and unrestricted,—they are a natural and true expression of the nation's thoughts and feelings. They were preserved, not on stone, but in the faithful memory of the people, who handed down the great heritage from century to century with a scrupulous exactitude which, in modern days, would be considered a miracle.

Scholars who have studied the Vedic hymns historically are aware that the materials they afford for constructing a history of civilisation are fuller and truer than any accounts which could have been recorded on stone or papyri. And those who have pursued Hindu literature through the different periods of ancient Hindu history, are equally aware that they form a complete and comprehensive story of the progress and gradual modifications of Hindu civilisation, thought, and religion through three thousand years. And the philosophical historian of human civilisation need not be a Hindu to think that the Hindus have preserved the fullest, the clearest, and the truest materials for his work.

We wish not to be misunderstood. We have made the foregoing remarks simply with a view to remove the very common and very erroneous impression that Ancient India has no history worth studying, no connected and reliable chronicle of the past which would be interesting or instructive to the modern reader.

Ancient India has a connected story to tell, and so far from being uninteresting, its special feature is its intense attractiveness. We read in that ancient story how a gifted Aryan people, separated by circumstances from the outside world, worked out their civilisation amidst natural and climatic conditions which were peculiarly favourable. We note their intellectual discoveries age after age; we watch their religious progress and developments through successive centuries; we mark their political career, as they gradually expand over India, and found new kingdoms and dynasties; we observe their struggles against priestly domination, their successes and their failures; we study with interest their great social and religious revolutions and their far-reaching consequences. And this great story of a nation's intellectual life—more thrilling in its interest than any tale which Shaharzadi told—is nowhere broken and nowhere disconnected. The great causes which led to great social and religious changes are manifest to the reader, and he follows the gradual development of ancient Hindu civilisation through thirty centuries, from 2000 B.C. to 1000 years after Christ.

The very shortcomings of Hindu civilisation, as compared with the younger civilisation of Greece or Rome, have their lessons for the modern reader. The story of our successes is not more instructive than the story of our failures. The hymns of Visvâmitra, the philosophy of Kapila, and the poetry of Kâlidâsa have no higher lessons for the modern reader than the decadence of our political life and the ascendency of priests. The story of the religious rising of the people under the leadership of Gautama Buddha and Asoka is not more instructive than the absence of any efforts after popular freedom. And the great heights to which the genius of Brâhmans and Kshatriyas soared in the infancy of the world's intellectual life are not more suggestive and not more instructive than the absence of genius in the people at large in their ordinary pursuits and trades,—in mechanical inventions and maritime discoveries, in sculpture, architecture, and arts, in manifestations of popular life and the assertion of popular power.

The history of the intellectual and religious life of the ancient Hindus is matchless in its continuity, its fulness, and its philosophical truth. But the historian who only paints the current of that intellectual life performs half his duty. There is another and a sadder portion of Hindu history,—and it is necessary that this portion of the story, too, should be faithfully told.

We have said before that the history of Ancient India divides itself into several distinct and long periods or epochs. Each of these periods has a distinct literature, and each has a civilisation peculiar to it, which modified itself into the civilisation of the next period under the operation of great political and social causes. It is desirable that we should, at the outset, give a brief account of these historical epochs and the great historical events by which they are marked. Such an outline-account of the different periods will make our readers acquainted with the plan and scope of this work, and will probably help them to grasp more effectually the details of each period when we come to treat them more fully. We begin with the earliest period, viz., that of Aryan settlements in the Punjab. The hymns of the Rig Veda furnish us with the materials for a history of this period.

FIRST EPOCH.

In this priceless volume, the Rig Veda, we find the Hindu Aryans as conquerors and settlers on the banks of the Indus and its five branches; and India beyond the Sutlej was almost unknown to them. They were a conquering race, full of the self-assertion and vigour of a young national life, with a strong love of action and a capacity for active enjoyments. They were, in this respect, far removed from the contemplative and passive Hindus of later days; they rejoiced in wealth and cattle and pasture-fields; and they carved out, with their strong right arm, new possessions and realms from the aborigines of the soil, who vainly struggled to maintain their own against the invincible conquerors. Thus, the period was one of wars and conquests against the aborigines; and the Aryan victors triumphantly boast of their conquests in their hymns, and implore their gods to bestow on them wealth and new possessions, and to destroy the barbarians. Whatever was bright and cheerful and glorious in the aspects of nature struck the Aryans with admiration and gladness, and such manifestations of nature were worshipped and invoked as gods.

It is needless to say that the entire body of Aryans was then a united community, and the only distinction of castes was between the Aryans and the aborigines. Even the distinction between professions was not very marked; and the sturdy lord of many acres, who ploughed his fields and owned large herds in times of peace, went out to defend his village or plunder the aborigines in times of war, and often composed spirited hymns to the martial gods in his hours of devotion. There were no temples and no idols; each patriarch of a family lighted the sacrificial fire in his own hearth, and offered milk and rice offerings, or animals, or libations of the Soma juice to the fire, and invoked the "bright" gods for blessings and health and wealth for himself and his children. Chiefs of tribes were kings, and had professional priests to perform sacrifices and utter hymns for them; but there was no priestly caste, and no royal caste. The people were free, enjoying the freedom which belongs to vigorous pastoral and agricultural tribes.

What is the date of this period of Aryan settlements in the Punjab as pictured in the Rig Veda? We think we agree with the general opinion on the subject when we fix 2000 to 1400 B.C. for this first period of Hindu history. And, for the sake of convenience, we will call this period the *Vedic Period.*

SECOND EPOCH.

When once the Hindu Aryans had come as far as the Sutlej, they did not lose much time in crossing that river and pouring down in numbers in the valley of the Ganges. We have rare mention of the Ganges and the Jumna in the Rig Veda, showing that they were not yet generally known to the Hindus in the first or Vedic Period, although adventurous colonists must have issued out of the Punjab and settled in the shores of those distant rivers. Such settlements must have multiplied in the second period, until, in the course of some centuries, the entire valley of the Ganges, as far down as modern Tirhut, were the seats of powerful kingdoms and nationalities, who cultivated science and literature in their schools of learning, and developed new forms of religion and of civilisation widely different from those of the Vedic Period.

Among the nations who flourished in the Gangetic valley, the most renowned have left their names in the epic literature of India. The Kurus had their kingdom round about modern Delhi. The Panchâlas settled further to the south-east, round about modern Kanouj. The Kosalas occupied the spacious country between the

Ganges and the Gunduck, which includes modern Oudh; the Videhas lived beyond the Gunduck, in what is now known as Tirhut; and the Kâsis settled down round about modern Benares. These were the most renowned nations of the second period, though other less powerful nationalities also flourished and extended their kingdoms from time to time.

When the first Kurus and Panchâlas settled in the Doab, they gave indications of a vigorous national life, and their internecine wars form the subject of the first National Epic of India, the Mahâbhârata. And, although this work, in its present shape, is the production of a later age — or rather of later ages — yet, even in its present form, it preserves indications of that rude and sturdy vigour and warlike jealousies which characterised the early conquerors of the Gangetic valley. The Hindus did not, however, live many centuries in the soft climate of this valley before losing their vigour and manliness, as they gained in learning and civilisation. As they drifted down the river they manifested less and less of the vigour of conquering races. The royal courts of the Videhas and the Kâsis were learned and enlightened, but contemporary literature does not bear witness to their warlike qualities. The Kosalas, too, were a polished nation, but the traditions of that nation, preserved in the second National Epic of India, the Râmâyana (in its present form, a production of later ages), show more devotion to social and domestic duties, obedience to priests, and regard for religious forms, than the sturdy valour and the fiery jealousies of the Mahâbhârata.

This gradual enervation of the Hindus was the cause of the most important results in religious and social rules. Religion changed its spirit. The manly but simple hymns with which the sturdy conquerors of the Punjab had invoked nature-gods scarcely commended themselves to the more effete and more ceremonious Hindus of the Gangetic valley. The hymns were still repeated, but lost their meaning and sense, and vast ceremonials and observances took the place of simple forms. The priestly class increased in number and in influence, until they formed a hereditary caste of their own. The kings and warriors of the Gangetic valley lived in more splendid courts, and had more gorgeous surroundings than the simple agricultural warriors of the Punjab, and soon separated themselves from the people and formed a caste of their own. The mass of the people—the Vaisyas or Visas of the Riga Veda—became more feeble than their forefathers in the Punjab, and wore, without a protest, the chains which priests and warriors — the Brâhmans and the Kshatriyas — threw around them. And as subjection means demoralisation, the people in Hindu kingdoms never afterwards became what the people in ancient and modern Europe have striven to be. And lastly, the aborigines who were subjugated and had adopted the Aryan civilisation formed the low caste of Sûdras, and were declared unfit to perform the Aryan religious rites or to acquire religious knowledge.

Such was the origin of the Caste-system in India, in the second period of Hindu history. The system arose out of weakness and lifelessness among the people, and, to a certain extent, it has perpetuated that weakness ever after.

It will be observed that this Second Period was a period of the submission of the people under the Brâhmans and the Kshatriyas, and of the submission of the Kshatriyas themselves under the Brâhmans. At the close of the period, however, there appears to have been a reaction, and the proud Kshatriyas at last tried to prove their equality with the Brâhmans in learning and religious culture. Wearied with the unmeaning rituals and ceremonials prescribed by priests, the Kshatriyas started new speculations and bold inquiries after the truth. The effort was unavailing. The priests remained supreme. But the vigorous speculations which the

Kshatriyas started form the only redeeming portion of the inane and lifeless literature of this period. And these speculations remained as a heritage of the nation, and formed the nucleus of the Hindu philosophical systems and religious revolutions of a later day.

It was in this period of Aryan expansion in the Gangetic valley that the Rig Veda and the three other Vedas —Sâman, Yajus, and Atharvan—were finally arranged and compiled. Then followed another class of compositions known as the Brâhmanas, and devoted to sacrificial rites; and these inane and verbose compositions reflect the enervation of the people and the dogmatic pretensions of the priests of the age. The custom of retirement from the world into forest life, which was unknown in the earlier ages, sprang up, and the last portions of the Brâhmanas are Âranyakas devoted to forest rites. And lastly, the bold speculations started by Kshatriyas are known as the Upanishads, and form the last portions of the literature of this period, and close the so-called *Revealed Literature* of India.

Scholars have generally held that a period of at least four or five centuries was required for the great social and political changes of this epoch. Within this period the valley of the Ganges, as far as Tirhoot, was cleared, colonised, and Hinduised, and formed into sites of powerful kingdoms. Religious observances were vastly elaborated; social rules were changed; the caste-system was formed; the supremacy of priests was established and confirmed, and ultimately questioned by the Kshatriyas; and lastly, within this age, a varied and voluminous literature was recorded. The Period may, therefore, be supposed to have extended approximately from 1400 to 1000 B.C.

One or two facts may be cited here which confirm these dates. The central historical fact of this period was a great war between the Kurus and the Panchâlas, which forms the subject of the Mahâbhârata, and of which we shall have something to say further on. The central literary fact of this period was the compilation of the Vedas. Tradition and the Epic itself inform us that the compiler of the Vedas was a contemporary of the war; but we may accept or reject this as we like. We will examine these two facts separately.

First, with regard to the compilation of the Vedas. Tradition has it that when the Vedas were compiled, the position of the solstitial points was observed and recorded to mark the date. The Jyotisha in which this observation is now found is a late work, not earlier than the third century before Christ, but the observation was certainly made at an ancient date, and Bentley and Archdeacon Pratt—both able mathematicians—have gone over the calculation and found that it was made in 1181 B.C.

Much has been written of late against the value of this discovery in Europe, America, and India, but we have found nothing in these discussions which goes against the genuineness of the astronomical observation. We are inclined to believe that the observation marks approximately the true date of the final compilation of the Vedas; and as the work of compilation occupied numerous teachers for generations together, we may suppose that the Vedas were compiled during the fourteenth and thirteenth centuries B.C. And this date falls within the period which we have assigned for the Second Epoch.

Next, with regard to the Kuru-Panchâla War. The annals of different kingdoms in India allude to this ancient war, and some of these annals are not unreliable. The founder of Buddhism lived in the sixth century B.C., and we learn from the annals of Magadha that thirty-five kings reigned between the Kuru-Panchâla War and the time of Buddha. Allowing twenty years to each reign, this would place the war in the thirteenth century B.C.

Again, we know from coins that Kanishka ruled in Kashmîra in the first century A.D., and his successor Abhimanyu probably reigned towards the close of that century. The historian of Kashmîra informs us that fifty-two kings reigned for 1266 years from the time of the Kuru-Panchâla War to the time of Abhimanyu, and this would place the war in the twelfth century B.C.

We do not ask the reader to accept any of the particular dates given above. It is almost impossible to fix any precise date in the History of India before Alexander the Great visited the land; and we may well hesitate, even when astronomical calculations point to a particular year, or historical lists point to a particular century. All that we ask, and all that we are entitled to ask, is that the reader will now find it possible to accept the fact that the Vedas were finally compiled and the Kuru-Panchâla War was fought sometime about the thirteenth century or the twelfth century B.C.

And, if the Kuru-Panchâla War was fought in the thirteenth century B.C. (*i.e.*, about a century before the Trojan War), it is impossible to fix a date later than 1400 B.C. for the commencement of the Second Epoch of which we are speaking. For at the time of the Kuru-Panchâla War, the tracts of country round modern Delhi and Kanouj were the seats of powerful nations who had developed a civilisation and literature of their own. And two centuries must be allowed between the date when the Aryans issued out of the Punjab and the date when these results had been achieved in the Gangetic valley.

To accept 1400 B.C. as the date when the Aryans issued out of the Punjab, is to confirm the dates we have given (2000 to 1400 B.C.) for the First Epoch, the Vedic Period.

Again, many of the Brâhmanas contain internal evidence that they were composed at the time or after the time of the Kurus and the Panchâlas. We may, therefore, suppose these to have been composed in the thirteenth and twelfth centuries B.C. And the Upanishads, which mark the close of Brâhmana literature, were composed about the eleventh century B.C. Janaka, the king of the Videhas, gave a start to the Upanishads; we may, therefore, suppose the Videhas and the Kosalas to have flourished about 1200 to 1000 B.C., as the Kurus and the Panchâlas flourished about 1400 to 1200 B.C.

For the sake of convenience we will call this second period the *Epic Period.* It was the period when the nations described in the national epics of India lived and fought; when the Kurus and the Panchâlas, the Kosalas and the Videhas, held sway along the valley of the Ganges.

THIRD EPOCH.

The Third Epoch is, perhaps, the most brilliant period of Hindu history. It was in this period that the Aryans issued out of the Gangetic valley, spread themselves far and wide, and introduced Hindu civilisation and founded Hindu kingdoms as far as the southernmost limits of India. Magadha or South Behar, which was already known to the Hindus in the Epic Period, was completely Hinduised in the Third Epoch; and the young and powerful kingdom founded here soon eclipsed all the ancient kingdoms of the Gangetic valley. Buddhism spread from Magadha to surrounding kingdoms, and Chandragupta, the contemporary of Alexander the Great, brought the whole of Northern India, from the Punjab to Behar, under the rule of Magadha. With this great political event, viz., the consolidation of all Northern India under one great empire, the Third Epoch ends and the Fourth Epoch begins.

Aryan colonists penetrated to Bengal and introduced Hindu religion and civilisation among the aborigines. The kingdoms founded in the south won greater distinction. The Andhras founded a powerful kingdom in the Deccan, and developed great schools of learning. Further south, the Aryans came in contact with the old Dravidian civilisation. The more perfect Hindu civilisation prevailed, and the Dravidians were Hinduised and founded kingdoms which became distinguished for learning and power. The three sister-kingdoms of the Cholas, the Cheras, and the Pandyas made their mark before the third century B.C., and Kânchî (Conjeveram), the capital of the Cholas, distinguished itself as the seat of Hindu learning at a later day.

In the west the Saurâshtras (including Gujrat and the Maharatta country) received Hindu civilisation; while, beyond a strip of the sea, Ceylon was discovered, and formed a great resort of Hindu traders.

The practical and enterprising spirit of the age shows itself in literature as well as in territorial conquests. The whole of the verbose teachings and rites of the Brâhmanas and Âranyakas were condensed into Sûtras or aphorisms so as to form handy manuals for the sacrifice. Other Sûtras were framed for laying down the rules of domestic rites and social conduct. Sûtra schools sprang all over India, in the north and in the south, and works multiplied. And besides these religious works, phonetics, metre, grammar, and lexicons were studied, and Yâska wrote his Nirukta, and Pânini his Vyâkarana early in this period. And the construction of sacrificial altars according to fixed rules gave rise to geometry, which was first discovered in India.

And, lastly, the lessons of the Upanishads were not lost. The bold speculations started in these works were pursued, until Kapila started the Sânkhya philosophy—the first closely-reasoned system of mental philosophy known in the world. Other systems of philosophy were started by other thinkers, but the Sânkhya philosophy was destined to have the greatest influence on the future of India; for Gautama Buddha was born in the sixth century B.C., and he added to the cold logic of the Sânkhya philosophy a world-embracing sympathy and love for mankind which has made his religion the religion of a third of the human race.

We have no difficulty in fixing the dates of this epoch. Chandragupta, the contemporary of Alexander the Great, united Northern India in 320 B.C. We may, therefore, date the Third Epoch from 1000 B.C. to 320 B.C. For the sake of convenience, we will call it the *Philosophical* or *Rationalistic Period.*

The great political, literary, and religious incidents of the period require the wide space of seven centuries that we have allotted to the epoch; and all the facts that we know confirm these dates. The dates which Dr. Bühler has given to the Sûtras of Gautama, Baudhâyana, Vasishtha, and Âpastamba fall within the limits given above. Dr. Thibaut assigns the eighth century to the Sulva Sûtras or geometry. Writers on Sânkhya philosophy assign the seventh century to Kapila's philosophy, and Gautama Buddha lived, as we know, in the sixth century.

These dates, which have been ascertained with tolerable certainty, confirm the dates which we have accepted for the previous or the Epic Period. For, if the philosophy of Kapila, which was a distant and matured result of the Upanishads, was started in the seventh century, the Upanishads themselves must have been composed several centuries earlier. And we are presumably correct in assigning B.C. 1000 for the Upanishads,—the works which closed the Epic Period.

FOURTH EPOCH.

The epoch begins with the brilliant reign of Chandragupta. His grandson Asoka the Great made Buddhism the state religion of India, settled the Buddhist Scriptures in the great council of Patna, and published his edicts of humanity on stone pillars and on rocks. He prohibited the slaughter of animals, provided medical aid to men and cattle all over his empire, proclaimed the duties of citizens and members of families, and directed Buddhist missionaries to proceed to the ends of the earth, to mix with the rich and the poor, and to proclaim the truth. His inscriptions show that he made treaties with Antiochus of Syria, Ptolemy of Egypt, Antigonus of Macedon, Magas of Cyrene, and Alexander of Epiros, and sent missionaries to these kingdoms to preach the Buddhist religion. "Both here and in foreign countries," says Asoka, "everywhere the people follow the doctrine of the religion of the Beloved of the Gods, wheresoever it reacheth." "Buddhist missionaries," says a Christian writer,* "preached in Syria two centuries before the teaching of Christ (which has so many moral points in common) was heard in Northern Palestine. So true is it that every great historical change has had its forerunner."

The Maurya dynasty, which commenced with Asoka's grandfather Chandragupta about 320 B.C., did not last very long after the time of Asoka. It was followed by two short-lived dynasties, the Sunga and the Kânva (183 to 26 B.C.), and then the great Andhras, who had founded a powerful empire in the South, conquered Magadha and were masters of Northern India for four centuries and a half, B.C. 26 to A.D. 430. They were generally Buddhists, but respected Brâhmans and orthodox Hindus; and throughout the Buddhist Epoch, the two religions flourished in India side by side, and persecution was almost unknown. The Andhras were followed by the great Gupta emperors, who were supreme in India till about 500 A.D., and then their power was overthrown. The Guptas were generally orthodox Hindus, but favoured Buddhism also, and made grants to Buddhist churches and monasteries.

In the meantime Western India was the scene of continual foreign invasions. The Greeks of Bactria, expelled by Turanian invaders, entered India in the second and first centuries before Christ, founded kingdoms, introduced

* Mahaffy, "Alexander's Empire," chapter xiii.

Greek civilisation and knowledge, and had varied fortunes in different parts of India for centuries after. They are said to have penetrated as far as Orissa. The Turanians of the Yu-Chi tribe next invaded India, and gave a powerful dynasty to Kashmîra; and Kanishka the Yu-Chi king of Kashmîra had an extensive empire in the first century A.D., which stretched from Kabul and Kashgar and Yarkand to Guzrat and Agra. He was a Buddhist, and held a great council of the Northern Buddhists in Kashmîra. The Cambojians and other tribes of Kabul then poured into India, and were in their turn followed by the locust-hordes of the Huns, who spread over Western India in the fifth century A.D. India had no rest from foreign invasions for several centuries after the time of Asoka the Great; but the invaders, as they finally settled down in India, adopted the Buddhist religion, and formed a part of the people.

Buddhism gradually declined during the centuries after the Christian Era, much in the same way as the Hinduism of the Rig Veda had gradually declined in the Epic Period when the Hindus had settled down in the Gangetic valley. Buddhist monks formed a vast and unmanageable body of priesthood, owning vast acres of land attached to each monastery, and depending on the resources of the people; and Buddhist ceremonials and forms bordered more and more on Buddha-worship and idolatry. Many of these forms and ceremonials, which were dear to the common people, were adopted by the Hinduism of the day, and thus a new form of Hinduism asserted itself by the sixth century after Christ. An effete form of Buddhism lingered on for some centuries in some parts of India after this, until it was stamped out by the Mahomedan conquerors of India.

We find an uninterrupted series of Buddhist rock-cut caves, chaityas or churches, and vihâras or monasteries, all over India, dating from the time of Asoka to the fifth century A.D.; but there are scarcely any specimens of Buddhist architecture of a later date. Temple-building and Hindu architecture flourished from the sixth century A.D. to long after the Mahommedan conquest.

The most valuable portions of Buddhist literature left to us are the scriptures as finally settled in the Council of Patna by Asoka, and sent by him all over India and India. These scriptures, preserved in the Pâli language beyond in Ceylon, form our best materials for the history of early Buddhism, while later forms of this literature have been found in Nepal, in Thibet, in China, in Japan, and in all Northern Buddhist countries.

We have said that Buddhism had a marked effect on Hinduism. Buddhism had questioned the sacredness of the Vedas, and modern or Puranic Hinduism, though nominally revering the Vedas, shows a complete estrangement and emancipation from those ancient works. Hindu astronomy, mathematics, laws, and philosophical speculations had sprung from the Vedas and the Vedic sacrifices, and belonged to different Vedic schools. But Hindu science and learning of the post-Buddhist age have no reliance on the Vedas and do not belong to any Vedic school. Puranic Hinduism is not a religion of Vedic sacrifices, but of the worship of images and gods unknown to the Vedas.

The Code of Manu represents Hindu thought and manners of the Buddhist Epoch. It is based on the ancient Dharmasûtras or social laws of the Philosophical Period; but while the Dharmasûtras belong to different Vedic schools, Manu's Sanhitâ knows of no Vedic schools and professes to be the law for all Aryans. On the other hand Manu adheres to the Vedic sacrifices, eschews image-worship, and does not know of the Trinity of Puranic Hinduism. Thus Manu marks the transition stage from Vedic Hinduism to Puranic Hinduism.

For reasons which will appear from the foregoing remarks, we date the fourth or *Buddhist Period* from 320 B.C. to 500 A.D.

FIFTH EPOCH.

The fifth or last epoch of Hindu history is the epoch of Hindu revival, and covers five centuries from 500 A.D. to 1000 A.D., the date of the first invasions of Mahmud of Ghazni.

The period begins with great deeds in politics and literature. Foreign invaders had harassed India for centuries before, and at last a great avenger arose. Vikramâditya the Great, of Ujjayinî, was the master of Northern India; he beat back the invaders known as the Sakas in the great battle of Korur, and asserted Hindu independence. Hindu genius and literature revived under his auspices, and a new form of Hinduism asserted itself.

The three centuries commencing with the time of Vikramâditya the Great (500 to 800 A.D.) may be called the Augustan era of later Sanscrit literature, and nearly all the great works which are popular in India to this day belong to this period. Kâlidâsa wrote his matchless dramas and poems in Vikrama's court. Amara Sinha, the lexicographer, was another of the "nine gems" of this court. And Bhâravi was Kâlidâsa's contemporary or lived shortly after. Silâditya II., a successor of Vikramâditya, ruled from 610 to 650 A.D., and is the reputed author of Ratnâvali. Dandin, the author of Dasakumâra Charita, was an old man when Silâditya II. reigned, and Bânabhatta, the author of Kâdambarî, lived in his court. Subandhu, the author of Vâsavadattâ, also lived at the same time; and there are reasons to believe that the Bhattikâvya was composed by Bhartrihari, the author of the Satakas, in the same reign.

In the next century Yasovarman ruled between 700 and 750 A.D., and the renowned Bhavabhûti composed his powerful dramas in this reign. Bhavabhûti, however was, the last of the galaxy of the poets and literary men of ancient India,—and no great literary genius arose in India after the eighth century.

It was in this Augustan era also that the great national epics of India, the production of many ages, received their last additions and touches, and assumed their final shape; and the voluminous Purânas, which have given their name to this period, began to be composed in their present shape.

In modern Hindu science, too, we have the brightest names in these three centuries. Âryabhatta, the founder of modern Hindu astronomy, was born in 476 A.D., and produced his work early in the sixth century. Varâhamihira, his successor, was one of the "nine gems" of Vikrama's court. Brahmagupta was born in 598 A.D., and was, therefore, a contemporary of Bânabhatta, the novelist. Other astronomers of note also lived about the sixth century.

This brilliant period of three centuries (500 to 800 A.D.) was followed by two centuries of impenetrable darkness! The history of Northern India from 800 to 1000 A.D. is a perfect blank. No great dynasties rose to power, no literary or scientific men rose to renown, no great work of architecture or art was constructed in Northern India. History is silent over these two dead centuries!

But we have indications of what was transpiring. The two dark centuries witnessed the fall of ancient dynasties, and the crumbling down of ancient kingdoms and nationalities. They resemble the dark ages of Europe, which witnessed the fall of the Roman power, and which cleared up when Feudal power arose. In India, too, the power of ancient races and dynasties was silently swept away during the period of darkness, and when light breaks in again, we see a new race of Hindu Feudal barons as the masters of India,—the modern Rajputs! In the general dissolution of ancient power and the struggle for supremacy, the youngest and the most vigorous race came to the forefront, and about 1000

A.D. we find Rajput dynasties ruling everywhere in Northern India. They inherited the throne of Vikramâditya and his successors in Ujjayinî and Kanouj; they usurped the power of the powerful Ballabhi kings of Gujrat and Western India; they ruled Bengal and the Deccan; and they tried to oppose the progress of Sabaktagin and Mahmud in the Punjab.

Different theories have been put forward as to the origin of the Rajputs. H. H. Wilson and other authorities maintain that they were descended from the Scythian invaders of India who poured in through successive centuries, who were once beaten back by Vikramâditya the Great, but who, like other invaders, settled down in the deserts of Western India, and ruled and conquered when they could. Be that as it may, the Rajputs certainly appear to have been new converts to Hindu civilisation, for there is no mention of them in older records. Like all new converts, they espoused Hinduism with exceptional zeal; they were proud to be styled Kshatriyas,—descended from the Solar and Lunar races; and wherever they conquered, Hindu temples arose. Priestly monopoly in its closest form and the unhealthiest restrictions of modern Hinduism date from this period, and were perpetuated during the seven centuries of national lifelessness under the Musalman rule.

It is impossible not to be struck with the resemblance between European history and Indian history at the period which marks the close of the Ancient Age. The efforts of Vikramâditya to beat back the Sakas have a close resemblance to the efforts of the last Roman Emperors and armies to keep back the hordes of barbarians who pressed eagerly forward for conquests. For centuries the Hindus and the Romans succeeded; but the waves of invasion and conquest at last overwhelmed the ancient empires in India and in Italy, and marked the fall of ancient thrones and institutions! For centuries after this event, Western Europe and Northern India have scarcely any history; or the history is one of violence and wars which closed the Ancient Age and ushered in the Modern Age! When, at last, the darkness clears up, we find a new feudal power in Europe, and a new feudal power in India. And the new dynasties of Europe had embraced Christianity, and exerted as zealously and enthusiastically for the mediæval priests, as the newly-converted Rajputs did for the Brâhmans and the modern form of Hinduism.

But the parallel does not end here. The new masters of India had to fight as hard against the waves of Mahommedan invasion as the new masters of Europe did in France, in Spain, and in Syria. Richard the Lion-hearted was fighting at the same period as Prithu Rai of Delhi, and against the same rising power. In Europe the Christian barons saved their independence, and ultimately expelled the Musalmans even from Spain; in India the Hindu barons struggled and fell. Shahabuddin Ghori overthrew the Rajput kingdoms of Delhi and Ajmere, Kanouj and Benares, in 1193 and 1194 A.D., and the boldest of the Rajputs retreated to their desert fastnesses, where they enjoy a sort of independence to the present day, through the generous sufferance of the British Government.

We have dated the Fifth or *Puranic Period* from 500 A.D. to 1000 A.D., but from what has been stated above it will appear that the Puranic Age really ends at 800 A.D. The history of Ancient India terminates at that date, and is followed by two centuries of Dark Age.

DATES.

There are two Eras prevalent in India, viz., the *Samvat Era*, running from 56 B.C., and the *Sakâbda Era*, running from 78 A.D. Scholars have experienced the greatest difficulty in finding out what great events these Eras really commemorate; and the conclusions arrived at are not yet beyond the pale of controversy.

It has been now ascertained that the Sakâbda or Saka Era is the Era of the Saka king Kanishka, who conquered Kashmir and Western India in the first century after Christ, and spread Buddhism over neighbouring countries. Thus the Sakâbda was originally a Buddhist Era. It was adopted in Buddhist India, and it was known and used in all Buddhist countries—in Thibet and Burma, in Ceylon and Java. It was after the Hindu revival of the sixth century that the date was adopted by Hindus, and the story was added, that the Era marked, not the reign of a Buddhist Saka king, but the defeat of the Sakas by a Hindu king. But wherever the Era is cited by ancient writers, it is cited as the Era of the Saka king;* and to the present day the Era is known in our almanacs as the Sakâbda, or more fully as *Saka Narapater Atîtâbda*, which means the Era of the Saka king, not the Era of the destruction of the Sakas by a Hindu king.

The Samvat Era is still more perplexing. Popularly it is known as the Era of a great victory of Vikramâditya. But history knows of no Vikramâditya of Ujjayinî in 56 B.C., and it is pretty certain, that Vikramâditya the Great, the patron of Kâlidâsa, lived in the sixth century after Christ.

It is still more curious that the Samvat Era has come into use in comparatively recent times. No instance has yet been discovered of the use of this Era in the centuries

* The exceedingly careful and observant scholar, Colebrooke, pointed out seventy years ago, that the astronomer, Varâhamihira, who lived in the sixth century A.D., cited the Saka Era as the *Saka Bhupa Kâla* or *Sakendra Kâla*, *i.e.*, the Era of the Saka king. His commentator explains this as the Era when the barbarians called Sakas "*were discomfited by Vikramâditya.*" Again, the astronomer Brahmagupta, who flourished in the seventh century A.D., cites the Era as *Saka Nripânte*, *i.e.*, after the Saka king. His commentator explains this as "*after the reign of Vikramâditya, who slew a people of barbarians called Sakas.*"—Colebrooke's Algebra, &c., from the Sanscrit, p. xliii. London, 1817.

immediately after the Christian Era. No trace of this Era is found in the inscriptions of the Buddhist Period in India, or in other Buddhist countries,—Thibet and Burma, Ceylon and Java.

There certainly seems to be some mystery about the Samvat Era, 56 B.C. It pretends to commemorate a victory of a king of whom history knows nothing; and it is an Era which does not seem to have been used in the numerous inscriptions of India for several centuries after it pretends to have been established.

Probably the true origin of the Era has been discovered by Mr. Fleet in his volume on the inscriptions of the Gupta kings. It would seem that the Era was originally an obscure Era of the Mâlava tribe, and came subsequently to be connected with the name of Vikramâditya, who in the sixth century after Christ raised the Mâlavas to the rank of the first nation in India.

We now proceed, for facility of reference, to give a table of dates for the different Epochs, premising, that the dates should be taken as only approximately correct, and that the earlier dates are supposed to be correct only within two or three centuries.

EPOCH I.—VEDIC PERIOD, B.C. 2000 to 1400.

Aryan settlement in the Indus valley Composition of the Rig Veda hymns	B.C. 2000 to 1400

EPOCH II.—EPIC PERIOD, B.C. 1400 to 1000.

Aryan settlements in the Ganges valley	B.C. 1400 to 1000
Lunar Zodiac fixed. Astronomical observations Compilation of the Vedas	B.C. 1400 to 1200
Flourishing Period of the Kurus and the Panchâlas	B.C. 1400 to 1200
Kuru-Panchâla War	B.C. 1250
Flourishing Period of the Kosalas, the Kâsis, and the Videhas	B.C. 1200 to 1000
Composition of the Brâhmanas and Âranyakas	B.C. 1300 to 1100
Composition of the Upanishads	B.C. 1100 to 1000

EPOCH III.—RATIONALISTIC PERIOD, B.C. 1000 to 320.

Aryan Conquest of all India	B.C. 1000 to 320
Yâska	B.C. 9th century.
Pânini	B.C. 8th century.
Sûtra Schools	B.C. 800 to 400
Sulva Sutras (Geometry)	B.C. 8th century.
Kapila and Sânkhya Philosophy	B.C. 7th century.
Other Schools of Philosophy	B.C. 600 to Christian Era.
Gautama Buddha	B.C. 557 to 477
Bimbisâra, King of Magadha	B.C. 537 to 485
Ajatasatru " "	B.C. 485 to 453
First Buddhist Council	B.C. 477
Second Buddhist Council	B.C. 377
Nine Nandas, Kings of Magadha	B.C. 370 to 320

EPOCH IV.—BUDDHIST PERIOD, B.C. 320 to A.D. 500.

Chandragupta, King of Magadha	B.C. 320 to 290
Bindusâra, King of Magadha	B.C. 290 to 260
Asoka, King of Magadha	B.C. 260 to 222
Third Buddhist Council	B.C. 242
The Maurya Dynasty in Magadha ends	B.C. 183
The Sunga Dynasty in Magadha	B.C. 183 to 71
The Kânva Dynasty in Magadha	B.C. 71 to 26
The Andhra Dynasty in Magadha	B.C. 26 to A.D. 430
The Gupta Emperors	A.D. 300 to A.D. 500
The Bactrian Greeks invaded India	B.C. 2nd and 1st centuries.
The Yu-Chi invaded India	A.D. 1st century.
Kanishka, the Yu-Chi King of Kashmîra, founded the Saka Era	A.D. 78
The Shah Kings ruled in Saurâshtra	A.D. 150 to 300
The Cambojians invaded India	A.D. 3rd and 4th centuries.
The White Huns invaded India	A.D. 5th century.

EPOCH V.—PURANIC PERIOD, A.D. 500 TO 1000.

Vikramâditya of Ujjayinî and Northern India	A.D. 500 to 550
Kâlidâsa, Amarasinha, Vararuchi, &c.	A.D. 500 to 550
Bhâravi, about	A.D. 550 to 600
Âryabhatta, founder of modern Hindu Astronomy	A.D. 476 to 530

Varâhamihira	A.D. 500 to 550
Brahmagupta	A.D. 598 to 650
Sîlâditya II., Emperor of Northern India. .	A.D. 610 to 650
Dandin	A.D. 570 to 620
Bânabhatta and Subandbu	A.D. 610 to 650
Bhartrihari and the Bhattikâvya . . .	
Bhavabhûti	A.D. 700 to 750
Sankarâchârya	A.D. 788 to 850
The Dark Ages in Northern India . . .	A.D. 800 to 1000

BOOK I.

VEDIC PERIOD, B.C. 2000 TO B.C. 1400.

CHAPTER I.

THE INDO-ARYANS.—THEIR LITERATURE.

THE site of the early home of the Aryans* has been a subject of endless controversies among scholars. Enthusiastic and patriotic Hindu scholars will not admit that the first home of the Aryans was anywhere outside India; while equally patriotic European scholars would place the seat of the primitive Aryans on the shores of the Baltic Sea. We need hardly say that it is not our object to enter into this discussion; and we merely repeat here the theory of many moderate thinkers that the early home of the Aryans was somewhere in Central Asia.

The main arguments on which this conclusion is based have been summed up by Professor Max Müller in a recent work, and we quote them for our readers:—

"Firstly, we have two streams of language, one tending south-east to India, and the other north-west to

* Recent anthropological researches have disclosed that the nations speaking Aryan languages are not descended from the same stock, and never belonged to the same race. At the same time it is admitted that the ancestors of these races must have derived their languages from a common source; they must have been subject to one great race which imposed its language on them, or lived in one common tract of country. When we speak of the early home of the Aryans, we mean this common country; and when we speak of Aryans, we mean races speaking Aryan languages.

Europe. The point where these two streams naturally intersect, points to Asia."

"Secondly, the earliest centres of civilised life were in Asia." And we may add that the most primitive form of all Aryan languages—the nearest approach to that language which was spoken by the primitive Aryan races —is the Vedic Sanscrit of Ancient India.

"Thirdly, we see in later times large ethnic waves, rising from Central Asia and overwhelming Europe. Such are the Huns in the fourth and the Mongols in the thirteenth century.

"Fourthly, if the migration had taken place from Europe to Asia, particularly from Scandinavia, we should naturally look in the common Aryan language for a number of words connected with maritime life." But this is not the case. While we find common names for particular animals and birds, and even common names for animals (*pasu*) and birds (*vi*) in general, we find no names for special fishes, and no general name for fish, nor even is there a common name for the sea!

Various pictures, more or less imaginary, of the civilisation of the early Aryans before they separated have been drawn by various scholars from the slender materials of the words which are found in common use among the different Aryan nations in the world. Pictet's work in two large volumes, published in Paris in 1859–63, created a wider interest than any preceding attempt of a similar nature; and this was followed by Dr. Fick's work in 1868, and Dr. Hehn's work in 1870. It is not our intention to draw such pictures here; we will only give a few facts about the life of the primitive Aryans about which there is no dispute.

The domestic economy among the early Aryans was much the same as it is among the Ayran nations of the present day. The historian of man does not find in Aryan history any traces of Hetairism (or of promiscuous relationship between the sexes), of families being reckoned on the mother's side, or of inheritance by the female line. On the contrary, the father was the protector and the nourisher of the family, the mother looked after and fed the children, the daughter milked the cattle, and relationship by marriage was recognised. Probably the primitive Aryans had already reached a higher state of civilisation than promiscuous living would imply. The family, and not the tribe, was the unit of society; and the father was the head of the family.

Many of the useful animals had been domesticated and brought under the service of man. The cow, the bull, the ox, the sheep, the goat, the swine, the dog, and the horse had all been domesticated. The wild bear, the wolf, the hare, and the dreaded serpent were known. Similarly among birds, the goose, the duck, the cuckoo, the raven, the quail, the crane, and the owl were well known to the early Aryans.

The various industries were still in their infancy; but a commencement in manufactures and arts had been made. The Aryans built houses, villages, and towns, made roads, and constructed boats for communication by water or for a humble kind of trade. Weaving, spinning, and plaiting were known, and furs, skins, and woollen fabrics were made into garments. Carpentry must have made considerable progress, and dyeing was known.

It need scarcely be stated that agriculture was practised by the primitive Aryans, and it was this occupation which probably gave them their name (*Árya* = cultivator). Many words familiar to cultivators, like the plough, the waggon, the cart, the wheel, the axle, the yoke, in common use among the Aryan nations, point to the same primitive roots from which they have been derived. Corn was ground, prepared, and cooked in various ways; while the flocks of sheep and cows by which every family was surrounded afforded milk and meat. There can be little doubt that, although agriculture was largely resorted to, many patriarchs of families used also to rove about from place to place with their attendants and flocks in search of new pastures, and a fairly large portion of the early Aryans led a nomad life. Of this we have some trace even in the Rig Veda, as we shall see farther on.

War was not infrequent in those primitive times, and weapons of bone and of wood, of stone and of metals, were known. The bow and the arrow, the sword and the spear seem to have been the weapons of war.

It argues some advance in civilisation that the use of gold and of silver was undoubtedly known to the early Aryans; and with the simplicity of early races, they called gold by the name "yellow" and silver by the name "white." A third metal (*ayas*) was also known, but it is doubtful if it was iron.

It is perhaps impossible to conjecture the sort of government which obtained in those olden days. Patriarchs of tribes and leaders of men undoubtedly obtained ascendency, and the simple subjects looked up to them and called them the protectors or nourishers of men, or the shining chief (*Pati, Vispati, Râja*) in war as well as in peace. The natural feelings of civilised man distinguished between right and wrong, and custom and a vague perception of what was good for the nation had the force of law.

And lastly, the primitive religion of the Aryans was suggested by whatever was beautiful and striking in the phenomena of Nature. The sky or the bright sky was an eternal object of wonder and of worship. The sun, the dawn, the fire, and the earth, the storms and the clouds and the thunder, all received worship. But religion was still simple and archaic. Myths and legends about the gods and their relationship had not yet multiplied; elaborate rites and ceremonials had not yet been fabricated. The bold forefathers of the Aryan nations looked up with a manly veneration to whatever was wondrous and beautiful in Nature, imagined such manifestations as instinct with deity, and offered their praise and their prayers with a grateful and fervent heart.

Adventurous bands of Aryans left their primitive home from time to time in quest of food or pasture, of kingdoms or plunder. The exact order in which the different nations left has not been ascertained, and will never be ascertained. Professor Max Müller holds that the first division of the Aryan races was into two branches, viz., the North-Western or European, and the South-Eastern or Asiatic; and that, after they became once separated, the two branches never met again. The North-Western branch travelled towards Europe; and five distinct races occupied five different portions of Europe at periods which cannot be ascertained. The Celts settled, or were more probably driven onwards by other races to settle in the extreme west of Europe, in France, Ireland, Great Britain, and Belgium; the robust Tutons settled in northern and central Europe, from which they issued after the downfall of Rome to conquer the whole of Europe; the Slavs settled in eastern Europe, *i.e.*, in Russia and other places; and the Italic and Greek races settled in the south of Europe.

The Asiatic branch travelled southwards, and according to Max Müller, the still undivided Indo-Iranians came as far as the Indus, to the land of the five rivers, or the Punjab. Here, "within sight of the Indus and its tributaries, the undivided South-Eastern Aryans spoke a language more primitive than the Sanscrit or Zend." Religious schism then separated them; the worshippers of the Devas or the Hindus remained in the Punjab, the worshippers of the Asuras or the Iranians went away to Persia.

It is the worshippers of the Devas—the Hindu Aryans—who have composed those hymns which are known as the Rig Veda, and we will say a few words here about this ancient work. Probably there is not another work in the literature of mankind which is so deeply interesting, so unique in the lessons it imparts. The hoary antiquity of this ancient work, the picture it affords of the earliest form of civilisation that the Aryans developed in any part of the world, and the flood of light it throws on the origin of the myths and religions of all Aryan nations,—make the Rig Veda deeply interesting.

But the work has a yet higher import, a deeper significance. To the philosophical historian of man the Rig Veda discloses the origin of religious faith and religious feelings. It explains how the mind of man in its infancy worships what is bright and glorious in nature, what is powerful and striking. Among less happy nations, religion began with the dread of diseases and of evils, as these made the most lasting impression on the mind. But among the Aryans, the brighter and pleasanter aspects of nature,—the bright sky, the blushing dawn, the rising sun, and the glowing fire,—created the deepest impression, and called forth songs of gratitude and praise and worship. This is the Rig Veda Sanhitâ,—this is the earliest form of Aryan religion known.

But the Rig Veda is more than this. It shows us how the mind is led from Nature up to Nature's God. For the sages of the Rig Veda do not always remain satisfied with the worship of the manifestations of Nature; they sometimes soar higher, and dare to conceive that all these phenomena—the sun, the sky, the storms, and the thunder—are but the actions of the Unknowable One.

And if such is the value of the Rig Veda to the historian of man, its value to the historian of Aryan nations is still greater. It is the oldest work in the Aryan world. It gives us a picture of the oldest civilisation which the Aryans developed in any part of the world. And as we have said before, it enlightens and clears up much that is dark and obscure in the religions and myths of Aryan nations all over the world. It would be entirely foreign to our present object to illustrate this by instances, but some instances are so well known as to merely require a mention to illustrate our views.

Zeus or Jupiter is the Vedic Dyu, or the sky; and Daphne and Athena are probably the Vedic Dahanâ and Ahanâ, the dawn. Uranus is Varuna, the sky; and probably Prometheus is the Vedic Pramantha, the fire which is produced by friction.

To the Hindus the Rig Veda is a work of still higher importance. It explains the whole fabric of the later Hindu religion; it clears all the complications of later mythology; it throws light on the history of the Hindu mind from its earliest stage of infancy. The Hindu learns from this ancient and priceless volume that Vishnu the supreme preserver, and his three steps covering the universe, mean the sun at its rise, its zenith, and its setting; that the terrible god Rudra the supreme destroyer originally meant the thunder or thunder-cloud; and that Brahmâ the supreme creator was originally prayer or the god of prayer.

The Rig Veda consists of 1028 hymns, comprising over ten thousand verses. The hymns are generally simple, and betray a child-like and simple faith in the gods, to whom sacrifices are offered, and libations of the Soma juice are poured, and who are asked for increase of progeny, cattle, and wealth, and implored to help the Aryans in their still doubtful struggle against the black aborigines of the Punjab.

The hymns of the Rig Veda are divided into ten Mandalas or Books, and with the exception of the first and last books, every one of the remaining eight books contains hymns said to have been composed or rather proclaimed by one Rishi,—by which we may understand one family or line of teachers. Thus the second book is by Gritsamada; the third is by Visvâmitra; the fourth is by Bâmadeva; the fifth is by Atri; the sixth is by Bhâradvâja; the seventh is by Vasishtha; the eighth is by Kanva; and the ninth is by Angiras. The first book contains 191 hymns, which, with scattered exceptions, are composed by fifteen Rishis; and the tenth book also contains 191 hymns, which are mostly ascribed to fictitious authors.

The hymns of the Rig Veda were handed down from father to son, or from teacher to pupil for centuries together, and it was in a later age, in the Epic Period, that they were arranged and compiled. The whole, or greater portion of the tenth book, seems to have been the production of this later period, but was thrown in and preserved with the body of the older hymns.

The arrangement and compilation of the Rig Veda hymns in their present shape must have been completed within the Epic Period. In Aitareya Âranyaka II, 2, we have fanciful derivations given of the names of the Rishis of the Rig Veda in the order in which the Mandalas are arranged. And this is followed by an account of a Sûkta or hymn, of a Rik or verse, of a half Rik, of a Pada or word, and of an Akshara or syllable. The Rig Veda Sanhitâ, therefore, had not only been arranged Mandala by Mandala, but had been carefully divided, subdivided, and analysed within the Epic Period.

By the close of the Epic Period, every verse, every word, every syllable of the Rig Veda had been counted. The number of verses, as computed, varies from 10,402 to 10,622, that of words is 153,826, that of syllables 432,000.

CHAPTER II.

AGRICULTURE, PASTURE, AND COMMERCE.

THE main industry of the ancient Hindus, as of the modern Hindus, was agriculture; and as might be expected, we have frequent allusions to it in the Rig Veda. The very name Ârya, by which the Aryan conquerors of India have distinguished themselves from the aborigines or Dâsas, is said to come from a root which means to cultivate. Professor Max Müller believes that traces of this root are to be found in the names of many Aryan countries, from Iran or Persia, to Erin or Ireland, and argues that the word was invented in the primeval home of the Aryans, to indicate their partiality to cultivation, as distinguished from the nomadic habits of the Turanians, whose name is supposed to indicate their rapid journeys or the fleetness of their horse. Certain it is that the word Ârya is the one word in the Rig Veda which distinguishes the conquerors as a class, or even as a caste, from the aborigines of the country. And there are remarkable passages also which show that the new settlers, in calling themselves Ârya, had not altogether forgotten the original signification of the word. One instance will suffice :—

"O ye two Asvins! you have displayed your glory by teaching the *Ârya* to cultivate with the plough and to sow corn, and by giving him rains for the production of his food, and by destroying the *Dasyu* by your thunderbolt" (I, 117, 21).

There are two other words in the Rig Veda which

are synonymous, not with the Aryan tribe, but rather with man generally; and both of them come from roots which indicate cultivation. The words are *Charshana* (I, 3, 7, &c.) and *Krishti* (I, 4, 6, &c.), and both these words come from modifications of the same root *Krish* or *Chrish* to cultivate.

Thus the very names which the Aryan conquerors of India gave themselves are names which are believed to indicate that useful occupation which distinguishes the civilised man from the barbarian, viz., cultivation of the soil.

There are numerous direct allusions in the Rig Veda to agriculture, but the most remarkable among them is a hymn which is dedicated to a supposed god of agriculture, the Lord of the Field as he is called, and which we will translate in full:—

"1. We will win (cultivate) this field with the Lord of the Field; may he nourish our cattle and our horses; may he bless us thereby.

"2. O Lord of the Field! bestow on us sweet and pure and butter-like and delicious and copious rain, even as cows give us milk. May the Lords of the water bless us.

"3. May the plants be sweet unto us; may the skies and the rains and the firmament be full of sweetness; may the Lord of the Field be gracious to us. We will follow him uninjured by enemies.

"4. Let the oxen work merrily; let the men work merrily; let the plough move on merrily. Fasten the traces merrily; ply the goad merrily.

"5. O Suna and Sîra! accept this hymn. Moisten this earth with the rain you have created in the sky.

"6. O fortunate Furrow! proceed onwards, we pray unto thee; do thou bestow on us wealth and an abundant crop.

"7. May Indra accept this Furrow; may Pûshan lead her onwards. May she be filled with water, and yield us corn year after year.*

* In these two remarkable verses, the furrow, Sitâ, is addressed as a female, and asked to yield copious harvests. In the Yajur Veda also, the

"8. Let the ploughshares turn up the sod merrily; let the men follow the oxen merrily; may Parjanya moisten the earth with sweet rains. O Suna and Sîra! bestow on us happiness" (IV, 57).

We shall seek in vain in the entire range of later Sanscrit literature for a passage in which the humble hopes and wishes of simple agriculturists are so naturally described. This is the unique charm of the Rig Veda as a literary composition. Whether it be an account of a battle with the aborigines, or a prayer to friendly Indra to come and have a cup of Soma, or a song of the simple cultivator,—the Rig Veda hymn always takes us nearer to the workings of a simple and manly heart than anything in the literature of later times.

We will translate a portion of another hymn, also relating to agriculture:—

"3. Fasten the ploughs, spread out the yokes, and sow the seed on this field which has been prepared. Let the corn grow with our hymns; let the scythes fall on the neighbouring fields where the corn is ripe.

"4. The ploughs have been fastened; the labourers have spread the yokes; the wise men are uttering prayers to gods.

"5. Prepare troughs for the drinking of the animals. Fasten the leather-string, and let us take out water from this deep and goodly well which never dries up.

"6. The troughs have been prepared for the animals; the leather-string shines in the deep and goodly well which never dries up, and the water is easily got. Take out water from the well.

"7. Refresh the horses; take up the corn stacked in the field; and make a cart which will convey it easily. This well full of water for the drinking of animals, is one

furrow is similarly worshipped. And when the Aryans gradually conquered the whole of India, and primeval jungles and waste lands were marked with the furrow, the furrow or Sîtâ assumed a more definite human character, and became the heroine of the Epic which describes the Aryan conquest of Southern India.

drona in extent, and there is a stone wheel to it. And the reservoir for the drinking of men is one *skanda.* Fill it with water" (X, 101).

Irrigation and cultivation in the Punjab are only possible by means of wells, and wells are reserved also for the drinking of men and of beasts; and it is not surprising therefore that we should find references to wells in the Rig Veda. Another remarkable fact which appears from the passages translated above is, that horses were used for cultivation in those days, a custom still common in Europe, but not in India in modern times.

In X, 25, 4, and in many other places we have allusions to wells. In X, 93, 13, we are told how water was raised from wells for irrigation. The contrivance is the same as is still in vogue in Northern India; a number of pots are tied to a string, and as the pots go up and down by the movement of a wheel, they are filled in the well and pulled up and emptied and sent down again. The contrivance is called *ghatichakra,* or the circle of pots, and bears the same name to the present day.

In X, 99, 4, we have another allusion to irrigation of fields by means of canals which were replenished with water by means of a *drona.* And in X, 68, 1, we are told that cultivators who irrigated their fields kept away birds by uttering loud cries.

As stated above, the allusions to pasture are by no means so frequent as the allusions to agriculture. Pûshan is the god of shepherds,—he is the sun as viewed by shepherds,—and is supposed to protect them and travellers generally in their wanderings over the country. And here and there in a hymn to Pûshan, we find that the Aryans of India had brought with them recollections and songs about those migrations which they occasionally undertook in their primitive home, if not after their settlement in India. We translate one such hymn below:—

"1. O Pûshan! help us to finish our journey, and

remove all dangers. O Son of the Cloud, do thou march before us !

"2. O Pûshan ! do thou remove from our path him who would lead us astray, who strikes and plunders and does wrong.

"3. Do thou drive away that wily robber who intercepts journeys.

"4. Do thou trample under thy foot the vile carcass of him who plunders us in both ways (by stealth and by force) and who commits outrages.

"5. O wise Pûshan, destroyer of enemies ! we implore of thee the protection with which thou didst shield and encourage our forefathers.

"6. O Pûshan, possessed of all wealth, possessed of golden weapons, and chief among beings ! bestow on us thy riches.

"7. Lead us so that enemies who intercept may not harm us ; lead us by an easy and pleasant path. O Pûshan ! devise means (for our safety) on this journey.

"8. Lead us to pleasant tracts covered with green grass ; let there be no extreme heat by the way. O Pûshan ! devise means (for our safety) on this journey.

"9. Be powerful in thy protection ; fill us with riches ; bestow on us wealth ; make us strong and give us food ! O Pûshan ! devise means (for our safety) on this journey.

"10. We do not blame Pûshan ; but we extol him in our hymns. We solicit wealth from the handsome Pûshan" (I, 42).

There is also another interesting hymn on the practice of taking out cattle to pasture fields, and bringing them back. A few verses are worth translating :—

"4. We call the cowherd, let him take out these cows ; let him pasture them in the fields ; let him know and pick out the animals ; let him bring them back to the house ; let him pasture them on all sides.

"5. The cowherd seeks for the cows and brings them

back to the house; he pastures them on all sides. May he come home safe.

"8. O cowherd! pasture the cows in all directions, and bring them back. Pasture them in various parts of the earth, and then bring them back" (X, 19).

There are allusions in the preceding passages to robbers who infested outlying tracts of the country, probably to the cattle-lifters and thieves among the aboriginal races, who hung around the Aryan villages and clearances, and lived by intercepting peaceful industry. We shall speak of them further on.

Allusions to trade and commerce must be necessarily rare in a collection of hymns to gods; but, nevertheless, we are here and there surprised by passages which throw a curious light on the manners of the times. Loans and usury were well understood in those days, and Rishis (who, we should always remember, were worldly men in those days, and not hermits or anchorites), occasionally lament their state of indebtedness with the simplicity of primitive times. In one remarkable verse again, we are reminded of the finality of a sale-transaction, when once the sale is completed:—

"One sells a large quantity for a small price, and then goes to the purchaser and denies the sale, and asks for a higher price. But he cannot exceed the price once fixed on the plea that he has given a large quantity. Whether the price was adequate or inadequate, the price fixed at the time of sale must hold good" (IV, 24, 9).

A passage like the above would indicate the existence of current money for the purposes of buying and selling. We have instances of Rishis acknowledging the gift of a hundred pieces of gold (V, 27, 2, &c.), and there can be no doubt, pieces of gold of a certain fixed value were used as money as indicated in these passages. At the same time it must be admitted that there is no distinct allusion to *coined* money in the Rig Veda. The word *Nishka* (I, 126, 2, &c.) is often used in the Rig

Veda in a dubious sense. In some passages it means money, in others it means a golden ornament for the neck. The two interpretations are not necessarily contradictory, for in India pieces of gold used as money have habitually been used as ornaments for the neck since times immemorial.

On the other hand, there are distinct references to voyages by sea, though of course the words used may mean rivers only, and not the sea. The shipwreck of Bhujyu, and his deliverance by the gods Asvins, is constantly alluded to (I, 116, 3, &c.), and in I, 25, 7, the god Varuna is said to know the paths of the birds through the sky, and the paths of the ships over the sea. In IV, 55, 6, the poet refers to the "people who desiring to acquire wealth pray to the sea before undertaking a voyage"; while in VII, 88, 3, Vasishtha says:—

"When Varuna and I went on a boat and took her out to sea, I lived in the boat floating on the water and was happy in it, rocking gracefully (on the waves)."

While there are these and other distinct allusions to voyage, there is absolutely no prohibition against it in the Rig Veda.

CHAPTER III.

FOOD, CLOTHING, AND THE ARTS OF PEACE.

BARLEY and wheat seem to have been the principal produce of the field, and the principal articles of food. The names of grain found in the Rig Veda are somewhat misleading, as they have come to bear a different signification in modern days from what they had in the ancient times. Thus the word *Yava,* which in modern Sanscrit implies barley only, was used in the Veda to imply food-grains generally, including wheat and barley. And the word *Dhâna,* which, in Bengal at least, means paddy or rice, implies in the Rig Veda fried barley, which was used as food and offered to the gods. There is no allusion to *vrîhi* (rice) in the Rig Veda.

We also find mention of various kinds of cakes prepared from these grains and used as food and offered to the gods. *Pakti* (from *pach,* to cook, or to prepare) means prepared cakes, and various other terms like *Purodâsa* and *Apûpa* and *Karambha,* are also used (III, 52, 1 and 2; IV, 24, 7, &c.)

It may be easily imagined that animal food was largely used by the early Hindus of the Punjab. We have frequent allusions to the sacrifice and to the cooking of cows, buffaloes, and bulls (I, 61, 12; II, 7, 5; V, 29, 7 and 8; VI, 17, 11; VI, 16, 47; VI, 28, 4; X, 27, 2; X, 28, 3, &c.)

In X, 89, 14, there is mention of a slaughter-house where cows were killed, and in X, 91, 14, there is an allusion to the sacrifice of horses, bulls, and rams. The allusions to the sacrifice of the horse are extremely rare, showing that, although the custom was introduced into India by the early Aryans from their primitive home, the flesh of horse as an article of food soon fell into disuse. In later times the sacrifice of the horse or the *Asvamedha* was performed on rare occasions with great pomp and circumstance by powerful kings, after they had subdued their neighbours and assumed a title answering to the Imperial title in Europe. There can be no doubt this great imperial rite rose out of the simple sacrifice of the horse practised in primitive times when the horse was still an article of food. The pomp and ceremony, as well as certain revolting rites connected with the horse-sacrifice of later days, were unknown in Vedic times.

A fairly complete account of the sacrifice of the horse, such as it prevailed in the Vedic times, is to be found in hymn 162 of the first Mandala of the Rig Veda. The body of the horse was marked with a cane and was then dissected along the lines marked, and the ribs and the different limbs were separated. The meat was roasted and boiled, while the soul of the horse was supposed to go to the gods.

Who could have believed that this simple horse-sacrifice of the Rig Veda, the carving and the roasting and the boiling of the horse for worship and for the purposes of food, would have developed into the imperial ceremony of *Asvamedha* in later times? But many a practice which we see in its simple and natural aspect in the Veda has developed into pompous ceremonials in later days; and many a simple Vedic allegory relating to the striking phenomena of Nature has also developed into elaborate Puranic legends. Herein constitutes the true value of the Veda; we trace in it Hindu rites and ceremonials and the Hindu religion itself to their simple natural beginnings.

The fermented juice of the plant called *Soma* appears

to have been the only intoxicating drink used in the Vedic times. So much were the ancient Aryans addicted to this drink that Soma was soon worshipped as a deity both in India and in Iran (under the name *Haoma* in the latter country), and we find one entire Mandala or Book of the Rig Veda dedicated to this deity. The Indo-Aryans appear to have been more addicted to fermented and intoxicating Soma than their peaceful brethren of Iran; and many are the allusions in the Zendavesta to the hated customs of their Indian brethren. Some antiquarians think that this was one great reason of those dissensions which broke out among the southern Aryans, and which led to the final separation of the Iranians from the Hindus.

The process by which the Soma-juice was prepared has been fully described in IX, 66, and in other hymns. We will translate a few verses from this hymn :—

"7. O Soma! you have been crushed; you flow as a stream to Indra, scattering joy on all sides; you bestow immortal food.

"8. Seven women stir thee with their fingers, blending their voices in a song to thee; you remind the sacrificer of his duties at the sacrifice.

"9. You mix with water with a pleasing sound; and the fingers stir you over a woollen strainer, and filter you. Your particles are thrown up then, and a sound arises from the woollen strainer.

"11. The woollen strainer is placed on a vessel, and the fingers repeatedly stir the Soma, which sends down a sweet stream into the vessel.

"13. O Soma! you are then mixed with milk. Water runs towards thee with a pleasing sound."

From this description it would appear that the juice of Soma used to be taken—much as *Siddhi* is taken in our times—mixed with milk. The poets of the Rig Veda go into ecstasy over the virtues and the exhilarating powers of the Soma; and some of their descriptions have developed into strange Puranic legends in subsequent times. One or two verses will illustrate this:—

"O Soma! there is nothing so bright as thou. When poured out, thou welcomest all the gods to bestow on them immortality" (IX, 108, 3).

"The praiseworthy Soma has from ancient times been the drink of the gods; he was milked from the hidden recesses of the sky; he was created for Indra and was extolled" (IX, 110, 8).

"In that realm where there is perennial light, and where the Heaven is placed, O Soma, lead me to that deathless and immortal realm! Flow thou for Indra" (IX, 113, 7).

Such passages as these are to be found throughout the ninth book of the Rig Veda. Who could have guessed that the strange Puranic legends of the churning of the ocean and the discovery of the *Amrita* or immortal drink would have arisen from these simple Vedic descriptions of Soma! The sky in the Veda is considered watery, and is often confused with the sea, and the milking of Soma from the sky is translated in the Purânas into the churning of the ocean for the *Amrita!*

It would appear from many passages in the Rig Veda that many arts were carried to a high state of excellence. Weaving was well known of course, and deft female fingers wove the warp and the woof in ancient times as in modern days (II, 3, 6; II, 38, 4, &c.). In one curious passage (VI, 9, 2), the Rishi laments his ignorance of the mysteries of religious rites by saying: "I know not the warp and I know not the woof" of religious rites; and in another place (X, 26, 6), the weaving and bleaching of sheep's wool are attributed to the god Pûshan, who, as we have already seen, is the god of shepherds.

Every Aryan village had probably its barber then as now; and the clearances of forests by fire are in one passage somewhat mysteriously described as the *shaving* of the earth (I, 164, 44). Carpentry was also well known, and we have frequent allusions to the construction of carts and chariots (III, 53, 19; IV, 2, 14; IV, 16, 20, &c.) The use of iron, of gold, and of other metals was well known ; in V, 9, 5, we have a reference to the work of an ironsmith, and in VI, 3, 4, we are told of goldsmiths melting gold.

But we get a better idea of working in metals in the Vedic times from the description of various gold ornaments and iron utensils and implements of war which is to be found throughout the Rig Veda. The allusions are numerous, and we can therefore only make a selection here which will convey a fair idea of the manufactures of those days. We are told of armours used in war in I, 140, 10 ; in II, 39, 4 ; in IV, 53, 2 ; and in various other places. In II, 34, 3, we have reference to golden helmets, and in IV, 34, 9, there is mention of armour for the shoulders or arms, probably a shield. The lightning has been compared to a javelin (*rishti*) in V, 52, 6, and in V. 54, 11 ; and also to a sword or battle-axe (*bâshi*), and to bows and arrows and quivers in V, 57, 2. Three thousand mailed warriors are spoken of in VI, 27, 6 ; feathered, sharp-pointed, shining shafts are described in VI, 46, 11 ; and sharp-edged swords are spoken of in VI, 47, 10. And in verses 26 and 29 of the same hymn we are told of war-chariots and kettle-drums. And lastly, in the 75th hymn of the sixth Mandala, we have a spirited account of the arms and accoutrements of war which we will translate for our readers further on.

In IV, 2, 8, we have a reference to horses with golden caparisons, and in IV, 37, 4, V, 19, 3, and many other places we have allusions to the *Nishka*, a golden ornament worn in the neck. In V, 53, 4, the lighting ornaments of the Maruts are compared with jewelry (*Anji*), with necklaces (*Srak*), with golden breastplates (*Rukma*), and with bracelets and anklets (*Khadi*). In V, 54, 11, we are again told of anklets for the feet, and golden breastplates for the breast, and of golden crowns (*Sipråh hiranmayih*) for the head.

Thus it will be seen that a very considerable advance was made in the manufacture of arms, weapons, and various kinds of ornaments. We have references also to skin vessels (VI, 48, 18), and iron vessels (V, 30, 15), and in several places to iron towns, which must be taken in a figurative sense as signifying strong forts (VII, 3, 7; VII, 15, 14; VII, 95, 1, &c.) We have also references to a hundred stone-built towns in IV, 30, 20, and other places.

There can be no doubt that in the various rocky and mountainous tracts where the early Hindus established their colonies, they soon learnt to utilise stone as a durable and cheap material for architecture; and there can be no difficulty in believing that in numerous Hindu towns many structures and surrounding walls were of stone. That the art of building was carried to some degree of excellence appears from many allusions to mansions with thousand pillars (II, 41, 5; V, 62, 6, &c.); but at the same time it must be admitted that there is no distinct allusion in the Rig Veda to the art of sculpture properly so-called. The researches of antiquarians have failed to discover in any part of India traces of sculptured stone of a time long previous to the Buddhist era; and in the numerous great museums of Europe, which are filled with the ancient stone monuments of Egypt and Babylon, India is not represented by any such monuments dating much before the Buddhist Period.

Most of the animals domesticated at the present day were domesticated in India in the remote period of the Rig Veda. We have spirited accounts of the war-horse in several places (VI, 46, 13 and 14, &c.)

Indeed, these war-horses were so highly prized by the early Aryans in their battles against the aborigines, that the horse, under the name of *Dadhikrâ*, soon became an object of worship; and in IV, 38, we have a spirited account of the respect paid to this god-like being.

In IV, 4, 1, we have a reference to a king riding with his ministers on an elephant. Among other domesticated animals, we have frequent mention of cows, goats, sheep, buffaloes, and dogs, which last were used in carrying burdens.

CHAPTER IV.

WARS AND DISSENSIONS.

As has been stated before, the early Hindus wrested the fertile tracts on the banks of the Indus and its tributaries from the primitive races of the Punjab; but the aborigines did not give up their birthright without a struggle. Retreating before the more civilised organisation and valour of the Hindus in the open field, they still hung round in fastnesses and forests near every Hindu settlement and village, harassed them in their communications, waylaid and robbed them at every opportunity, stole their cattle, and often attacked them in considerable force. Well might they exclaim with the Gaels of Scotland, who had been similarly dispossessed of their fertile soil by the conquering Saxons, and had similarly retreated to barren fastnesses:—

> "These fertile plains, that softened vale,
> Were once the birthright of the Gael;
> The stranger came with iron hand,
> And from our fathers reft the land.
> Where dwell we now? See rudely swell
> Crag over crag, and fell o'er fell.
>
> . . . .
>
> Pent in this fortress of the North,
> Think'st thou we will not sally forth,
> To spoil the spoiler as we may,
> And from the robber rend the prey?
> Ay, by my soul! While on yon plain
> The Saxon rears one shock of grain,
> While, of ten thousand herds, there strays
> But one along yon river's maze,—
> The Gael, of plain and river heir,
> Shall, with strong hand, redeem his share!"

Unfortunately, however, they had no poet to hand down to us their view of the case, and the only account we have of this long war of centuries is from the conquering Hindus. It is needless to say that the conquerors viewed the aborigines with the contempt and hatred which have marked the conduct of all conquering nations, whether on the banks of the Indus seventeen hundred years before Christ, or on the banks of the Mississippi seventeen hundred years after Christ! History repeats itself; and the Punjab was cleared of its non-Aryan aborigines just as the United States of America have, in modern times, been cleared of the many powerful and brave Indian races who lived and hunted and ruled within its primeval forests.

Of these wars with the aborigines we have frequent allusions in the Rig Veda; and a translation of some of these passages will give a better idea of these interminable hostilities than any account that we can give of them. The allusions are so numerous that our only difficulty is in making a selection.

"Indra, who is invoked by many, and is accompanied by his fleet companions, has destroyed by his thunderbolt the *Dasyus* and *Simyus* who dwelt on earth, and then he distributed the fields to his white-complexioned friends (Aryans). The thunderer makes the sun shine and the rain to fall" (I, 100, 18). "Indra with his weapon, the thunderbolt, and in his vigour, destroyed the towns of the *Dasyus*, and wandered at his will. O holder of the thunderbolt! be thou cognisant of our hymns, and cast thy weapon against the *Dasyu*, and increase the vigour and the fame of the *Arya*" (I, 103, 3).

In the very next hymn, we come across a curious allusion to aboriginal robbers who dwelt on the banks of four small streams called the Sifâ, the Anjasî, the Kulisî, and the Vîrapatnî, whose courses cannot now be determined. These robbers issued from their fastnesses and harassed the civilised Aryan villages, much in the same way as a true descendant of those aborigines, the Bhil Tantia in our own times, harassed the peaceful villages of Central India! We translate the two verses below:—

"Kuyava gets scent of the wealth of others and appropriates it. He lives in water and pollutes it. His two wives bathe in the stream; may they be drowned in the depths of the Sifâ river!

"Ayu lives in water in a secret fastness. He flourishes amidst the rise of waters. The rivers Anjasî, Kulisî, and Vîrapatnî protect him with their waters" (I, 104, 3 and 4).

We proceed with some more extracts:—

"Indra protects his *Ârya* worshipper in wars. He who protects him on countless occasions, protects him in all wars. He subdues the people who do not perform sacrifices for the benefit of men (Aryans). He flays the enemy of his black skin and kills him and reduces him to ashes. He burns down all who do injury, and all who are cruel" (I, 130, 8).

"O destroyer of foes! collect together the heads of these marauding troops, and crush them with thy wide foot! Thy foot is wide!

"O Indra! destroy the power of these marauding troops! Throw them into the vile pit—the vast and vile pit!

"O Indra! thou hast destroyed three times fifty such troops! People extol this thy deed; but it is nothing compared to thy prowess!

"O Indra! destroy the Pishâchis, who are reddish in appearance and utter fearful yells. Destroy all these Râkshasas"* (I, 133, 2–5).

"O Indra! the poet prays to thee for pleasant food. Thou hast made the earth the bed (burial-ground) of the *Dâsas.* Indra has beautified the three regions with his gifts; he has slayed *Kuyavâcha* for King *Daryoni.*

"O Indra! Rishis still extol that ancient deed of

* Pishâchis and Râkshasas may mean imaginary demons. We would rather think, however, that they here refer to the aborigines.

prowess! Thou hast destroyed many marauders to put an end to war; thou hast stormed the towns of enemies who worship no gods; and thou hast bent the weapons of foes who worship no gods" (I, 174, 7 and 8).

"O Asvins! destroy those who are yelling hideously like dogs, and are coming to destroy us! Slay those who wish to fight with us! You know the way to destroy them. Let each word of those who extol you bring wealth in return. O you truthful ones! accept our prayers" (I, 182, 4).

"The far-famed and graceful Indra is gracious to men (Aryans)! The destroying and powerful Indra has cast down the head of the malignant *Dâsa!*

"Indra, who slayed Vritra and stormed towns, has destroyed the troops of the black *Dâsas*, and has made the earth and the water for Manu.* May he fulfil the wishes of the sacrificer" (II, 20, 6 and 7).

We know how the Spaniards, the conquerors of America, owed their successes to a very great extent to their horses, animals previously unknown to the American aborigines, and therefore regarded with a strange terror. It would seem that the war-horses of the early Indo-Aryans inspired the aborigines of India with a similar fear. The following passages, translated from a hymn to *Dadhikrâ*, or the deified war-horse, will therefore be regarded with interest:—

"As people shout and raise a cry after a thief who has purloined a garment, even so the enemies yell and shout at the sight of Dadhikrâ! As birds make a noise at the sight of the hungry hawk on its descent, even so the enemies yell and shout at the sight of Dadhikrâ careering in quest of plunder of food and cattle!

"Enemies fear Dadhikrâ, who is radiant and destroying as a thunderbolt. When he beats back a thousand

* Here, as elsewhere, Manu is spoken of as the ancestor of the Aryan man. In many places he is spoken of as the originator of cultivation and of the worship of fire which distinguished the Aryans.

men around him, he becomes excited and uncontrollable in his strength" (IV, 38, 5 and 8).

It would seem from numerous passages in the Rig Veda that Kutsa was a powerful warrior and a mighty destroyer of the black aborigines. We are told in hymn 16 of the fourth Mandala, that Indra slew the "*Dasyu*, who is wily and impious," to bestow wealth on Kutsa (verse 9); that he helped Kutsa and came to his house with the common object of slaying the *Dasyu* (verse 10); and that he slew fifty thousand "black-complexioned enemies" in battle (verse 13). In IV, 28, 4, we are told that Indra has made the *Dasyus* devoid of all virtues, and the object of hatred of all men; and in IV, 30, 15, we learn that Indra destroyed five hundred and a thousand *Dâsas.*

We have similar allusions to the subjugation and destruction of *Dasyus* or *Dâsas* in V, 70, 3; VI, 18, 3; and VI, 25, 2; while there is a curious reference to an unknown region inhabited by the *Dasyus* in VI, 47, 20, which deserves translation:—

"O ye gods! We have travelled and lost our way, and come to a region where cattle do not pasture. The extensive region gives shelter to *Dasyus* only. O Brihaspati! lead us in our search for cattle. O Indra! show the way to your worshippers who have lost their way."

It will be seen that the Aryan poets are sufficiently uncomplimentary in speaking of the shouts and yells of the aboriginal barbarians. The civilised conquerors could scarcely imagine that these yells could form a language, and have therefore in some places described the barbarians as without a language (V, 29, 10, &c.)

We have spoken before of Kuyava and Ayu, two aboriginal robbers who dwelt in fastnesses surrounded by rivers, and harassed the Aryan villages. We have frequent allusions to another powerful aboriginal leader who is called Krishna, probably because of his black complexion. One of the passages relating to him deserves translation :—

"The fleet Krishna lived on the banks of the Ausumatî river with ten thousand troops. Indra of his own wisdom became cognisant of this loud-yelling chief. He destroyed the marauding host for the benefit of men (Aryans).

"Indra said: 'I have seen the fleet Krishna. He is lurking in the hidden region near the Ausumatî, like the sun in a cloud. O Maruts! I desire you to engage in fight, and to destroy him.'

"The fleet Krishna then appeared shining on the banks of the Ausumatî. Indra took Brihaspati as his ally, and destroyed the fleet and godless army" (VIII, 96, 13—15).

Not only have the aborigines been described as fond of yelling and devoid of a language, but they are in other places considered as scarcely human. We are told in one place:

"We are surrounded on all sides by *Dasyu* tribes. They do not perform sacrifices; they do not believe in anything; their rites are different; they are not men! O destroyer of foes! kill them. Destroy the *Dâsa* race!" (X, 22, 8).

In X, 49, Indra proclaims that he has deprived the *Dasyu* race of the name of *Ârya* (verse 3); that he has destroyed Navavâstva and Brihadratha of the *Dâsa* race (verse 6); that he cuts the *Dâsas* in twain,—"it is for this fate that they have been born!" (verse 7).

Such were the aborigines with whom the early Hindus carried on an interminable war, and such was the fate to which they consigned their less civilised neighbours, the primeval owners of the Indian soil! It is abundantly evident that no love was lost between the conquerors and the conquered. It was by ceaseless fighting that the conquerors protected themselves in their newly-conquered country, gradually extended the limits of cultivation, built new villages, threw out new colonies in primeval jungles, and spread the light of civilisation and the fame of their prowess around. They hated the despised barbarians with a genuine hatred, killed numbers of them when they could, thinned their ranks with their horses, called them yelling hounds and men without a tongue and brutes below the rank of men, and almost believed they were born to be slain,—"it is for this fate that they have been born!" On the other hand, the stubborn barbarians had their revenge too. Retreating before the more civilised valour of the Hindus, they hung about in every fastness and every bend of a river, they waylaid and robbed travellers, harassed villages, killed or stole cattle, and sometimes fell on the Hindus in great numbers. With that dogged tenacity which is peculiar to barbarians they disputed every inch of ground as they retreated, they interrupted the religious rites of the conquerors, despised their gods, and plundered their wealth. But in spite of every resistance the colonies of the more civilised races extended in every direction, the area of civilisation widened, jungles and wastes were brought under cultivation and dotted with villages and royal towns, and the kingdoms of the early Hindus extended over the whole of the Punjab. The barbarians were either exterminated, or retreated before the ever-advancing line of Aryan civilisation into those hills and fastnesses which their children still inhabit.

It may be imagined, however, that some among the weaker barbarians preferred abject subjection to extermination or exile. We find traces accordingly in the Rig Veda of *Dasyus* who at last owned the domination of the more powerful race, and who adopted their civilisation and their language. These, then, were the first *Hinduised aborigines* of India.

Our extracts on the subject of the wars of the Aryans with the aborigines have been numerous. We will now quote one or two passages to show that the Aryan conquerors were not always at peace among themselves! Sudâs was an Aryan king and conqueror, and we are frequently told that various Aryan tribes and kings combined against him, and he was victorious over them all. The allusions to these internecine wars among Aryan races, and to the particular tribes who fought against Sudâs, are historically among the most important passages in the Rig Veda.

"8. The wily foes planned destruction, and broke down the embankment of the Adîna (to cause an inundation). But Sudâs filled the earth with his prowess, and Kavi, the son of Chayamâna, fell like a victim.

"9. For the waters of the river flowed through their old channel and did not take a new course; and Sudâs' horse marched over the country. Indra placed the hostile and talkative men and their children under Sudâs.

"11. Sudâs earned glory by killing twenty-one men of both regions. As the young priest cuts the kusa grass in the house of sacrifice, even so Sudâs cut his enemies. The hero Indra sent the Maruts for his succour.

"14. The sixty-six thousand six-hundred and sixty-six warriors of Anu and Druhya, who had desired for cattle, and were hostile to Sudâs, were laid low. These deeds proclaim the glory of Indra!

"17. It was Indra who enabled the poor Sudâs to achieve these deeds. Indra enabled the goat to kill the strong lion. Indra felled the sacrificial post with a needle. He bestowed all the wealth on Sudâs" (VII, 18).

The poet Tritsu or Vasishtha, who sang these deeds of Sudâs' glory, was not unrewarded for his immortal verse. For in verses 22 and 23, he acknowledges with gratitude that the valiant Sudâs rewarded him with two hundred cows and two chariots and four horses with gold trappings! We quote below another hymn relating to Sudâs.

"1. O Indra and Varuna! Your worshippers, relying on your help and seeking to win cattle, have marched eastwards with their weapons. Crush, Indra and Varuna, your enemies, whether *Dâsas* or *Âryas*, and defend Sudâs with your protection.

"2. Where men raise their banners and meet in battle, where nothing seems to favour us, where the men look up to the sky and tremble, then, O Indra and Varuna! help us and speak to us words of comfort.

"3. O Indra and Varuna! the ends of the earth seem to be lost, and the noise ascends to the skies! The troops of the enemy are approaching. O Indra and Varuna! who ever listen to prayers, come near us with your protection.

"4. O Indra and Varuna! you pierced the yet unassailed Bheda, and saved Sudâs. You listened to the prayers of the Tritsus. Their priestly vocation bore fruit in the hour of battle.

"5. O Indra and Varuna! the weapons of the enemy assail me in all directions, the foes assail me among marauding men. You are the owners of both kinds of wealth! Save us in the day of battle.

"6. Both parties invoked Indra and Varuna for wealth at the time of war. But in this battle you protected Sudâs with the Tritsus who were attacked by ten kings.

"7. O Indra and Varuna! the ten kings who did not perform sacrifices were unable, though combined, to beat Sudâs."

"8. You bestowed vigour, Indra and Varuna, to Sudâs, when surrounded by ten chiefs; when the white-robed Tritsus, wearing braided hair, worshipped you with oblations and hymns" (VII, 83).

Another remarkable hymn gives an account of the weapons used in war in those days. We make some extracts:—

"1. When the battle is nigh, and the warrior marches in his armour, he appears like the cloud! Warrior, let not thy person be pierced; be victorious; let thy armour protect you!

"2. We will win cattle with the bow, we will win with the bow; we will conquer the fierce and proud enemy with the bow! May the bow foil the desires of the enemy! We will spread our conquests on all sides with the bow!

"3. The string of the bow when pulled approaches the ear of the archer, making way in battle. It whispers words of consolation to him, and with sound it clasps the arrow, even as a loving wife clasps her husband.

"5. The quiver is like the parent of many arrows; the many arrows are like its children. It makes a sound, and hangs on the back of the warrior, and furnishes arrows in battle, and conquers the enemy.

"6. The expert charioteer stands on his chariot and drives his horses wheresoever he will. The reins restrain the horses from behind. Sing of their glory!

"7. The horses raise the dust with their hoofs, and career over the field with the chariots, with loud neighings. They do not retreat, but trample the marauding enemies under their feet.

"11. The arrow is feathered; the deer (horn) is its teeth. Well pulled and sent by the cow-leather-string, it falls on the enemy. Wherever men stand together or are separate, there the shafts reap advantage.

"14. The leather guard protects the arm from the abrasion of the bow-string, and coils round the arm like a snake in its convolutions. It knows its work, and is efficient, and protects the warrior in every way.

"15. We extol the arrow which is poisoned, whose face is of iron; * whose stem is of Parjanya" (VI, 75).

Before concluding our extracts, we will make one more from a hymn about the coronation of victorious kings.

"1. O king! I place you in the station of a king. Be the lord of this country! Be immovable and fixed! Let all the subjects cherish thee! Let not your kingdom be destroyed!

"2. Remain here fixed as the mountain; do not be

* This passage shows that the arrow-heads were of iron. Parjanya is the god of rains. Stems of Parjanya probably mean stems of reed growing in the rains. Verse 11 shows that arrow-heads were sometimes of deer-horn.

dethroned! Remain fixed like Indra, and support the kingdom!

"3. Indra has received the sacrificial offerings, and supports the newly-coronated king! Soma blesses him.

"4. The sky is fixed, the earth is fixed, the mountains are fixed, this universe is fixed. He also is fixed as king among his subjects!

"5. May King Varuna make you immovable! May the good Brihaspati make you immovable; may Indra and Agni support you and make you immovable.

"6. See, I mix these immortal offerings with the immortal Soma-juice. Indra has brought your subjects under your rule, and made them willing to pay you revenue!" (X, 173).

These extracts are enough. We have elsewhere shown that the warriors used not only armour and helmets, but also protecting armour for the shoulder, probably shields. They used javelins and battle-axes, and sharp-edged swords, beside bows and arrows. All the weapons of war known elsewhere in ancient times were known in India four thousand years ago. Drums assembled men in battle, banners led them on in compact masses, and the use of war-horses and chariots was well known. Tame elephants were in use too, and we have allusions to kings riding on richly-caparisoned elephants with their ministers (IV, 4, 1). But it does not appear that elephants were regularly used in war in the Vedic Period, as they were in the third and fourth centuries before Christ when the Greeks came to India.

For the rest, it was a turbulent time when the Vedic warriors lived and fought. They had not only to wage an interminable war against the aborigines, but the Hindu States were divided among themselves, and a powerful leader was often bent on annexing his neighbour's state. Rishis engaged in sacrifices asked for prowess to conquer the foes, or prayed to the gods for sons who would win victory in battles. Every able-bodied man was a warrior, and was ever prepared to defend his home and his fields and his cattle with his strong right arm. Every Hindu colony or tribe, while attentive to the worship of the gods and to the cultivation of the various arts of peace, was at the same time alive to the fact that its national existence depended on a constant preparedness for war. And the great conglomeration of Hindu tribes, which spread from the banks of the Indus to the banks of the Sarasvatî, consisted of hardy, brave, and warlike peoples, who maintained their footing in the land, and their independence and national existence by constant struggles, and a determination to win or die.

It is sad to contemplate this state of things. But where is the country in which, in ancient times, tribes and nations had not to maintain a ceaseless war for their aggrandisement, or even for their very existence? And even in modern times, during the two thousand years which have elapsed since Gautama Buddha and Jesus Christ preached their messages of peace, where shall we seek for the tribe or nation which could hope to reap the results of its peaceful industry without a constant struggle against its neighbours? With the exception of a few countries advantageously situated, all the nations of Europe are armed to the teeth; all the individuals, by millions, of great kingdoms and empires, are eternally prepared for war, ready on a week's notice to leave their homes and occupations and march to the frontier! Civilisation has done much for the cause of humanity; but civilisation has not converted the sword into the scythe, or enabled man to reap the results of his peaceful industry without a struggle to the death against his neighbour.

CHAPTER V.

SOCIAL LIFE.

IT was by such continuous wars against the aborigines of the soil that the Aryans at last conquered the whole of the Punjab from the Indus to the Sarasvatî, and from the mountains probably to the sea.

As might be expected, we have frequent allusions to the Indus and its five tributaries. Hymn 75 of the tenth Mandala is a remarkable instance, and we will give our readers a translation of the entire hymn :—

"1. O ye streams! The bard celebrates your excellent prowess in the house of the worshipper. They flow in three systems, seven streams in each system. The prowess of the Indus is superior to that of all others.

"2. O Indus! when you ran towards lands rich in food, Varuna opened out the way for you. You flow over a spacious path on the land. You shine above all flowing rivers.

"3. The mighty sound of the Indus ascends above the earth to the sky! She flows with mighty force and in radiant form. Her mighty sound is heard as if rains are descending from the clouds with great noise. The Indus comes roaring like a bull.

"4. As cows bring milk to their calves, even thus, O Indus, the other streams come sounding to you with their waters! As a king marches with his forces to battle, even thus you march in front with two systems of rivers flowing by your side! *

* *i.e.*, the tributaries coming from Cabul in the west, and the tributaries flowing through the Punjab in the east, as named in the two following verses.

"5. O Gangâ! O Yamunâ and Sarasvatî and Sutudrî (Sutlej) and Parushnî (Ravi)! share this my praise among you! O river combined with Asiknî (Chinab)! O Vitastâ (Jhilam)! O Ârjîkîyâ (Beas), combined with Sushomâ (Indus)! hear my words.

"6. O Indus! first thou flowest united with Trishtâmâ, then with Susartu and Rasâ and the Svetî. You unite Krumu (Kurum river) and Gomatî (Gomal river) with Kubhâ (Cabul river) and Mehatnu. You proceed together with these rivers.

"7. The irresistible Indus proceeds straight, white and dazzling in splendour! She is great, and her waters fill all sides with mighty force. Of all the flowing rivers, none is flowing like her! She is wild like a mare, beautiful like a well-developed woman!

"8. The Indus is ever young and beautiful. She is rich in horses, in chariots, and in garments; she is rich in gold and is beauteously clad! She is rich in corn and in wool and in straw, and has covered herself with sweet flowers.

"9. The Indus has fastened horses to her easy chariot, and has brought food therein to us. The greatness of the chariot is extolled as mighty; it is irresistible and great and rich in its fame!"

The hymn is remarkable for its power and its beauty, and remarkable also for the extensive vision of the poet who, as Professor Max Müller says, takes in at one swoop three great river-systems, those flowing from the north-west into the Indus, those joining it from the north-east, and in the distance the Ganges and the Jumna with their tributaries. "It shows the widest geographical horizon of the Vedic poets, confined by the snowy mountains in the north, the Indus and the range of the Suleiman mountains in the west, the Indus or the sea in the south, and the valley of the Jumna and Ganges in the east. Beyond that the world, though open, was unknown to the Vedic poets."

The rivers of the Punjab are sometimes spoken of together as the "seven rivers," and it is explained in one place (VII, 36, 6), that the seven rivers have the Indus for their mother and the Sarasvatî as the seventh. The Indus and its five branches still water the primeval home of the early Hindus, but the Sarasvatî, which was the most sacred of ancient rivers and was worshipped even in that remote time as a goddess, has since ceased to flow. Its bed is still visible near Kurukshetra and Thanesvar, and these places are still considered sacred by the Hindus.

There is one somewhat curious passage in which the Rishi Visvâmitra, encumbered with the chariots and horses and other rewards bestowed on him by King Sudâs, finds a difficulty in crossing the confluence of the Beas and the Sutlej, and pours out an entire hymn (III, 33) to appease the anger of the roaring flood! We have seen that this Sudâs was a mighty conqueror and subjugated ten surrounding kings, and was the victor of great battles which form the theme of some spirited hymns. This mighty conqueror seems also to have been a patron of learning and religion, and liberally rewarded the sages of the houses of Visvâmitra and Vasishtha alike. As a consequence, there was jealousy between these two priestly houses to which we will allude further on.

While references to the rivers of the Punjab are thus frequent, allusions to the Ganges and the Jumna are rare. We have already translated a hymn in which both those rivers are named.

The only other passage in the Rig Veda where the Ganges is alluded to, is VI, 45, 31, where the high banks of the Ganges are the subject of a simile. The famed cattle in the pasture-fields along the banks of the Jumna are alluded to in V, 52, 17.

Thus the land of the five rivers was the earliest home of the Aryan settlers in India; and it would seem that the settlers along the five rivers gradually formed themselves into five tribes or nations. The "five lands"

(*Pancha-Kshiti*) are alluded to in I, 7, 9; I, 176, 3; VI, 46, 7, and in other places. Similarly we read of the "five cultivating tribes" (*Pancha-Krishti*) in II, 2, 10; IV, 38, 10; and other places, and we read of "five peoples" (*Pancha-Jana*) in VI, 11, 4; VI, 51, 11; VIII, 32, 22; IX, 65, 23, and other places.

It was these "five tribes" of simple, bold, and enterprising Aryans, living by agriculture and by pasture on the fertile banks of the Indus and its tributaries, which have spread their civilisation from the Himâlayas to Cape Comorin.

We now turn to the interesting and pleasing subject of the social and domestic manners and the home-life of these five tribes of the Punjab. The first thing that strikes us here is the absence of those unhealthy rules and restrictions, those marked distinctions between man and man and between class and class, which form the most unpleasant feature of later Hindu society. We have already seen that the sturdy Hindus of the Vedic times recognised no restrictions against the use of beef, and that they refer with pride to their merchants going to the sea. We have seen too, that the Rishis did not form a separate and exclusive class, and did not pass their lives away from the world in penance and contemplation. On the contrary, the Rishis were practical men of the world who owned large herds of cattle, cultivated fields, fought against the aboriginal enemies in times of war, and prayed to their gods for wealth and cattle, for victory in wars, and for blessings on their wives and children. Every father of a family was in fact a Rishi on a small scale, and worshipped his gods in his own house in his own humble fashion, and the women of the family joined in the worship, and helped in the performance of the ceremonies. Some among the community were of course prominent in the composition of hymns and the performance of great sacrifices; and kings and rich men sent for them on great occasions, and rewarded them handsomely. But even these great composers—these great Rishis of the Rig Veda—did not form an exclusive caste of their own. They were worldly men, mixed and married with the people, shared property with the people, fought the wars of the people, and were of the people.

One martial Rishi for instance (in V, 23, 2) prays for a son who will conquer enemies in war. Another (in VI, 20, 1) prays for wealth and corn-fields and a son who will destroy his foes. Another (in IX, 69, 8) prays for wealth and gold, for horses and cows, for profuse harvests, and excellent progeny. Another Rishi, with naïve simplicity, says that his cattle are his wealth and his Indra! (VI, 28, 5.) Throughout the Rig Veda the Rishis are the people. There is not the shadow of any evidence that the Rishis or priests were a "caste" of their own, different from the fighters and cultivators.*

This will be considered by impartial judges to be very good evidence that the caste-system did not exist. It proves a negative much more convincingly than many positive facts can be proved. In a vast collection of hymns, composed during six hundred years and more, and replete with references to the habits and manners and customs of the people,—replete with allusions to agriculture and pasture and manufacture, to wars against aborigines, to marriage and domestic rules, and the duties and position of women, to religious observances and to elementary astronomy as then known,—we have not one single passage to show that the community was cut up into hereditary "*Castes.*" Is it possible to suppose

* The solitary mention of the four castes, in X, 90, 12, will not be considered an exception, or weaken our argument. The hymn itself was composed centuries after the time when the Rig Veda hymns were generally composed, as is proved by its language and its ideas. It was composed after the Rik, and the Saman and the Yajur Vedas had been separately classified (verse 9), and after the idea of the sacrifice the Supreme Being (unknown elsewhere in the Rig Veda) had found a place in the Hindu religion. It was composed, as Colebrooke states, after the rude versification of the Rig Veda had given place to the more sonorous metre of a later age. All scholars agree as to this hymn being comparatively modern.

that that wonderful system existed, and yet there is no allusion to that fundamental principle of society in the ten thousand verses of the Rig Veda? Is it possible to find a single religious work of later times, of one-tenth the dimensions of the Rig Veda, which is silent on that system?

So far, then, we have proved a negative in the only way in which a negative can be proved. But curiously enough there is positive proof, and various passages in the Rig Veda show, that the caste-system did not exist. The very word "*varna*," which in later Sanscrit indicates caste, is used in the Rig Veda to distinguish the Aryans and the non-Aryans, and nowhere indicates separate sections in the Aryan community (III, 34, 9, &c.). The very word *Kshatriya*, which in later Sanscrit means the military caste, is used in the Veda simply as an adjective which means strong, and is applied to gods (VII, 64, 2; VII, 89, 1, &c.). The very word *Vipra*, which in later Sanscrit means the priestly caste, is used in the Rig Veda merely as an adjective which means wise, and which is applied to gods (VIII, 11, 6, &c.). And the very word *Brâhmana*, which in later Sanscrit means also the priestly caste, is used in a hundred places in the Rig Veda to imply the composers of hymns, and nothing else (VII, 103, 8, &c.).

We would gladly multiply evidence, but our limits forbid. But we cannot help producing one piece of evidence. With that charming simplicity which is the characteristic beauty of the Rig Veda, one Rishi says pathetically of himself:—

"Behold, I am a composer of hymns, my father is a physician, my mother grinds corn on stone. We are all engaged in different occupations. As cows wander (in various directions) in the pasture-fields for food, so we (in various occupations) worship thee, O Soma! for wealth. Flow thou for Indra!" (IX, 112, 3). Those who suppose that the hereditary caste-system existed in the Vedic times will find some difficulty in explaining passages like the above, where father, mother, and son are described as physician, corn-grinder, and composer of hymns!

Later asserters of the caste-system have sometimes tried to explain these passages, and with the most wonderful results! Like most other Rishis of the Rig Veda (who, we have seen before, constantly prayed for warlike sons), Visvâmitra was a warrior and a composer of hymns. Later Hindus were shocked at this, and invented a beautiful Puranic myth to explain how Visvâmitra was first a Kshatriya and then became a Brâhman. Needless endeavour, for Visvâmitra was neither a Kshatriya nor a Brâhman! He was a Vedic Rishi, *i.e.*, a warrior and priest, long before the Brâhmans and the Kshatriyas, as such, were known! *

As we have seen, then, every father of a family was his own priest, and his home was his temple. There is no mention of idols in the Rig Veda, none of temples or places of worship where the people were to congregate. The sacred fire was lighted in the house of every householder, and he chanted the beautiful and simple hymns which we now find collected in the Rig Veda. We have a pleasing picture of women who assisted at these sacri-

* It gives us much pleasure to be able to cite here the authority of three scholars who have devoted their lifetime to the study of the Veda, and who form the Triumvirate of Vedic scholarship in Europe :—

" If then, with all the documents before us, we ask the question, does caste, as we find it in Manu, and at the present day, form part of the most ancient religious teaching of the Vedas? We can answer with a decided 'No.'"—Max Müller, *Chips from a German Workshop*, vol. ii. (1867), p. 307.

" There are no castes as yet, the people are still one united whole, and bear but one name, that of *Visas*."—Weber, *Indian Literature* (translation), p. 38.

And lastly, Dr. Roth shows how in the Vedic Age the domestic priests of petty kings were called Brâhmans, and had not yet formed into a caste. And the great scholar explains how in a later age,—that of the Mahâbhârata,—" powerful communities should arise among the domestic priests of petty kings, and their families should attain to the highest importance in every department of life, and should *grow into a caste*."—Quoted in Muir's *Sanscrit Texts*, vol. i. (1872), p. 291.

fices, who ordered the necessary things, prepared them with pestle and mortar, extracted the Soma-juice, stirred it with their figures, and strained it through a woollen strainer. In numerous places we find mention of wives joining their husbands, and performing the sacrifice together. They offer the oblations together, and hope thereby to go to heaven together (I, 131, 3; V, 43, 15, &c.). A few verses from a pious hymn on this subject will no doubt interest our readers.

"5. O ye gods! The married couple who prepare oblations together, who purify the Soma-juice and mix it with milk,

"6. May they obtain food for their eating, and come united to the sacrifice. May they never have to go in quest of food.

"7. They do not make vain promises of offerings to the gods, nor withhold your praise. They worship you with the best offerings.

"8. Blest with youthful and adolescent offspring, they acquire gold, and they both attain to a mature age.

"9. The gods themselves covet the worship of such a couple who are fond of sacrifices, and offer grateful food to the gods. They embrace each other to continue their race, and they worship their gods!" (VIII, 31).

Still more grateful to us is the picture of cultured ladies who were themselves Rishis, and composed hymns and performed sacrifices like men. For there were no unhealthy restrictions against women in those days, no attempt to keep them secluded or uneducated or debarred from their legitimate place in society. There is mention of veiled wives and brides, but no allusion to women being kept in seclusion. On the contrary, we meet them everywhere in their legitimate spheres of action, taking a share in sacrifices, and exercising their influence on society. We cherish the picture of the cultured lady Visvavârâ, which has been handed down to us through thousands of years,—a pious lady who composed hymns, performed sacrifices, and with true fervency invoked the god Agni to regulate and keep within virtuous bounds the mutual relations of married couples (V, 28, 3). We meet with the names of other ladies also who were Rishis of the Rig Veda.

In a society so simple as that of the Vedic times, the relations of life were determined by the needs and requirements of individuals rather than by cast-iron rules as in later days; and there was no religious obligation, therefore, that every girl must be married. On the contrary, we find allusions to unmarried women who remained in the homes of their fathers, and naturally claimed and obtained a share of the paternal property (II, 17, 7). On the other hand, we have frequent references to careful and industrious wives who superintended the arrangements of the house, and like the dawn roused and sent every one in the house to his work in the morning (I, 124, 4), and who possessed those domestic virtues for which Hindu wives have always been noted from the earliest to the present times. Occasionally we have allusions to women who went astray (II, 29, 1); to maidens who had no brothers to watch over their morals; and wives who were faithless to their husbands (IV, 5, 5; X, 34, 4). And we are told of the wife of a ruined gambler who becomes the object of other men's lust (X, 34, 4).

It would seem that girls had some voice in the selection of their husband. Their selection was not always happy, for "many a woman is attracted by the wealth of him who seeks her. But the woman who is of gentle nature and of graceful form selects, among many, her own loved one as her husband" (X, 27, 12). We can almost imagine we see the *Svayamvara* system of later times foreshadowed in the above verse. There can be no doubt, however, that fathers always exercised a wise control in the selection of husbands for their daughters; and as at the present day, fathers gave away their girls gracefully adorned and decked with golden ornaments (IX, 46, 2; X, 39, 14).

The ceremony of marriage was an appropriate one, and the promises which the bridegroom and bride made to each other were suitable to the occasion. We will translate some verses from a hymn in the later portion of the Rig Veda, in which we find a pleasing picture of the ceremony. The first two among the following verses will show that the unnatural custom of child-marriage was unknown, and that girls were married after they had attained their youth:—

"21. O Visvâvasu! (god of marriage), arise from this place, for the marriage of this girl is over. We extol Visvâvasu with hymns and prostrations. Go to some other maiden who is still in her father's house and has attained the signs of the age of marriage. She will be your share, know of her.

"22. O Visvâvasu! arise from this place. We worship thee, bending in adoration. Go to an unmarried maiden whose person is well developed; make her a wife and unite her to a husband.

"23. Let the paths by which our friends go in quest of a maiden for marriage be easy and free of thorns. May Aryaman and Bhaga lead us well. O gods! may the husband and wife be well united.

"24. O maiden! the graceful sun had fastened thee with ties (of maidenhood), we release thee now of those ties. We place thee with thy husband in a place which is the home of truth and the abode of righteous actions.

"25. We release this maiden from this place (her father's house), but not from the other place (her husband's house). We unite her well with the other place. O Indra! may she be fortunate and the mother of worthy sons.

"26. May Pûshan lead thee by the hand from this place. May the two Asvins lead thee in a chariot. Go to thy (husband's) house and be the mistress of the house. Be the mistress of all, and exercise thine authority over all in that house.

"27. Let children be born unto thee, and blessings attend thee here. Perform the duties of thy household with care. Unite thy person with the person of this thy husband; exercise thy authority in this thy house until old age.

"40. First Soma accepts thee; then Gandharva accepts thee; Agni is thy third lord; the son of man is the fourth to accept thee.*

"41. Soma bestowed this maiden to Gandharva, Gandharva gave her to Agni, Agni has given her to me with wealth and progeny.

"42. O bridegroom and bride! do ye remain here together; do not be separated. Enjoy food of various kinds; remain in your own home, and enjoy happiness in company of your children and grandchildren.

"43. (The bride and bridegroom say, May Prajapati bestow on us children; may Aryaman keep us united till old age. (Address to the bride), O bride! Enter with auspicious signs the home of thy husband. Do good to our male servants and our female servants, and to our cattle.

"44. Be thine eyes free from anger; minister to the happiness of thy husband; do good to our cattle. May thy mind be cheerful; and may thy beauty be bright. Be the mother of heroic sons, and be devoted to the gods. Do good to our male servants and our female servants, and to our cattle.

"45. O Indra! make this woman fortunate and the mother of worthy sons. Let ten sons be born of her, so that there may be eleven men in the family with the husband.

"46. (Address to the bride), May thou have influence over thy father-in-law, and over thy mother-in-law, and be as a queen over thy sister-in-law and brother-in-law.

* This and the following verse would show that the bride was offered to the three gods before she was united to the bridegroom.

"47. (The bridegroom and bride say), May all the gods unite our hearts; may Mâtarisvan and Dhâtri and the goddess of speech unite us together" (X, 85).

Our extract has been somewhat lengthy, but our readers will not regret it. The extract shows at once the appropriate nature of the ceremony that was performed, and the position which the young bride occupied in the home and the affections of her lord.

Polygamy was allowed among kings and the rich people in Vedic times, as it was allowed in olden times in all countries and among all nations. Domestic dissensions were the natural result in such instances, and we have hymns in the latter part of the Rig Veda in which wives curse their fellow-wives (X, 145; X, 159). The evil seems, however, to have grown in the latter part of the Vedic Age, for there are scarcely any allusions to it in the earlier hymns.

There are two curious verses which seem to lay down the law of inheritance, and are therefore of peculiar interest. We give a translation below:—

"1. The father who has no son honours his son-in-law, capable of begetting sons, and goes (*i.e.*, leaves his property) to the son of his daughter. The sonless father trusts in his daughter's offspring, and lives content.

"2. A son does not give any of his father's property to a sister. He gives her away to be the wife of a husband. If a father and mother beget both son and daughter, then one (*i.e.*, son) engages himself in the acts and duties of his father, while the other (daughter) receives honour" (III, 31).

This is the first germ of the Hindu law of inheritance, which makes the son, and not the daughter, the inheritor of his father's property and religious duties, and which allows the property to go to the daughter's son only in the absence of male issue. We think we discover the first germs of the Hindu law of adoption too in such passages as the following:—

"As a man who is not indebted gets much wealth, so we too shall get the treasure that endures (*i.e.*, a son). O Agni! let us not have son begotten of another. Do not follow the ways of the ignorant.

"A son begotten of another may yield us happiness, but can never be regarded or accepted as one's own. And verily he ultimately goes back to his own place. Therefore, may a son be newly born unto us who will bring us food and destroy our foes" (VII, 4, 7 and 8).

We have spoken in this chapter of marriage and inheritance; we will complete our account of domestic customs by making some extracts with regard to funeral rites. Yama in the Rig Veda is not the god of hell, but the god of the heaven of the righteous, the god who rewards the virtuous man after his death, in a happy land. His two dogs, however, are objects to be avoided or propitiated.

"7. O thou deceased! proceed to the same place where our forefathers have gone, by the same path which they followed. The two kings, Yama and Varuna, are pleased with the offerings; go and see them.

"8. Go to that happy heaven and mix with the early forefathers. Mix with Yama and with the fruits of thy virtuous deeds. Leave sin behind, enter thy home.

"9. O ye ghosts! leave this place, go away, move away. For the forefathers have prepared a place for the deceased. That place is beautiful with day, with sparkling waters and with light; Yama assigns this place to the dead.

"10. O thou deceased! these two dogs have four eyes each, and a strange colour. Go past them quickly. Then proceed by the beautiful path to those wise forefathers, who spend their time in joy and happiness with Yama" (X, 14).

These verses give us some idea of the belief in future happiness as it prevailed among the Hindus of the Vedic

Age. The rites of cremation and burial are alluded to in the following passages:—

"O fire! do not reduce this deceased into ashes; do not give him pain. Do not mangle his skin or his person. O fire! send him to the home of our fathers as soon as his body is burnt in thy heat" (X, 16, 1).

"10. O thou deceased! go to the extended earth who is as a mother; she is extensive and beautiful. May her touch be soft as that of wool or of a female. You have performed sacrifices, may she save thee from unrighteousness.

"11. O earth! rise up above him, do not give him pain. Give him good things, give him consolation. As a mother covers her child with the hem of her cloth, so cover the deceased.

"12. Let the earth, raised on him as a mound, lie light. Let a thousand particles of dust rest on him. Let them be to him as a house filled with butter, let them form a shelter to him" (X, 18).

It remains only to allude to one more remarkable verse of this hymn, which distinctly sanctions the marriage of widows:—

"Rise up, woman, thou art lying by one whose life is gone; come to the world of the living, away from thy husband, and become the wife of him who holds thy hand, and is willing to marry thee" (X, 18, 8).

The translation is based on Sâyana's rendering of the passage in the *Taittirîya Áranyaka*, and there can be little doubt as to its correctness, because the word Didhishu used in the passage has only one meaning in the Sanscrit language, viz., the second husband of a woman. We quote here with pleasure the following remarks with which Dr. Rajendra Lala Mitra winds up a paper on Funeral Ceremony in Ancient India:—"That the remarriage of widows in Vedic times was a national custom, can be established by a variety of proofs and arguments; the very fact of the Sanscrit language having, from ancient times, such words as Didhishu, 'a man that has married a widow,' Parapûrvâ, 'a woman that has taken a second husband,' Paunarbhava, 'a son of a woman by her second husband,' are enough to establish it."

It is with pain and regret that we refer to another passage, also belonging to this remarkable hymn, which is perfectly harmless in the Rig Veda itself, but which was altered and mistranslated in later times to sanction the barbarous custom of *Satî*, or the burning of the widow on the pyre of her husband. That most cruel of all modern Hindu institutions finds no sanction in the Rig Veda. There is a perfectly harmless passage (X, 18, 7), which refers to a procession of women at a funeral ceremony. The passage may be thus translated:—

"May these women not suffer the pangs of widowhood. May they who have good and desirable husbands, enter their houses with collyrium and butter. Let these women, without shedding tears, and without any sorrow, first proceed to the house, wearing valuable ornaments."

There is not a word in the above relating to the burning of widows. But a word in it *Agre* was altered into *Agne*, and the text was then mistranslated and misapplied in Bengal to justify the modern custom of the burning of widows. In the words of Professor Max Müller, "This is, perhaps, the most flagrant instance of what can be done by an unscrupulous priesthood. Here have thousands of lives been sacrificed and a fanatical rebellion been threatened on the authority of a passage which was mangled, mistranslated, and misapplied."

CHAPTER VI.

VEDIC RELIGION.

THE religion of the Rig Veda is well known. It is pre-eminently the worship of Nature in its most imposing and sublime aspects. The sky which bends over all, the beautiful and blushing dawn which like a busy housewife wakes men from slumber and sends them to their work, the gorgeous tropical sun which vivifies the earth, the air which pervades the world, the fire which cheers and enlightens us, and the violent storms which in India usher in those copious rains which fill the land with plenty,—these were the gods whom the early Hindus loved to extol and to worship. And often when an ancient Rishi sang the praises of any of the gods with devotion and fervour, he forgot that there was any other god besides, and his sublime hymn has the character and the sublimity of a prayer to the one God of the universe. This is what makes many scholars often pause and hesitate before they give the Vedic religion any other name than Monotheism. Indeed the Rishis themselves often rose higher than the level of Nature-worship, and they boldy declared that the different gods were but different manifestations or different names of the one Primal Cause. The landmarks between Nature-worship and Monotheism have been passed, and the great Rishis of the Rig Veda have passed from Nature up to Nature's God.

The sky was naturally the most prominent object of worship, and as the sky assumes various aspects, various names were given to it, and the conception of various deities was formed. The oldest probably is Dyu (literally the shining), the Zeus of the Greeks, the first syllable of the Jupiter of the Romans, the Tiu of the Saxons, and the Zio of the Germans. This common name among many Aryan races indicates that the deity was worshipped by the ancestors of all these nations in their first primeval abode.

But while Zeus and Jupiter maintained their supremacy among the gods of Greece and Rome, in India he soon lost his place, and the sky *in one of its peculiar functions* soon usurped his place. For in India the annual rise of rivers, the fertility of land, and the luxuriance of crops depend, not on the sky which shines above us, but on the *sky that rains*, and *Indra,* which means the rain-giver, soon became the first among the Vedic gods.

Another ancient name of the sky was Varuna, the Uranus of the Greeks. The word signifies to cover, and Varuna was the sky which covered the earth, probably the sky without light, the nightly sky. For we find another name for the bright sky of day, viz., Mitra, the Mithra of the Zendavesta. Sanscrit commentators naturally explain Varuna as night and Mitra as day, and the Iranians worshipped the sun under the name of Mithra, and gave the name of Varuna to a happy region, if not the sky.

These facts show that the idea and name of Varuna as a god of sky was known to the ancestors of the Aryan nations before those nations separated and migrated to Greece, to Persia, and to India. Indeed the eminent German scholar Dr. Roth is of opinion that before the Indo-Aryans and the Iranians separated, Varuna was the highest and holiest of the gods of their ancestors, and represented the spiritual side of their religion. After the separation had taken place, this deity of righteousness was translated in Iran into Ahura Mazd, the supreme Deity. And although in India, Varuna yielded the foremost place among gods to the young and vigorous rain-giver Indra, still he never became divested of that sanctity and holiness which entered into his first conception, and the holiest hymns of the Rig Veda are his, not Indra's. Whatever be the value of these opinions, the fact of Varuna's pre-eminent sanctity in the Rig Veda cannot be denied, and we will give a few short translations from the hymns to Varuna to illustrate this :—

"6. O Varuna! the birds that fly have not attained thy power, or thy vigour; the water which flows ceaselessly and the moving wind do not surpass thy speed.

"7. King Varuna of unsullied power remains in the firmament, and holds on high the rays of light. Those rays descend downwards, but proceed from above. May they sustain our existence.

"8. King Varuna has spread out the path for the course of the sun. He has made the path for the sun to traverse in pathless space. May he rebuke our enemies who pierce our hearts.

"9. O King Varuna! a hundred and a thousand medicinal drugs are thine; may thy beneficence be vast and deep. Keep unrighteousness away from us, deliver us from the sins we have committed.

"10. Yonder stars * which are placed on high, and are seen by night,—where do they go by day? The acts of Varuna are irresistible; the moon shines brightly by his mandate" (I, 24).

"3. O Varuna! with an anxious heart I ask thee about my sins. I have gone to learned men to make inquiry;

* The word used in the text is Riksha, which may either mean stars generally, or the stars of the constellation Great Bear. The root *rich* means to shine, whence in course of time the word Riksha came to have two meanings—the shining stars of a particular constellation, and an animal with bright eyes and shining glossy hair. By a natural confusion of ideas, therefore, the constellation itself ultimately came to be called the Bear. The question is discussed with remarkable eloquence and learning by Max Müller in his Science of Language, and he explains that "the surprise with which many a thoughtful observer has looked at these seven bright stars, wondering why they were ever called the Bear, is removed by reference to the early annals of human speech."

the sages have all said to me,—'Varuna is displeased with thee.'

"4. O Varuna! what have I done that thou wishest to destroy thy friend, thy worshipper? O thou of irresistible power, declare it to me, so that I may quickly bend in adoration, and come unto thee.

"5. O Varuna! deliver us from the sins of our fathers. Deliver us from the sins committed in our persons. O royal Varuna! deliver Vasishtha, like a calf from its tether, like a thief who has feasted on a stolen animal.

"6. O Varuna! all this sin is not wilfully committed by us. Error or wine, anger or dice, or even thoughtlessness, has begotten sin. Even an elder brother leads his younger astray, sin is begotten even in our dreams.

"7. Freed from sin, I will faithfully serve, as a slave, the Varuna who fulfils our wishes and supports us. We are ignorant, may the Ârya god bestow on us knowledge. May the wise deity accept our prayer and bestow on us wealth" (VII, 86).

"1. O King Varuna! may I never go to the earthen home. O thou of great power! have mercy, have mercy.

"2. O Varuna with thy weapons! I come trembling even like a cloud driven by the wind. O thou of great power! have mercy, have mercy.

"3. O rich and pure Varuna! I have been driven against righteous acts through weakness. O thou of great power! have mercy, have mercy.

"4. Thy worshipper hath thirsted even when living in water. O thou of great power! have mercy, have mercy.

"5. O Varuna! we are mortals. In whatever way we have sinned against gods, in whatever manner we have through ignorance neglected thy work—O! do not destroy us for these sins" (VII, 89).

These and many other hymns show that Varuna was never divested in India of that idea of holiness which is said to have entered into his original conception. But nevertheless, Varuna like Dyu was supplanted in power by the younger Indra, a god who is peculiarly Indian, and is unknown to other Aryan nations.

One of the most famous legends about Indra, the most famous legend probably in the Aryan world, is about the production of rain. The dark heavy clouds to which man looks up with wistful eyes, but which often disappoint him in seasons of drought, are called by the ancient name of Vritra.

Vritra is supposed to confine the waters, and will not let them descend until the sky-god or rain-god Indra strikes the monster with his thunderbolt. The captive waters then descend in copious showers, rivers rise almost instantaneously, and gods and men rejoice over the changed face of nature. Many are the spirited hymns in the Rig Veda in which this combat is narrated with much glee and rejoicing. The storm-gods, Maruts, help Indra in the combat, the sky and earth tremble at the noise, Vritra long wages an unequal combat, and then falls and dies,—the drought is over, and rains begin.

We have said that Indra is a peculiarly Indian name, and is unknown to other Aryan nations. But the legend given above and the name of Vritra appear in various shapes among various Aryan nations. Vritraghna, or the slayer of Vritra, is worshipped in the Zendavesta as Verethraghna, and we also find in the same work an account of the destruction of Ahi, which in the Veda is another name for Vritra. Threyetana is the slayer of Ahi, and the genius of the great French scholar Burnouf has recognised this identical Threyetana in the Ferudin of Ferdusi's Shah Nama,—translated from mythology to history after thousands of years! It will probably surprise modern readers more to know that scholars have traced this Ahi of the Veda and the Zendavesta in the dragon Echis and Echidna of Greek mythology; that in the dog Orthros, the offspring of Echidna, they have recognised our old friend Vritra or the rain-cloud, and

Hercules therefore, the slayer of Orthros, is the counterpart of Threyetana of the Zendavesta, and of Indra of the Rig Veda!

It would be easy to multiply such legends, but our limits forbid such a course. We will therefore only make a passing mention of one more legend, viz., that about the recovery of light by Indra after the darkness of night. The rays of light are compared to cattle which have been stolen by the powers of darkness, and Indra (the sky) seeks for them in vain. He sends *Saramâ, i.e.*, the dawn, after them, and Saramâ finds out the *Bilu*, or fortress, where the *Panis*, or powers of darkness, have concealed the cattle. The Panis try to tempt Saramâ, but in vain. Saramâ comes back to Indra, and Indra marches with his forces, destroys the fort, and recovers the cattle; darkness is gone, and it is day! This is a well-known Vedic legend, and there are constant allusions to it in the hymns to Indra.

Professor Max Müller maintains that the story of the siege of Troy is a development of this simple Vedic myth, and is "but a repetition of the daily siege of the East by the Solar powers that every evening are robbed of their brightest treasures in the west." Ilium according to the Professor is *Bilu*, the cave or the fortress of the Rig Veda. Paris is the *Panis* of the Veda who tempt, and Helena is the Vedic *Saramâ* who resists the temptation in the Veda, but succumbs to it in Greek mythology.

We cannot say that Max Müller has proved his theory, but the evidence of a historical siege of Troy does not necessarily disprove it, for nothing is more common in ancient history than the blending of mythical names and incidents with historical events. Arjuna the hero of a historical Kuru-Panchâla war is a myth, and is a name of the rain-god Indra; and it is not impossible that the poet who sang of a historical siege of Troy blended with it a solar myth with its names and incidents. We will now make short extracts from the Rig Veda illustrating these two legends:—

"1. We sing the heroic deeds which were performed by Indra the thunderer. He destroyed Ahi (cloud) and caused rains to descend, and opened out the paths for the mountain streams to roll.

"2. Indra slayed Ahi resting on the mountains; Twashtri had made the far-reaching thunderbolt for him. Water in torrents flowed towards the sea, as cows run eagerly towards their calves.

"3. Impetuous as a bull, Indra quaffed the Soma-juice; he drank the Soma libations offered in the three sacrifices. He then took the thunderbolt, and thereby slayed the eldest of the Ahis.

"4. When you killed the eldest of the Ahis, you destroyed the contrivances of the artful contrivers. You cleared the sun and the morning and the sky, and left no enemies behind.

"5. Indra with his all-destructive thunderbolt slayed the darkling Vritra (cloud), and lopped his limbs. Ahi now lies touching the earth like the trunk of a tree felled by the axe.

"6. The proud Vritra thought that he had no equal, and defied the destroyer and conqueror Indra to combat. But he did not escape destruction, and Indra's foe fell, crushing the rivers in his fall.

"8. Glad waters are bounding over the prostrate body as rivers flow over fallen banks. Vritra when alive had withheld the water by his power; Ahi now lies prostrate under that water.

"10. The prostrate body lies concealed and nameless under ceaseless and restless waters, and the waters flow above. Indra's foe sleeps the long sleep" (I, 32).

The above is a hymn relating to the legend of Vritra. We now turn to a hymn relating to the legend of Saramâ:—

1. The *Panis* say:—"O Saramâ! why hast thou come here? It is a long distance. He who looks back cannot come this way. What have we with us for which

thou hast come ? How long hast thou travelled ? How didst thou cross the Rasâ ?"

2. *Saramâ* replies :—"I come as the messenger of Indra. O Panis! it is my object to recover the abundant cattle which you have hidden. The water has helped me; the water felt a fear at my crossing, and thus I crossed the Rasâ."

3. The *Panis.*—"What is that Indra like, whose messenger thou art, and hast come from a long distance? How does he look ? (To one another:) Let her come, we will own her as a friend. Let her take and own our cows."

4. *Saramâ.*—"I do not see any one who can conquer the Indra whose messenger I am, and have come from a long distance. It is he who conquers everybody. The deep rivers cannot restrain his course. O Panis! you will surely be slain by Indra and will lie down."

5. *Panis.*—"O beautiful Saramâ ! thou hast come from the farthest ends of the sky; we will give thee without any dispute these cows as thou desirest. Who else would have given the cattle without a dispute ? We have many sharp weapons with us."

9. *Panis.*—"O Saramâ ! thou hast come here because the god threatened thee and sent thee here. We will accept thee as a sister; do not return. O beautiful Saramâ! we will give thee a share of this cattle."

10. *Saramâ.*—"I do not comprehend your words about brothers and sisters. Indra and the powerful sons of Angiras know all. They sent me here to guard the cattle until recovery. I have come here under their shelter. O Panis! run away far far from here" (X, 108).

It will be seen from the few extracts we have made that the hymns to Indra are characterised by force and vigour, as those to Varuna are marked with a feeling of righteousness. Indra is, in fact, the most vigorous of the Vedic gods, fond of Soma wine, delighting in war, leading his comrades the Maruts to fight against drought, leading hosts of the Aryans against the black aborigines, and helping them to carve out for themselves with their strong right arm the most fertile spots along the five rivers of the Punjab. The sky and earth gave him birth as a cudgel for the enemies (III, 49, 1). The young and vigorous infant went to his mother Aditi for food, and saw Soma wine on her breast; he drank Soma before he drank from his mother's breast (III, 48, 2 and 3). And the great drinker and fighter often hesitates between the temptation of Soma libations at sacrifices, and the temptation of his home where a beautiful wife awaits him (III, 53, 4–6).

We have thus far spoken of Dyu and Varuna and Mitra and Indra as the principal sky-gods of the Rig Veda. All these gods may, however, also be considered as gods of light, as the idea of the bright light of sky enters into the conception of all these deities, even of Varuna in some passages. We will now, however, speak of some deities who have more distinctly a solar character, and some of whom are grouped together under the common name of Âdityas or sons of Aditi, and this brings us to the most remarkable name that occurs in the Rig Veda mythology. Unlike Indra, which comes from *Ind* to rain, and Dyu, which comes from *Dyu* to shine, the word Aditi involves a more complicated idea. Aditi means the undivided, the unlimited, the eternal. It is in reality, as has been stated, the earliest name invented by man to express the Infinite,—the visible infinite, the endless expanse, beyond the earth, beyond the clouds, beyond the sky. The fact that such an idea should enter into the conception of a deity argues a remarkable advance in the culture and thought of the early Hindus. The word has no counterpart among the names of the deities of other ancient Aryan nations, and must have been coined in India after the Indo-Aryan section had settled in this country. It means, according to the eminent German scholar Dr. Roth, the eternal and inviolable principle, the celestial light.

There is much confusion in the Rig Veda as to who

the Âdityas are,—the sons of this celestial light. In II, 27, Aryaman and Bhaga and Daksha and Ansa are named besides Varuna and Mitra, of whom we have spoken before. In IX, 114, and in X, 72, the Âdityas are said to be seven in number, but are not named. We have seen before that Indra is called a son of Aditi. Savitri, the sun, is often described as an Âditya, and so are Pûshan and Vishnu, who are also different names of the sun. When, in course of time, the year was divided into twelve months, the number of the Âdityas was fixed at twelve, and they were the suns of the twelve months.

Sûrya and Savitri are the most common names of the sun in the Rig Veda, the former word answering to the Greek Helios, the Latin Sol, and the Iranian Khorshed. Commentators draw a distinction between Savitri, the rising or the unrisen sun, and Sûrya, the bright sun of day. The golden rays of the sun were naturally compared with arms until a story found its place in Hindu mythology that Savitri lost his arm at a sacrifice, and it was replaced by a golden arm. The same story reappears in a different form in German mythology, in which the sun-god placed his hand in the mouth of a tiger and lost it!

The only extract we will make from the hymns to the sun will be that most celebrated of all the verses in the Rig Veda, the Gâyatrî, or the morning hymn of the later Brâhmans. But the Rig Veda recognised no Brâhmans, the caste-system was not formed then, and the sublime hymn was the *national* property of the early Hindus who dwelt on the banks of the Indus. We give the original verse and Dr. Wilson's translation :—

" *Tat savitur varenyam bhargo devasya dhîmahi*
" *Dhiyo yo nah prachodayât.*"

"We meditate on the desirable light of the divine Savitri who influences our pious rites" (III, 62, 10).

Pûshan is the sun as viewed by shepherds in their wanderings in quest of fresh pasture-lands. He travels in a chariot yoked with goats, guides men and cattle in their travels and migrations, and knows and protects the flocks. The hymns to Pûshan, therefore, often breathe a simplicity which is truly pastoral. A few extracts from such hymns have been given before.

Vishnu has obtained such a prominent place as the Supreme Deity in later Hinduism that there is a natural reluctance among orthodox modern Hindus to accept him in his Vedic character as a mere sun-god. Yet such he is in the Rig Veda, and he is quite a humble deity in the Vedic pantheon, far below Indra or Varuna, Savitri or Agni. It was not till the Puranic times, long after the Christian Era, that Vishnu was considered a Supreme Deity. In the Veda, Vishnu is said to traverse space in three steps, viz., the sun at rising, at zenith, and at setting. In the Purânas this simple metaphor has led to a long story.

Fire was an object of worship among all ancient nations, and in India sacrificial fire received the highest regard. As no sacrifice could be performed without fire, Agni or fire was called the invoker of the gods. He was called Yavishtha, or the "youngest" among the gods, because he was kindled anew at each time of sacrifice by the friction of *arani*, or the sacrificial wood. For this reason, he also received the name of Pramantha, *i.e.*, produced by friction.*

So high was the esteem in which fire was held among the gods of the Rig Veda, that when the ancient commentator Yâska tried to reduce the number of the Vedic gods

* According to Mr. Cox, many of the Greek and Latin deities owe their name to the Sanscrit names of Fire. "In this name, Yavishtha, which is never given to any other Vedic god, we may recognise the Hellenic Hephaistos. *Note.*—Thus with the exception of Agni, all the names of the Fire and the Fire-gods were carried away by the Western Aryans; and we have Prometheus answering to Pramantha, Phoronus to Bharanyu, and the Latin Vulcanus to the Sanscrit Ulka."—Cox's *Mythology of Aryan Nations.*

"Agni is the god of fire; the Ignis of the Latins, the Ogni of the Sclavonians."—Muir's *Sanscrit Texts.*

into three, he named Agni or fire as the god of the earth, Indra or Vâyu as the god of the firmament, and the Sun as the god of the sky.

But Agni is not only the terrestrial fire in the Rig Veda; he is also the fire of the lightning and the sun, and his abode is the invisible heaven. The Bhrigus discovered him there, Mâtarisvan brought him down, and Atharvan and Angiras, the first sacrificers, first installed him in this world as the protector of men.

Vâyu, or the air, has received less consideration from the Vedic bards, and there are but few hymns assigned to him. But the Maruts or the storm-gods are oftener invoked, as we have seen before, probably because they inspired more terror; and they are considered as the companions of Indra in obtaining rain from the reluctant clouds! The earth trembles as they move in their deer-yoked chariots, and men see the flashing of their arms or the sparkle of their ornaments, the lightning. But they are benevolent all the same, and they milk from the udder of their mother Prisni (cloud) copious showers for the benefit of man.

Rudra, a fierce deity, is the father of the Maruts, loud-sounding as his name signifies, and a form of fire as the commentators Yâska and Sâyana explain. There can be no doubt, therefore, as to the correctness of Dr. Roth's conclusion, that the original meaning of this loud-sounding fire, this father of storms, is Thunder. Like Vishnu, Rudra is a humble deity in the Rig Veda, and only a few hymns are assigned to him. But like Vishnu, Rudra has attained prominence in later times, and is one of the Hindu Trinity of the Puranic religion, a portion of the Supreme. In some of the Upanishads we find the names Kâlî, Karâlî, &c., used as the names of different kinds of flame, and in the White Yajus Sanhita, we find Ambikâ spoken of as the sister of Rudra. But when Rudra assumed a more distinct individuality in the Purânas, all these names were construed as the different names of his wife! We have only to add that none of these goddesses, nor Lakshmî, the wife of Puranic Vishnu, is so much as mentioned by name in the Rig Veda.

Another god who has also changed his character in the Purânas (and very much for the worse!) is Yama, the king of the dead. In the Purânas he is called the child of the Sun, and there are some reasons (which Professor Max Müller explains with his usual eloquence) for supposing that the original conception of Yama in the Rig Veda is the conception of the departing sun. The sun sets and disappears, just as a man's life ends: and the imagination of a simple race would easily conjure up an after-world, where that departed deity would preside over departed spirits.

According to the Rig Veda, Vivasvat the sky is the father, and Saranyu the dawn is the mother, of Yama and his sister Yamî.

Who can be the offspring of the sky and the dawn but the sun or the day? It is difficult to resist the conclusion that the twins Yama and Yamî are day and night in their original conception. There is a curious passage in the Rig Veda in which the amorous sister Yamî desires to embrace her brother as her husband, but the brother declines such union as unholy (X, 10). It is not difficult to fathom the import of this conversation:—Day and Night, though eternally pursuing each other, can never be united.

But whatever the original conception of Yama may be, there is no doubt that even in the Rig Veda itself, that deity has attained a distinct individuality, and he is the king of the departed. So far his Vedic character agrees with his Puranic character, but here the parallel ends. In the Veda, he is the beneficent king of the happy world where the virtuous live and enjoy themselves in after-life. Clothed in a glorious body, they sit by the side of Yama in the realms of light and sparkling waters, they enjoy endless felicity there, and are adored here below under the name of Pitris or fathers. How different is the character which Yama bears in the Purânas as the cruel and dread Punisher of the guilty!

"1. Worship Yama the son of Vivasvat with offerings. All men go to him. He takes men of virtuous deeds to the realm of happiness. He clears the way for many.

"2. Yama first discovered the path for us. That path will not be destroyed again. All living beings will, according to their acts, follow by the path by which our forefathers have gone" (X, 14).

We may also quote here another passage from a hymn to Soma, which contains a fuller allusion to the future world. Soma, it is well known, was the juice of a plant made into wine, and used as libation in sacrifices. Soma soon attained the rank of a deity, and all the hymns of the ninth Mandala are dedicated to him.

"7. O flowing Soma! take me to that immortal and imperishable abode where light dwells eternal, and which is in heaven. Flow, Soma! for Indra.

"8. Take me where Yama is king, where there are the gates of heaven, and where mighty rivers flow. Take me there and make me immortal. Flow, Soma! for Indra.

"9. Take me where there is the third heaven, where there is the third realm of light above the sky, and where one can wander at his will. Take me there and make me immortal. Flow, Soma! for Indra.

"10. Take me where every desire is satiated, where Pradhma has his abode, where there is food and contentment. Take me there and make me immortal. Flow, Soma! for Indra.

"11. Take me where there are pleasures and joys and delights, where every desire of the anxious heart is satiated. Take me there, and make me immortal. Flow, Soma! for Indra" (IX, 113).

We have spoken above of Yama and Yamî as the twin children of Vivasvat the sky, by Saranyu the dawn. It is remarkable that the same parents had another twin children, the two Asvins. There can be little doubt that they too, like Yama and Yamî, were in their original conception the day and the night, or the dawn and the evening.

But whatever the original conception of the Asvins may be, they appear in the Rig Veda as great physicians, healers of the sick and the wounded, and tending many persons with kindness. Long lists of the kind acts of the two Asvins are given in several hymns, and the same cures are spoken of over and over again. On their three-wheeled chariot, they make the circuit of the world day by day, and succour men in their distress.

Brihaspati or Brahmanaspati is the lord of hymns, Brahman in the Rig Veda meaning hymn. The conception of this deity arose in much the same way as the conception of the deities Fire and Soma. As there is power in the flame and the libation of the sacrifice, so there is power in the prayer uttered; and this power of prayer is personified in the Vedic god Brahmanaspati.

He is quite a humble god in the Rig Veda, but has a great future. For in course of centuries, the thinkers of the Upanishads conceived of a Supreme Universal Being, and gave him the Vedic name Brahman. Then, when Buddhism flourished in the land, the Buddhists themselves tolerated Brahmâ as a gentle and beneficent spirit in their pantheon. And when at last Puranic Hinduism supplanted Buddhism in India, the Puranic thinkers gave the name of Brahmâ to the Supreme Creator of the Universe. Thus, by looking into our national records of the farthest antiquity, we trace the simple beginnings of that gorgeous Puranic mythology which has for over a thousand years swayed the opinions and conduct of hundreds of millions of our countrymen and countrywomen. It is like tracing one of our great Indian rivers, which spreads for miles together at its mouth, to its very source, where a narrow but pure and crystal streamlet issues from the eternal mountains! Ideas develop in the course of time, just as rivers expand and receive fresh supplies of water in their course, until they lose all their primitive character, although still bearing the same names. And we can no more recognise the simple Vedic character of Brahman the prayer, of Vishnu the sun, and of Rudra the thunder, in the Supreme Creator, the Preserver and the Destroyer of the Purânas, than we can recognise the crystal streamlet at Hardwar in the sea-like expanse of the Ganges where it mingles with the Bay of Bengal.

These are the important gods of the Rig Veda. Of the goddesses there are only two who have any marked individuality, viz., Ushas, the dawn, and Sarasvatî, the goddess of the river of that name, and afterwards the goddess of speech.

There is no lovelier conception in the Rig Veda than that of the dawn. There are no hymns in the Veda more truly poetical than those dedicated to her, and nothing more charming is to be found in the lyrical poetry of any ancient nation. We can make room here for only a few extracts :—

"20. What mortal knoweth thee, O immortal Ushas fond of our praise! Whom, O mighty one, dost thou favour?

"21. Far-extending, many-tinted, brilliant Ushas! we know not thy abode, whether it be nigh or remote.

"22. Daughter of the sky! accept these offerings, and perpetuate our welfare" (I, 30).

"7. She, the young, the white-robed daughter of the sky, the mistress of all earthly treasure, dawns upon us, dissipating darkness! Auspicious Ushas! shine upon us to-day on this spot.

"8. Following the path of mornings that have passed, to be followed by endless mornings to come, bright Ushas dispels darkness, and awakens to life all beings, unconscious like the dead in sleep.

"10. How long have the Dawns risen? How long will the Dawns arise? The present morning pursues those that are gone, future mornings will pursue this resplendent Ushas.

"11. Mortals who beheld the pristine Ushas have passed away; we behold her now; and men will come after us who will behold Uṣhas in the future" (I, 113).

"4. Ahanâ gently proceeds to every house; she comes ever diffusing light, and blesses us and accepts our offerings.

"11. Radiant as a bride decorated by her mother, thou displayest thy person to the view. Auspicious Ushas! remove the investing darkness; no other dawns but thee will disperse it" (I, 123).

The Dawn was known by various names, and most of these names and the legends connected with them were brought by the Hindus from their original abode, since we find phonetical equivalents of these names, and a repetition of some of the legends too, in Greek mythology. Ushas is the Eos of the Greeks and the Aurora of the Latins. Arjunî, according to philologists, is the Greek Argynoris, Brisayâ is Briseis, and Dahanâ is Daphne. Saramâ is phonetically equivalent to the Greek Helena. Saranyu, the mother of Yama and of the Asvins, is the Greek Erinys, and Ahanâ is the renowned goddess Athena.

We have already alluded to the legend of Saranyu running away from her husband Vivasvat, and then giving birth to the twin Asvins. We find the same legend among the Greeks who believed in Erinys Demeter running away in the same manner, and giving birth to Areion and Despoina. The idea in both cases is the same; it is the dawn or gloaming disappearing as the day and night advance. The same idea has given rise to another beautiful Greek legend whose origin, too, we trace in the Rig Veda. In many passages (I, 115, 2, for instance), we find allusions to the sun pursuing the dawn as a man pursues a woman. The Greek Apollo in the same way pursues the Greek Daphne, until she is metamorphosed, *i.e.*, the dawn disappears!

Sarasvatî, as her name signifies, is the goddess of the

river of that name, which was considered holy because of the religious rites performed on its banks and the sacred hymns uttered there. By a natural development of ideas, she was considered the goddess of those hymns, or in other words the goddess of speech, in which character she is worshipped now. She is the only Vedic goddess whose worship continues in India to the modern day; all her modern companions, Durgâ, Kalî, Lakshmî, and others, are creations of a later day.

Such is the nature-worship of the Rig Veda; such were the gods and goddesses whom our forefathers worshipped four thousand years ago on the banks of the Indus. The conception of the nature-gods and the single-hearted fervency with which they were adored, argue the simplicity and vigour of a manly race, as well as the culture and thoughtfulness of a people who had already made a considerable progress in civilisation. And the very conception of the Vedic gods argues an elevated sentiment, a high tone of morality in the men who conceived such deities. As M. Barth justly observes, the Vedic gods are masters close at hand, and require a due performance of duty by man. "He must be sincere towards them, for they cannot be deceived. Nay he knows that they in turn do not deceive, and that they have a right to require his affection and confidence as a friend, a brother, a father. . . . How could it be permitted to men to be bad when the gods are good, to be unjust while they are just, to be deceitful when they never deceive? It is certainly a remarkable feature of the hymns that they acknowledge no wicked divinities, and no mean and harmful practices. . . . We must acknowledge then that the hymns give evidence of an exalted and comprehensive morality, and that in striving to be 'without reproach before Aditi and the Adityas,' the Vedic minstrels feel the weight of other duties besides those of multiplying offerings to the gods." *

* *The Religions of India* (translation), p. 32 *et seq.*

There are no indications in the Rig Veda of any "temples reared by mortal hands" and consecrated as places of worship. On the contrary, every householder, every patriarch of his family, lighted the sacrificial fire in his own home, and poured libations of the Soma-juice, and prayed to the gods for happiness to his family, for abundant crops and wealth and cattle, for immunity from sickness, and for victory over the black aborigines. There was no separate priestly caste, and men did not retire into forests, and subject themselves to penances in order to meditate on religion, and chant these hymns. On the contrary, the old Rishis,—the real Rishis as we find them in the Rig Veda, and not the fabled ones of whom we have legendary accounts in the Purânas,—were worldly men, men with considerable property in crops and in cattle and surrounded by large families, men who in times of danger exchanged the plough for the spear and the sword, and defended against the black barbarians those blessings of civilisation which they solicited from their gods, and secured with so much care.

But though each householder was himself the priest, the warrior and the cultivator, yet we find evidence of kings performing rites on a large scale by help of men specially proficient in the chanting of hymns and other religious rites, and engaged and paid for the purpose. And as we go towards the later hymns of the Rig Veda, we find this class of professional priests gaining in reputation and in wealth, honoured by chiefs and kings, and rewarded by gifts of cattle and cars. We find mention of particular families specially proficient in the performance of religious rites, and in the composition of hymns; and it is probable that the existing hymns of the Rig Veda were composed by members of these families, and were traditionally learnt by rote and preserved in those families.

The hymns of the Rig Veda are divided into ten *Mandalas*, so arranged according to the Rishis by whom they were composed. The first and the last Mandalas contain hymns composed by numerous Rishis, but the remaining eight Mandalas belong, each of them, to a particular Rishi, or rather to a particular house or school of Rishis. As we have stated before, the second Mandala is a collection of hymns composed by Gritsamada of the house of Bhrigu, the third Mandala belongs to Visvâmitra, the fourth Mandala belongs to Vâmadeva, the fifth to Atri, the sixth to Bhâradvâja, the seventh to Vasishtha, the eighth to Kanva, and the ninth to Angiras. All these names are familiar to modern Hindus through the numberless legends which have surrounded them in Puranic times, and modern Hindus still love to trace their descent from these ancient and revered houses. We shall have something to say about these Rishis and their legends in our next chapter.

It is to these and other venerable houses that the Aryan world owes the preservation of the most ancient compositions of the Aryan race. From century to century the hymns were handed down without break or intermission, and the youths of the priestly houses spent the prime of their life in learning by rote the sacred songs from the lips of their grey-headed sires. It was thus that the inestimable treasure, the Rig Veda, was preserved for hundreds of years.

In course of time the priests boldly grappled with the deeper mysteries of nature, they speculated about creation and about the future world, and they resolved the nature-gods into the Supreme Deity.

"1. That all-wise Father saw clearly, and after due reflection created the sky and the earth in their watery form, and touching each other. When their boundaries were stretched afar, then the sky and the earth became separated.

"2. He who is the Creator of all is great; he creates and supports all, he is above all and sees all. He is beyond the seat of the seven Rishis. So the wise men say, and the wise men obtain fulfilment of all their desires.

"3. He who has given us life, he who is the Creator, he who knows all the places in this universe—*he is one, although he bears the names of many gods.* Other beings wish to know of him.

"7. You cannot comprehend him who has created all this; he is incomprehensible to your mind. People make guesses, being shrouded in a mist; they take their food for the support of their life, and utter hymns and wander about" (X, 82).

This sublime hymn teaches us in unmistakable words that the different Vedic gods are but different *names* of the One incomprehensible Deity. We quote another such hymn below.

"1. At that time what is, was not, and what is not, was not. The earth was not, and the far-stretching sky was not. What was there that covered? Which place was assigned to what object? Did the inviolate and deep water exist?

"2. At that time death was not, nor immortality; the distinction between day and night was not. There was only ONE who lived and breathed without the help of air, supported by himself. Nothing was, except HE.

"3. At first darkness was covered in darkness. All was without demarcation; all was of watery form. The world that was a void was covered by what did not exist and was produced by meditation.

"4. Desire arose in the mind, the cause of creation was thus produced. Wise men reflect, and in their wisdom ascertain the birth of what is from what is not.

"5. Males with generating seed were produced, and powers were also produced. Their rays extended on both sides and below and above, a self-supporting principle beneath, an energy aloft.

"6. Who knows truly? Who will describe? When was all born? Whence were all these created? *The gods have been made after the creation.* Who knows whence they were made ?

"7. Whence all these were created, from whom they came, whether any one created them or did not create, —is only known to Him who lives as Lord in the highest place. If He knows not (no one else does)" (X, 129).

Such is the first recorded attempt among the Aryan nations of the earth to pierce into the mysteries of creation; such are the bold and sublime if vague ideas which dawned in the minds of our forefathers thousands of years ago, regarding the commencement of this great universe. One more hymn we will quote here, a remarkable hymn, showing, again, how the later Rishis soared beyond the conception of the nature-gods to the sublime idea of One Deity :—

"1. In the beginning the Golden Child existed. He was the Lord of all from his birth. He placed this earth and sky in their respective places. Whom shall we worship with offerings ?

"2. Him who has given life and strength ; whose will is obeyed by all the gods ; whose shadow is immortality, and whose slave is death. Whom shall we worship with offerings ?

"3. Him who by his power is the sole king of all the living beings that see and move ; him who is the Lord of all bipeds and quadrupeds. Whom shall we worship with offerings ?

"4. Him by whose power these snowy mountains have been made, and whose creations are this earth and its oceans. Him whose arms are these quarters of space. Whom shall we worship with offerings ?

"5. Him who has fixed in their places this sky and this earth ; him who has established the heavens and the highest heaven ; him who has measured the firmament. Whom shall we worship with offerings ?

"6. Him by whom the sounding sky and earth have

been fixed and expanded; him whom the resplendent sky and earth own as Almighty; him by whose support the sun rises and gains its lustre. Whom shall we worship with offerings?

"7. Mighty waters pervaded the universe, they held in their womb and gave birth to fire. The One Being, who is the life of the gods, appeared. Whom shall we worship with offerings?

"8. He who by his own prowess controlled the waters which gave birth to energy, he who is the Lord above all gods, he was One. Whom shall we worship with offerings?

"9. He, the True, who is the creator of this earth, who is the creator of the sky, who is the creator of the glad and mighty waters,—may he not do us harm. Whom shall we worship with offerings?

"10. O Lord of creatures! None but thee has produced all these created things. May the object with which we worship be fulfilled. May we acquire wealth and happiness" (X, 121).

We now see the force of the remark that the religion of the Rig Veda travels from Nature up to Nature's God. The worshipper appreciates the glorious phenomena of nature, and rises from these phenomena to grasp the mysteries of creation and its great Creator.

CHAPTER VII.

VEDIC RISHIS.

WE have stated in the last chapter that certain pious and learned families obtained pre-eminence in the Vedic Period by their knowledge of performing religious sacrifices and their gift of composing hymns; that kings delighted to honour and reward these families; and that it is to them that the Aryan world is indebted for handing down the Vedic hymns from generation to generation. Modern Hindus take a pride in tracing their descent from these ancient families, and their names are a household word in modern Hindu society. Some account of these ancient Rishis,—the revered pioneers of the Hindu religion, —will therefore not be unwelcome to Hindu readers.

Pre-eminent among the Vedic Rishis, or rather Rishi families, stand the Visvâmitras and the Vasishthas. The learned and industrious scholar Dr. Muir has, in the first volume of his "Sanscrit Texts," collected many legends about these Rishis from later Sanscrit literature; but there is no Hindu who has not heard from his boyhood innumerable legends of this kind, connected with those revered names.

The Vasishthas and the Visvâmitras were both honoured by the powerful conqueror, Sudâs. The hymns of the third Mandala are ascribed to the Visvâmitras, and in the 53rd hymn we find the following passage:—"The great god-born, god-commissioned Rishi, the beholder of men, has stayed the watery current. When Visvâmitra sacrificed for Sudâs, then Indra was propitiated through the

Kausikas." Again, the hymns of the seventh Mandala are ascribed to the Vasishthas, and in the 33rd hymn we find the following passage:—"The Vasishthas in white robes, with their hair knots on the right, devoted to sacred rites, have gladdened me. Rising up, I call the people round the sacrificial grass. Let not the Vasishthas depart from my door."

There was naturally some jealousy between these two priestly houses, and hard words were exchanged. The following verses in III, 53, are said to contain an imprecation against the Vasishthas:—

"21. Indra, approach us to-day with many excellent succour: be propitious to us. May he who hates us fall low; and let the breath of life forsake him whom we hate.

"22. As the tree suffers from the axe, as the Simbala flower is broken, as the cauldron boiling over casts forth foam, so may the enemy, O Indra.

"23. The might of the destroyer is not perceived. Men lead away the Rishi as if he were a beast. The wise do not condescend to ridicule the fool. They do not lead the ass before the horse.

"24. These Bhâratas have learnt to turn away from, not to associate with (the Vasishthas). They urge the horse against them as against a foe. They bear about the bow in battle."

Vasishtha is supposed to have hurled back the imprecation in the following verses of VII, 104:—

"13. Soma does not bless the wicked nor the ruler who abuses his power. He slays the demon; he slays the untruthful man; both are bound by the fetters of Indra.

"14. If I had worshipped false gods, or if I had called upon the gods in vain,—but why art thou angry with me, O Jâtavedas? May vain talkers fall into thy destruction.

"15. May I die at once if I be a Yâtudhana, or if I

hurt the life of any man. But may he be cut off from his ten friends who falsely called me a Yâtudhana.

"16. He who called me a Yâtudhana, when I am not so, or who said I am a bright devil,—may Indra strike him down with his great weapon, may he fall the lowest of all beings."

So far the jealousy of the two angry priests is intelligible and even natural, however unbecoming of their great learning and sanctity. But when we proceed from the Rig Veda to later Sanscrit literature, incidents which are human and natural become lost in a cloud of miraculous and monstrous legends.

It is assumed from the commencement in these later legends that Vasishtha was a Brâhman and Visvâmitra was a Kshatriya, although the Rig Veda justifies no such assumption and knows no Brâhmans and Kshatriyas as castes. On the contrary, Visvâmitra is the composer of some of the finest hymns cherished by later Brâhmans, including the sacred Gâyatrî, the morning prayer of modern Brâhmans.

Having assumed that Visvâmitra was born a Kshatriya, the Mahâbhârata, the Harivansa, the Vishnu Purâna, and other later works repeat an amusing story to account for the sage's attaining Brâhmanhood. Satyavatî, a Kshatriya girl, had been married to Richîka, a Brâhman. Richîka prepared a dish for his wife, which would make her conceive a son with the qualities of a Brâhman, and another dish for his mother-in-law (a Kshatriya's wife), which would make her conceive a son with the qualities of a Kshatriya. The two ladies, however, exchanged dishes; and so the Kshatriya's wife conceived and bore Visvâmitra with the qualities of a Brâhman, and the Brâhman's wife Satyavatî bore Jamadagni, whose son, the fiery Parasurâma, though a Brâhman, became a renowned and destructive warrior! Such were the childish stories which the later writers had to invent to remove the difficulty they had created for themselves.

by assuming that Vedic Rishis belonged to particular castes!

In the celebrated legend of Harischandra, Visvâmitra appears as a rapacious Brâhman. He not only made the king give up his whole empire, but compelled him to sell his queen, his boy, and himself as slaves to pay the inexorable Brâhman's fee! If such stories are invented to teach respect and duty due to Brâhmans, they fail in their object and inspire other sentiments. The bereaved Harischandra was, however, rewarded in the end, and Visvâmitra anointed his son as king, and Harischandra went to heaven. Vasishtha became angry and cursed Visvâmitra to be a Vaka or crane, and Visvâmitra, too, transformed Vasishtha into an Ari bird! The two birds began a furious contest which shook the whole world, until Brahmâ had to interpose, and restored the saints to their own forms, and reconciled them!

In the legend of Trisanku, we are told that that prince wished to go bodily to heaven. Vasishtha declared the thing impossible, and in return for the king's angry words changed him to a Chandâla. The fiery Visvâmitra now appeared on the scene. He declared the thing quite possible, and began a great sacrifice and proceeded with it in spite of Vasishtha's absence. Trisanku ascended to heaven, but Indra refused to receive him, and threw the intruder, head downwards, towards the earth. The irrepressible Visvâmitra, however, threatened to create another heaven with Indra and gods and stars! The gods had to give in, and Trisanku ascended to heaven, and shone like a star beyond the sun's course, but in a somewhat uncomfortable position, with his head still downwards!

In various other legends, which have almost become household stories for Hindu boys and girls, these two sages continually appear, in defiance of chronology and date, and are always at enmity with each other. The rival priests appear in courts of kings, twenty, thirty, or fifty generations removed from each other, and there is hardly a classical composition of note about a royal house or a semi-divine hero in which we do not find mention of Vasishtha and Visvâmitra, eternally the rivals of each other. Thus the Vishnu Purâna makes Vasishtha the priest of Ikshvâku's son Nimi, as well as the priest of Sagara, who was thirty-seventh in descent from Ikshvâku; and the Râmâyana makes Vasishtha the priest of Râma, who was sixty-first in descent from Ikshvâku! Such is the use which later romancers have made of the simple materials furnished by the Rig Veda, and such is the manner in which they have piled story upon story, and myth upon myth in connection with incidents which in the ancient Veda are simple, natural, and human. Not only the Rishis of the Veda, but every deity, and we may almost say every simile or allegory in the Rig Veda about a natural phenomenon, have received such treatment in the hands of the later imaginative Hindus.

But while a hundred wild stories were invented in later days to account for Visvâmitra's attaining Brâhmanhood, there was no thought of denying that accepted fact. Every legend, every learned disquisition, every childish tale, every great work, from the Mahâbhârata to Manu and the Purânas,—admit that Visvâmitra was a Kshatriya and a Brâhman. Yudhisthira in the Anusâsana Parva (section 3) of the Mahâbhârata inquires of Bhîshma how Visvâmitra had not only become a Brâhman but had established "the great and wise family of the Kusikas, *which included Brâhmans and hundreds of Brâhman Rishis.*" The question would be a difficult one to answer in the Puranic Age in which the Mahâbhârata received its last touches. The question would not be difficult of solution in the Epic Age when the caste-system was still a pliable institution. And the question would not arise at all in the Age of Visvâmitra himself, *i.e.*, in the Vedic Age, when caste as such did not exist.

From the legends of the Visvâmitras and the Vasishthas, let us now turn to the scarcely less renowned houses of the Angirases, the Vâmadevas, the Bhâradvâjas, and the Bhrigus. All these were families of Vedic Rishis, composers of Vedic hymns; and later writers therefore feel somewhat uncertain about their caste. They are sometimes called Brâhmans with the character of Kshatriyas, sometimes Kshatriyas with the character of Brâhmans; and occasionally the bold truth is conjectured that these Rishis lived before the institution of caste was formed.

The Angirases are the reputed authors of the ninth Mandala of the Rig Veda. About the Angirases, the Vishnu Purâna (IV, 2, 2) has the following:—"The son of Nabhâga was Nâbhâga; his son was Ambarîsha; his son was Virûpa; from him sprang Prishadasva, and from him Rathînara. On this subject there is this verse: These persons *descended from a Kshatriya stock and afterwards known as Angirases* were the chief of the Rathînaras, *Brâhmans possessing also the character of Kshatriyas.*"

Vâmadeva and Bhâradvâja are reputed to be the authors of the fourth and sixth Mandalas of the Rig Veda. The Matsya Purâna includes them (section 132) among the Angirases of whom we have spoken before.

To the Gritsamadas are attributed the hymns of the second Mandala of the Rig Veda. The commentator Sâyana says of him that he was formerly of the Angiras race, but he afterwards became Gritsamada, of the Bhrigu race. This somewhat mystic legend is elaborated in the Mahâbhârata, Anusâsana Parva (section 30), in which we are told that Vîtahavya, a Kshatriya king, had taken shelter with Bhrigu, and Bhrigu, in order to save the fugitive from his pursuer, stated "there is no Kshatriya here, all these are Brâhmans." The word of Bhrigu could not prove untrue, and the fugitive Kshatriya Vîtahavya forthwith bloomed into Brâhmanhood and became Gritsamada! It must be allowed that this was an easier process than the penance of thousands of years which Visvâmitra is said to have performed,—not to mention that his mother had exchanged dishes with a Brâhman's wife!

But the story of Gritsamada's change of caste is not universally accepted. The Vishnu Purâna and the Vâyu Purana conjecture the bold truth that Gritsamada lived before the caste institution was formed. "From Gritsamada was descended Saunaka, *who originated the four castes*" (*Vish. Pur.*, IV, 8).

Lastly, let us turn to the Kanvas and the Atris. The Kanvas are the authors of the eighth Mandala of the Rig Veda, and we find the same uncertainty about their caste. The Vishnu Purâna (IV, 19), and the Bhâgavata Purâna (IX, 20, 6, 7), maintain that Kanva was a descendant of Puru, a Kshatriya. Nevertheless the Kanvas were regarded as Brâhmans. "From Ajamîdha sprang Kanva, and from him Medhâtithi, *from whom were descended the Kanvanaya Brâhmans*" (*Vish. Pur.*, IV, 19).

The Atris are the reputed authors of the fifth Mandala of the Rig Veda, and we find the same uncertainty about their caste also. Thus the Vishnu Purâna (IV, 6), calls Atri the grandfather of Pururavas, *who belonged to the Kshatriya race.*

These extracts are enough. They are made from works composed or revised two or three thousand years after the time of the Vedic Rishis, but those extracts enable us to comprehend the status and position of the Vedic religious leaders and warriors, and are therefore not out of place in an account of the Vedic Period. Writing at such a long distance of time from the Vedic Age the modern authors often misapprehended ancient facts and traditions. But nevertheless, the unswerving loyalty to the past which has ever characterised Hindu writers prevented them from tampering with such traditions. Those traditions pointed to a state of society which had long passed away, and which had become almost unintelligible. Puranic writers could scarcely comprehend that priests and warriors could spring from the same race, that a Rishi could be a warrior, or that a warrior could be a priest. They tried to explain such traditions by a hundred different theories and legends, but nevertheless they have faithfully and piously handed down the traditions unchanged and unaltered. Thus, to make only one more extract, the Matsya Purâna enumerates 91 Vedic Rishis, and concludes with the following suggestive passage, (section 132):—"Thus 91 persons have been declared, by whom the hymns have been given forth. *They were Brâhmans, Kshatriyas, and Vaisyas,* all sons of Rishis. They were the offspring of the Rishikas, sons of Rishis, Vedic Rishis."

Thus the Purâna faithfully preserves the ancient tradition that the Vedic hymns were the common property of the entire Aryan population. And when the writer tells us that the composers of those hymns were Brâhmans, Kshatriyas, and Vaisyas, we have little difficulty in discovering in that statement a dim recollection of the truth that the hymns were composed by the *undivided ancestors of those castes.*

Modern writers have classed Rishis under three classes, viz., Devarshis, or saintly gods like Nârada; Brahmarshis, or saintly Brâhmans like Kanva of the Sakuntalâ drama; and Râjarshis, or saintly Kshatriyas like Janaka, king of the Videhas. The ancient Vedic Rishis did not answer to any of these classes, did not belong exclusively to any of these categories, and were therefore a standing puzzle to modern writers. Hence the numerous legends to account for what was unaccountable; and often in the midst of these wild conjectures, the modern writer made a bold guess after the truth, and maintained that the Vedic Rishis must have lived before caste was originated. We do not wonder at the theories and legends which were multiplied in such profusion; we admire the boldness with which the truth was sometimes conjectured.

For the rest, these invaluable traditions—that priests

and warriors were descended from the same races, and that the same Rishis were often both priests and warriors, —enable us to comprehend the true position of Vedic Rishis. For, divested of their miraculous and legendary character, what do these traditions indicate? They indicate that the venerable families of the olden times,—like those of the Vasishthas, the Visvâmitras, the Angirases, and the Kanvas,—furnished renowned warriors and eminent priests at the same time. A Percy or a Douglas might be an ambitious priest or a fiery warrior, and so might a Kanva or an Angiras. To be sure, the Hindu houses were pre-eminently priestly as the European houses were military, but *caste* was as unknown to the one as to the other. Many a baron of Mediæval Europe, whose name is still preserved in the history of the crusades, had his father or uncle, son or nephew, immured in the solitude of holy monasteries; and many a Vasishtha or Visvâmitra, whose religious hymns we still cherish and revere, had his son or nephew engaged in the wars of the Vedic Period, in the unending contests against the aborigines of the soil. These facts are proved by the texts of the Rig Veda itself which we have quoted in a previous chapter; and they are confirmed by the legends and traditions which we have quoted in this chapter from later Sanscrit literature. The Vedic Rishis composed their hymns, fought their wars, and ploughed their fields; but were neither Brâhmans, nor Kshatriyas, nor Vaisyas. The great Rishi houses of the Vedic Age furnished priests and soldiers, but were no more Brâhmans or Kshatriyas than the Percies or Douglases of Mediæval Europe were Brâhmans or Kshatriyas.

BOOK II.

EPIC PERIOD, B.C. 1400 TO 1000.

CHAPTER I.

LITERATURE OF THE PERIOD.

WE have closed our account of the Vedic Age, when the Hindu Aryans gradually conquered and occupied the whole tract of the country watered by the Indus and its five tributaries. We have seen that the sole work of this period which remains to us is the collection of hymns known as the Rig Veda Sanhitâ, and we have also seen how these hymns illustrate the civilisation of the Vedic Period. We now proceed to describe the civilisation of the Epic Period, when the Hindus crossed the Sutlej, moved down the basin of the Ganges and the Jumna, and founded powerful kingdoms along the entire valley as far down as modern Benares and North Behar. And as in the case of the Vedic Age, so in the case of the Epic Age, we will base our account on contemporaneous literature.

What is the contemporaneous literature of the Epic Age? And what is the contemporaneous literature of the Philosophical or Rationalistic Age that followed? The Brâhmanas, the Âranyakas, and the Upanishads, which constantly refer to the actions of the Kurus, the Panchâlas, the Kosalas, and the Videhas *living in the valley of the Ganges*, form the literature of the Epic Age. The Sûtras, which presuppose the rise of rationalism in

India, and which were composed when the Aryans *had expanded all over India*, form the literature of the Rationalistic Age.

About thirty years ago Professor Max Müller published his great work on Sanscrit literature, and gave reasons, which have since generally been accepted, for considering the mass of Sûtra literature as subsequent to the Brâhmana literature. He showed that the Sûtra literature presupposed and quoted from the Brâhmana literature, and the converse was never the case. He showed that the Brâhmana literature reflected an age of priestly supremacy and unquestioning obedience on the part of the people, which was anterior to the practical and philosophical and sceptical age of the Sûtras. He showed that the Brâhmana literature down to the Upanishads was considered *revealed* in India, while all Sûtra works were ascribed to human authors. And he enforced these arguments by a wealth of illustrations and a degree of erudition which left nothing to be desired.*

It is needless to say that we cannot enter into the

* Later researches have confirmed the view. Not only are the Sûtras of a particular school subsequent to the Brâhmanas of the same school, but the body of the Sûtra literature as a whole is subsequent to the body of the Brâhmana literature. Thus, to quote one instance only, Dr. Bühler, who does not altogether agree with Max Müller on this point, nevertheless points out in his Introductions to the Dharma Sûtras that those Sûtras repeatedly quote from Brâhmanas of different schools. He shows that Gautama's Dharma Sûtra, which is the oldest extant, presupposes an Âranyaka of the Black Yajur Veda, a Brâhmana of the Sâma Veda and even an Upanishad of the Atharva Veda! He points out that Vasishtha's Dharma Sûtra quotes from a Brâhmana of the Rig Veda, an Âranyaka of the Black Yajur Veda and a Brâhmana of the White Yajur Veda, and also mentions an Upanishad of the Atharva Veda. So also Baudhâyana's Dharma Sûtra quotes from the Brâhmanas both of the Black and the White Yajur Veda. On the other hand, no Brâhmana ever quotes from any Sûtra work.

No scholar maintains that the last Brâhmana work was composed before the first Sûtra work was written. But there can be little doubt on the evidence now before us, that there was a period when the *prevailing style* of writing was the prose style of the Brâhmanas, and that this period was followed by a period when the *prevailing style* was aphorisms or Sûtras.

details of these learned discussions. True to the plan of the present work, we will make only a few remarks not on the *literary*, but on the *historical* bearings of the facts stated above. What is the historical import of this sequence in the different classes of Ancient Sanscrit literature? What is the historical reason of this sequence? Why did the Ancient Hindus compose their works in one particular form, the Vedic hymns, for a number of centuries? Why did they gradually abandon that style of composition, and write the prolix and dogmatic prose Brâhmanas, for some succeeding centuries? And why again did they gradually change this for the concise aphorisms of the Sûtras during the next few centuries? What is there in the nature of things that would induce the Ancient Hindus to take up different styles of composition at different periods of their history,—as if to afford the future historian a clue to the dates of their writings?

The question is more easily asked than answered. It may be answered, however, by a counter-question. What is there in the nature of things which prevented the Chronicles and Romances of Mediæval Europe being composed after the fourteenth and fifteenth centuries? Why did not Hume and Gibbon compose Chronicles? Why did not Fielding and Scott compose Mediæval Romances? The subjects were still the same;—why was the composition so different that it would be possible to demarcate the feudal ages from the modern period on the testimony of European literature, even if every vestige of European history was destroyed?

An Englishman would answer: It was impossible that Chronicles and feudal Romances should be continued after Elizabeth had reigned and Shakespeare and Bacon had written. A new light had dawned on Europe. The human mind had expanded. Religion was purified. A new world had been discovered. Modern philosophy had taken its rise. Commerce and maritime enterprise had received a wonderful development. Feudalism had died a natural death. The face of the European world had been changed.

Were it possible to bring before the reader the history of Hindu civilisation as vividly as he has before him the history of European civilisation, he would give similar replies with regard to the epochs of Indian History. It was impossible in the nature of things that Hymns like those of the Rig Veda should be composed after the Hindus had achieved the elaborate civilisation, and adopted the pompous religious rites of the Epic Period. The simple fervency with which the Punjab Aryans looked up to the Sky, the Dawn, or the Sun, had passed, once and for ever. Simple natural phenomena did not excite the wonder and religious admiration of the cultured and somewhat artificial Gangetic Aryans engaged in solemn rites and pompous sacrifices. The fervent prayer to the rain-god Indra, or the loving address to the dawn-goddess Ushas, was almost impossible. The very import and object of the old simple hymns were forgotten, and sacrifices of various descriptions, from the simple morning and evening libations to the elaborate royal sacrifices lasting for many years, formed the essence of the later religion. The rules of the sacrifices, the import and object of every minute rite, the regulations for each insignificant observance,—these occupied the religious minds of the people, these formed the subjects of discussion between learned kings and royal priests, these formed the bulk of the Brâhmana literature. It was as impossible for the cultured writers and thinkers of the day to go back to the buried past and disinter the simple faith of the Vedic Hymns, as it was impossible for the erudite schoolmen of Mediæval Europe to produce the wild and simple Norwegian Sagas of a bygone age.

Again, the elaborate and dogmatic trifling of the scholastic philosophy of Europe was impossible after Descartes had lived and Bacon had written. In the same way, and for the same reason, the elaborate trifling of the Brâhmanas were impossible in the Hindu world after Kapila had taught and Gautama Buddha had preached. The human mind in India had received a new impetus. A new world had been discovered beyond the Vindhya range, though the name of the Indian Columbus, who first planted the Hindu flag in a southern kingdom, is forgotten. The earnest and fervent Upanishads had been written, and marked a strong reaction against priestly pedantry. Kapila—the Descartes of India—had startled the Hindu world by his Sânkhya philosophy; and Gautama—the Luther of India—had proclaimed a reformed faith for the poor and the lowly, and protested against the privileges of priests. New sciences had started into existence. A new light had dawned in the Hindu world.

The Brâhmana literature died a natural death. The elaborate and unmeaning dogmas were left in the shade; the rules for the performance of the ancient sacrifices were condensed for practical purposes. It was a practical age, when everything was condensed and codified. The rules of life were codified. Philosophy was condensed into aphorisms, science and learning in every department were condensed. Treatises were composed in every branch of human knowledge in a concise style, in which teachers could teach and learners could learn by rote. And thus it is that we have the entire literature of the Rationalistic Age in the shape of aphorisms,—of Sûtras.

This is the historical import of the three different classes of Ancient Sanscrit literature, which represent three distinct epochs of Hindu history. The Hymns reflect the manly simplicity of the Vedic Age. The Brâhmanas reflect the pompous ceremonials of the Epic Age. The Sûtras reflect the science and learning, and even the scepticism of the Rationalistic Age.

We have said before that the tide of Hindu colonisation rolled eastward and southward in each successive period, and the different classes of Sanscrit literature spoken of attest to this onward movement. In Europe feudal literature and modern literature were developed on the same arena, in Italy and Germany, in France and England. In India the case was different. For the Aryans of India went on conquering through successive periods, and the literature of each period speaks of the portion of India under the Aryan influence and domination in that particular period. This in itself is an invaluable index to the dates of the different classes of literature.

The Hymns of the Rig Veda speak of the Punjab alone,—India beyond the Punjab is unknown to the Rig Veda. The banks of the distant Ganges and the Jumna are rarely alluded to; the scenes of all the wars and social ceremonies and religious sacrifices of the Rig Veda are the banks of the Indus and its tributaries and the Sarasvatî. This was the Hindu world when the hymns were composed.

But the Hindus soon threw out colonies all over Northern India. In course of centuries these colonies rose into importance and were formed into powerful kingdoms, and by their progress and learning threw the mother-country, the Punjab, into the shade. In the Brâhmanas we hear of the mighty Kurus in the tract of the country round modern Delhi; we hear of the powerful Panchâlas in the country round modern Kanouj; we read of the Videhas in the country now known as North Behar; we read of the Kosalas in Oudh; and we read of the Kâsîs in the country round modern Benares. These colonists developed pompous sacrificial rites, and had illustrious and learned kings like Janaka and Ajâtasatru and Janamejaya Pârikshita. They founded schools or parishads in villages and towns, and they developed a new social system based on caste distinctions. It is of these colonists and their civilisation that we mostly read in the Brâhmanas;—the Punjab is almost forgotten, and Southern India is still unknown, or is referred to as the home of wild beasts and wild men.

And lastly, the Sûtra literature makes us familiar with great Hindu kingdoms in Southern India, and some of the existing Sûtras were composed in Southern India. Thus the countries and nations described by the different classes of literature point to their respective ages.

We have spoken of the Vedic Period and the Rig Veda Hymns in the First Book of this work. We will speak of the Epic Period and the Brâhmana literature in this Second Book. And we will speak of the Rationalistic Period and the Sûtra literature in the Third Book.

We have seen before that the Rig Veda Hymns were *composed* in the Vedic Age and were finally *compiled* in the Epic Age. The other three Vedas known as the Sâma Veda, the Yajur Veda (White and Black), and the Atharva Veda, were also compiled in this Epic Age.

The reasons which led to the compilation of the Sâma Veda and the Yajur Veda have been ascertained with a fair degree of certainty. We find mention in the hymns of the Rig Veda of different classes of priests who performed different duties at sacrifices. The Adhvaryus were entrusted with the material performance of sacrifice. They measured the ground, built the altar, prepared the sacrificial vessels, fetched wood and water, and immolated animals. The Udgâtris, on the other hand, were entrusted with the duty of singing, as according to ancient custom some parts of the sacrifice had to be accompanied by songs. The Hotris had to recite hymns. And lastly, the Brahmans presided at sacrifices over all the rest.

Of these four classes of priests, neither the Brahman nor the Hotri required any special manual. For the Brahman was required to know the entire ceremonial, to be able to superintend the performance of the sacrifice, to advise the other priests on doubtful points, and to correct their mistakes. The Hotri too had simply to recite, and if he knew the hymns of the Rig Veda, he did not require any separate compilation. But the duties of the Adhvaryu and the Udgâtri required special training. Special sacrificial formulas must have existed for the former, and a stock of the Rig Veda Hymns, set to music, must have also existed for the latter in the Vedic Period, for we find the names Yajus and Sâman in the Rig Veda Hymns. These formulas and chants were, however, separately collected and compiled at a later age, *i.e.*, in the Epic Period; and these separate compilations, in the shape which they last took, are the Yajur Veda and the Sâma Veda as we have them now.

No name has been handed down to us as the compiler of the Sâma Veda. Professor Benfey has pointed out, what Dr. Stevenson previously suspected, that all the verses of the Sâma Veda, with the exception of a few, are to be found in the Rig Veda; and it is supposed that these few verses too must have been contained in some other recension of the Rig Veda now lost to us. It is quite clear, therefore, that the Sâma Veda is only a selection from the Rig Veda set to music for a special purpose.

Of the compilers of Yajur Veda, we have some information. The more ancient or Black Yajur Veda is called the Taittirîya Sanhitâ from Tittiri, who probably compiled or promulgated it in its present shape. In the Anukramanî of the Âtreya recension of this Veda, however, we are told that the Veda was handed down by Vaisampâyana to Yâska Paingi, by Yâska to Tittiri, by Tittiri to Ukha, and by Ukha to Âtreya. This would show that the existing oldest recension of the Yajur Veda was not the first recension.

We have fuller information with regard to the more recent White Yajur Veda. It is called the Vâjasaneyi Sanhitâ, from Yâjnavalkya Vâjasaneya, the compiler or promulgator of that Veda. Yâjnavalkya held the influential position of chief priest in the court of Janaka, king of the Videhas, and the promulgation of this new

Veda proceeded probably from the court of that learned king.

There is a striking difference in arrangement between the White Yajur Veda and the Black Yajur Veda. In the latter, the sacrificial formulas are followed by dogmatic explanations, and by accounts of ceremonials belonging to them. In the former, the formulas only find place in the Sanhitâ, the explanation and the ritual being assigned to the Brâhmana. It is not improbable, as has been supposed, that it was to improve the old arrangement, and to separate the exegetic matter from the formulas, that Yâjnavalkya, of the court of Janaka, founded the new school known as the Vâjasaneyins, and that their labours resulted in a new (Vâyasaneyi) Sanhitâ and an entirely separate (Satapatha) Brâhmana.

But although the promulgation of the White Yajur Veda is ascribed to Yâjnavalkya, a glance at its contents will show that it is not the compilation of any one man or even of one age. Of its 40 chapters only the first 18 are cited in full and explained in due order in the first nine books of the Satapatha Brâhmana; and it is the formulas of these 18 chapters only which are found in the older Black Yajur Veda. These 18 chapters then are the oldest portion of the White Yajur Veda, and may have been compiled or promulgated by Yâjnavalkya Vâjasaneya. The next 7 chapters are very likely a later addition. The remaining 15 chapters are undoubtedly a still later addition, and are expressly called Parisishta or Khila, *i.e.*, supplement.

Of the Atharva Veda, we need only state that it was not generally recognised as a Veda till long after the period of which we are speaking, though a class of literature known as the Atharvângiras was growing up during the Epic Period, and is alluded to in the later portions of some of the Brâhmanas. Throughout the first three Periods of Hindu history, and even in Manu and other metrical codes, three Vedas are generally recognised.

And although the claims of the Atharvan were sometimes put forward, still the work was not generally recognised as a fourth Veda till long after the Christian Era. Numerous passages recognising three Vedas only could be cited from the literature of the period of which we are now speaking; but we are unable to make room for such passages. We will only refer our readers to some of them, viz.: Aitareya Brâhmana, V, 32; Satapatha Brâhmana, IV, 6, 7; Aitareya Âranyaka, III, 2, 3; Brihadâranyaka Upanishad, I, 5; and Chhândogya Upanishad, III and VII. In this last work, after the three Vedas are named, Atharvângiras is classed with Itihâsa. It is only in the Brâhmana and Upanishads of the Atharva Veda itself that we find a uniform recognition of this work as a Veda. For instance, it is the principal object of the Gopatha Brâhmana to show the necessity of four Vedas. A carriage, we are told, does not proceed with less than four wheels, an animal cannot walk with less than four feet, nor can sacrifice be perfect with less than four Vedas! Such special pleading only proves that the fourth Veda was not yet recognised generally, even in the comparatively recent times when the Gopatha Brâhmana was composed.

Atharvan and Angiras are, as Professor Whitney remarks, half mythical names of ancient and venerated Indian families, and it was sought to bring the recent Veda into connection with these ancient names! The Veda is divided into twenty books, and contains nearly six thousand verses, and a sixth of this is in prose. Of the remaining, one-sixth is found among the hymns of the Rig Veda, mostly in the tenth book. The nineteenth book is a kind of supplement to the previous eighteen, while the twentieth book is made up of extracts from the Rig Veda.

The entire Veda principally consists of formulas intended to protect men against the baneful influences of divine powers, against diseases, noxious animals, and curses of enemies. It knows a host of "imps and hobgoblins," and offers homage to them to prevent them from doing harm. The hymns are supposed to bring from the unwilling hands of gods the favours that are wanted. Incantations calculated to procure long life or wealth or recovery from illness, and invocations for good luck in journeys, in gaming, &c., fill the work. These hymns resemble similar hymns in the last book of the Rig Veda; only, as Professor Weber has pointed out, in the Rig Veda they are apparently additions made at the time of the compilation, while in the Atharva Veda they are the natural utterance of the present.

We must now hasten to an account of the compositions called Brâhmanas, after which the literature of this Age has been named the Brâhmana literature. We have seen that in the Black Yajur Veda the texts are as a rule followed by their dogmatic explanations. These explanations were supposed to elucidate the texts and to explain their hidden meanings, and they contained the speculations of generations of priests. A single discourse of this kind was called a Brâhmana; and in later times collections or digests of such discourses were called Brâhmanas.

The Rig Veda has two Brâhmanas, viz., the Aitareya and the Kaushîtaki. The composition of the former is attributed to Mahidâsa Aitareya, son of Itarâ. In the Kaushîtaki Brâhmana, on the other hand, special regard is paid to the sage Kaushîtaka, whose authority is considered to be final. For the rest, these two Brâhmanas seem to be only two recensions of the same work, used by the Aitaryins and the Kaushîtakins respectively, and they agree with each other in many respects, except that the last ten chapters of the Aitareya are not found in the Kaushîtaki, and belong probably to a later age.

The Sâma Veda has the Tândya or Panchavinsa Brâhmana, the Sadvinsa Brâhmana, the Mantra Brâhmana, and the better known Chhândogya.

The Black Yajur Veda or Taittirîya Sanhitâ has its

Taittirîya Brâhmana, and the White Yajur Veda or Vâjasaneyi Sanhitâ has its voluminous Satapatha Brâhmana. We have already stated that the Satapatha Brâhmana is attributed to Yâjnavalkya, though it is more likely the handiwork of the school he founded, as he is often quoted in the work. Nor does the work belong entirely to one school or to one age. On the contrary, as in the case of the White Yajur Veda Sanhitâ so in the case of its Brâhmana, there are reasons to think that the work belongs to different periods. The first 18 chapters of the Sanhitâ are the oldest part of the work, and the first nine books of the Brâhmana, which comment on these 18 chapters, are the oldest part of the Brâhmana. The remaining five books are of later date than the first nine books.

The Atharva Veda has its Gopatha Brâhmana, a comparatively recent production, the contents of which are a medley, derived to a large extent from other sources.

Next after the Brâhmanas come the Âranyakas, which may indeed be considered as the last portions of the Brâhmanas. They are so called, as Sâyana informs us, because they had to be read in the forest, while the Brâhmanas were for use in sacrifices performed by householders in their homes.

The Rig Veda has its Kaushîtaki Âranyaka and its Aitareya Âranyaka, the latter ascribed to Mahidâsa Aitareya. The Black Yajur Veda has its Taittirîya Âranyaka, and the last book of the Satapatha Brâhmana is called its Âranyaka. The Sâma Veda and the Atharva Veda have no Âranyakas.

What gives these Âranyakas a special importance, however, is, that they are the proper repositories of those celebrated religious speculations known as the Upanishads. The Upanishads which are the best known, and which are undoubtedly ancient, are the Aitareya and the Kaushîtaki, found in the Âranyakas of those names, and belonging to the Rig Veda; the Chhândogya and the

Talavakâra (or Kena) belonging to the Sâma Veda; the Vâjasaneyi (or Isa) and the Brihadâranyaka belonging to the White Yajur Veda; the Taittirîya and Katha and Svetâsvatara belonging to the Black Yajur Veda; and the Mundaka and Prasna and Mândukya belonging to the Atharva Veda. These twelve are the ancient Upanishads to which Sankarâcharya principally appeals in his great commentary on the Vedânta Sûtras. But once after the Upanishads had come to be considered sacred and authoritative works, new compositions of the class began to be added, until the total number reaches 200 or more. The later Upanishads, which are generally known as the Atharva Upanishads, come down as far as the Puranic times, and enter the lists in behalf of sectarian views, instead of being devoted to an inquiry into the nature of Brahman or the Supreme Spirit, like the old Upanishads. Indeed, the later Upanishads come down to a period long subsequent to the Mahommedan Conquest of India, and the idea of a universal religion which was cherished by the great emperor Akbar finds expression in an Upanishad called the Allah Upanishad! We need hardly say that we will refer in this work only to the ancient Upanishads, and not to the later Upanishads.

With the Upanishads the Epic Period ends, and the so-called revealed literature of India ends also. Other classes of works, besides those named herein, undoubtedly existed in the Epic Period, but have now been lost to us, or more frequently replaced by newer works. A fragment only of the vast literature of the Epic Period has come down to us, and the principal works which remain have been detailed above.

Of the Epics themselves, the Mahâbhârata and the Râmâyana, we will speak in the next two chapters.

CHAPTER II.

KURUS AND PANCHÂLAS.

THE tide of Aryan conquests rolled onward. If the reader will refer to a map of India, he will find that from the banks of the Sutlej to the banks of the Jumna and the Ganges, there is not a very wide strip of country to cross. The Aryans, who had colonised the whole of the Punjab, were not likely to remain inactive on the banks of the Sutlej or of the Sarasvatî. Already in the Vedic Period bands of enterprising colonists had crossed those rivers and explored the distant shores of the Jumna and the Ganges, and those noble streams, though alluded to in the hymns as on the very horizon of the Hindu world, were not unknown. In course of time the emigrants to the fertile banks of the two rivers must have swelled in number, until the colonists founded a powerful kingdom of their own in the country near modern Delhi,—the kingdom of the Kurus.

The colonists were no others than the Bhâratas renowned in the wars of Sudâs, but their kings belonged to the house of Kurus, and hence the tribe went by both names, Bhâratas and Kurus. From what part of the Punjab the Kurus came, is a question still involved in obscurity. In the Aitareya Brâhmana (VIII, 14), it is stated that the Uttara Kurus and the Uttara Mâdras lived beyond the Himalaya. In later works, the Mahâbhârata (I, 47, 19, &c.) and the Râmâyana (IV, 44, 88, &c.), the land of the Uttara Kurus, has already become a mythical country. Uttara Kuru is identified with Ottorakorra of Ptolemy, and Lassen places the country somewhere east of modern Kashgar; but we would place the Uttara Kuru alluded to in the Aitareya Brâhmana somewhere north of the Sub-Himalayan range, *i.e.*, in Kashmir. We assume that the colony of the Kurus on the Ganges rose to prowess and fame about 1400 B.C.

When the Hindus had once begun to colonise the fertile banks of the Jumna and the Ganges, swarms of the colonists marched down the course of those streams and soon occupied the whole of the Doab, *i.e.*, the tract of country between those rivers. While we find the Kurus or Bhâratas settling down in the country near modern Delhi, we find another adventurous tribe, the Panchâlas, occupying the tract of country near modern Kanouj. The original seat of the Panchâlas is still less known than that of the Kurus, and it has been supposed that they also came from the northern hills, like the Kurus. Their name, however, which means "Five tribes," would seem to indicate that they were of the Pancha-Krishti or Pancha-jana, "five cultivating tribes" of whom we read so often in the Rig Veda.

The Panchâla kingdom probably rose to distinction about the same time as the kingdom of the Kurus, and the Brâhmana literature frequently refers to these allied tribes as forming the very centre of the Hindu world, and renowned by their valour, their learning, and their civilisation. Many of the Brâhmanas allude to the culture of their schools, the sanctity of their priests, the ostentatious religious sacrifices of their kings, and the exemplary lives of the people.

For centuries had elapsed since the Aryans had first settled on the banks of the Indus, and the centuries had done their work in progress and civilisation. The Kurus and the Panchâlas were no longer like the warrior-cultivators who battled against the black aborigines and won the banks of the Indus and its tributaries. Manners had changed, society had become more refined and polished, learning and arts had made considerable progress. Kings invited wise men to their courts, held learned controversies with their priests, performed elaborate sacrifices according to the rules of the age, led respectable and trained armies to the field, appointed duly qualified men to collect taxes and to administer justice, and performed all the duties of civilised administrators. The relations and friends of the king and all the warriors of the nation learnt archery and driving the war chariot from their early youth, and also learned the Vedas and all the holy learning that was handed down from generation to generation. The priests multiplied religious rites and observances, preserved the traditional learning of the land, and instructed and helped the people in their religious duties. And the people lived in their towns and villages, cherished the sacred sacrificial fire in their houses, cultivated the arts of peace, trained their boys from early youth in the Vedas and in their social and religious duties, and gradually developed those social customs which in India have the force of laws. Women had their legitimate influence in society, and moved without restriction or restraint. Society in India, fourteen hundred years before Christ, was more polished and refined than that of the preceding Vedic Age, and had more of healthy life and vigour than Hindu society has had in succeeding ages.

Civilisation, however, does not necessarily put a stop to wars and dissensions; and of the political history of the Kurus and the Panchâlas, the only reminiscences we possess are those of a sanguinary war in which many neighbouring tribes took part, and which forms the subject of one of the two great epics of India.

The incidents of the war described in the Mahâbhârata are undoubtedly mythical, as the incidents described in the Iliad are mythical. The five Pândava brothers and their common wife are myths, as Achilles and Paris and Helen are myths. But nevertheless the great epic is based on the recollections of a true war of the great Bhâratas (hence the name of the epic), and faithfully describes the manners and customs of the ancient Hindus, as the Iliad describes the manners of the ancient Greeks.

It is because the story of the existing epic throws valuable side-lights on the state of the society of the ancient Hindus that we think it necessary to briefly narrate it here. Let the reader attach no value to the names, which are mostly mythical, or to the incidents, which are mostly imaginary; let him only endeavour to draw from the story a picture of Hindu life in the Epic Period, *i.e.*, the period of Aryan expansion in the Gangetic valley.

The capital of the Kurus at the time of which we are speaking was the city of Hastinâpura, the supposed ruins of which have been discovered on the upper course of the Ganges, about sixty-five miles to the north-east of Delhi. Sântanu, the old king of Hastinâpura, died, leaving two sons, Bhîshma, who had taken a vow of celibacy, and a younger prince who became king. This young prince died in his turn, leaving two sons, Dhritarâshtra who was blind, and Pandu who ascended the throne.

Pându died, leaving five sons who are the heroes of the epic. Dhritarâshtra remained virtually the king during the minority of the five Pândavas and of his own children, while Dhritarâshtra's uncle Bhîshma, a renowned warrior, remained the chief councillor and friend of the state.

The account of the training of the young Pândavas and the sons of Dhritarâshtra to arms throws much light on the manners of royal houses. Drona was a Brâhman, and a renowned warrior, for caste had not yet completely formed itself, Kshatriyas had not yet obtained the monopoly of the use of arms, nor Brâhmans of religious learning. He had been insulted by his former friend the king of the Panchâlas, and had retired in disgust to the court of the Kurus and undertook to train the princes in arms.

Yudhisthira, the eldest of the Pândavas, never became much of a warrior, but became versed in the religious learning of the age, and is the most righteous character in the epic. Bhîma, the second, learnt to use the club, and was renowned for his gigantic size and giant strength, and is indeed the Ajax of the poem. The third, Arjuna, excelled all other princes in the skill of arms, and aroused the jealousy and hatred of the sons of Dhritarâshtra, even in their boyhood. Nakula, the fourth, learned to tame horses, and Sahadeva, the fifth, became proficient in astronomy. Duryodhana, the eldest son of Dhritarâshtra, was proficient in the use of the club, and was a rival to Bhîma.

At last the day came for a public exhibition of the proficiency which the princes had acquired in the use of arms. A spacious area was enclosed. Seats were arranged all round for the accommodation of ancient warriors and chieftains, of ladies and courtiers. The whole population of Kuruland flocked to see the skill of their young princes. The blind king Dhritarâshtra was led to his seat; and foremost among the ladies were Gândhârî, the queen of Dhritarâshtra, and Kuntî, the mother of the first three Pândavas. The last two were Pându's sons by another wife.

There was shooting of arrows at a butt, and there was fighting with swords and bucklers and clubs. Duryodhana and Bhîma soon began to fight in right earnest, and rushed towards each other like mad elephants. Shouts ascended to the sky, and soon the fight threatened to have a tragic end. At last the infuriated young men were parted, and peace was restored.

Then the young Arjuna entered the lists in golden mail, with his wondrous bow. His splendid archery surprised his most passionate admirers and thrilled the heart of his mother with joy, while shouts of admiration rose from the multitude like the roar of the ocean. He played with his sword, which flashed like lightning, and also with his sharp-edged quoit or chakra, and never missed his mark. Lastly, he brought down horses and deer to the ground by the noose, and concluded by doing obeisance to his worthy preceptor Drona, amidst the ringing cheers of the assembled multitude.

The dark cloud of jealousy lowered on the brow of Dhritarâshtra's sons, and soon they brought to the field an unknown warrior, Karna, who was a match for Arjuna in archery. King's sons could only fight with their peers, like the knights of old, and Dhritarâshtra therefore knighted the unknown warrior, or rather made him a king on the spot, so that Arjuna might have no excuse for declining the fight. To awkward questions which were put to him, the haughty Karna replied that rivers and warriors knew not of their origin and birth,—their prowess was their genealogy. But the Pândavas declined the fight, and the haughty Karna retired in silence and in rage.

Drona now demanded the reward of his tuition. Like doughty warriors of old he held revenge to be the dearest joy of a warrior, and for his reward he asked the help of the Kurus to be revenged on Drupada, king of the Panchâlas, who had insulted him. The demand could not be refused. Drona marched against Drupada, conquered him, and wrested half his kingdom. Drupada swore to be avenged.

Dark clouds now arose on the horizon of Kuruland. The time had come for Dhritarâshtra to name a Yuvarâja, *i.e.*, or a prince who would reign during his old age. The claim of Yudhisthira to the throne of his father could not be gainsaid, and he was appointed Yuvarâja. But the proud Duryodhana rebelled against the arrangement, and the old monarch had to yield, and sent the five Pândavas in exile to Vâranâvata, said to be near modern Allahabad, and then the very frontier of Hindu settlements. The vengeance of Duryodhana pursued them there, and the house where the Pândavas lived was burnt to ashes. The Pândavas and their mother escaped by an underground passage, and for a long time roamed about disguised as Brâhmans.

Heralds now went from country to country, and proclaimed in all lands that the daughter of Drupada, king of the Panchâlas, was to choose for herself a husband among the most skilful warriors of the time. As usual on such occasions of *Svayamvara*, or choice of a husband by a princess, all the great kings and princes and warriors of the land flocked to the court of Drupada, each hoping to win the lovely bride, who had already attained her youth, and was renowned for her beauty. She was to give her hand to the most skilful archer, and the trial ordained was a pretty severe one. A heavy bow of great size was to be wielded, and an arrow was to be shot through a whirling chakra or quoit into the eye of a golden fish, set high on the top of a pole!

Not only princes and warriors, but multitudes of spectators flocked from all parts of the country to Kâmpilya, the capital of the Panchâlas. The princes thronged the seats, and Brâhmans filled the place with Vedic hymns. Then appeared Draupadî with the garland in her hand which she was to offer to the victor of the day. By her appeared her brother Dhrishtadyumna, who proclaimed the feat which was to be performed.

Kings rose and tried to wield the bow, one after another, but in vain. The skilful and proud Karna stepped forth to do the feat, but was prevented.

A Brâhman suddenly rose and drew the bow, and shot the arrow through the whirling chakra into the eye of the golden fish. A shout of acclamation arose! And Draupadî, the Kshatriya princess, threw the garland round the neck of the brave Brâhman, who led her away as bride. But murmurs of discontent arose like the sound of troubled waters from the Kshatriya ranks at this victory of a Brâhman, and the humiliation of the warriors; and they gathered round the bride's father and threatened violence. The Pândavas now threw off their disguise, and the victor of the day proclaimed himself to be Arjuna, a true-born Kshatriya!

Then follows the strange myth that the Pândavas went back to their mother and said, a great prize had been won. Their mother, not knowing what the prize was, told her sons to share it among them. And as a mother's mandate cannot be disregarded, the five brothers wedded Draupadî as their wife. It is needless to say that the story of Draupadî and of the five Pândavas is a myth. The Pândavas now formed an alliance with the powerful king of the Panchâlas, and forced the blind king Dhritarâshtra to divide the Kuru country between his sons and the Pândavas. The division, however, was unequal; the fertile tract between the Ganges and the Jumna was retained by the sons of Dhritarâshtra, while the uncleared jungle in the west was given to the Pândavas. The jungle Khândava Prastha was soon cleared by fire, and a new capital called Indraprastha was built, the supposed ruins of which are shown to every modern visitor to Delhi.

Military expeditions were now undertaken by the Pândavas on all sides, but these need not detain us, especially as the accounts of these distant expeditions are modern interpolations. When we find in the Mahâbhârata accounts of expeditions to Ceylon, or to Bengal, we may unhesitatingly put them down as later interpolations.

And now Yudhishthira was to celebrate the Râjasûya or coronation ceremony, and all the princes of the land, including his kinsmen of Hastinâpura, were invited. The place of honour was given to Krishna, chief of the Yâdavas of Gujrat. Sisupâla of Chedi violently protested, and Krishna killed him on the spot. Krishna is only a great chief, and not a deity, in the older portions of the Mahâbhârata, and his story shows that Gujrat was colonised from the banks of the Jumna in the Epic Age.

The tumult having subsided, the consecrated water was

sprinkled on the newly-created monarch, and Brâhmans went away loaded with presents.

But the newly-created king was not long to enjoy his kingdom. With all his righteousness, Yudhishthira had a weakness for gambling like the other chiefs of the time, and the unforgiving and jealous Duryodhana challenged him to a game. Kingdom, wealth, himself and his brothers, and even his wife were staked and lost,—and behold now, the five brothers and Draupadî the slaves of Duryodhana! The proud Draupadî refused to submit to her position, but Duhsâsana dragged her to the assembly-room by her hair, and Duryodhana forced her down on his knee in the sight of the stupefied assembly. The blood of the Pândavas was rising, when the old Dhritarâshtra was led to the assembly-room and stopped a tumult. It was decided that the Pândavas had lost their kingdom, but should not be slaves. They agreed to go in exile for twelve years, after which they should remain concealed for a year. If the sons of Dhritarâshtra failed to discover them during the year, they would get back their kingdom.

Thus the Pândavas again went in exile; and after twelve years of wanderings in various places, disguised themselves in the thirteenth year and took service under the king of Virâta. Yudhishthira was to teach the king gambling; Bhîma was the head cook; Arjuna was to teach dancing and music to the king's daughter; Nakula and Sahadeva were to be master of horse and master of cattle respectively, and Draupadî was to be the queen's handmaid. A difficulty arose. The queen's brother was enamoured of the new handmaid of superb beauty, and insulted her and was resolved to possess her. Bhîma interfered and killed the lover in secret.

Cattle-lifting was not uncommon among the princes of those days, and the princes of Hastinâpura carried away some cattle from Virâta. Arjuna, the dancing master, could stand this no longer; he put on his armour, drove out in chariot, and recovered the cattle, but was discovered! The question whether the year of secret exile had quite expired was never settled.

And now the Pândavas sent an envoy to Hastinâpura to claim back their kingdom. The claim was refused, and both parties prepared for a war, the like of which had never been seen in India. All the princes of note joined one side or the other, and the battle which was fought in the plains of Kurukshetra, north of Delhi, lasted for eighteen days, and ended in fearful slaughter and carnage.

The long story of the battle with its endless episodes need not detain us. Arjuna killed the ancient Bhishma unfairly, after that chief was forced to desist from fighting. Drona, with his impenetrable "squares" or phalanxes, killed his old rival Drupada, but Drupada's son revenged his father's death and killed Drona unfairly. Bhîma met Duhsâsana, who had insulted Draupadî in the gambling room, cut off his head, and in fierce vindictiveness drank his blood! Lastly, there was the crowning contest between Karna and Arjuna, who had hated each other through life; and Arjuna killed Karna unfairly when his chariot wheels had sunk in the earth, and he could not move or fight. On the last or eighteenth day, Duryodhana fled from Bhîma, but was compelled by taunts and rebukes to turn round and fight, and Bhîma by a foul blow (because struck below the waist) smashed the knee on which Duryodhana had once dragged Draupadî. And the wounded warrior was left there to die. The bloodshed was not yet over, for Drona's son made a midnight raid into the enemy's camp and killed Drupada's son, and thus an ancient feud was quenched in blood.

The remainder of the story is soon told. The Pândavas went to Hastinâpura, and Yudhishthira became king. He is said to have subdued every king in Aryan India, and at last celebrated the Asvamedha ceremony or the great horse-sacrifice. A horse was let loose and wandered at its will for a year, and no king dared to stop it.

This was a sign of the submission of all the surrounding kings, and they were then invited to the great horse-sacrifice. We have seen that in the Vedic times the horse was sacrificed simply for eating; in the Epic Period the horse-sacrifice became a means of expiation of sin, and of the assumption of supremacy among kings.

Such is the story of the great epic divested of its numerous legends and episodes, its supernatural incidents and digressions. Krishna, the Island-born, and compiler of the Vedas, (not Krishna the Yâdava chief), is said to have been the son of the unmarried girl who afterwards married Sântanu. He was therefore the half-brother of Bhîshma. He often appears on the scene abruptly and in a supernatural manner, and imparts instruction and advice. The story has a historical interest, and shows that the Vedas were compiled before the time of the Kuru-Panchâla war.

For the rest, it will appear from the above brief account that the first Hindu colonists of the Gangetic valley had not yet lost the sturdy valour and the stubborn warlike determination of the preceding Vedic Age. Kings now ruled over larger countries and peoples, manners were more polished, the rules of social life and of chivalry were more highly developed, and the science of war itself was better organised. But nevertheless the stern and relentless valour of the Vedic warriors breaks through the polished manners of the Kurus and the Panchâlas, and those nations, if they had gained in civilisation, had scarcely yet lost much in the vigour of national life. How imperfectly the caste-system flourished among these sturdy races is shown by many facts which still loom out in bold outline amidst the interpolations and additions of later writers. Sântanu, the ancient king of Hastinâpura, had a brother Devâpi, who was a priest. The most learned character in the epic, Yudhishthira, is a Kshatriya, and the most skilful warrior Drona is a Brâhman. And the venerable compiler of the Vedas, Krishna Dvaipâyana himself—was he a Brâhman or a Kshatriya?

CHAPTER III.

VIDEHAS, KOSALAS, AND KÂSÎS.

THE tide of Aryan conquests rolled onward. When the country between the Jumna and the Ganges had been completely conquered, peopled, and Hinduised, new bands of adventurous settlers crossed the Ganges and marched further eastwards to found new colonies and new Hindu kingdoms. Stream after stream was crossed, forest after forest was explored and cleared, region after region was slowly conquered, peopled, and Hinduised in this onward march towards the unknown east. The history of the long struggles and the gradual development of the Hindu power in these regions has been lost to us; and we only see, in the literature which has been preserved, the establishment of powerful and civilised Hindu kingdoms east of the Ganges,—the kingdom of the Kosalas in the country known as modern Oudh, that of the Videhas in North Behar, and that of the Kâsîs round modern Benares.

Some recollection of the eastern march of the Videhas has been preserved in a stray passage in the Satapatha Brâhmana, quoted below:—

"10. Mâdhava the Videgha carried Agni Vaisvânara in his mouth. The Rishi Gotama Râhûgana was his family priest. When addressed by the latter he made no answer, fearing lest Agni might fall from his mouth.

"13. Still he did not answer. (The priest continued): 'Thee, O butter-sprinkled one, we invoke!' (Rig Veda,

V, 26, 2). So much he uttered when, at the very mentioning of butter, Agni Vaisvânara flashed forth from the king's mouth; he was unable to hold him back; he issued from his mouth and fell down on this earth.

"14. Mâdhava the Videgha was at that time on the river Sarasvatî. He (Agni) thence went burning along this earth towards the east; and Gotama Râhûgana and the Videgha Mâdhava followed after him as he was burning along. He burnt over (dried up) all these rivers. Now that river which is called Sadânîra (Gunduck river) flows from the northern (Himâlaya) mountain: that one he did not burn over. That one the Brâhmans did not cross in former times, thinking it has not been burnt over by Agni Vaisvânara.

"15. Nowadays, however, there are many Brâhmans to the east of it. At that time it (the land east of the Sadânîra) was very uncultivated, very marshy, because it had not been tasted by Agni Vaisvânara.

"16. Nowadays, however, it is very cultivated, for the Brâhmans have caused Agni to taste it through sacrifices. Even in late summer that river, as it were, rages along; so cold it is, not having been burnt over by Agni Vaisvânara.

"17. Mâdhava the Videgha then said to Agni, 'Where am I to abide?' 'To the east of this river be thy abode!' said he. Even now this river forms the boundary of the Kosalas and Videhas; for these are the Mâdhavas (or descendants of Mâdhava)" (*Satapatha Brâhmana*, I, 4, 1).

Here then we have an account, in a legendary form, of the gradual march of the colonists from the banks of the Sarasvatî eastwards until they came to the Gunduck. That river formed the boundary between the two kingdoms; the Kosalas lived to the west of it, and the Videhas to the east of it.

In course of years, probably of centuries, the kingdom of the Videhas rose in power and in civilisation, until it became the most prominent kingdom in Northern India.

Janaka, king of the Videhas, is probably the most prominent figure in the history of the Epic Period in India. That monarch had not only established his power in the farthest confines of the Hindu dominions in India, but he gathered round him the most learned men of his time, he entered into discussion with them, and instructed them in holy truths about the Universal Being. It is this that has surrounded the name of Janaka with undying glory. King Ajâtasatru of the Kâsîs, himself a learned man and a most renowned patron of learning, exclaimed in despair, "Verily, all people run away, saying, Janaka is our patron!" (*Brihadâranyaka Upanishad*, II, 1, 1).

The great fame of Janaka is partly owing to the culture and learning of the chief priest of his court, Yâjnavalkya Vâjasaneyin. Under the royal auspices of Janaka this priest conceived the bold idea of revising the Yajur Veda as it then existed, of separating the formulas from the exegetic matter, of condensing the former in the shape of a new Yajur Veda (the White Yajur Veda), and of amplifying the latter into a vast body of Brâhmana (the Satapatha Brâhmana). Generations of priests laboured at this stupendous work, but the glory of starting the work belongs to the founder of the school, Yâjnavalkya Vâjasaneyin, and his learned patron, King Janaka of the Videhas.

But Janaka has a still higher claim to our respect and admiration. While the priestly caste was still multiplying rituals and supplying dogmatic explanations for each rite, the royal caste seems to have felt some impatience at this priestly pedantry. Thinking and earnest Kshatriyas asked themselves if these rites and dogmas were all that religion could teach. Learned Kshatriyas, while still conforming to the rites laid down by priests, gave a start to healthier speculations, and inquired about the destination of the Soul and the nature of the Supreme Being. So bold, so healthy and vigorous were these new and earnest speculations, that the priestly classes, who were wise in their own esteem, at last felt their inferiority, and came to Kshatriyas to learn something of the wisdom of the new school. The Upanishads contain the healthy and earnest speculations which were started at the close of the Epic Period; and King Janaka of Videha is honoured and respected,—more than any other king of the time,—as an originator of the earnest speculations of the Upanishads.

The teaching of the Upanishads will be dwelt on more fully in a subsequent chapter of this Book, but an account of Janaka and of the other kings of the period and their place in Hindu literature will not be complete unless we cite a few passages here, illustrating their relations with their priests, and their labours in the cause of earnest philosophical thought in India.

"Janaka of Videha once met some Brâhmans who had just arrived. They were Svetaketu Âruneya, Somasushma Satyayajni and Yâjnavalkya. He said to them: 'How do you perform the Agnihotra?'"

The three Brâhmans replied as best they could; but not correctly. Yâjnavalkya came very near the mark, but was not quite correct. Janaka told them so, and mounted his car and went away!

The priests said: "This fellow of a Râjanya has insulted us." Yâjnavalkya mounted his car, followed the king, and had the difficulty explained (*Satapatha Brâhmana*, XI, 4, 5). "Henceforth Janaka became a Brâhman" (*S. Br.* XI, 6, 2, 1).

We find in Chhândogya Upanishad, V, 3, that one of the three Brâhmans named above, Svetaketu Âruneya, came to an assembly of the Panchâlas, and Pravâhana Jaivali, a Kshatriya, asked him some questions which puzzled him. He came back sorrowful to his father and said: "That fellow of a Râjanya asked me five questions, and I could not answer one of them." The father,

Gautama, was himself puzzled and went to the Kshatriya to have his difficulty removed. Pravâhana Jaivali replied, "Gautama, this knowledge did not go to any Brâhman before you, and therefore this teaching belonged in all the worlds to the Kshatra class alone." And then he imparted the knowledge to Gautama.

In another place in this Upanishad (I, 8), this Pravâhana silenced two boastful Brâhmans, and then imparted the true knowledge of the Highest God to them.

A story is told in the Satapatha Brâhmana (X, 6, 1, 1), and is repeated in the Chhândogya Upanishad (V, II), that five Brâhman householders and theologians became anxious to know, 'What is our Self and what is God?' They came to Uddâlaka Âruni to obtain the knowledge, but Âruni had his misgivings, and therefore took them to the Kshatriya king, Asvapati Kaikeya, who courteously invited them to stay at a sacrifice he was going to perform. He said: "In my kingdom there is no thief, no miser, no drunkard, no man without an altar in his house, no ignorant person, no adulterer, much less an adulteress. I am going to perform a sacrifice, sirs, and as much wealth as I give to each Ritvik priest, I shall give to you, sirs. Please to stay here."

They stayed and told him what they had come for, and "on the next morning they approached him, carrying fuel in their hands (like students), and he, without any preparatory rites," imparted to them the knowledge they had come for.

It is curious how we meet the same names over and over in the different Upanishads, and often the same story too in different forms, showing that the old Upanishads were composed at much the same time. We find Uddâlaka Âruni, also called Gautama, and his son Svetaketu again in the Kaushîtaki Upanishad; and the father and the son went to Chitra Gângyâyani, fuel in hand, to learn the truth. Chitra, a Kshatriya king, said: "You are worthy of Brahman, O Gautama, because you were not led away by pride. Come hither, I shall make you know clearly" (I, 1).

A celebrated story is told in the Kaushîtaki Upanishad (IV), of a conversation between Gârgya Bâlâki, a celebrated man of learning, and Ajâtasatru, the learned king of the Kâsîs. The boastful Brâhman challenged the king, but in course of the learned dispute which followed, he collapsed and became silent. Ajâtasatru said to him: 'Thus far do you know, O Bâlâki?' 'Thus far only,' replied Bâlâki. Then Ajâtasatru said to him: 'Vainly did you challenge me, saying, Shall I tell you of God?' 'O Bâlâki, He who is the maker of those objects (which you mentioned), He of whom all this is the work, He alone is to be known.'

"Then Bâlâki came, carrying fuel in his hand, saying: 'May I come to you as a pupil?' Ajâtasatru said to him: 'I deem it improper that a Kshatriya should initiate a Brâhman. Come, I will make you know clearly.'"

This story, as well as the story of Svetaketu Âruneya and the Kshatriya king Pravâhana Jaivali, are repeated in the Brihadâranyka Upanishad.

There are numerous such passages in the Upanishads in which the Kshatriyas are represented as the wisest teachers in true religious knowledge. But it is needless to multiply instances here. What we have said is enough to indicate the place which belongs to the royal caste at the close of the Epic Period in the history of Hindu religion and philosophy. The Upanishads mark a new era in the history of human knowledge, and this knowledge, which dates about 1000 B.C., "did not belong to any Brâhman before," "it belonged in all the worlds to the Kshatra class alone."

These are real claims of Janaka, king of the Videhas, to the admiration and gratitude of posterity. Curiously enough, posterity remembers him and the Videhas and the Kosalas also through a myth which has clung round their revered names. That myth relates to the Aryan conquest of Southern India; and with a fervid and blind gratitude poets of subsequent ages have connected that great historical event with the names of ancient kings who had nothing to do with the conquest! Historical knowledge in Europe, even in the dark ages, was never so dim as to allow a poet to attribute the recovery of Jerusalem to Charlemagne or Alfred the Great! But the second great epic of India conceives and describes the conquest of Ceylon by a king of the Kosalas who had married the daughter of Janaka, king of the Videhas.

It is not possible with our present knowledge to state when the Râmâyana was composed in its original shape. We find references to the Mahâbhârata in the Sûtra literature, but we find no such reference to the Râmâyana. The discovery and conquest of Ceylon by Vijaya from Bengal took place in the fifth century B.C., and at first sight one would be inclined to refer the first conception of the epic, which has its scene of action in that island, to that date. On the other hand, the existence of the island was well known to the Hindus for centuries before its conquest by Vijaya. And the composition of the Râmâyana, which makes no allusion to Vijaya's conquest, may be referred to an age anterior to Vijaya, when the island was still very imperfectly known to the Hindus.

That this view is more probable appears from the fact that the whole of India south of the Vindhya chain is described in the Râmâyana as one interminable forest, inhabited by aborigines who are described as monkeys and bears. Now we know that the banks of the Godâvarî and even of the Krishnâ river were colonised by the Aryans early in the Rationalistic Period, and great empires like that of the Andhras rose to power and started new schools of science and learning several centuries before Christ. The first conception of the Râmâyana must be referred to a period anterior to these movements in the South, for the Râmâyana speaks of no Aryan civilisation south of the Vindhyas. The original Râmâyana, like the original Mahâbhârata, belongs therefore to the Epic Age.

Like the Mahâbhârata, the Râmâyana is utterly valueless as a narrative of historical events and incidents. As in the Mahâbhârata, so in the Râmâyana, the heroes are myths, pure and simple.

Sîtâ, the field furrow, had received divine honours from the time of the Rig Veda, and had been worshipped as a goddess. When cultivation gradually spread in Southern India, it was not difficult to invent a poetical myth that Sîtâ was carried to the South. And when this goddess and woman—the noblest creation of human imagination,—had acquired a distinct and lovely individuality, she was naturally described as the daughter of the holiest and most learned king on record, Janaka of the Videhas!

But who is Râma, described in the epic as Sîtâ's husband and the king of the Kosalas? The later Purânas tell us that he was an incarnation of Vishnu, but Vishnu himself had not risen to prominence at the time of which we are speaking! Indra was still the chief of the gods of the Epic Period. And in the Sûtra literature (*e.g.*, Pâraskara Grihya Sûtra, II, 17, 9) we learn that Sîtâ, the furrow goddess, is the wife of Indra. Is it then an untenable conjecture that Râma, the hero of the Râmâyana, is in his original conception, like Arjuna, the hero of the Mahâbhârata, only a new edition of Indra battling with the demons of drought? The myth of Indra has thus been mixed up with the epic which describes a historic war in Northern India, and with the epic which describes the historic conquest of Southern India!

But though the Râmâyana is utterly valueless as a narrative of events, still, like the Mahâbhârata, it throws side-lights on the state of ancient society in India, and the story of the epic therefore needs be briefly told. Only we must premise that, even as a picture of life, the Râmâyana is long posterior to the Mahâbhârata, and belongs to the very close of the Epic Period. We miss in the Râmâyana the fiery valour and the proud self-assertion of the Kshatriyas of the Mahâbhârata; and the subordination of the people to the priestly caste is more complete. Janaka himself is not described as the proud asserter of Kshatriya learning and dignity that he was, but as a humble servant of priests. And Râma himself, the hero of the epic, though he encounters and defeats a Brâhman warrior Parasu Râma, does so with many apologies and due submission! The story of Parasurâma probably conceals a great historic truth. He is said to have fought against the Kshatriyas and exterminated the caste; and then he was conquered by the Kshatriya Râma, the hero of the epic. It would seem that this story indicates the real rivalry and hostilities between the priestly and warrior castes,—indications of which we have found in a literary form in the Upanishads.

For the rest, one feels on reading the Râmâyana that the real heroic age of India had passed, and that centuries of residence in the Gangetic valley had produced an enervating effect on the Aryans. We miss the heroic if somewhat rude and sturdy manners and incidents which mark the Mahâbhârata. We miss characters distinguished by real valour, and battles fought with real obstinacy and determination. We miss men of flesh and blood, and pride and determination, like Karna and Duryodhana and Bhîma; and the best developed characters in the Râmâyana are women like the proud and scheming Kaikeyî or the gentle and ever suffering Sîtâ. The heroes of the Râmâyana are somewhat tame and commonplace personages, very respectful to priests, very anxious to conform to the rules of decorum and duty, doing a vast amount of fighting work mechanically, but without the determination, the persistence of real fighters! A change had come over the spirit of the nation; and if princes and men had become more polished and law-abiding, they had become less sturdy and heroic. For a picture of Hindu life of the thirteenth century, when the hardy and conquering Kurus and the Panchâlas ruled in the Doab, we would refer our readers to the Mahâbhârata. For a picture of Hindu life of the eleventh century, when the Kosalas and the Videhas had, by a long residence in the Gangetic valley, become law-abiding and priest-ridden, learned and enervated, we would refer our readers to the Râmâyana. The two epics represent the change which Hindu life and society underwent from the commencement to the close of the Epic Age.

We proceed now with the story of the Râmâyana. The people who lived in the wide tract of country between the Ganges and the Gunduck were known by the general name of the Kosalas, as we have seen before. Dasaratha, a distinguished king of this nation, had his capital in Ayodhyâ, or Oude, the ruins of which ancient town are still shown to travellers in some shapeless mounds. Dasaratha had three queens honoured above the rest, of whom Kausalyâ bore him his eldest born Râma, Kaikeyî was the mother of Bharata, and Sumitrâ of Lakshmana and Satrughna. Dasaratha in his old age decided on making Râma the Yuvarâja or reigning prince, but the proud and beauteous Kaikeyî insisted that her son should be Yuvarâja, and the feeble old king yielded to the determined will of his wife.

Before this Râma had won Sîtâ, the daughter of Janaka king of the Videhas, at a *Svayamvara*. Kings and princes had assembled there, but Râma alone could lift the heavy bow, and bent it till it broke in twain. But now, when Ayodhyâ was still ringing with acclamation at the prospect of Râma's being installed as Yuvarâja, it was decided in queen Kaikeyî's chambers that Bharata must be the Yuvarâja, and further that Râma must go into exile for fourteen years.

Râma was too obedient and dutiful to resist or even resent this decision. His faithful half-brother Lakshmana accompanied him, and the gentle Sîtâ would not hear of parting with her lord. Amidst the tears and lamentation of the people of Ayodhyâ, Râma and Sîtâ and Lakshmana walked out of the city.

The exiles first went to the hermitage of Bhâradvâja in Prayaga or Allahabad, and then to that of Vâlmîki in Chitrakûta, somewhere in modern Bandelkund. Vâlmîki is reputed to be the author of the epic Râmâyana, just as Krishna Dvaipâyana Vyâsa, the compiler of the Vedas, is said to be the author of the Mahâbhârata.

Dasaratha died of grief for Râma, and Bharata followed Râma to Chitrakûta, and informed him of their father's death, and implored his return. But Râma felt himself bound by the promise he had made, and it was agreed that Râma would return after fourteen years and ascend the throne. Bharata returned to Ayodhyâ.

Leaving Chitrakûta, Râma wandered in the Dandaka forest and towards the sources of the Godâvarî among jungles and non-Aryan tribes. For Southern India had not yet been colonised by the Aryans. Thirteen years thus passed away.

Râvana, the monster king of Lankâ or Ceylon, and of Southern India, heard of the beauty of Sîtâ now dwelling in jungles; and in the absence of Râma took her away from their hut, and carried her off to Ceylon. Râma, after a long search, obtained clue of her; he made alliances with the non-Aryan tribes of Southern India, who are described as monkeys and bears, and made preparations for crossing over to Ceylon to recover his wife.

Bâli was a great king among the non-Aryans, but his brother Sugrîva thirsted after his kingdom and his wife. Râma fought and killed Bâli, helped Sugrîva to win the kingdom and Bâli's widow, and Sugrîva then marched with his army to Lankâ.

Hanuman, the commander-in-chief of the non-Aryan army, led the way. He leaped over the strait of sixty miles which separates India from Ceylon, found Sîtâ, and gave her the ring sent by Râma. He then caused a conflagration in the capital of Râvana, and returned to Râma.

A causeway was then built across the strait by boulders and stones. The reader is aware that a natural causeway runs nearly across the strait, and there is no doubt that the physical aspect of this locality suggested to the poet the idea that the causeway was built by the superhuman labours of Râma's army. The whole army then crossed over and laid siege to the capital of Râvana.

The account of the war which follows, though full of poetical incidents and stirring description, is unnatural and tedious. Chief after chief was sent out by Râvana to beat back the invaders, but they all fell in the war, Râma using his supernatural weapons and mystic mantras. Indrajit, the proud son of Râvana, battled from the clouds, but Lakshmana killed him. Râvana came out in rage and killed Lakshmana, but the dead hero revived under the influence of some medicine brought by the faithful Hanuman. One of Râvana's brothers, Bibhîsana, had left his brother and had joined Râma, and told him the secret by which each warrior would be killed, and thus chief after chief of Râvana's proud host fell. At last Râvana himself came out, and was killed by Râma. Sîtâ was recovered, but she had to prove her untainted virtue by throwing herself into a lighted pyre, and then coming out of it uninjured.

The fourteenth year of exile having now expired, Râma and Sîtâ returned to Ayodhyâ and ascended the throne. But the suspicions of the people fell on Sîtâ, who had been in Râvana's house, and could not, they thought, have returned untainted. And Râma, as weak as his father had been, sent poor, suffering Sîtâ—then gone with child—to exile.

Vâlmîki received her at Chitrakûta, and there her two sons, Lava and Kusa, were born. Vâlmîki composed the poem of the Râmâyana and taught the boys to repeat the piece, and thus years were passed.

Then Râma decided to celebrate the Asvamedha sacrifice, and sent out the horse. The animal came as far as Vâlmiki's hermitage, and the boys, in a playful humour, caught it and detained it. Râma's troops tried in vain to recover the animal. At last Râma himself saw the princely boys, but did not know who they were; he heard the poem Râmâyana chanted by them, and it was in a passion of grief and regret that he at last knew them and embraced them as his own dear boys.

But there was no joy in store for Sîtâ. The people's suspicions could not be allayed, and Râma was too weak to act against his people. The earth which had given poor Sîtâ birth yawned and received its long-suffering child. The Vedic conception of Sîtâ, as the field-furrow, manifests itself in the Epic in this incident. But to the millions of Hindus, Sîtâ is a real human character,—a pattern of female virtue and female self-abnegation. To this day Hindus hesitate to call their female children by the name of Sîtâ; for if her gentleness, her virtue, her uncomplaining devotion, and her unconquerable love for her lord, were more than human, her sufferings and woes too were more than usually fall to the lot of woman. There is not a Hindu woman in the length and breadth of India to whom the story of suffering Sîtâ is not known, and to whom her character is not a model to strive after and to imitate. And Râma too, though scarcely equal to Sîtâ in the worth of character, has been a model to men for his truth, his obedience, and his piety. And thus the epic has been for the millions of India a means of moral education, the value of which can hardly be over-estimated.

CHAPTER IV.

ARYANS AND NON-ARYANS.

THE great river systems of Northern India determined the course of Aryan conquests; when we survey the course of these rivers, we comprehend the history of Aryan conquests during ten centuries. And when we have traced the course of the Indus and its tributaries, and of the Ganges and the Jumna as far as Benares and North Behar, we have seen the whole extent of Indo-Aryan world as it existed at the close of the Epic Period, or about 1000 B.C. Beyond this wide tract of Hindu kingdoms lay the whole extent of India yet unexplored or rather unconquered by the Aryans, and peopled by various aboriginal tribes. A wide belt of this Non-Aryan tract, surrounding the Hindu world to the east, south, and west, was becoming known to the Hindus about the very close of the Epic Period. South Behar, Malwa, and a portion of the Deccan and the regions to the south of the Rajputana desert, formed a wide semi-circular belt of country, as yet not Hinduised, but becoming gradually known to the Hindus, and therefore finding occasional mention in the latest works of the Brâhmana literature, as regions peopled by *Satvas, i.e.*, living creatures, hardly human beings. We can imagine hardy colonists penetrating into this encircling belt of unknown and uncivilised regions, obtaining a mastery over the aborigines wherever they went, establishing some isolated settlements on the banks of fertile rivers, and presenting to the astonished barbarians some of the results of civilised administration and civilised life. We can imagine also saintly anchorites retiring into these wild jungles, and fringing the tops of hills or fertile valleys with their holy hermitages, which were the seats of learning and of sanctity. And lastly, adventurous royal huntsmen not unoften penetrated into these jungles, and unhappy princes, exiled by their more powerful rivals, often chose to retire from the world and took up their abodes in these solitudes. In such manner was the belt of Non-Aryan country gradually known to the Hindus, and we will cite a passage or two which will show how far this knowledge extended, and how the civilised Hindus named the different aboriginal tribes dwelling in this tract, probably in the eleventh century B.C.

There is a passage in the last book of the Aitareya Brâhmana which, along with an account of the principal Hindu kingdoms of the time, makes some mention of aboriginal races in the south and south-west; and the passage deserves to be quoted:—

"The Vâsavas then inaugurated him (Indra) in the eastern direction during thirty-one days by these three Rik verses, the Yajus verse, and the great words (all just mentioned), for the sake of obtaining universal sovereignty. Hence all kings of eastern nations are inaugurated to universal sovereignty and called *Samrâj*, *i.e.*, universal sovereign, after this precedent made by the gods.

"Then the Rudras inaugurated Indra in the southern region during thirty-one days, with the three Rik verses, the Yajus, and the great words (just mentioned), for obtaining enjoyment of pleasures. Hence all kings of living creatures* in the southern region, are inaugurated for the enjoyment of pleasures and called *Bhoja*, *i.e.*, the enjoyer.

"Then the divine Âdityas inaugurated him in the western region during thirty-one days, with those three Rik

* *Satvânâm* is the word in the original.

verses, that Yajus verse, and those great words for obtaining independent rule. Hence all kings of the *Nîchyas* and *Apâchyas* in the western countries* are inaugurated to independent rule, and called "independent rulers."†

"Then the Visvedevâh inaugurated him during thirty-one days in the northern region by those three Rik verses, &c., for distinguished rule. Hence all people living in northern countries beyond the Himâlaya, such as the *Uttara Kurus*, *Uttara Mâdras*, are inaugurated for living without a king (*Vairâjyam*), and called *Virâj*, *i.e.*, without king.

"Then the divine Sâdhyas and Aptyas inaugurated Indra during thirty-one days in the middle region, which is a firmly established footing (the immovable centre) to the kingship (*Râjya*). Hence the kings of the *Kuru Panchâlas*, with the *Vasas* and *Usînaras*, are inaugurated to kingship and called kings (Râja)."

This passage shows us at one glance the whole of the Hindu world as it existed at the close of the Epic Period. To the farthest east lived the Videhas and the Kâsîs and the Kosalas, as we have seen before, and those newest and youngest of the Hindu colonists excelled in learning and reputation their elder brethren in the west. Their kings, Janaka and Ajâtasatru and others, took the proud title of *Samrâj*, and worthily maintained their dignity by their learning and their prowess.

In the south, some bands of Aryan settlers must have worked their way up the valley of the Chumbal, and become acquainted with the aboriginal tribes inhabiting the country now known as Malwa. These tribes were called *Satvas*, *i.e.*, living creatures, scarcely human beings! We note, however, that the kingdoms in this direction already went by the name of *Bhoja* (however fanciful the derivation which the author gives to the word), and *Bhoja* was in later times the name of the same region, lying

* *Pratîchyâm* is the word in the original.

† *Svarât* is the word in the original, whence *Saurâshtra* and Surat.

immediately to the north of the Vindhya chain, and along the valley of the Chumbal.

Westwards from this place surged the waves of Aryan settlers or adventurers, until the invaders came to the shores of the Arabian sea, and could proceed no further. The aboriginal races in these distant tracts were looked upon with some degree of contempt by the civilised colonists or invaders, and were significantly called *Nîchyas* and *Apâchyas*, and their rulers had the significant name of *Svarât* or independent rulers. These, races dimly known at the very close of the Epic Period, were the ancestors of the proudest and most warlike Hindu tribe of later times, viz., the Maharattas.

To the north the Uttara Kurus and the Uttara Mâdras and other tribes lived—beyond the Himâlaya we are told—but which probably means beyond the lower ranges and among the valleys of the Himalayas. To the present day men in these hills live in independent primitive communities, and have very little concern with chief or king; and it is no wonder that in ancient times they should be known as peoples without kings.

And then, in the very centre of the Hindu world, along the valley of the Ganges, lived the powerful tribes of the Kurus and the Panchâlas, and the less known tribes, the Vasas and the Usînaras.

In the west, the deserts of Rajputana were wholly unexplored by the Aryans. The Bhil aborigines of those deserts and mountains were left undisturbed until new and hardy tribes of invaders entered India after the Christian era and settled down in these parts.

In the far east, South Behar was not yet Hinduised. In a passage in the Atharva Veda pointed out by Professor Weber, special and hostile notice is taken of the Angas and the Magadhas. The passage shows that the people of South Behar did not yet belong to the Hindu confederation of nations; but were nevertheless becoming known to the Aryans. Bengal proper was as yet unknown.

And the whole of Southern India, *i.e.*, India south of the Vindhya range, was yet unoccupied by the Hindus. The Aitareya Brâhmana gives (VII, 18), the names of certain degraded barbarous tribes, and among others that of the Andhras. We shall see that in the Rationalistic Period the Andhras rose to be a great civilised Hindu power in the Deccan.

We have now spoken of all the principal Aryan races and kingdoms which flourished in the Epic Period, and of the non-Aryan kingdoms, which formed a semicircular belt in the south of the Hindu world. It will be our pleasant task in the following chapters to give some account of the social customs and the domestic life of the people. But before we take leave of kings, we must make some mention of the great coronation ceremony, as it has been described in many works of the Epic Period. This ceremony and the horse-sacrifice were the most imposing and ostentatious royal ceremonials of Ancient India, and we have already said something about both these rites, in connection with the two Epics of the Hindus. An extract or two about the coronation ceremony are all that is needed here:—

"He spreads the tiger-skin on the throne in such a manner that the hairs come outside, and that part which covered the neck is turned eastward. For the tiger is the Kshattra (royal power) of the beasts in the forests. The Kshattra is the royal prince; by means of this Kshattra, the king makes his Kshattra (royal power) prosper. The king, when taking his seat on the throne, approaches it from behind, turning his face eastwards, kneels down with crossed legs, so that his right knee touches the earth, and holding the throne with his hands, prays over it an appropriate mantra.

"The priest then pours the holy water over the king's head, and repeats the following: 'With these waters, which are happy, which cure everything, increase the royal power, the immortal Prajâpati sprinkled Indra, Soma sprinkled the royal Varuna, and Yama sprinkled Manu; with the same sprinkle I thee! Be the ruler over kings in this world. The illustrious mother bore thee as the great universal ruler over men; the blessed mother has borne thee, &c.' And the ceremony concludes with a drink of the Soma wine which the priest hands over to the king" (*Aitareya Brâhmana*, VIII, 6–9).

We are then told that with this ceremony priests invested a number of kings whose names are already known to us. Tura, the son of Kavasha, thus inaugurated Janamejaya, the son of Parikshit. "Thence Janamejaya went everywhere, conquering the earth up to its ends, and sacrificed the sacrificial horse." Parvata and Nârada thus invested Yudhamsraushti, the son of Ugrasena. Vasishtha invested Sudâs, the great conqueror of the Rig Veda hymns; and Dîrghatamas invested Bhârata, the son of Duhshanta, with this ceremony.

We have another excellent account of the coronation rite in the White Yajur Veda, from which we quote a remarkable passage in which the priest blesses the newly-crowned king: "May God who rules the world bestow on you the power to rule your subjects. May fire, worshipped by householders, bestow on you supremacy over the householders. May Soma, the lord of trees, bestow on you supremacy over forests. May Vrihaspati, the god of speech, bestow on you supremacy in speech. May Indra, the highest among gods, bestow on you the highest supremacy. May Rudra, the cherisher of animals, bestow on you supremacy over animals. May Mitra, who is truth, make you supreme in truth. May Varuna, who cherishes holy works, make you supreme in holy acts" (IX, 39).

In the address to the people which follows, the priest tells them: "This is your king, O ye such and such tribes." The Kânva text reads thus: "This is your king, O ye Kurus, O ye Panchâlas."

We will conclude this chapter with an excellent piece

of advice which is given to kings further on, in the same Veda, which modern rulers will do well to remember:— "*If thou shalt be a ruler, then from this day judge the strong and the weak with equal justice, resolve on doing good incessantly to the public, and protect the country from all calamities*" (X, 27).

CHAPTER V.

CASTE.

THE entire isolation in which the Hindu Aryans lived from the outer world for centuries and thousands of years, —an isolation which has no parallel in the history of any other nation,—had its advantages and also its disadvantages. Among other results it led to social institutions being more and more crystallised into hard and fast rules, which gradually contracted the liberties and the free energies of the people. Four or five centuries of peaceful residence in a genial climate in the fertile basin of the Ganges and the Jumna enabled the Hindus to found civilised kingdoms, to cultivate philosophy, science, and arts, and to develop their religious and social institutions; but it was under the same gentle but enervating influences that they also divided themselves into those separate social classes known as "castes."

We have seen that about the close of the Vedic Period the priests had already formed themselves into a separate profession, and sons stepped forward to take up the duties of their fathers. When religious rites became more elaborate in the Epic Period, when with the founding of new kingdoms along the fertile Doab kings prided themselves on the performance of vast sacrifices with endless rites and observances, it is easy to understand that the priests who alone could undertake such complicated rites rose in the estimation of the people, until they were naturally regarded as aloof from the ordinary people, as a distinct and superior race,—as a caste. They devoted their lifetime to learn these rites, and they alone were able to perform them in all their details, and the natural inference in the popular mind was that they alone were worthy of the holy task. And when hereditary priests were thus completely separated from the people by their fancied sanctity and their real knowledge of elaborate rites, it was scarcely considered "good form" on their part to form misalliances with the people outside their holy rank. They might still condescend to honour particular families by choosing brides from among them, but young ladies of priestly houses must never give their hands to men outside their ranks. What is a feeling and a custom among modern nations soon became an inviolable and religious rule among a custom-abiding people like the Gangetic Hindus, isolated from the outside world.

The very same causes led to the rise of a royal caste. Royalty had not assumed a very high dignity among the Punjab Hindus. Warlike chiefs led clans from conquests to conquests; and the greatest of them, like Sudâs the patron of the Vasishthas and the Visvâmitras, were locked upon more as leaders of men and protectors of clans than as mighty kings. Far different was the state of things with the Gangetic Hindus. Probably in the early days of the martial Kurus and Panchâlas, caste distinctions had not yet been fully matured. But later in the day, the kings of the peaceful Kosalas and Videhas, surrounded by all the pomp and circumstance of royalty, were looked upon by the humble and lowly and extremely law-abiding people as more than human. It was scarcely possible, under these circumstances, that maidens of the royal or warlike classes should condescend to marry men from the ranks. The stigma which attaches to such misalliances all over the world gave rise to an inviolable rule in India. And when priests and warriors were thus separated by absolute and inviolable rules from the people, the humblest girls of the former classes were debarred from marriage with the greatest and richest among the Vaisyas.

It is difficult to find in the history of European institutions any parallel to the caste-system of India. Yet there was a time in Europe when institutions somewhat similar to the caste-system of India sprang from the same causes which operated in India, viz., the feebleness of the people, and the power of warriors and priests. When the Roman Empire fell to pieces, and barbarian chiefs and barons carved out among themselves the fairest portions of Europe, the mass of the people were devoid of political life and political freedom. Never in Europe was there such a wide distinction between a powerful clergy and a powerful soldiery on the one hand, and a lifeless and powerless people on the other, as in the days of feudalism in Europe. Vast monasteries arose all over Europe; great feudal towers frowned on every navigable river and every humble village; and the dwellers of villages and the humble artisans in little towns were scarcely regarded as better than slaves. The clergy, the knighthood, and the people of Europe in the Middle Ages answered in some respects to the Brâhmans, the Kshatriyas, and the Vaisyas of India.

But the resemblance is in appearance only. The clergy of Feudal Europe did not marry, and their ranks were recruited from the ablest, the cleverest, the most learned among the people. The knights too were glad to welcome into their ranks doughty squires and brave warriors among the people. The people, too, soon formed leagues to protect their commerce, fortified their towns to meet the marauding barons, formed municipal corporations, and trained themselves to arms to defend their interests in those insecure times. Ambitious scions of baronial houses often mixed with the people, and fought their battles in the field and at the council board; and this healthy admixture, which the caste-system prevented in India, revived and strengthened the people in Europe. Feudalism and the absolute power of the clergy decayed as trade and commerce and political life rose among the people; and the danger of the people being divided into three "castes," if it ever existed in Europe, passed away once and for ever.

The simple origin of the caste institution as narrated above is obscured in later Hindu literature in a cloud of strange myths and legends. But in spite of such wonderful legends, later Hindu writers never completely lost sight of the fact that caste was originally only a distinction based on professions. And this simple and natural account of the origin of caste often occurs in the same Puranic works which elsewhere delight in strange and monstrous myths about the origin of the institution. We have room only for one or two extracts.

In the Vâyu Purâna we are told that in the first or Krita Age, *there were no castes*, and that subsequently Brahma established divisions among men *according to their works*. "Those of them who were suited for command and prone to deeds of violence, he appointed to be Kshatriyas, from their protecting others. Those disinterested men who attended upon them, spoke the truth, and declared the Veda aright, were Brâhmans. Those of them who formerly were feeble, engaged in the work of husbandmen, tillers of the earth, and industrious, were Vaisyas, cultivators and providers of subsistence. Those who were cleansers and ran about on service, and had little vigour or strength, were called Sûdras." Accounts more or less similar to this occur in the other Purânas also.

The Râmâyana in its present shape is, as we have seen before, the work of later ages. In the Uttarâ Kânda, chapter 74, we are told that in the Krita Age Brâhmans alone practised austerities: that in the Tretâ Age, Kshatriyas were born, *and then was established the modern system of four castes*. Reduced from mythical to historical language, the above account may be read thus:—In the Vedic Age, the Hindu Aryans were a united body and practised Hindu rites. In the Epic Age, however, priests and kings separated themselves as distinct castes, and the people also formed themselves into the lower orders, the Vaisyas and Sûdras.

The Mahâbhârata also, as we have seen before, is in its present shape a work of later ages, but here also we occasionally meet with a sensible and honest attempt to account for caste. In the Sânti Parva, section 188, we are told that "red-limbed twice-born men who were fond of sensual pleasure, fiery, irascible, daring, and forgetful of their sacrificial duties, fell into the caste of Kshatriyas. Yellow twice-born men, who derived their livelihood from cows and agriculture, and did not practise religious performances, fell into the caste of Vaisyas. Black twice-born men who were impure and addicted to violence and lying, and were covetous and subsisted by all kinds of works, fell into the caste of Sûdras. *Being thus separated by these their works, the twice-born men become of other castes.*"

The composers of these and similar passages no doubt knew of the legend of the four castes springing from four members of Brahma's body; but they ignored it, and treated it as an allegory, which it is. They maintain that in the earliest age there were no castes, and they make a very fair and sensible conjecture that castes were developed in a later age from distinctions in work and professions. We must now, however, return from this digression, and examine the caste-system as it prevailed in the Epic Period.

As we have stated before, the caste-system first formed itself among the peaceful citizens of Gangetic India; it never should be forgotten, however, that the worst results of that system did not appear, and could not appear, until the Hindus had ceased to be a free nation. In the Epic Period the body of the people were still entitled to acquire religious knowledge and learning, and to perform religious rites, just like Brâhmans and Kshatriyas. And even intermarriage between Brâhmans, Kshatriyas, and

Vaisyas was allowed under certain restrictions. However much, therefore, the historian of Ancient India may deplore the commencement of the caste-system, he should never forget that the worst results of that system were unknown in India until after the Mahommedan conquest.

In the sixteenth chapter of the White Yajur Veda we meet with the names of various professions which throw some light on the state of society at the time the chapter was compiled. It is apparent, however, the list is one of different professions, not of different castes. Thus, various kinds of thieves are enumerated in Kandikâs, 20 and 21, and horsemen, charioteers, and infantry are spoken of in 26. Similarly the carpenter, the chariot-maker, the potter, and the blacksmith, mentioned in 27, also formed different professions, and not castes. The Nishâda and others, also mentioned in the same Kandikâ, were obviously aboriginal tribes, who, then as now, formed the lowest strata of Hindu society.

The list is very much enlarged in the 30th chapter of the same work, which, as we have seen before, is of a considerably later date, and indeed belongs to the *Khila* or the supplement. But here, too, we meet with many names which indicate professions only, and many others which undoubtedly refer to the aborigines; and we find no evidence that the mass of the Vaisya population had been divided into sub-castes. We find names of dancers, orators, and frequenters in assemblies; of chariot-makers, carpenters, potters, jewellers, cultivators, arrow-makers, and bow-makers; of dwarfs and crookedly formed men, and blind and deaf persons; of physicians and astronomers; of keepers of elephants, horses, and cattle; of servants, cooks, gate-keepers, and wood-cutters; of painters and engravers; of washermen, dyers, and barbers; of learned men and proud men and women of various descriptions; of tanners, fishermen, hunters and fowlers; of goldsmiths and merchants and men with various diseases; of wig-makers and poets and musicians of various kinds.

It is plain that this is not a list of castes. On the other hand, the Mâgadha and Sûta and Bhîmala and Mrigayu and Svanin, and Nishâda, and Durmada, and others mentioned in the list, are clearly aborigines, living under the shadow of the Aryan society. We have only to add that the same list, with slight modifications, is given in the Taittirîya Brâhmana.

The above lists throw some light on the state of the society and the professions which were recognised in the period of which we speak; but they have nothing to do with caste. Throughout the Epic Period, and throughout the succeeding periods almost to the time of the Mahommedan conquest, the great body of the Aryan people were Vaisyas, although they followed numerous professions. Along with the Brâhmans and the Kshatriyas they formed the Aryan nation, and were entitled to all the rights and privileges, and the literary and religious heritages of the nation. The conquered aborigines, who formed the Sûdra caste, were alone debarred from the heritage of the Aryans.

This is the cardinal distinction between the ancient caste-system, and the caste-system of the present age. Caste reserved some privileges for priests, and some privileges for warriors, in ancient times; but *never divided and disunited the Aryan people.* Priests and warriors and citizens, though following their hereditary professions from generation to generation, felt that they were one nation and one race, received the same religious instructions, attended the same schools of learning, possessed the same literature and traditions, ate and drank together, intermarried and intermixed in all respects, and were proud to call themselves the Aryan race as against the conquered aborigines. Caste in modern times has cut up the Aryan people, the Vaisyas, into scores of communities, has opened the wide gulf of race distinctions among these different communities, has interdicted marriage and social communion among them, has starved the entire body of the people of religious knowledge and literature, and has degraded them to the rank of Sûdras.

There are numerous passages in the Brâhmana literature which show that the distinctions between the castes were by no means so rigid in the early times as at a later period. A remarkable passage, for instance, occurs in the Aitareya Brâhmana (VII, 29). When a Kshatriya eats at a sacrifice the portion assigned for Brâhmans, his progeny has the characteristics of a Brâhman "ready to take gifts, thirsty after drinking Soma, and hungry of eating food, and ready to roam about everywhere according to pleasure." And "*in the second or third generation he is capable of entering completely the Brâhmanship.*" When he eats the share of Vaisyas his "offspring will be born with the characteristic of Vaisyas, paying taxes to another king;" "and in the second or third degree they are capable of entering the caste of Vaisyas." When he takes the share of Sûdras, his progeny "will have the characteristics of Sûdras; they are to serve the three higher castes, to be expelled and beaten according to the pleasure of their masters." And "in the second or third degree, he is capable of entering the condition of Sûdras."

In a previous chapter we have seen that Janaka, king of the Videhas, imparted to Yâjnavalkya learning unknown to the priest before, and was thenceforward considered a Brâhman (Satapatha Brâhmana, XI, 6, 2, 1). In Aitareya Brâhmana (II, 19), we are told of Kavasha, the son of Ilushâ, whom the other Rishis expelled from a sacrificial session, saying, "How should the son of a slave girl, a gamester, who is no Brâhman, remain among us and become initiated! But Kavasha knew the gods and all the gods knew him, and he was admitted as a Rishi. Similarly, in the beautiful legend of Satyakâma Jabâla in the Chhândogya Upanishad (IV, 4), is exemplified the fact that truth and learning opened out in those days a path to the highest honour and to the highest caste. The legend is so beautiful in its simplicity and its poetry, that we feel no hesitation in quoting a portion of it :—

"1. Satyakâma, the son of Jabâlâ, addressed his mother and said: 'I wish to become a Brahmachârin (religious student), mother. Of what family am I?'

"2. She said to him: 'I do not know, my child, of what family thou art. In my youth when I had to move about much as a servant, I conceived thee. I do not know of what family thou art. I am Jabâlâ by name, thou art Satyakâma; say that thou art Satyakâma Jabâla.'

"3. He, going to Gautama Haridrumata, said to him: 'I wish to become a Brahmachârin with you, sir. May I come to you, sir?'

"4. He said to him: 'Of what family are you, my friend?' He replied: 'I do not know, sir, of what family I am. I asked my mother, and she answered—"In my youth when I had to move about much as a servant, I conceived thee. I do not know of what family thou art. I am Jabâlâ by name, thou art Satyakama." I am therefore Satyakâma Jabâla, sir.'

"5. He said to him: 'No one but a true Brâhman would thus speak out. Go and fetch fuel, friend; I shall initiate you. You have not swerved from the truth.'"

And this truth-loving young man was initiated, and, according to the custom of the times, went out to tend his teacher's cattle. In time he learnt the great truths which nature, and even the brute creation, teach those whose minds are open to instruction. Yes, he learned truths from the bull of the herd that he was tending, from the fire that he had lighted, and from a flamingo and a diver-bird which flew near him, when in the evening he had penned his cows and laid wood on the evening fire, and sat behind it. The young student then came back to his teacher, and his teacher at once said: "Friend, you shine like one who knows Brahman: who then has taught you?" "Not men," was the young student's reply. And the truth which the young student had learnt, though clothed in the fanciful style of the period, was that the four quarters, and the earth, the sky, the heaven and the ocean, and the sun, the moon, the lightning, and the fire, and the organs and minds of living beings, yea the whole universe, was Brahman or God.

Such is the teaching of the Upanishads, and such are the poetical legends in which the teaching is clothed, as we shall see further on. A legend like that of Satyakâma Jabâla, which is full of human feeling and pathos and the highest moral lessons, cheers and refreshes the student after he has waded through pages of the dry and meaningless dogmas and rituals of the Brâhmanas. But our purpose in quoting the legend here is to show that the rules of caste had not become yet rigid when such legends were composed. We find in the legend that the son of a servant girl, who did not know his own father, became a religious student simply through his love of truth, learnt the lessons which nature and the learned men of the time could teach him, and subsequently became classed among the wisest religious teachers of the time. Surely the caste-system of that ancient time must have been freedom itself compared to the narrow system of later times, when the entire nation except the priests was cruelly debarred from religious knowledge,—that knowledge which is the food of a nation's mind, and the life of a nation's life.

It was in the Epic Period that the sacrificial cord Yajnopavîta came into use. We are told in the Satapatha Brâhmana (II, 4, 2) that when all beings came to Prajâpati, the gods and the fathers came, wearing the sacrificial cord. And we are told in Kaushîtaki Upanishad (II, 7) that the all-conquering Kaushîtaki adores the sun when rising, having put on the sacrificial cord.

The Yajnopavîta was worn in this ancient period by

Brâhmans, Kshatriyas and Vaisyas alike, but only at the time of performing Yajna or Vedic sacrifice.

Things have changed since those ancient times. The Yajnopavîta is now habitually and ostentatiously worn at all times, by the members of one caste only—the Brâhmans—and that caste has forgotten to perform Vedic Yajna!

CHAPTER VI.

SOCIAL LIFE.

THE great distinction, then, between the society of the Vedic times and the society of the Epic Period was that the caste-system was unknown in the former, and had grown up in the latter. But this was not the only distinction. Centuries of culture and progress had their influence on society, and the cultured Hindus of the Epic Period were as widely different in their social manners from the warrior-cultivators of the Vedic Period, as the Greeks of the time of Pericles were different from the Greeks of the time of Agamemnon and Ulysses.

The Hindus of the period of which we are speaking had attained a high degree of refinement and civilisation, and had developed minute rules to regulate their domestic and social duties. Royal courts were the seats of learning, and the learned and wise of all nations were invited, honoured, and rewarded. Justice was administered by learned officers, and laws regulated every duty of life. Towns, with their strong walls and beautiful edifices, multiplied among all nations, and had their judges, their executive officers, and their police. Agriculture was fostered, and the king's officers looked to the collection of taxes and the comforts of cultivators.

We have said that the courts of enlightened and learned kings, like those of the Videhas, the Kâsîs, and the Kuru-Panchâlas, were the principal seats of learning in those times. Learned priests were retained in such courts for the performance of sacrifices, and also for the purpose of the cultivation of learning; and many of the Brâhmanas which have been handed down to us, were composed in the schools which these priests founded. On great occasions men of learning came from distant towns and villages, and discussions were held not only on ritualistic matters, but on such subjects as the human mind, the destination of the soul after death, the future world, the nature of the gods, the fathers, and the different orders of being, and lastly, on the nature of that Universal Being who has manifested himself in all the works we see.

But learning was not confined to royal courts. There were Parishads or Brâhmanic establishments for the cultivation of learning, answering to the Universities of Europe, and young men went to these Parishads to acquire learning. Thus in Brihadâranyaka Upanishad VI, 2, we learn that Svetaketu went to the Parishads of the Panchâlas for his education. Professor Max Müller, in his History of Sanscrit Literature, quotes passages which show that, according to modern writers, a Parishad ought to consist of twenty-one Brâhmans well versed in philosophy, theology, and law; but these rules, as he points out, are laid down in later law books, and do not describe the character of the Parishads of the Epic Period. Parâsara says that four, or even three, able men from amongst the Brâhmans in a village, who know the Veda and keep the sacrificial fire, form a Parishad.

Besides these Parishads, individual teachers established what would be called private schools in Europe, and often collected round themselves students from various parts of the country. These students lived with their teachers, served them in a menial capacity during the time of their studentship, and after twelve years or longer, made suitable presents to their teachers and returned to their homes and their longing relatives. Learned Brâhmans too, who retired to forests in their old age, often collected students round them, and much of the boldest speculations of this period has proceeded from these sylvan and retired seats of sanctity and learning. Such is the way in which learning has been cultivated and preserved during thousands of years among the Hindus, a nation who valued learning and knowledge perhaps more than any other nation in ancient or modern times. Good works and religious rites lead, according to the Hindu creed, to happier states of life and to their due reward; but true knowledge alone leads to final union with God.

When students had thus acquired the traditional learning of the age either in Parishads or under private teachers, they returned to their homes, married, and settled down as householders. With marriage began their duties as householders, and the first duty of a householder was to light the sacrificial fire under an auspicious constellation, to offer morning and evening libations of milk to the fire, to perform other religious and domestic rites, and above all, to offer hospitality to strangers. The essence of a Hindu's duties are inculcated in passages like the following:—

"Say what is true! Do thy duty! Do not neglect the study of the Veda! After having brought to thy teacher the proper reward, do not cut off the lives of children! Do not swerve from the truth! Do not swerve from duty! Do not neglect what is useful! Do not neglect greatness! Do not neglect the learning and teaching of the Veda!

Do not neglect the works due to the gods and fathers! Let thy mother be to thee like unto a god! Let thy father be to thee like unto a god! Let thy teacher be to thee like unto a god! Whatever actions are blameless, those should be regarded, not others. Whatever good works have been performed by us, those should be observed by thee" (*Taittirîya Upanishad*, I, 2).

Pleasing pictures of a happy state of society are presented in many passages which we meet with in the literature of the period: "May the Brâhmans in our kingdom," says the priest at a horse-sacrifice, "live in piety; may our warriors be skilled in arms and mighty; may our cows yield us profuse milk, our bullocks carry their weights, and our horses be swift; may our women defend their homes, and our warriors be victorious; may our youths be refined in their manners. . . . May Parjanya shower rain in every home and in every region; may our crops yield grains and ripen, and we attain our wishes and live in bliss" (*White Yajur Veda*, XXII, 22).

The wealth of rich men consisted in gold and silver and jewels; in cars, horses, cows, mules and slaves; in houses and fertile fields, and even in elephants (Chhândogya Upanishad, V, 13, 17, and 19; VII, 24; Satapatha Brâhmana, III, 2, 48; Taittirîya Upanishad, I, 5, 12, &c., &c.). Gold is considered a proper gift at sacrifice, the gift of silver being strictly prohibited. The reason is sufficiently grotesque, as the reasons given in the Brâhmanas generally are: When the gods claimed back the goods deposited with Agni, he wept, and the tears he shed became silver; and hence if silver is given as *dakshinâ*, there will be weeping in the house! The reason scarcely veils the cupidity of priests, which was the real cause of gifts in gold.

Not only was the use of gold and silver known, but several other metals are mentioned in White Yajur Veda, XVIII, 13. The following passage from the Chhândogya Upanishad specifies some metals then in use:—

"As one binds gold by means of *lavana* (borax), and silver by means of gold, and tin by means of silver, and lead by means of tin, and iron by means of lead, and wood by means of iron, and also by means of leather" (IV, 17, 7).

In Aitareya Brâhmana (VIII, 22), we are told, evidently in the language of exaggeration, that the son of Atri presented ten thousand elephants and ten thousand slave girls, "well endowed with ornaments on their necks, who had been gathered from all quarters."

As in the Vedic Period, the food of the people consisted of various kinds of grain as well as the meat of animals. In the Brihadâranyaka Upanishad (VI, III, 13), ten kinds of seeds are mentioned, viz., rice and barley (brîhiyavâs), sesamum and kidney beans (tilamâshâs), millet and panic seed (anupriyangavâs), wheat (godhûmâs) lentils (masûrâs), pulse (khalvâs) and vetches (khalakulâs).

In the White Yajur Veda (XVIII, 12) we have a list of these grains, beside mudga, nîvâra, and syâmâka. Grains were ground and sprinkled with curds, honey, and clarified butter, and made into different kinds of cake. Milk and its various preparations have ever been a favourite food in India.

Animal food was in use in the Epic Period, and the cow and the bull were often laid under requisition. In Aitareya Brâhmana (I, 15) we learn that an ox or a cow is killed when a king or an honoured guest is received; and an honoured guest is called, even in comparatively modern Sanscrit, a cow-killer.

In the Brâhmana of the Black Yajur Veda, the kind and character of the cattle which should be slaughtered in minor sacrifices, for the gratification of particular divinities, are laid down in detail. The same Brâhmana lays down instructions for carving, and the Gopatha Brâhmana tells us who received the different portions. The priests got the tongue, the neck, the shoulder, the rump, the legs, &c.; while the master of the house (wisely) appropriated to himself the sirloin, and his wife had to content herself with the pelvis! Plentiful libations of the Soma beer were taken to wash down the meat!

In III, 1, 2, 21 of the Satapatha Brâhmana there is an amusing discussion as to the propriety of eating the meat of an ox or a cow. The conclusion is not very definite: "Let him (the priest) not eat the flesh of the cow and the ox." Nevertheless Yâjnavalkya said (taking apparently a very practical view of the matter), "I for one eat it, provided that it is tender!"

The practical Yâjnavalkya could scarcely, however, have contemplated the wonderful effects of vegetable and animal diets respectively, as laid down in the following passage in the Brihadâranyaka Upanishad (VI, 4, 17 and 18):—

"And if a man wishes that a learned daughter should be born to him, and that she should live to her full age, then after having prepared boiled rice with sesamum and butter they (the husband and wife) should both eat, being fit to have offspring.

"And if a man wishes that a learned son should be born to him, famous, a public man, a popular speaker, that he should know all the Vedas, and that he should live to his full age, then, after having prepared boiled rice with meat and butter, they (the husband and wife) should both eat, being fit to have offspring. The meat should be of a young or of an old bull."

We scarcely thought that the venerable composers of the Vedic Brâhmanas ever suspected any sort of connection between beef-eating and public-speaking, such as has manifested itself in later days!

And now let our readers construct for themselves a picture of the social life which the Hindus of the Epic Period—which the citizens of Hastinâpura and Kâmpilya and Ayodhyâ and Mithila—lived three thousand years ago. The towns were surrounded by walls, beautified by edifices, and laid out in streets, which would not bear comparison with the structures and roads of modern days, but were probably the finest of their kind in ancient times. The king's palace was always the centre of the town, and was frequented by boisterous barons and a rude soldiery, as well as by holy saints and learned priests. The people flocked to the palace on every great occasion, loved, respected and worshipped the king, and had no higher faith than loyalty to the king. Householders and citizens had their possessions and wealth in gold, silver, and jewels; in cars, horses, mules, and slaves; and in the fields surrounding the town. They kept the sacred fire in every respectable household, honoured guests, lived according to the law of the land, offered sacrifices with the help of Brâhmans, and honoured knowledge. Every Aryan boy was sent to school at an early age. Brâhmans and Kshatriyas and Vaisyas were educated together, learnt the same lessons and the same religion, and returned home, married, and settled down as householders. Priests and soldiers were a portion of the people, intermarried with the people, and ate and drank with the people. Various classes of manufacturers supplied the various wants of a civilised society, and followed their ancestral professions from generation to generation, but were not cut up into separate castes. Agriculturists lived with their herds and their ploughs in their own villages, and according to the ancient custom of India, Hindu village communities managed and settled their own village concerns. The picture of ancient life can be indefinitely enlarged; but each reader will probably do this for himself. We will turn from this general account of ancient society to examine the position which women held in that society.

We have seen that the absolute seclusion of women was unknown in ancient India. Hindu women held an honoured place in society from the dawn of Hindu civilisation four thousand years ago; they inherited and possessed property; they took a share in sacrifices and religious duties; they attended great assemblies on state occasions; they openly frequented public places; they often distinguished themselves in science and in the learning of their times; and they even had their legitimate influence on politics and administration. And although they never mixed so freely in the society of men as women do in modern Europe, yet absolute seclusion and restraint were not Hindu customs; they were unknown in India till the Mahommedan times, and are to this day unknown in parts of India like the Mahârâshtra, where the rule of the Moslems was brief. No ancient nation held their women in higher honour than the Hindus, but the Hindus have been misjudged and wronged by writers unacquainted with their literature, and who received their notions of the women of the East from Turkish and Arab customs.

Innumerable passages could be quoted from the Brâhmana literature, showing the high esteem in which women were held, but we will content ourselves with one or two. The first is the celebrated conversation between Yâjnavalkya and his learned wife Maitreyî on the eve of his retirement into forests:—

"1. Now when Yâjnavalkya was going to enter upon another state, he said: 'Maitreyî, verily I am going away from this my house. Forsooth let me make a settlement between thee and Kâtyâyanî.'

"2. Maitreyî said: 'My Lord, if this whole earth full of wealth belonged to me, tell me, should I be immortal by it?' 'No,' replied Yâjnavalkya; 'like the life of rich people will be thy life. But there is no hope of immortality by wealth?'

"3. And Maitreyî said: 'What should I do with that by which I do not become immortal? What my lord knoweth of immortality, tell that to me?'

"4. Yâjnavalkya replied: 'Thou who art truly dear to me, thou speakest dear words. Come, sit down, I will explain it to thee, and mark well what I say.'"

And then he explained the principle which is so often and so impressively taught in the Upanishads, that the Universal Soul dwells in the husband, in the wife, in the sons, and in wealth; in the Brâhmans and Kshatriyas, and in all the worlds; in the Devas, in all living creatures, yea, in all the universe. Maitreyî,—the wise, the accomplished, the learned lady—received and grasped this great truth, and valued it more than all the wealth of the world (*Brihadâranyaka Upanishad*).

Our next quotation, which is also from the same

Upanishad, relates to a great assembly of learned men in the court of Janaka, king of the Videhas:—

"Janaka Videha sacrificed with a sacrifice at which many presents were offered to the priests of (the Asvamedha). Brâhmans of the Kurus and the Panchâlas had come thither, and Janaka wished to know which of those Brâhmans was the best read. So he enclosed a thousand cows, and ten padas (of gold) were fastened to each pair of horns.

"And Janaka spoke to them: 'Ye venerable Brâhmans, he who among you is the wisest, let him drive away these cows.' Then those Brâhmans durst not, but Yâjnavalkya said to his pupil, 'Drive them away, my dear.' He replied, 'O glory of the Sâman!' and drove them away."

On this the Brâhmans became angry, and plied the haughty priest Yâjnavalkya with questions, but Yâjnavalkya was a match for them all. Asvala the Hotri priest, Jâratkarava Ârtabhâga, Bhujyu Lâhyâyani, Ushasta Châkrâyana, Kahola Kaushîtakeya, Uddâlaka Âruni, and others plied Yâjnavalkya with questions, but Yâjnavalkya was not found wanting; the learned men, one by one, held their peace.

There was one in the great assembly—and this is a remarkable fact which throws light on the manners of the time—who was not deficient in the learning and the priestly lore of those times, because she was a lady. She rose in the open assembly, and said: "O Yâjnavalkya, as the son of a warrior from the Kâsîs or Videhas might string his loosened bow, take two pointed foe-piercing arrows in his hand and rise to battle, I have risen to fight thee with two questions. Answer me these questions." The questions were put and were answered, and Gârgî Vâchaknavî was silent.

Do not these passages and such passages as these indicate that women were honoured in ancient India, more perhaps than among any other ancient nation in the face of the globe? Considered as the intellectual companions of their husbands, as their affectionate helpers in the journey of life, and as the inseparable partners of their religious duties, Hindu wives received the honour and respect due to their position. They also had their rights to property and to inheritance, which indicate the regard in which they were held. It would be scarcely fair to compare ancient customs with the institutions of modern civilisation; but the historian of India, who has studied the literature of the ancient Hindus, will have no hesitation in asserting that never in the most polished days of Greece or Rome were women held in such high regard in those countries as in India three thousand years ago.

As we have said before, early marriage and child-marriage were still unknown in the Epic Period, and we have numerous allusions, in the Epics and elsewhere, to the marriage of girls at a proper age. Widow-marriage was not only not prohibited, but there is distinct sanction for it; and the rites which the widow had to perform before she entered into the married state again are distinctly laid down. As caste was still a pliable institution, men belonging to one caste not unoften married widows of another, and Brâhmans married widows of other castes without any scruple. "And when a woman has had ten former husbands, not Brâhmans, if a Brâhman then marries her, it is he alone who is her husband" (*Atharva Veda*, V, 17, 8).

Polygamy was allowed among the Hindus as among many other ancient nations, but was confined to kings and wealthy lords as a rule. Modern readers, who would judge harshly of ancient Hindu civilisation from the prevalence of this custom, should remember that polygamy was nearly universal among the wealthy people of all nations in ancient times, and that, to take some instances, Alexander the Great and his successors Lysimachus, Seleucus, Ptolemy, Demetrius, Pyrrhus, and others were all polygamists! Polyandry, we need hardly say, was unknown in Aryan India: "For one man has many wives, but one wife has not many husbands at the same time" (*Aitareya Brâhmana*, III, 23).

There is in the Satapatha Brâhmana (I, 8, 3, 6) a curious passage prohibiting marriages among blood relations to the third or fourth generation: "Hence from one and the same man spring both the enjoyer (the husband) and the one to be enjoyed (the wife);" "for now kinsfolk live sporting and rejoicing together, saying, in the fourth or third generation we unite." The rule of prohibition became more strict in later times.

Women in India have ever been remarkable for their faithfulness and their duteous affection towards their husbands, and female unfaithfulness is comparatively rare. It would appear that Hindu priests, like Roman Catholic priests, found a way to discover the most hidden secrets of frail women, and the following reads like a rule of Catholic confessional :—

"Thereupon the Pratiprasthâtri returns to the place where the sacrificer's wife is seated. When he is about to lead the wife away, he asks her : 'With whom holdest thou intercourse ?' Now when a woman who belongs to one man carries on intercourse with another, she undoubtedly commits a sin against Varuna. He therefore asks her, lest she should sacrifice with a secret pang in her mind ; for when confessed, the sin becomes less, since it becomes truth : this is why he thus asks her. And whatever connection she confesses not, that indeed will turn out injurious to the relatives" (*Satapatha Brâhmana*, II, 5, 2, 20).

CHAPTER VII.

LAW, ASTRONOMY, AND LEARNING.

THE punishment of criminals and the proper administration of laws are foundations on which all civilised societies are built, and we find a true appreciation of laws in some passages in the Brâhmana literature: "Law is the kshatra (power) of the Kshatra, therefore there is nothing higher than the law. Thenceforth even a weak man rules a stronger with the help of the law as with the help of a king. Thus the law is what is called the true. And if a man declares what is true, they say he declares the law; and if he declares the law, they say he declares what is true. Thus both are the same" (*Brihadâranyaka*, I, 4, 14). No nobler definition of law has been discovered by all the jurists in the world.

The judicial procedure was still however crude, and, as among other ancient nations, criminals were often tried by the ordeal of fire.

"They bring a man hither whom they have taken by the hand, and they say: 'He has taken something, he has committed theft.' (When he denies, they say): 'Heat the hatchet for him.' If he committed the theft, then he . . . grasps the heated hatchet, he is burnt, and he is killed. But if he did not commit the theft, then he . . . grasps the heated hatchet, he is not burnt, and he is delivered" (*Chhândogya*, VI, 16). Murder, theft, drunkenness, and adultery are considered the most heinous offences.

We will now turn to Astronomy. The first elementary knowledge of the astronomical science is discernible in the Rig Veda itself. The year was divided into twelve lunar months, and a thirteenth or intercalary month was added to adjust the lunar with the solar year (I, 25, 8). The six seasons of the year were named Madhu, Mâdhava, Sukra, Suchi, Nabha, and Nabhasya, and were connected with different gods (II, 36). The different phases of the moon were observed and were personified as deities. Râkâ is the full moon, Sinîvâli is the last day before the new moon, and Gungu is the new moon (II, 32). The position of the moon with regard to the Nakshatras or the lunar mansions is also alluded to (VIII, 3, 20), and some of the constellations of the lunar mansions are also named in X, 85, 13. It would appear from this that the Nakshatras were observed and named in the Vedic Age, and it was in the Epic Period that the lunar zodiac was finally settled.

As might be expected, there was a considerable progress made in the Epic Period. Astronomy had now come to be regarded as a distinct science, and astronomers by profession were called Nakshatra Darsa and Ganaka (Taittirîya Brâhmana, IV, 5, and White Yajur Veda, XXX, 10, 20). The twenty-eight lunar mansions are also enumerated in the Black Yajur Veda, and a second and later enumeration occurs in the Atharva Sanhitâ and in the Taittirîya Brâhmana. An interesting passage in Satapatha Brâhmana (II, 1, 2) shows how sacrificial rites were regulated by the position of the moon in reference to these lunar asterisms. It is too long to be quoted, and we will therefore give extracts :—

"1. He may set up two fires under the *Krittikâs* (the pleiades), for they, the Krittikâs, are doubtless Agni's asterism. . . .

"6. He may also set up his fires under *Rohinî.* For under Rohinî it was that Prajâpati, when desirous of progeny, set up his fires. . . .

"8. He may also set up his fires under the asterism of *Mrigasîrsha.* For Mrigasîrsha, indeed, is the head of Prajâpati. . . . He may also set up his fires under the *Phalgunîs.* They, the Phalgunîs, are Indra's asterism, and even correspond to him in name; for, indeed, Indra is also called Arjuna, this being his mystic name; and they (Phalgunîs) are also called Arjunîs. . . .

"12. Let him set up his fire under the asterism *Hastâ*, whosoever should wish that presents should be offered him: then indeed that will take place forthwith; for whatever is offered with the hand (hasta), that indeed is given to him.

"13. He may also set up his fires under *Chitrâ*," &c., &c.

It will thus appear that the setting up of the sacrificial fires was regulated by the constellations. In the same way, sacrifices lasting for a year were regulated by the sun's annual course. Dr. Martin Haug, the editor and translator of the Aitareya Brâhmana, has made some excellent remarks on this subject, which deserve to be quoted:—

"The great sacrifices take place generally in spring in the months *Chaitra* and *Vaisâkha* (April and May). The *Sattras*, which lasted for a year, were, as one may learn from a careful perusal of the fourth book of the Aitareya Brâhmana, nothing but an imitation of the sun's yearly course. They were divided into two distinct parts, each consisting of six months of thirty days each; in the midst of both was the Vishuvan, *i.e.*, equator or central day, cutting the whole *Sattra* into two halves. The ceremonies were in both the halves exactly the same; but they were in the latter half performed in an inverted order. This represents the increase of the days in the northern and their decrease in the southern progress; for both increase and decrease take place exactly in the same proportions" (*Introduction*, p. 47).

We have said that the lunar zodiac was finally arranged in India towards the commencement of the Epic Period, say, B.C. 1400. The illustrious Colebrooke first stated

Jagannâtha. Later on, Purushottama Deva (1479 to 1504) is said to have defeated the king of Kânchî in Southern India, and married his daughter; and his successor, Prâtapa Rudra Deva, was on the throne when the great Vaishuava reformer Chaitanya visited Orissa.

Govinda Vidyâdhara murdered the last king of the Gangetic house and ascended the throne; but conflict with the Mahommedans began in his reign, 1534 to 1541 A.D. Four kings then successively ascended the throne, Chakra Pratâpa (1541 to 1549), Narasinga Jana (1549 to 1550), Raghurâma Chotra (1550 to 1551), and Mukunda Deva (1551 to 1559 A.D). It was in this last reign that the famous Mahommedan general Kalapahar invaded the province, defeated and slew the king in a battle near Jajpur, plundered the city of Jagannâtha, and overthrew the Hindu monarchy.

Thus, after maintaining its independence for nearly four centuries after the conquest of Northern India and Bengal, Orissa was conquered by the Mahommedans about 1560 A.D.

any trace of a lunar zodiac among the archives of old Babylonian learning; but Professor Whitney of America supports this "suspicion," as he calls it, because he thinks the Hindus "were not a people of such habits of mind" as to make observations in the heavens and settle the lunar zodiac. The argument is so amusing that the learned professor almost withdraws it himself, stating that the argument "is not of a character to compel belief."

When scholars condescend to such wild reasoning, it is idle to pursue the controversy. We will therefore conclude this subject with a passage in which Professor Max Müller puts forward the common sense view of the subject. "The 27 Nakshatras, or the 27 constellations which were chosen in India as a kind of lunar zodiac, were supposed to have come from Babylon. Now the Babylonian zodiac was solar, and in spite of repeated researches, no trace of a lunar zodiac has been found, where so many things have been found, in the cuneiform inscriptions. But supposing even that a lunar zodiac had been discovered in Babylon, no one acquainted with Vedic literature, and with the ancient Vedic ceremonial, would easily allow himself to be persuaded that the Hindus had borrowed that simple division of the sky from the Babylonians." *

Besides fixing the lunar zodiac, the Hindus of this period observed the solstitial points to fix the dates of momentous events, and divided the year into months, naming each month after the lunar constellation in which the moon was at its full in the particular month. According to Bentley the lunar zodiac was fixed in 1426 B.C., and the months were named in 1181 B.C.† A knowledge of the solar zodiac was borrowed from the Greeks, after the Christian era, as we will see in a subsequent book.

Besides astronomy, other branches of learning were

* India: What can it teach us (1883), p. 126.

† Hindu Astronomy (London, 1825), pp. 3 and 10.

also cultivated in the Epic Period. Thus in Chhândogya Upanishad (VII, 1, 2) we find Nârada saying to Sanatkumâra, "I know the Rig Veda, sir, the Yajur Veda, the Sâma Veda, as the fourth the Atharvana, as the fifth the Itihâsa Purâna, the Veda of the Vedas (grammar); the Pitrya (rules for sacrifices for the ancestors); the Râsi (the science of numbers); the Daiva (the science of portents); the Nidhi (the science of time); the Vâkovâkya (logic); the Ekâyana (ethics); the Deva Vidyâ (etymology); the Brahma Vidyâ (pronunciation, prosody, &c.); the Bhûta Vidyâ (the science of demons); the Kshatra Vidyâ (the science of weapons); the Nakshatra Vidyâ (astronomy); the Sarpa Devanjana Vidyâ (the science of serpents and of genii). All this I know, sir."

In Brihadâranyaka (II, 4, 10) we are told that "Rig-Veda, Yajur Veda, Sâma Veda, Atharvângirasas, Itihâsa (legends), Purâna (cosmogonies), Vidyâ (knowledge), the Upanishads, Slokas (verses), Sûtras (prose rules), Anu Vyâkhyânas (glosses), Vyâkhyânas (commentaries), have all been breathed forth from the Supreme Being."

Again, in the eleventh book of the Satapatha Brâhmana, we have mention of the three Vedas, the Atharvângirasas, the Aunsâsanas, the Vidyâs, the Vâkovâkya, the Itihâsa Purâna, the Narasansîs, and the Gâthâs.

Professor Weber is of opinion that these names do not necessarily imply distinct works which existed in the Epic Period, and which have been since lost to us. He points out that many of the names merely imply the different subjects which we will still find in the Brahmanas. It was at a later age, in the Rationalistic Period, that these different subjects which we find interwoven in the Brâhmanas and Upanishads branched out as separate subjects of study, and were taught in the separate Sûtra works and compositions which have came down to us.

There is some force in this supposition, but, at the same time, many of the subjects enumerated above could scarcely have been taught properly and handed down from teacher to pupil without the help of special works on those subjects. We therefore believe that such separate works existed in the Epic Period, which have been lost to us, because they have been replaced by more elaborate and scientific works of a later age on the same subjects.

CHAPTER VIII.

THE SACRIFICIAL RITES OF THE BRÂHMANAS.

THE main feature which distinguishes the religion of the Epic Period from that of the preceding age is the great importance which came to be attached to *sacrifice*. In the earlier portion of the Vedic Period, men composed hymns in praise of the most imposing manifestations of nature; they deified these various natural phenomena, and they worshipped these deities under the name of Indra or Varuna, of Agni or the Maruts. And the worship took the shape of sacrifice, *i.e.*, the offering of milk or grain, of animals or libations of the Soma-juice to the gods.

A gradual change, however, is perceptible towards the close of the Vedic Age, and in the Epic Age sacrifice as such,—the mere forms and ceremonials and offerings,—had acquired such an abnormal importance, that everything else was lost in it. This was inevitable when the priests formed into a caste. They multiplied ceremonials, and attached the utmost importance to every minute rite, until both they and the worshippers almost lost sight of the deities they worshipped in the voluminous rites they performed.

Sacrifices were generally accompanied by gifts of cattle, gold, garments, and food, and by the offering of animals as victims. There is a curious passage in Satapatha Brâhmana, 1, 2, 3, 7 and 8, about animal sacrifice, which deserves to be quoted :—

"At first, namely, the gods offered up a man as a victim. When he was offered up, the sacrificial essence went out of him. It entered into the horse. They offered up the horse. When it was offered, the sacrificial essence went out of it. It entered into the ox. When it was offered up, the sacrificial essence went out of it. It entered into the sheep. They offered up the sheep. When it was offered up, the sacrificial essence went out of it. It entered into the goat. They offered up the goat. When it was offered up, the sacrificial essence went out of it. It entered into this earth. They searched for it by digging. They found it in the shape of those two substances, the rice and barley: therefore even now they obtain those two by digging; and as much efficacy as all those sacrificed animal victims would have for him, so much efficacy has this oblation (of rice, &c.) for him who knows this."

Professor Max Müller infers from this passage that human sacrifices prevailed among the ancient Hindus, not in the Epic Period, not even in the Vedic Period, but at a still remoter age. Dr. Rajendra Lala Mitra, we regret to observe, follows the lead of Professor Max Müller, and infers from certain other passages which he quotes from the literature of this period, that the inhuman custom prevailed in the remote past. We demur to the conclusions of both these scholars.

If human sacrifice had prevailed in India before the Rig Veda hymns were composed, we should certainly have found allusions to it in the hymns themselves—allusions far more frequent than we find in the later Brâhmana literature. We find no such allusions. The story of Sunahsepha, as told in the Rig Veda, is no evidence of human sacrifice. And there is absolutely nothing else in the Rig Veda which can be construed as evidence of this custom. It is impossible to suppose that such a striking and fearful custom should have existed and gradually fallen into disuse without leaving the slightest trace in the Vedic hymns, some of which have come down from a very ancient date.

And where do we find allusions to this custom in the

literature of the Epic Period? The Sâma Veda is compiled from the Vedic hymns, and of course there is no mention of human sacrifice in this Veda. There is no mention of the custom in the Black Yajur Veda, and there is no mention of it in the White Yajur Veda, properly so-called. It is in the very latest compositions of the Epic Period,—in the *khila* or supplementary portion of the White Yajur Veda, in the Brâhmana of the Black Yajur Veda, in the Aitareya Brâhmana of the Rig Veda, and the last but one book of the Satapatha Brâhmana, that we have accounts of human sacrifice. Is it possible to postulate the existence of a horrible custom in India in the remote past of which we find no mention in the Rig Veda, in the Sâma Veda, in the Black or White Yajur Veda, but the memory of which suddenly revived after a thousand years in the supplements and Brâhmanas of the Vedas? Or is it not far more natural to suppose that all the allusions to human sacrifice in the later compositions of the Epic Period are the speculations of priests, just as there are speculatious about the sacrifice of the Supreme Being Himself? If the priests needed any suggestion, the customs of the non-Aryan tribes with whom they became familiar in the Epic Period would yield that suggestion.

We will now give a brief account of the principal sacrifices which were performed in this ancient age. We know from the Yajur Veda what these sacrifices were.

The *Darsa pûrnamâsa* was performed on the first day after the full and new moon, and Hindus down to the present time consider these days as sacred. The *Pinda-pitri yajna* was a sacrifice to the departed ancestors, and is one of the few ancient sacrifices which are performed to this day.

The *Agni hotra* was the daily libation of milk to the sacred fire, performed morning and evening. And the *Châturmâsya* was a sacrifice which was performed only once every four months.

The *Agni shtoma* was a Soma sacrifice; while the

Sautrâmanî was originally an expiation for over-indulgence in Soma. The *Râja sûya* was the imperial coronation sacrifice which was performed by great kings after they had established their prowess and fame by conquests; and the *Asva medha* was the celebrated horse-sacrifice which was also performed after great wars and conquests. Humbler than these, but far more important for our purpose, was the *Agniâdhâna* or setting up of the sacrificial fires, which had an important bearing on the life of every Hindu, and which deserves a few words in explanation.

Asvapti, as has been observed before, boasted that in his kingdom there was no thief, no miser, no drunkard, no ignorant person, no adulterer or adulteress, and "no man without an altar in his house." In those days, to keep the sacred fire in the altar was a duty incumbent on every householder, and the breach of this rule was regarded as positive impiety and irreligiousness. The student who had returned home from his teacher or his Parishad married in due time, and then set up the sacrificial fires. This was generally done on the first day of the waxing moon, but sometimes also at full moon, probably to enable the newly married couple to enter on the sacred duties as early as possible. The performance of the Agniâdhâna, or the establishment of the sacred fires, generally required two days. The sacrificer chose his four priests, the Brahman, the Hotri, the Adhvaryu, and the Agnîdhra, and erected two sheds or fire-houses, for the Gârhapatya and the Âhavanîya fires respectively. A circle was marked for the Gârhapatya fire, and a square for the Âhavanîya fire; and if a southern or Dakshinâgni was required, a semicircular area was marked to the south of the space between the other two.

The Adhvaryu then procured a temporary fire, either producing it by friction, or obtaining it from certain specified sources in the village, and after the usual five-fold lustration of the Gârhapatya fire-place, he laid down the fire thereon. Towards sunset the sacrificer invoked the gods and manes. He and his wife then entered the Gârhapatya house, and the Adhvaryu handed him two pieces of wood, the *Arani*, for the production of the Âhavanîya fire on the next morning. And the sacrificer and his wife laid them on their laps, performed propitiatory ceremonies, and remained awake the whole night and kept up the fire. In the morning the Adhvaryu extinguished the fire, or if there was to be a Dakshinâgni, he kept it till that fire was made up. Such in brief is the ceremony of the Agniâdhâna, or the setting up of sacrificial fires, which formed an important duty in the life of every Hindu householder in ancient days, when the gods were worshipped by each man in his fire-place, and temples and idols were unknown.

The illustrious scholar Dr. Roth first pointed out in 1854, from a passage in the Rig Veda (X, 18, 11), that in ancient ages burial was practised by the Hindus. This custom was followed by the burning of the dead and the burial of the ashes. That this latter custom was also in vogue in the Rig Veda Period appears from other passages, such as X, 15, 14, and X, 16, 1. In the Epic Period, of which we are now speaking, the custom of burying had ceased altogether, and the dead were burnt, and the ashes were buried. We find an account of this in the 35th chapter of the White Yajur Veda. The bones of the deceased were collected in a vessel and buried in the ground near a stream, and a mound was raised as high as the knee and covered with grass. The relatives then bathed and changed their clothes and left the funeral ground. The same ceremony is more fully described in the Âranyaka of the Black Yajur Veda. It is scarcely necessary to add that the custom which now prevails among the Hindus is simple cremation, without the burial of the ashes. This recent custom began, according to Dr. Rajendra Lala Mitra, shortly after the commencement of the Christian Era.

Another important rite which deserves some explanation is the Pindapitri yajna, or the gift of cakes to the departed ancestors. The cakes were offered to Fire and to Soma, and the Fathers were invoked to receive their shares. Then followed an address to the Fathers with reference to the six seasons of the year. The worshipper then looked at his wife and said: "Fathers! you have made us domestic men—we have brought these gifts to you according to our power." Then offering a thread or wool or hair, he said: "Fathers! this is your apparel, wear it." Then the wife ate a cake with a desire to have children, and said: "Fathers! let a male be born in me in this season. Do you protect the son in this womb from all sickness." Departed spirits, according to the Hindu religion, receive offerings from their living descendants, and get none when the family is extinct. Hence the extreme fear of Hindus to die without male issue, and the birth or adoption of a son is a part of their religion.

We do not propose to give an account of the other sacrificial rites; what we have already said will convey a general idea as to how sacrifices were performed. We will now turn to some of the legends of the Brâhmanas, which are curious and interesting. A most remarkable legend is told of Manu, who in the Vedic hymns is alluded to as the ancient progenitor of man, who introduced cultivation and worship by fire. The legend in the Satapatha Brâhmana (I, 8, 1) is not unlike the account of the Deluge in the Old Testament. As Manu was washing his hands a fish came unto him and said: "Rear me, I will save thee." Manu reared it, and in time it told him "in such and such a year that flood will come. Thou shalt then attend to me (*i.e.*, to my advice) by preparing a ship." The flood came, and Manu entered into the ship which he had built in time, and the fish swam up to him and carried the ship beyond the northern mountain. The ship was fastened to a tree there, and as the flood subsided, Manu gradually descended. "The flood then swept away all these creatures, and Manu alone remained here."

The legends relating to the creation of the world are also interesting. There is a beautiful Vedic simile in which the Sun, pursuing the Dawn, is compared to a lover pursuing a maiden. This gave rise to the legend which is found in the Brâhmanas (Satapatha, I, 7, 4; Aitereya, III, 33, &c.) that Prajâpati, the supreme god, felt a passion for his daughter, and this was the origin of creation! This legend in the Brâhmanas was further developed in the Purânas, where Brahmâ is represented as amorous of his daughter. The whole of these monstrous legends arose from a simple metaphor in the Rig Veda about the Sun following the Dawn. That such is the origin of the Puranic fables was known to Hindu thinkers and commentators, as will appear from the following well-known argument of Kumârila, the great opponent of Buddhism, and the predecessor of Sankarâchârya:—

"It is fabled that Prajâpati, the Lord of Creation, did violence to his daughter. But what does it mean? Prajâpati, the Lord of Creation, is a name of the sun; and he is called so because he protects all creatures. His daughter Ushas is the dawn. And when it is said that he was in love with her, this only means that at sunrise the sun runs after the dawn, the dawn being at the same time called the daughter of the sun because she rises when he approaches. In the same manner it is said that Indra was the seducer of Ahalyâ. This does not imply that the god Indra committed such a crime; but Indra means the sun, and Ahalyâ the night; and as the night is seduced and ruined by the sun of the morning, therefore is Indra called the paramour of Ahalyâ."

There is another legend of creation in the Taittirîya Brâhmana (I, 1, 3, 5). In the beginning there was nothing except water, and a lotus leaf standing out of it. Prajâpati dived in the shape of a boar and brought up some earth and spread it out and fastened it down by pebbles. This was the earth.

A similar story is told in the Satapatha Brâhmana (II, 1, 1, 8), that after the creation, the gods and asuras both sprung from Prajâpati, and the earth trembled like a lotus leaf when the gods and asuras contended for mastery. We know that in the Rig Veda, the word Asura is an adjective which means strong or powerful, and is invariably applied to gods except in the very last hymns of the last Mandala. In the Brâhmanas the word has changed its meaning altogether, and is applied to the enemies of the gods, about whom many new legends were invented.

Another account of creation is given in the Satapatha Brâhmana (II, 5, 1): "Verily in the beginning Prajâpati alone existed here." He created living beings and birds and reptiles and snakes, but they all passed away for want of food. He then made the breasts in the forepart of their body (*i.e.*, of the mammals) teem with milk, and so the living creatures survived. And thus the world was originally peopled.

While thus legends and sacrificial rites multiplied in the Epic Period, religion was still the same as in the Vedic Period. The gods of the Rig Veda were still worshipped, and the hymns of the Rik, Sâman, or Yajus were still uttered as texts. Only the veneration with which the gods were looked up to in the Vedic Period was now merged in the veneration for the sacrificial ceremonies.

New gods, however, were slowly finding a place in the Hindu pantheon—names which have acquired importance in later times. We have already seen that Arjuna was another name of Indra, even in the Satapatha Brâhmana. In Chapter XVI of the White Yajur Veda, we find Rudra already assuming his more modern Puranic names, and acquiring a more distinct individuality. In the Rig Veda, as we have already seen, Rudra is the father of the storms, he is the thunder. In the White Yajur Veda he is also described as the thunder-cloud, but is specially represented as a fearful god, and often the god of thieves and criminals, and altogether a destructive power. He is called Girisha (because clouds rest on mountains); he is called *Tâmra* or *Aruna* or *Babhru* (from the colour of the clouds); he is named Nîlakantha or blue-necked (also from the same reason); Kapardin or the long-haired; Pasupati or the nourisher of animals; Sankara or the benefactor; and Siva or the beneficent. Thus in the Epic Period we find Rudra in a transition stage, and we already see the origin of some of the Puranic legends about him. But nowhere in the Brâhmana literature do we find those legends fully developed, or Rudra represented as the Puranic Siva, the consort of Durgâ or Kâlî. In the Kaushîtaki Brâhmana, we find great importance attached in one passage to Isâna or Mahâdeva. In Satapatha Brâhmana, we find the following remarkable passage:—"This is thy share, O Rudra! Graciously accept it together with thy sister Ambikâ!" (II, 6, 2, 9). And in a celebrated passage in the Mundaka Upanishad, an Upanishad of the Atharva Veda, we find Kâlî, Karâlî, Manojavâ, Sulohitâ, Sudhûmarvarnâ Sphulinginî, and Bisvarupî as the names of the seven tongues of fire. In Satapatha Brâhmana (II, 4, 4, 6), we are told of a sacrifice being performed by Daksha Pârvati; and in the Kena Upanishad we find mention of a female called Umâ Haimavatî, who appeared before Indra and explained to Indra the nature of Brahman. These are a few specimens of the scattered materials in the Brâhmana literature, out of which the gorgeous Puranic legend of Siva and his consort was reared.

In Aitareya Brâhmana (VI, 15), and in Satapatha Brâhmana (I, 2, 5), we are told the story of the gods obtaining from the Asuras the part of the world which Vishnu could stride over or cover, and thus they managed to get the whole world. It is in the last book of the

Satapatha Brâhmana (XIV, 1, 1), that Vishnu obtains a sort of supremacy among gods, and his head is then struck off by Indra. Krishna, the son of Devakî, is not yet a deity; he is a pupil of Ghora Ângirasa in the Chhândogya Upanishad (III, 17, 6.)

While in these scattered allusions we detect materials for the construction of the gorgeous Puranic mythology of a later day, we also find in the Epic Period traces of that disbelief in Brâhmanical rites and creed which broke out also at a later day in the Buddhist revolution. The Tândya Brâhmana of the Sâma Veda contains the Vrâtya-stomas, by which the Vrâtyas or *Aryans not living according to the Brâhmanical system* could get admission into that community. Some of them are thus described :—"They drive in open chariots of war, carry bows and lances, wear turbans, robes bordered with red and having fluttering ends, shoes, and sheep skins folded double; their leaders are distinguished by brown robes and silver neck ornaments; they pursue neither agriculture nor commerce; their laws are in a state of confusion; they speak the same language as those who have received Brâhmanical consecration, but nevertheless call what is easily spoken hard to pronounce." For the rest, a Vrâtya was not yet looked upon with contempt, and the Supreme Being is addressed in Prasna Upanishad as a Vrâtya.

CHAPTER IX.

THE RELIGIOUS DOCTRINES OF THE UPANISHADS.

IT is a relief to pass from the rituals and legends of the Brâhmanas to the more vigorous speculations of the Upanishads. Some impatience appears to have been felt with the elaborate but unmeaning rites, the dogmatic but childish explanations, and the mystic but grotesque reasoning which fill the voluminous Brâhmanas; and thinking men asked themselves if this was all that religion could teach. Earnest men, while still conforming to the rites laid down in the Brâhmanas, began to speculate on the destination of the Soul and on the nature of the Supreme Being. Learned Kshatriyas must have given a start to these healthier speculations, or at least carried them on with vigour and success, until Brâhmans came to them to learn something of the wisdom of the new school. And even after the lapse of nearly three thousand years, it is impossible not to be struck with the vigour, the earnestness, and the philosophy which characterise the doctrines of the Upanishads. The most important among them are (1) the Doctrine of a Universal Soul, (2) the Doctrine of Creation, (3) the Doctrine of Transmigration of Souls, and (4) the Doctrine of Final Beatitude.

We begin with the Doctrine of a Universal Soul, an all-pervading Breath which is the keystone of the philosophy and thought of the Upanishads. This idea is somewhat different from monotheism as it has been generally understood in later days. For monotheism generally recognises a God and Creator as distinct from the created beings; but the monotheism of the Upanishads, which has been the monotheism of the Hindu religion ever since, recognises God as the Universal Being;—all things else have emanated from him, are a part of him, and will mingle in him, and have no separate existence. This is the lesson which Satyakâma Jabâla learnt from nature, and this is the lesson which Yâjnavalkya imparted to his beloved and esteemed wife Maitreyî. This too is the great idea which is taught in the Upanishads in a hundred similes and stories and beautiful legends, which impart to the Upanishads their unique value in the literature of the world.

"All this is Brahman (the Universal Being). Let a man meditate on the visible world as beginning, ending, and breathing in the Brahman. . . .

"The Intelligent, whose body is spirit, whose form is light, whose thoughts are true, whose nature is like ether (omnipresent and invisible), from whom all works, all desires, all sweet odours and tastes proceed; he who embraces all this, who never speaks and is never surprised.

"He is my self within the heart, smaller than a corn of rice, smaller than a corn of barley, smaller than a mustard seed, smaller than a canary seed or the kernel of a canary seed. He also is my self within the heart, greater than the earth, greater than the sky, greater than heaven, greater than all these worlds.

"He from whom all works, all desires, all sweet odours and tastes proceed, who embraces all this, who never speaks and is never surprised, he—my self within the heart—is that Brahman. When I shall have departed from hence, I shall obtain him" (*Chhândogya*, III, 14).

Such is the sublime language in which the ancient Hindus expressed their sublime conception of the minute but all-pervading and Universal Being whom they called Brahman or God.

We proceed with other extracts from the Chhândogya.

Svetaketu, as we have seen before, stayed with his teacher from his twelfth year to his twenty-fourth, and then returned home, "having then studied all the Vedas, conceited, considering himself well read, and stern." But he had yet things to learn which were not ordinarily taught in the schools of the age, and his father Uddâlaka Âruneya taught him the true nature of the Universal Being in beautiful similes:—

"As the bees, my son, make honey by collecting the juices of distant trees, and reduce the juice into one form. And as these juices have no discrimination, so that they might say, I am the juice of this tree or that, in the same manner, my son, all these creatures, when they have become merged in the True, know not that they are merged in the True. . . .

"These rivers, my son, run, the eastern (like the Ganges) towards the east, the western (like the Indus) towards the west. They go from sea to sea (*i.e.*, the clouds lift up the water from the sea to the sky and send it back as rain to the sea). They become indeed sea. And as those rivers, when they are in the sea, do not know, I am this or that river, in the same manner, my son, all these creatures, proceeding from the True, know not that they have proceeded from the True. . . .

"'Place this salt in water, and then wait on me in the morning.'

"The son did as he was commanded. The father said to him: 'Bring me the salt which you placed in the water last night.' The son having looked for it found it not, for, of course, it was melted.

"The father said: 'Taste it from the surface of the water. How is it?' The son replied: 'It is salt.' 'Taste it from the middle. How is it?' The son replied: 'It is salt.' 'Taste it from the bottom. How is it?' The son replied: 'It is salt.' The father said: 'Throw it away, and then wait on me.'"

"The son waited on the father, and the father explained to his son that the Universal Being, though invisible, dwells in us, as the salt is in the water" (*Chhândogya*, VI).

These extracts from the Chhândogya bring home to us the Hindu idea of a Universal Being. We will now quote one or two passages from the Kena and the Îsâ :—

"At whose wish does the mind, sent forth, proceed on its errand?" asks the pupil. "At whose command does the first breath go forth? At whose wish do we utter this speech? What god directs the eye or the ear?"

The teacher replies: "It is the ear of the ear, the mind of the mind, the speech of the speech, the breath of the breath, and the eye of the eye. . . .

"That which is not expressed by speech, and by which speech is expressed. . . . That which does not think by mind, and by which mind is thought. . . . That which does not see by the eye, and by which one sees. . . . That which does not hear by the ear, and by which the ear is heard. . . . That which does not breathe by breath, and by which breath is drawn,—*that alone know as Brahman,—not that which people here adore*" (*Kena Upanishad*, I).

The italics are, of course, ours. But who does not see in the above passage an effort of the human mind to shake itself from the trammels of meaningless ceremonials which priests taught and the "people here" practised, to soar into a higher region of thought and to comprehend the incomprehensible,—the breath of the breath and the soul of the soul? Who is not struck by this manly and fervent effort made by the Hindu nation, three thousand years ago, to know the unknown Maker, to comprehend the incomprehensible God.

And the joy of him who has comprehended, however feebly, the incomprehensible God, has been well described :—

"He who beholds all beings in the Self, and Self in all beings, he never turns away from it.

"When to a man who understands, the Self has become

all things, what sorrow, what trouble can there be to him who once beheld that unity?

"He, the Self, encircled all, bright, incorporeal, scatheless, without muscles, pure, untouched by evil, a seer, wise, omnipresent, self-existent, he disposed all things rightly for eternal years" (*Îsâ Upanishad*).

Lastly, in the Brihadâranyaka Upanishad we are told that all gods are the manifestation of Self or Purusha, "for he is all gods" (I, 4, 6). And likewise that he exists in all men, in the Brâhman, the Kshatriya, the Vaisya, and the Sûdra (I, 4, 15).

Our extracts on this subject have been somewhat lengthy, but the reader will not regret it. For the Doctrine of a Universal Soul is the very keystone of the Hindu religion, and it is necessary to know how this idea was first developed in India in the Upanishads. We will now pass on to another important doctrine, viz., the Doctrine of Creation.

The Creation of the world was still a mystery to those early thinkers, and the attempts to solve it were necessarily fanciful. A few passages may be quoted:—

"In the beginning this was non-existent. It became existent as it grew. It turned into an egg. The egg lay for the time of a year. The egg broke open. The two halves were one of silver, the other of gold.

"The silver one became this earth, the golden one the sky, the thick membrane (of the white) the mountains, the thin membrane (of the yolk) the mist with the clouds, the small veins the rivers, the fluid the sea.

"And what was born from it was Âditya, the Sun. When he was born shouts of hurrah arose, and all beings arose, and all things which they desired" (*Chhândogya*, III, 19).

A different account is given in VI, 2, of the same Upanishad, where we are told that—"In the beginning there was that only, which is,—One only, without a second." And that sent forth fire, and fire sent forth water, and the water sent forth the earth.

The Aitareya Âranyaka describes how Prâna, the Universal Breath, created the world, and then discusses the question of the material cause out of which the world was created. As in the Rig Veda (X, 129), and as in the Jewish account of creation, water is said to be the first material cause.

"Was it water really? Was it water? Yes, all this was water indeed. The water was the root, the world was the shoot. He (the person) is the father, they (earth, fire, &c.), are the sons." Mahidâsa Aitareya knew this. (II, 1, 8, 1).

Elsewhere in the same Upanishad the following account of Creation is given:—

"Verily in the beginning all this was Self,—one only. There was nothing else blinking whatsoever." And that Self sent forth the water (above the heaven), the lights which are the sky, the mortal which is the earth, and the waters under the earth. He then formed the Purusha, and the universe was produced from the Purusha.

Some of these extracts clearly recognise an original Creator,—the Breath or the Soul or the Self—and also a material cause, water or fire. We shall see hereafter how this doctrine of a Primal Soul and Primal Matter is developed in later Hindu Philosophy. We must now turn to the most important Doctrine of Transmigration of Souls. It is to the Hindus what the doctrine of Resurrection is to Christians. And while the Christians believe that our souls will live in another sphere after death, the Hindus believe that our souls have lived in other spheres before, and will live again in other spheres after death.

The central idea is that which has been adopted as the cardinal principle of the Hindu religion, that good acts lead to their rewards in future existences, but it is true knowledge only which leads to union with the Universal Spirit. "As here on earth, whatever has been acquired by exertion perishes, so perishes whatever is acquired for the next world by sacrifices and other good actions performed on earth. Those who depart from hence without having discovered the Self and those true desires, for them there is no freedom in all the worlds" (*Chhândogya*, VIII, 1, 6).

The doctrine of transmigration of souls is fully and beautifully explained in the Brihadâranyaka (IV, 4), and we will make an extract from that Upanishad :—

"As a caterpillar, after having reached the end of a blade of grass, and after having made another approach to another blade, draws itself together towards it, thus does the Self, after having thrown off this body, and dispelled all ignorance, and after making another approach to another body, draw itself together towards it.

"And as a goldsmith, taking a piece of gold, turns it into another newer and more beautiful shape, so does the Self, after having thrown off this body, and dispelled all ignorance, make unto himself another newer and more beautiful shape, whether it be like the Fathers, or like the Gandharvas, or like the Devas, or like Prajâpati, or like Brahman, or like other beings. . . .

"So much for the man who desires. But as to the man who does not desire; who, not desiring, free from desires, is satisfied in his desires, or desires the Self only, his vital spirits do not depart elsewhere; being Brahman, he goes to Brahman. . . .

"And as the slough of a snake lies on an anthill, dead and cast away, thus lies the body; but that disembodied immortal spirit is Brahman only, is only light."

And this brings us to the Doctrine of Final Beatitude and Salvation. There is nothing sublimer in the literature of the ancient Hindus than the passages in which they fervently recorded their hope and faith that the disembodied Soul, purified from all stains and all sins, will at last be received in the Universal Soul even as light mingles with light. We quote another passage from the Brihadâranyaka :—

"He, therefore, that knows it, after having become

quiet, subdued, satisfied, patient, and collected, sees self in Self, sees all in Self. Evil does not overcome him, he overcomes all evil. Evil does not burn him, he burns all evil. Free from evil, free from spots, free from doubt, he becomes a true Brahman;—enters the Brahma world."

It was this Doctrine of Final Beatitude which Death explained to Nachiketas in that beautiful idyll of an Upanishad called *Katha*. We will close the present chapter with an extract from that beautiful creation of fancy and of piety.

Nachiketas was given by his father unto Death and entered the abode of Yama Vaivasvata, and asked him for three boons, the last of which was this:—

"There is that doubt, when a man is dead;—some saying, he is; others, he is not. This I should like to know taught by thee; this is the third of my boons."

But Death was unwilling to reveal his secrets, and told Nachiketas to ask for other boons.

"Choose sons and grandsons who shall live a hundred years, herds of cattle, elephants, gold, horses. Choose the wide abode of the earth, and live thyself as many harvests as thou desirest.

"If you can think of any boon equal to that, choose wealth and long life. Be king, Nachiketas, on the whole earth. I make thee the enjoyer of all desires.

"Whatever desires are difficult to attain among mortals, ask for them, anything to thy wish;—these fair maidens with their chariots and musical instruments,—such are indeed not to be obtained by men; be waited on by them whom I give thee, but do not ask me about dying."

Nachiketas said: "These things last till to-morrow, O Death, for they wear out this vigour of all the senses. Even the whole of life is short. Keep thou thy horses, keep dance and song for thyself."

Pressed by the pious inquirer, Death at last revealed the great secret, which is the principle of the Upanishads and the principle of the Hindu religion:—

"The wise who, by means of meditation on his self, recognises the Ancient, who is difficult to be seen, who has entered into the dark, who has hidden in the cave, who dwells in the abyss, as God,—he indeed leaves joy and sorrow far behind.

"A mortal who has heard this and embraced it, who has separated from it all qualities, and has thus reached the subtle Being, rejoices because he has obtained what is a cause for rejoicing. The house of Brahman is open, I believe, O Nachiketas!"

Who can, even in the present day, peruse these pious inquiries and fervent thoughts of a long buried past, without feeling a new emotion in his heart, without seeing a new light before his eyes! The mysteries of the unknown future will never be solved by human intellect or by human science; but the first recorded attempts to solve them in a pious, fervent, philosophical spirit will ever have an abiding interest for every patriotic Hindu and for every thoughtful man.

In the words of the eminent German writer and philosopher Schopenhauer: "From every sentence deep, original and sublime thoughts arise, and the whole is pervaded by a high and holy and earnest spirit. Indian air surrounds us, and original thoughts of kindred spirits. . . . In the whole world there is no study except that of the originals, so beneficial and so elevating as that of the Oupnekhat.* It has been the solace of my life; it will be the solace of my death."

* Latin translation of the Upanishads.

BOOK III.

RATIONALISTIC PERIOD, B.C. 1000 TO 320.

CHAPTER I.

LITERATURE OF THE PERIOD.

A CHANGE came over the spirit of the Hindu world in the third period, and the change is reflected in the Sûtra literature of India. The Vindhya range was the extreme southern limit of the Hindu world in the Epic Period; but now the Hindus crossed that chain of mountains, and penetrated beyond the wastes and jungles of Central India, and founded powerful Hindu kingdoms on the banks of the Godâvarî and the Krishnâ, extending to the blue waters of the ocean. In the east the kingdom of Magadha rose to power and greatness and threw out colonies into Bengal and Orissa, and in the west the kingdom of Saurâshtra extended its limits to the Arabian Sea. This expansion of the Hindu world had its effect on the Hindu mind; the Hindus became more venturesome, and their ideas became more expanded. Whatever literature was handed down from ancient times was put in a condensed, practical shape, and new discoveries in every department of science were made with the boldness of new explorers and conquerors.

The practical spirit of the age showed itself in the form which literature assumed. All learning, all sciences, all religious teachings, were reduced to concise practical manuals. Brevity is the characteristic of the Sûtra literature, as verbosity is of the Brâhmana literature. Indeed, the writers went from one extreme to another;—verbose prose was replaced by aphorisms, and the proverbial saying which applies to the Sûtra literature is often quoted, that "an author rejoiceth in the economising of half a short vowel as much as in the birth of a son!"

One main reason which led to this extreme conciseness was that young Hindu students were expected in their early years to learn these Sûtras by rote. Aryan boys were expected to place themselves under some teacher at the early age of eight or ten or twelve, and for twelve years or more they remained in their teacher's house, doing menial service under him, begging alms for him, and learning day by day the ancestral religion by rote. The diffuse details of the Brâhmanas were therefore compressed into short treatises in order that they might be imparted and learnt with ease, and a separate body of Sûtras was thus composed for each Sûtra Charana or school. The names of the authors of many of these compositions have been handed down to us, and while the Vedas and the Brâhmanas are declared to be *revealed*, no such claim is put forward for the Sûtras, which are admitted to be human compositions. The so-called *revealed* literature of India closes therefore with the Upanishads, which form the last portions of the Brâhmanas.

When once the Sûtras began to be composed, the system spread rapidly all over India, and Sûtra schools multiplied. The Châranyavyûha names five Charanas of the Rig Veda, twenty-seven of the Black Yajur Veda, fifteen of the White Yajur Veda, twelve of the Sâma Veda, and nine of the Atharva Veda. Each Sûtra Charana must have had a separate body of Sûtras for itself, and the adherents of any particular Charana,—in whatever part of India they might live,—learnt and imparted to students the Sûtras of that particular school. A vast mass of Sûtra literature thus gradually sprung up in India, but of the numerous bodies of Sûtras which must have been composed and taught in these numerous Sûtra Charanas a lamentably small number has been left to us! As with the Brâhmanas, so with the Sûtras, a limited number of works only have been saved from the shipwreck of ancient Sanscrit literature.

We will now rapidly survey the different branches of learning which gradually assumed the Sûtra form, and we will begin with religion. Details of ceremonials relating to Vedic sacrifices were compressed into concise manuals, and these manuals are called *Srauta Sûtras.* Two collections of these Srauta Sûtras belonging to the Rig Veda, called Âsvalâyana and Sânkhâyana; three belonging to the Sâma Veda, and called Mâsaka, Lâtyâyana and Drâhyâyana; four belonging to the Black Yajur Veda, and called Baudhâyana, Bhâradvâja, Âpastamba, and Hiranyakesin; and one belonging to the White Yajur Veda, and called Kâtyâyana, have been left entire. An account of these Srauta Sûtras will not be interesting to our readers, but nevertheless, some facts about them deserve mention.

Âsvalâyana is said to have been the pupil of the celebrated Saunaka, and the teacher and pupil are said to have been the joint authors of the last two books of the Aitareya Âranyaka. The fact clearly points to the interesting fact that the earliest works of the Sûtra literature connect themselves with the last works of the Brâhmana or Epic Period.

Saunaka is indeed an interesting character of the Epic Period. In an anterior state of existence he is said to have been Gritsamada, the "seer" of the second book of the Rig Veda, and by this legend we may probably understand that he belonged to the line of teachers or families by whom that book of the Rig Veda was handed down from century to century. Saunaka was again the priest of Janamejaya Pârikshita in the famous horse-sacrifice which he celebrated. We may infer therefore that a line of Saunakas were celebrated priests and men of learning in the Epic Period. No wonder that the earliest compilers of Sûtras seek to connect themselves with this honoured name.

The Sânkhâyana Srauta Sûtra, it has been conjectured, belongs to the Western part of Hindustan, as the Âsvalâyana belongs to the Eastern.

Of the Sâma Veda the Mâsaka Srauta Sûtra is only a tabular enumeration of prayers belonging to different ceremonies, the Lâtyâyana embodies the opinions of various teachers, and both these Sûtras connect themselves with the great Tândya or Panchavinsa Brâhmana of the Sâma Veda. The Drahyâyana differs but little from the Lâtyâyana.

The Sûtras of the Black Yajur Veda have been chronologically arranged as those of Baudhâyana, Bhâradvâja, Âpastamba, and Hiranyakesin, and Dr. Bühler, who has recovered the lost Bhâradvâja Sûtra, justly remarks that the distance in years between Baudhâyana and Âpastamba must be measured not by decades but by centuries. In a most valuable introduction to his translation of the Dharma Sûtra of Âpastamba, Dr. Bühler states that a powerful Hindu kingdom, *i.e.*, of the Andhras, had been founded in Southern India before the Christian era, that the capital of the empire was probably situated near modern Amarâvatî on the river Krishnâ, that Âpastamba was probably born or naturalised in this country and founded his Sûtra school there, and that the date of his work cannot be put down later than the third century before Christ. And as Âpastamba speaks not only of the six Vedângas, but also of the Pûrva Mîmânsa and the Vedânta schools of philosophy, we can conclude that the philosophical schools of India had begun their work previous to that date.

The Srauta Sûtra of the White Yajur Veda is by Kâtyâyana, who also claims to be a pupil of the renowned Saunaka. Kâtyâyana was a critic of Pânini the grammarian, and lived, according to Max Müller, in the fourth century before Christ. An interesting "battle of books" has been waged by scholars about the date of Pânini, but we must avoid entering into the arena reserved for doughty scholars, and only express our assent to the prevailing opinion that the grammarian must have lived some centuries before his critic. The Kâtyâyana Sûtra strictly follows the Satapatha Brâhmana, and the first eighteen chapters of the Sûtra correspond with the first nine books of the Brâhmana. As in Lâtyâyana, so in Kâtyâyana we find allusion to Mâgadhadesîya Brahma-bandhu, who are supposed to be the first Buddhists.

We turn with pleasure from the Srauta Sûtras to the *Dharma Sûtras*, which present to us the customs and manners and laws of the times, and are, therefore, far more valuable for our historical purpose. In the Srauta Sûtras we see the Hindus as sacrificers; in the Dharma Sûtras we see them as citizens.

But the Dharma Sûtras of this ancient period have a still further claim to our attention, because they are the originals which have been modified and put into verse at a later age, and transformed into those law-books with which modern Hindus are familiar, such as Manu and Yâjnavalkya. This was pointed out by Professor Max Müller thirty years ago, and the researches which have been made since have fully confirmed the fact. A world of conjectures and fancies about the Code of Manu, previously supposed to be the work of legislators and rulers, has been exploded by this discovery, and we now know what the so-called codes are, and how and why they were framed. In their original Sûtra form (often in prose, sometimes in prose and verse, but never in continuous verse like the later codes), they were composed, just as the Srauta Sûtras were composed, by the founders of the Sûtra Charanas, and were learnt by rote by young Hindus, so that they might, in later life, never forget their duties as citizens and as members of society. No nation has taken greater precautions than the Hindus to implant in the mind of every member of society his religious, social, and legal duties.

Among the Dharma Sûtras which are lost, and have not yet been recovered, was the Mânava Sûtra or Sûtra of Manu, from which the later metrical Code of Manu has been compiled. It seems that the Dharma Sûtra of Manu was held in high honour in the Sûtra Period, as the metrical Code of Manu is held in honour in the present day. The references to Manu are frequent in the Sûtra literature, and Dr. Bühler has pointed out two quotations from Manu in Vasishtha's and Gautama's Dharma Sûtras.

Among the Dharma Sûtras still extant, Vasishtha belonging to the Rig Veda, Gautama belonging to the Sâma Veda, and Baudhâyana and Âpastamba belonging to the Black Yajur Veda, have been translated by Dr. Bühler.

In point of time Gautama is the oldest, and we find Baudhâyana transferring a whole chapter of Gautama's into his Sûtra, and Vasishtha again has borrowed the same chapter from Baudhâyana. And we have seen before that Âpastamba also comes after Baudhâyana.

We have spoken of the Srauta Sûtras which treat of the duties of a worshipper, and of the Dharma Sûtras which treat of the duties of a citizen. But man has other duties and responsibilities beyond those of a worshipper and a citizen. As a son, a husband, and a father, he has duties to perform towards the members of his family. He has little rites to perform in connection with domestic occurrences, which are quite different from the more elaborate ceremonials taught in the Srauta Sûtras. A distinct class of rules was necessary to fix the details of these Grihya or domestic rites, and these rules are given in the *Grihya Sûtras.*

A great deal of interest attaches to these simple domestic rites performed at the domestic fireside, and not at the hearths which had to be specially lighted at great sacrifices. The domestic fire was lighted by each householder on his marriage, and the simple rites, the

Pâkayajnas, were easily performed. "A log of wood," says Professor Max Müller, "placed on the fire of the hearth, an oblation poured out to the gods, or alms given to Brâhmans, this is what constitutes a Pâkayajna." Gautama enumerates seven Pâka sacrifices, viz.:—(1) Astakâ, performed in the four winter months; (2) Pârvana, at full and new moon; (3) Srâddha, or monthly funeral oblations; (4 to 7) Srâvanî, Âgrahâyanî, Chaitrî, and Âsvajujî, performed on the days of full moon in the months from which the rites have been named. The account of these rites contained in the Grihya Sûtras is deeply interesting to Hindus, because after a lapse of over two thousand years we are still practising, as will be seen further on, the same interesting rites, sometimes under the same name, and often under a different name and in a somewhat different way. The Grihya Sûtras also contain accounts of social ceremonies performed at marriage, at the birth of a child, at his first feeding, at his assuming the life of a student, &c. And thus we get a complete idea of domestic life among the ancient Hindus from these invaluable Grihya Sûtras.

The Sânkhâyana and Âsvalâyana Grihya Sûtras belonging to the Rig Veda, and the Pâraskara Grihya Sûtra belonging to the White Yajur Veda, have been translated by Herman Oldenberg. A second volume, which promises to contain a translation of Gobhila, &c., has been announced but has not yet been published.*

The Srauta Sûtra, the Dharma Sûtra, and the Grihya Sûtra go collectively under the name of Kalpa Sûtra. Indeed, each Sûtra Charana is supposed to have had a complete body of Kalpa Sûtra including the divisions mentioned above, but much of what existed has been lost, and we have only fragments of the Sûtra literature left. The entire Kalpa Sûtra of Âpastamba still exists, and is divided into thirty prasnas or sections. The first twenty-four of these treat of Srauta sacrifices; the 25th

* It has been published since the above was written.

contains the rules of interpretation; the 26th and 27th treat of the Grihya rites; the 28th and 29th contain the Dharma Sûtra, and the 30th section, the *Sulva Sûtra*, teaches the geometrical principles according to which the altars for the Srauta sacrifices had to be constructed. These interesting Sulva Sûtras have been made known to the western world by Dr. Thibaut. The publication of his work confirms the conclusions of Von Schrader, that Pythagoras learnt not only his theory of transmigration but his mathematics also from India in the sixth century before Christ.

We have so long spoken of the Kalpa Sûtra, as the Kalpa Sûtra forms the most important and, historically, the most valuable portion of the literature of the period. Our ancient writers enumerate five other Vedângas or departments of Vedic study, and we will briefly allude to them here.

Sikshâ or Phonetics is the science of pronunciation, and there is reason to believe that rules on the subject were formerly embodied in the Âranyakas and even in the Brâhmanas of the Epic Period, but that they have disappeared in consequence of the appearance of more scientific works on the same subject in the Rationalistic Period. These works are called Prâtisâkhyas, which were collections of phonetic rules applicable to each Sâkhâ or recension of each Veda.

Many of the Prâtisâkhyas, however, have been lost, and only one Prâtisâkhya for each Veda (except the Sâma Veda) has been preserved to us. The Prâtisâkhya of the Rig Veda is ascribed to the renowned Saunaka. Similarly, a Prâtisâkhya of the White Yajur Veda is also extant and is ascribed to Kâtyâyana. A Prâtisâkhya of the Black Yajur Veda and one of the Atharva Veda are also extant, but the names of the authors are forgotten. It will interest our readers to learn that among the teachers named in the Prâtisâkhya of the Black Yajur Veda we have the name of a Vâlmîki!

Chhandas or Metre is spoken of in the Vedas, and whole chapters in the Âranyakas and Upanishads are devoted to it. But as in the case of Sikshâ, so in the case of Chhandas, we have a clear scientific treatment of the subject for the first time in the Sûtra literature. There are some chapters on the metre of the Rig Veda at the end of the Prâtisâkhya of that Veda. For the Sâma Veda we have the well-known Nidâna Sûtra.

The deservedly great fame of Pânini in the department of *Vyâkarana* or Grammar has eclipsed that of all other grammarians of the period. Pânini belonged to the extreme north-west corner of India, where the Brâhmanas and Âranyakas and Upanishads, composed mostly on the banks of the Ganges and the Jumna, were little known or respected; and Pânini therefore knew little of them. Dr. Goldstücker is right in holding Pânini to be anterior to Buddha.

Similarly, the great fame of Yâska (anterior to Pânini according to Dr. Goldstücker and other scholars) in the department of *Nirukta* has eclipsed the fame of his predecessors, of whom we know little except from the mention made of them in Yâska's work. A common mistake is made in calling Yâska's work the Nirukta. Nirukta is a work, as Sâyana says, where only a number of words is given. Yâska takes up such an old existing Nirukta, and on this text he writes a commentary, which is his work.

Colebrooke speaks of different treatises on *Jyotisha* or Astronomy for each Veda, and he calls one which has a commentary, the Jyotisha of the Rig Veda. Professor Max Müller, however, has found the works to be different manuscripts of the same work, and he believes the work to have been composed after the Sûtra Period, although the doctrines and rules propounded in it belong to the earliest stage of Hindu astronomy. Its practical object is to convey a knowledge of the heavenly bodies necessary for fixing the time for sacrifices, and to establish a sacred calendar. However recent the date of the existing work may be, it contains observations made in India during the Epic Period, *i.e.*, when the Vedas were collected and arranged, and it furnishes evidence therefore of the date of that period, which should not be lightly rejected or ignored.

Besides the six Vedângas detailed above, there is another class of works called the Anukramanî or Index to the Vedas, which also belongs to Sûtra literature. The Anukramanî of the Rig Veda is ascribed to Kâtyâyana, and gives the first words of each hymn, the number of verses, the name of the poet, the metre, and the deity. There were some older Anukramanîs of the Rig Veda, which have all been replaced by Kâtyâyana's fuller work.

The Yajur Veda has three Anukramanîs, viz., one for the Âtreya recension of the Black Yajur Veda, one for the recension of the Charakas, and the third for the Mâdhyandina recension of the White Yajur Veda.

Of the Sâma Veda we have an ancient index in the Ârsheya Brâhmana, and some more among the Parisishtas or supplementary works. An Anukramanî of the Atharva Veda has been discovered in the British Museum.

We have still to refer to the most important product of the Hindu mind in the Rationalistic Period. The doctrines and philosophical inquiries started at the close of the Epic Period in the Upanishads led to those deeper investigations and profound researches which are known as the six schools of Hindu Philosophy. Professor Weber justly remarks that it was in Philosophy as well as in Grammar that the speculative Hindu mind attained the highest pitch of its marvellous fertility. The abstrusest questions of matter and spirit, of creation and future existence, were dealt with in Sânkhya Philosophy, not as in the Upanishads in guesses and speculations, but with the strictest method and relentless logic. Other schools of Philosophy followed the lead of Sânkhya Philosophy, and inquired boldly into the mysteries of soul and mind, of creation and of the Creator.

Orthodox Hindus became alarmed at the spread of sceptical ideas, and a reaction set in. The result is the Vedânta system of Philosophy, which reasserts the great doctrines of the Upanishads, and which forms to this day the basis of Hindu beliefs and religious convictions. In the meantime, however, a far mightier movement than that caused by philosophical opinions had been set on foot. Gautama Buddha was born in the sixth century before Christ, and proclaimed to the poor and the lowly that Vedic rites were useless, that a holy and tranquil and benevolent life is the essence of religion, that caste-distinctions do not exist among those who strive after holiness and purity. Thousands responded to his appeal, and thus a catholic religion began to spread in India, which has since become the religion of Asia.

From the brief account of the literature of the age given above, the reader will have some idea of the intellectual activity of this most brilliant period of Hindu civilisation. Religious rights and duties were laid down lucidly and concisely for householders; civil and criminal laws were compiled; phonetics, metre, and grammar were dealt with with scientific accuracy; geometry and mathematics were cultivated; mental philosophy and logic were studied and developed with marvellous success; and a noble religion was proclaimed which is now the religion of a third of the human race.

CHAPTER II.

EXPANSION OF THE HINDUS.

THE History of India receives a new light in the Rationalistic Period, as it was in this period that the Greeks visited India and also compiled accounts of it from report. Greek civilisation and national life had not commenced during the long centuries of the Vedic Age in India. Again, the rude heroes of the Trojan War knew little of their civilised but distant contemporaries, the Hindus of the Epic Age. The first two epochs of Hindu history receive no light therefore from Greek literature. The first Greek who is supposed to have borrowed his learning from the Hindus is the philosopher Pythagoras. He lived in the sixth century before Christ, *i.e.*, in the Rationalistic Period of Hindu history, and his theories and ideas throw some light on the prevailing ideas of the Hindus of that age. He learnt the Doctrine of Transmigration of Souls and the Doctrine of Final Beatitude from the Upanishads and the current faith of the Hindus, and his ascetic observances and prohibition to eat flesh and beans were also borrowed from India. He learnt his elementary geometry from the Sulva Sûtras; his notion of the virtues of numbers was borrowed from Sânkhya Philosophy; and lastly, his idea of the five elements was essentially an Indian idea.

Herodotus, the father of Greek history, lived in the fifth century before Christ; and although he never visited India, he gives accounts of the Hindus from report which are valuable, although he mixes them up with legends and stories, and often confounds the customs of the Hindus with those of the uncivilised aborigines who still inhabited large tracts in India. Herodotus tells us that the Indians were the greatest nation of the age, that they were divided into various tribes and spoke different tongues, that they procured great quantities of gold in their country, that India abounded in quadrupeds and birds larger than any other country, and produced wild trees which bore wool (cotton) from which the Indians made their clothing (III, 94–106). Elsewhere he says, speaking of the Thracians, that they were the greatest of nations among men excepting only the Indians (V, 3). Herodotus also mentions the fact, which is probably historically true, that Darius, king of Persia, subjugated a part of India, and his ships sailed down the Indus to the sea (IV, 44).

And lastly, Megasthenes came to India in the fourth century before Christ, and lived in the court of Chandragupta in Pâtaliputra or ancient Patna. And although his original account is lost, still extracts from his writings are found scattered in many subsequent works. These have been carefully collected by Dr. Schwanbeck of Bonn and translated into English by Mr. MacCrindle, and are invaluable for the purposes of Indian History, and we shall frequently have occasion to quote them. Pythagoras, Herodotus, and Megasthenes are unimpeachable witnesses to the high civilisation of India during three successive centuries which fall within the Rationalistic Period, viz., the sixth, fifth, and fourth centuries before Christ.

We have seen that by the end of the Epic Period the whole of the valley of the Ganges and Jumna from Delhi to North Behar had been conquered, peopled, and Hinduised. We have seen that towards the very close of that period, *i.e.*, about 1000 B.C., Hindu settlers and adventurers, colonists, and "pilgrim fathers" had left the valley of the Ganges and had penetrated into remote unknown lands, into Southern Behar, Malwa, the Deccan, and Gujrat. And we have seen that these non-Aryan provinces were becoming gradually known to the Hindus, and were slowly coming under Hindu influence and power when the Epic Period closed and the Rationalistic Period began.

The waves of Hindu conquests rolled onwards, and the aborigines submitted themselves to a higher civilisation and a nobler religion. Rivers were crossed, forests were cleared, lands were reclaimed, wide wastes were peopled, and new countries hitherto aboriginal witnessed the rise of Hindu power and of Hindu religion. Where a few scanty settlers had penetrated at first, powerful colonies arose, where religious teachers had retired in seclusion, quiet villages and towns arose. Where a handful of merchants had made their way by some unknown river, boats navigated up and down with valuable cargoes for a civilised population. Where hardy warriors or scions of royal houses had dwelt in exile or by the chase, powerful monarchs reigned over a conquered, civilised, Hinduised aboriginal population. And where foresters had felled trees and cleared small tracts of land, smiling fields covered with waving corn spread for miles and miles around, betokening the spread of civilisation and of the civilised arts of life.

Such was the history of Aryan conquests from generation to generation and from century to century in the Rationalistic Period, and each succeeding Sûtra work that we take up shows that the circle of civilisation has spread wider, and that the zone of unreclaimed barbarism has receded further and further. And long before we come to the close of the Rationalistic Period, *i.e.*, the fourth century B.C., we find that the entire peninsula has been reclaimed, civilised, and Hinduised, and that primitive barbarians dwelt only in rocks, forests, and deserts which the Aryans disdained to conquer. It is not a story of conquests only, which would have little interest for the philosophical reader. It is a story of the spread of Hindu civilisation among hitherto unknown countries and aboriginal nations. It was the acceptance, by the Andhras of the Deccan and the Saurâshtras of Gujrat, by the Cholas,

Cheras, and Pândyas of Southern India, by the Magadhas, the Angas, the Vangas, and the Kalingas of Eastern India —of that superior religion and language and civilisation which the Hindu Aryans offered to them. The gift was accepted and cherished, and henceforth the Dravidian and other tribes of Southern and Eastern India bore the livery of Aryan religion, Aryan language, and Aryan civilisation. This was the great work and result of the Rationalistic Period.

Baudhâyana lived probably in the sixth century before Christ, and was, as we have seen before, one of the earliest of the Sûtrakâras. In his time the zone of Hindu kingdoms and civilisation extended as far south as Kalinga or the eastern seaboard, stretching from modern Orissa southward to the mouth of the Krishnâ. The passage we refer to is interesting, because it shows that the ancient Aryan region along the Ganges and the Jumna was still regarded as the suitable home of the Aryans, while tracts of country in which the non-Aryan tribes had been recently Hinduised were looked upon with some degree of contempt.

"9. The country of the Âryas (Âryâvarta) lies to the east of the region where the River (Sarasvatî) disappears, to the west of the Black Forest (Kâlakavana), to the north of the Pâripâtra (Vindhya mountains), and to the south of the Himâlaya. The rule of conduct which prevails there is authoritative.

"10. Some declare the country between the Yamunâ and Gangâ (to be the Âryâvarta).

"11. Now the Bhâllavins quote also the following verse.

"12. In the west the boundary river, in the east the region where the sun rises, as far as the black antelopes wander, so far spiritual pre-eminence is found.

"13. The inhabitants of Avanti (Malwa), of Anga (East Behar), of Magadha (South Behar), of Saurâshtra (Gujrat), of the Deccan, of Upâvrit, of Sindh, and the Sauvîras (South Punjab) are of mixed origin.

"14. He who has visited the Ârattas (in the Punjab), Kâraskaras (in South India), Pundras (in North Bengal), Sauvîras (in the Punjab), Vangas (in Eastern Bengal), Kalingas (in Orissa), or Prânûnas shall offer a Punastoma or a Sarvaprishtha sacrifice" (*Baudhâyana*, I, 1, 2).

The passage is interesting, because it shows us the extent of the Hindu world in the early part of the Rationalistic Period, and also because it divides the Hindu world into three circles as it were, which were regarded with different degrees of esteem. Âryâvarta, stretching from the Sarasvatî to the confines of Behar, and from the Himâlayas to the Vindhyas, forms the first circle; and it is remarkable that the Punjab, which was the earliest home of the Aryans in the Vedic Age, is not included in this sacred circle. That realm had since then been backward in the later developments of Hindu religion and culture, and was rarely alluded to even in the literature of the Epic Period. The second circle, the people of which are said to be of mixed origin, includes Southern Punjab, Sindh, Gujrat, Malwa, the Deccan, and South and East Behar. If the reader refers to the fourth chapter of our last Book, he will find that these were the very regions which were becoming dimly known to the Hindus at the very close of the Epic Period. Early in the Rationalistic Age they had already become recognised as Hindu kingdoms, and Hindu influence and civilisation had travelled *beyond* these kingdoms to other regions which are included in the third circle. That third or last circle embraces the country of the Ârattas in the Punjab, some parts of Southern India, Eastern and Northern Bengal, and Orissa. A person travelling in these places had to expiate the sin by a sacrifice. This was the extreme limit of the Hindu world,—say in the sixth century before Christ.

That portions of Southern India had not only been colonised by this date, but had become the seats of Hindu kingdoms and of distinct schools of laws and learning, is proved by the writings of Baudhâyana. Baudhâyana himself may have been a southerner, at any rate he takes care to mention the peculiar laws and customs of Southern India. We will cite one passage:—

"1. There is a dispute regarding five practices, in the south and in the north.

"2. We will explain those peculiar to the south.

"3. They are to eat in the company of an uninitiated person, to eat in the company of one's wife, to eat stale food, *to marry the daughter of a maternal uncle or of a paternal aunt.**

"4. Now the customs peculiar to the north are, to deal in wool, to drink rum, to sell animals that have teeth in the upper and in the lower jaws, to follow the trade of arms, *and to go to sea.*†

"5. He who follows these practices in any other country than where they prevail commits sin.

"6. For each of these customs the rule of the country should be the authority.

"7. Gautama declares that that is false" (*Baudhâyana*, I, 1, 2).

Let us now take leave of Baudhâyana and come to the next Sûtrakâra of India. If Baudhâyana be supposed to have flourished in the sixth century before Christ, Âpastamba probably flourished in the fifth.‡ There can be little doubt that Âpastamba lived and taught in the Andhra country, and the limits of that great monarchy embraced all the districts between the Godâvarî and the Krishnâ. Dr. Bühler supposes that the capital of this southern empire was situated near modern Amarâ-

* Dr. Bühler points out that such marriages still prevail among the Desastha and Karhâda Brâhmans of the Deccan.

† Later degeneracy has fabricated a prohibition against going to sea for all Hindus.

‡ Dr. Bühler would on linguistic grounds place Âpastamba in the third century B.C., but on other grounds he would put back that Sûtrakâra by another 150 or 200 years, *i.e.*, to the fifth century B.C.

vatî on the lower Krishnâ. It was the Andhra text of the Taittirîya Âranyaka which Âpastamba recognised and followed, and his teachings are to this day held in regard by the Brâhmanas of Nasik, Puna, Ahmadabad, Satara, Sholapur, and Kolhapur, and other places in the Deccan who are Âpastambîyas.

Thus we find that the conquest of Southern India which was commenced at the close of the Epic Period went on through succeeding centuries; that by the sixth century, Bengal, Orissa, Gujrat, and the Deccan had been conquered and Aryanised; and that by the fifth century the Deccan as far south as the Krishnâ river was the seat of a powerful Hindu Empire. By the fourth century B.C., the whole of Southern India south of the Krishnâ river had been Hinduised, and three great Hindu kingdoms, those of the Cholas, the Cheras, and the Pândyas had been founded, stretching as far south as Cape Comorin; and Ceylon too had been discovered. And when we come towards the close of this (fourth) century, we issue now from the obscurity of isolated passages in the Sûtra works to the sunlight of Greek accounts of India! For it was in this century that Megasthenes, the ambassador of Seleucus, came to India and resided in the royal court of Chandragupta in Pâtaliputra (or ancient Patna) between 317 and 312 B.C.

The account of the races and kingdoms in India given by Megasthenes is full and intelligible, and gives us a clear idea of the state of the country at the close of the Rationalistic Period.

The Prâchyas, by which name we are now to understand the Magadhas, had become the most powerful and foremost nation in India in the fourth century B.C., as the Kurus, the Panchâlas, the Videhas and the Kosalas had been in the Epic Period. They had their capital at Pâtaliputra, a flourishing town described at 80 stadia or 9 miles long (a stadium = 202¼ yards) and 15 stadia or nearly 2 miles wide. It was of the shape of a parallelogram, girded with a wooden wall * pierced with loopholes for the discharge of arrows, and defended by a ditch in front.

It would seem that the whole of Northern India was now included in the powerful and extensive empire of Chandragupta, for the Jumna flowing through Mathura and Caresbora, was said to run through the kingdom of Pâtaliputra. The nation surpassed in power and glory every other people in India, and their king Chandragupta had a standing army of 600,000 foot soldiers, 30,000 cavalry, and 9000 elephants, "whence may be formed some conjecture as to the vastness of his resources."

Speaking of South Bengal, Megasthenes mentions the Calingœ living nearest the sea, the Mandu and the Malli living higher up, the Gangerides, near the mouths of the Ganges, and the Modo-Galingœ in an island in the Ganges. It is impossible not to recognise in the first and last of these names the ancient name of Kalinga, which included Orissa and the sea-coast of Bengal.

* The wooden wall was still standing in the fifth century after Christ, when the Chinese traveller Fa Hian saw it. Fa Hian writes: "The palaces of the king which are in the city have walls of which the stones have been collected by the genii. The carvings and the sculptures which ornament the windows are such as this age could not make; they still actually exist." The fall of Pâtaliputra was accomplished shortly after Fa Hian's time, for when Houen Tsang visited the place in the seventh century after Christ, he found nothing but ruins, and a village with two or three hundred houses. In an excavation made in 1876 for the construction of a public tank, some remains were discovered of what is supposed to have been the wooden wall spoken of by Megasthenes. In a part of Patna, half way between the railway station and the *chauk* or market-place, the excavators discovered, some twelve or fifteen feet below the surface, a long brick wall running from north-west to south-east. Parallel to this wall was found a line of palisades, the strong timber of which it was composed, being inclined slightly towards the wall. In one place there appeared to be an outlet or gate, two wooden pillars rising to a height of eight or nine feet, with no palisades between them. A number of wells were also found covered with fragments of broken mud vessels, and one of the wells being cleared yielded capital drinking water, while among the rubbish taken out were discovered several iron spear heads—See MacCrindle's *Megasthenes and Arrian*, p. 207, *note*.

Megasthenes describes Parthalis as the capital of the Calingœ. The powerful king of this place had 60,000 foot soldiers, 1000 horse, and 700 elephants. A large island in the Ganges is said to have been inhabited by the Modo-Galingœ (Madhya-Kalinga), and beyond them several powerful tribes lived under a king who had 50,000 foot soldiers, 4000 cavalry, and 400 elephants. Beyond them again lived the Andarœ, in whom it is impossible not to recognise the Andhras of Southern India. The Andhras were a great and powerful nation who had settled originally between the Godâvarî and the Krishnâ, but who before the time of Megasthenes had extended their kingdom as far north as the Narmadâ. Megasthenes writes that they were a powerful race, possessed numerous villages and thirty walled towns, and supplied their king with 100,000 infantry, 2000 cavalry, and 1000 elephants.

In the extreme North-West, Megasthenes speaks of the Isari, the Cosyri, and other tribes located probably in Kashmir or its neighbourhood. The Indus is said to skirt the frontiers of the Prâchyas, by which we understand that the powerful and extensive empire of Magadha extended as far as the frontiers of the Punjab, and embraced all Northern India.

A great portion of modern Rajputana was still the home of aboriginal tribes in the time of Megasthenes, of men who lived in woods, among tigers noted for their ferocity. He speaks of the tribes who lived in the fertile tracts surrounded by deserts, and of tribes who inhabited the hills, which ran in an unbroken chain parallel to the shores of the ocean. He also speaks of the tribes who lived enclosed by the loftiest mountain, Capitalia, which has been identified with Abu. He speaks further on of the Horatœ, who were undoubtedly the Saurâshtras. They had a capital on the coast, which was a noble emporium of trade, and their king was the master of 1600 elephants, 150,000 foot, and 5000 horse.

"Next come the Pandœ, the only race in India ruled by women. They say that Hercules having but one daughter, who was on that account all the more beloved, endowed her with a noble kingdom. Her descendants rule over 300 cities and command an army of 150,000 foot and 500 elephants."

Such is the half mythical account which Megasthenes gives us of the Pândyas, who were the ruling nation in the extreme south of India. These Pândyas have a history which is remarkable.

The Yâdavas, who under the leadership of Krishna left Mathurâ and settled in Dwârkâ in Gujrat, did not flourish there long. They fell fighting among themselves, and the remainder left Dwârkâ by sea. It is believed that they came to Southern India, where they founded a new kingdom. They called themselves Pândyas probably because they pretended to be of the same race with the Pândavas, and they named their new southern capital Mathurâ or Madura, as the town is called to the present day. Megasthenes no doubt refers to Krishna under the name of Hercules, and he probably heard some legend, which was then current in India, about the foundation of the southern kingdom by Krishna for his daughter.

And lastly, the Island of Ceylon too was known in the time of Megasthenes. It was conquered by Vijaya, a prince of Magadha who had been exiled by his father for his misdeeds in the fifth century before Christ. When Megasthenes came to India, Ceylon was already a Hindu kingdom. The island was called Taprobanê by the Greeks, the name being slightly altered from the Pali name Tambapannî, which corresponds to the Sanscrit Tâmraparni or the copper-leaved. Megasthenes says that the island was separated from the mainland by a river, and that the country was productive of gold and large pearls, and elephants much larger than the Indian breeds. Ælian who wrote long after Megasthenes, but like most other Greek and Roman writers got much of his information about India from the account of Megasthenes, says that Taprobanê was a large mountainous island full of palm groves, that the inhabitants dwelt in huts of reeds, and transported their elephants in boats which they constructed for the purpose, and sold them to the king of Kalingai.

We have surveyed the political results of the seven centuries included in the Rationalistic Period, as we surveyed the literary results in the last chapter. Within this period Hindu colonists issued in bands from the Gangetic valley, came to strange lands, conquered strange nations, and gradually imposed upon them their language, their religion, and their civilisation. The Magadhas of South Behar were not only Hinduised, but became the foremost nation in India. The Saurâshtras of Gujrat and the Angas, the Vangas, and the Kalingas of the east were Hinduised. The great Andhra tribe not only accepted Hindu religion and civilisation, but distinguished itself by schools of Hindu learning rivalling the great schools of the Gangetic valley. Further down, other nations accepted the superior civilisation, religion, and language of the Aryans; and all India, Aryan and non-Aryan, wore the mantle of Hindu-Aryan civilisation.

CHAPTER III.

ADMINISTRATION, AGRICULTURE, AND ARTS.

AN account of the system of administration which prevailed in India over two thousand years ago will naturally interest our readers, and fortunately, both Hindu Sûtrakâras and Greek writers furnish us with reliable information on the subject. We will begin our account with some extracts from Sûtra works. The king is directed to build a royal town, and a palace for himself, looking towards the south :—

"3. The palace shall stand in the heart of the town.

"4. In front of that there shall be a hall. That is called the hall of invitation.

"5. At a little distance from the town to the south he shall cause to be built an assembly house with doors on the south and on the north sides, so that one can see what passes inside and outside."

Fires shall burn constantly and oblations shall be offered in these fires, and—

"8. In the hall he shall put up his guests, at least those who are learnt in the Vedas.

"9. Rooms, a couch, meat and drink should be given to them according to their good qualities."

A table with dice should also be provided, and Brâhmans, Vaisyas, and Sûdras may be allowed to play there. Assaults of arms, dancing, singing and music are allowed in the houses of the king's servants; and the king shall constantly take care of his subjects :—

"15. That king only takes care of the welfare of his

subjects in whose dominions, be it in villages or forests, there is no danger from thieves" (*Âpastamba*, II, 10, 25).

Vasishtha thus details the duties of the king :—

"1. The particular duty of a king is to protect all beings ; by fulfilling it he obtains success.

"3. Let him appoint a domestic priest to perform the rites obligatory on the order of householders.

"8. Let him punish those who stray from the path of duty.

"11. Let him not injure trees that bear fruit and flowers.

"12. He may injure them in order to extend cultivation.

"13. The measures and weights of objects necessary for households must be guarded (against falsification).

"14. Let him not take property for his own use from the inhabitants of his realm.

"15. The measures and price of such property shall only be liable to deductions in the shape of taxes" (*Vasishtha*, XIV).

Vasishtha (I, 42) and Baudhâyana (I, 10, 18, 1) declare that the king is entitled to a sixth portion of the income of his subjects as taxes, but exempt many classes who are unable to pay. Gautama details the taxes thus :—

"24. Cultivators pay to the king a tax amounting to one-tenth, one-eighth, or one-sixth (of the produce).

"25. Some declare that the tax on cattle and gold amounts to one-fiftieth (of the stock).

"26. In the case of merchandise one-twentieth (must be paid by the seller) as duty.

"27. Of roots, fruits, flowers, medicinal herbs, honey, meat, grass, and firewood, one-sixtieth.

"31. Each artisan shall monthly do one day's work (for the king).

"32. Hereby the taxes payable by those who support themselves by personal labour have been explained.

"33. And those payable by owners of ships and carts.

"34. He must feed these persons while they work for him" (*Gautama*, X).

Megasthenes gives us a valuable account of the manner in which the work of administration was actually carried on, and the following passages will be read with interest:—

"Those who have charge of the city are divided into six bodies of five each. The members of the first look after everything relating to the industrial arts. Those of the second attend to the entertainment of foreigners. To these they assign lodgings, and they keep watch over their modes of life by means of those persons whom they give to them for assistants. They escort them on the way when they leave the country, or in the event of their dying, forward their property to their relatives. They take care of them when they are sick, and if they die bury them. The third body consists of those who inquire when and how births and deaths occur, with the view not only of levying a tax, but also in order that births and deaths among both high and low may not escape the cognisance of Government. The fourth class superintends trade and commerce. Its members have charge of weights and measures, and see that the products in their season are sold by public notice. No one is allowed to deal in more than one kind of commodity unless he pays a double tax. The fifth class supervises manufactured articles, which they sell by public notice. What is new is sold separately from what is old, and there is a fine for mixing the two together. The sixth and last class consists of those who collect the tenths of the prices of the articles sold."

The military officers "also consist of six divisions with five members to each. One division is appointed to co-operate with the Admiral of the fleet; another with the Superintendent of the bullock trains which are used for transporting engines of war, food for the soldiers, provender for the cattle, and other military requisites. . . .

The third division has charge of the foot soldiers, the fourth of the horses, the fifth of the war chariots, and the sixth of the elephants."

Besides the municipal officers and military officers, there was yet a third class of officers who superintended agriculture, irrigation, forests, and generally the work of administration in rural tracts. "Some superintend the rivers, measure the land as is done in Egypt, and inspect the sluices by which water is let out from the main canals into their branches, so that every one may have an equal supply of it. The same persons have charge also of the huntsmen, and are entrusted with the power of rewarding or punishing them according to their deserts. They collect the taxes, and superintend the occupations connected with land as those of the woodcutters, the carpenters, the blacksmiths, and the miners. They construct roads, and at every ten stadia set up a pillar to show the by-roads and distances" (*MacCrindle's Translation*).

Of the personal habits and occupations of kings, Megasthenes has given us a picture which agrees in the main with the picture given in Sanscrit literature. The care of the king's person was entrusted to female slaves, who were bought from their parents, and the guards and the rest of the soldiery were stationed outside the gates. The king attended the court every day, and remained there during the day without allowing the business to be interrupted. The only other occasions on which he left the palace were when he performed sacrifices or went out for the chase. Crowds of women surrounded him when he went out for the chase, and outside this circle the spearmen were ranged. Armed women attended the king in chariots, on horses, or on elephants, when he hunted in the open grounds from the back of an elephant. Sometimes he shot arrows from a platform inside an enclosure, and two or three armed women stood by him on the platform. These accounts show that the sturdy and warlike manners of the Kurus and the Panchâlas of the Epic Age had already been replaced by more luxurious and effeminate habits in the Rationalistic Age. The age of chivalry had gone, and that of luxury had come!

Arrian gives an account of the mode in which the Hindus equipped themselves for war:—"The foot soldiers carry a bow made of equal length with the man who bears it. This they rest upon the ground, and pressing against it with their left foot, thus discharge the arrow, having drawn the string far backwards: for the shaft they use is little short of being three yards long, and there is nothing which can resist an Indian archer's shot,—neither shield nor breastplate, nor any stronger defence, if such there be. In their left hand they carry bucklers made of undressed ox-hide, which are not so broad as those who carry them, but are about as long. Some are equipped with javelins instead of bows, but wear a sword, which is broad in the blade, but not longer than three cubits; and this, when they engage in close fight (which they do with reluctance), they wield with both hands to fetch down a lustier blow. The horsemen are equipped with two lances like the lances called *Saunia*, and with a shorter buckler than that carried by the foot soldiers. For they do not put saddles on their horses; nor do they curb them with bits in use among the Greeks or the Kelts, but they fit on round the extremity of the horse's mouth a circular piece of stitched raw ox-hide studded with pricks of iron or brass pointing inwards, but not very sharp; if a man is rich he uses pricks made of ivory" (*MacCrindle's Translation*).

The laws of war were more humane among the Hindus than among other nations in the world. "The Aryans forbid the slaughter of those who have laid down their arms, of those who beg for mercy with flying hair or joined hands, and of fugitives" (*Âpastamba*, II, 5, 10, 11). "Let him not fight with those who are in fear, intoxicated, insane, or out of their minds, nor with those who have lost their armour, nor with women, infants, aged men, and Brahmans" (*Baudhâyana*, I, 10, 18, 11). "The wives (of slain soldiers) shall be provided for" (*Vasishtha*, XIX, 20). And Megasthenes too vouches for the humane laws of war among the Hindus. "For whereas among other nations it is usual in the contests of war to ravage the soil, and thus to reduce it to an uncultivated waste, among the Indians, on the contrary, by whom husbandmen are regarded as a class that is sacred and inviolable, the tillers of the soil, even when battle is raging in their neighbourhood, are undisturbed by any sense of danger; for the combatants on either side, in waging the conflict, make carnage of each other, but allow those engaged in husbandry to remain quite unmolested. Besides, they neither ravage an enemy's land with fire, nor cut down its trees."

Megasthenes tells us that the Indian tribes numbered 118 in all. On the north of India, and beyond the Himâlaya, the country "is inhabited by those Scythians who are called the Sakai." Such is the brief mention made of that powerful tribe which hung like an ominous cloud on the northern slopes of the Himâlaya in the fourth century before Christ, but which in course of a few centuries burst like a hurricane on the plains of Western India, and convulsed and shattered Hindu kingdoms.

Of the peaceful and law-abiding people in India, Megasthenes gives an account which every Hindu will read with legitimate pride:—"They live happily enough, being simple in their manners and frugal. They never drink wine, except at sacrifices. Their beverage is a liquor composed from rice instead of barley, and their food is principally a rice pottage. The simplicity of their laws and their contracts is proved by the fact that they seldom go to law. They have no suits about pledges and deposits, nor do they require either seals or witnesses, but make their deposits and confide in each other. Their houses and property they generally leave unguarded. These things indicate that they possess sober sense. . . . Truth and virtue they hold alike in esteem. Hence they accord no special privileges to the old unless they possess superior wisdom."

Megasthenes further states that the Indians did "not even use aliens as slaves, and much less a countryman of their own," that thefts were very rare among them, that their laws were administered from memory, and even that they were ignorant of the art of writing. We have the evidence of Nearchos that writing *was* known in India in the Rationalistic Period, and the statement of Megasthenes only shows that writing was in very little use, either in schools where boys received their learning and their religious lessons by rote, or even in Courts of Justice where laws, *i.e.*, the Dharma Sûtras, were administered by learned Judges entirely from memory.

Arrian quotes a passage from Nearchos, and says that the Indians "wear an under-garment of cotton which reaches below the knee half way down to the ankles, and also an upper garment which they throw partly over their shoulders and partly twist in folds round their head. . . . They wear shoes made of white leather, and these are elaborately trimmed, while the soles are variegated, and made of great thickness." And the great mass of the "people of India live upon grain and are tillers of the soil, but we must except the hillmen, who eat the flesh of beasts of chase."

Our faithful guide Megasthenes also gives us an account of cultivation in Ancient India which, on the whole, corresponds with the system of cultivation prevalent at the present time. Megasthenes speaks of a double rainfall in the year, considering the winter showers as a regular rainfall. He speaks of "many vast plains of great fertility, more or less beautiful, but all alike intersected by a multitude of rivers. *The greater part of the soil moreover is under irrigation,* and consequently bears two crops in the course of the year. It teems at the same time with animals of all sorts, beasts of the field and fowls of the air, of all different degrees of strength and size. It is prolific, besides, in elephants which are of monstrous bulk. . . . In addition to cereals, there grows throughout India much millet, which is kept well watered by the profusion of river streams, and much pulse of different sorts, and rice also, and what is called *bosporum,* as well as many other plants useful for food, of which most grow spontaneously. The soil yields, moreover, not a few other edible products fit for the subsistence of animals about which it would be tedious to write. It is accordingly affirmed that *famine has never visited India, and that there has never been a general scarcity in the supply of nourishing food.* For since there is a double rainfall in the course of each year,—one in the winter season, when the sowing of wheat takes place as in other countries, and the second at the time of the summer solstice, which is the proper season for sowing rice and *bosporum,* as well as sesamum and millet,—the inhabitants of India almost always gather in two harvests annually; and even should one of the sowings prove more or less abortive, they are always sure of the other crop. The fruits moreover of spontaneous growth, and the esculent roots which grow in marshy places and are of varied sweetness, afford abundant sustenance for man."

It is impossible for a Hindu in the modern day to read without a feeling of pride this impartial testimony of an intelligent and observant foreigner regarding the prosperous condition of India as administered by Hindus over two thousand years ago. An industrious and peaceful peasantry peopled the fair villages, and cultivated and irrigated, carefully and laboriously, the endless expanse of fertile fields, while the artisans in towns carried the various manufactures and arts of peace to a high state of excellence. It is impossible to suppose that these results were achieved without a careful and watchful system of administration, without a fair degree of security of life and property, and without the help of laws which were on the whole just and fair. And even when kings fell out among themselves, and riotous Kshatriya chiefs were engaged in their frequent wars, a humane custom, unknown elsewhere in the ancient world, mitigated the horrors of war, and saved the peaceful villagers and industrious cultivators from disturbance and danger.

The excellent manufactures of India were known to the traders of Phœnicia and in the markets of Western Asia and Egypt long before the Christian era. Megasthenes naïvely says that the Indians were "well skilled in the arts, as might be expected of men who inhale a pure air and drink the very finest water." The soil, too, has "under ground numerous veins of all sorts of metals, for it contains much gold and silver, and copper and iron in no small quantity, and even tin and other metals, which are employed in making articles of use and ornament, as well as the implements and accoutrements of war."

With regard to finery and ornament, Megasthenes says that "in contrast to the general simplicity of their style, they love finery and ornament. Their robes are worked in gold and ornamented with precious stones, and they wear also flowered garments made of the finest muslin. Attendants walking behind hold up umbrellas over them: for they have a high regard for beauty, and avail themselves of every device to improve their looks."

More striking, however, is a passage in which Strabo describes a gorgeous procession, such as Megasthenes must have seen paraded in the streets of Pâtaliputra:—

"In processions at their festivals, many elephants are in the train, adorned with gold and silver; numerous carriages drawn by four horses and several pairs of oxen; then follows a body of attendants in full dress (bearing) vessels of gold, large basins and goblets an *orguia* in breadth, tables, chairs of state, drinking cups and lavers of Indian copper, most of which are set with precious stones, as emeralds, beryls, and Indian carbuncles; garments embroidered and interwoven with gold; wild beasts, as buffaloes, panthers, tame lions, and a multitude of birds of variegated plumage and of fine song" (*Bohn's Translation of Strabo*, III, p. 117).

CHAPTER IV.

LAWS.

THE equality of laws between the conquerors and the conquered, between priests and laymen, has not been known in the world's past history. There was not the same law in the past ages for the Greek and the Helot, the Patrician and the Plebeian, the baron and the serf, the monk and the layman, the white man and the negro, or the white man and the red man. And as in other parts of the world, so in India too, we find inequality in laws among the different classes of the people. There was one law for the Brâhman, another for the Sûdra; the former was treated with undue leniency, the latter with excessive and cruel severity. If a Brâhman committed one of the four or five heinous crimes enumerated in the law-books, *i.e.*, if he slew a Brâhman, violated his guru's bed, stole the gold of a Brâhman, or drank spirituous liquor, the king branded him on the forehead with a heated iron and banished him from his realm. If a man of a lower caste slew a Brâhman, be was punished with death and the confiscation of his property. If such a man slew a man of equal or lower caste, other suitable punishments were meted out to him (*Baudhâyana*, I, 10, 18 and 19).

Adultery has always been looked upon in India not only as a criminal offence, but as an offence of a heinous nature; but the punishment for this offence also was regulated by the caste of the offender. A man of the first three castes who committed adultery with a Sûdra woman was banished; but a Sûdra who committed adultery with a woman of the first three castes suffered capital punishment (*Âpastamba*, II, 10, 27).

Indeed Brâhman legislators have painted themselves worse than they really were. In order to point out the vast distinction between themselves and the Sûdras, they prescribed monstrous punishments for insolent Sûdras, which, it is safe to assert, always remained an empty threat, and were meant as a threat only. The tongue of a Sûdra who spoke evil of a virtuous person belonging to one of the first three castes was to be cut out, and a Sûdra who assumed an equal position with those castes was to be flogged (*Âpastamba*, II, 10, 27). Similarly we are told that a Sûdra who reviled a twice-born man or assaulted him with blows should lose the limb with which he offended; that if he listened to a recitation of the Veda, his ears should be stopped with molten lac or tin; that if he recited the Veda, his tongue should be cut out; and if he remembered Vedic texts, his body should be split in twain! (*Gautama*, XII). The reader will easily perceive, that the Brâhman composers of the Sûtras were anxious to emphasise the distinction between themselves and the other castes and specially Sûdras, and have therefore represented the laws as ten times more iniquitous than they were as actually administered by sensible kings and Kshatriya officers, or even by Brâhman judges.

A Kshatriya abusing a Brâhman pays 100 kârshâpanas, and beating a Brâhman pays 200 kârshâpanas. A Vaisya abusing a Brâhman pays 150 kârshâpanas, and we suppose pays 300 for beating him. But a Brâhman pays only 50 kârshâpanas for abusing a Kshatriya, 25 for abusing a Vaisya, and for abusing a Sûdra,—nothing! (*Gautama*, XII, 8–13).

Death or corporal punishment seems to have been the punishment for theft at least in some cases; and the thief is directed to appear before the king with flying hair, holding a club in his hand, and proclaiming his deed. If the king pardons him and does not slay him or strike him, the guilt falls on the king (*Gautama*, XII, 45). The prerogative of mercy was the king's alone, but a guru, a priest, a learned householder or a prince could intercede for an offender, except in the case of a capital offence (*Âpastamba*, II, 10, 27, 20).

Vasishtha reserves the right of self-defence in the case of a person attacked by an Âtatâyin, and that term includes an incendiary, a poisoner, one ready to kill with a weapon in his hand, a robber, a man who takes away another's land, or abducts another's wife. A man may slay an Âtatâyin who comes to slay, even if the latter "knows the whole of the Veda, together with the Upanishads" (*Vasishtha*, III, 15–18).

Agriculture and trade were the means of the people's subsistence, and crimes relating to a cultivator's land or to an artisan's trade were punished with the utmost severity. We have seen that defence of land was one of the cases in which the right of self-defence was allowed, and false evidence given about land was looked upon with the utmost detestation. By giving false evidence concerning small cattle, a witness commits the sin of killing ten men; by false evidence concerning cows, horses, and men, he commits the sin of killing a hundred, a thousand, and ten thousand men respectively; but by false evidence concerning land, he commits the sin of killing the whole human race. "Hell is the punishment for a theft of land" (*Gautama*, XIII, 14–17). Similarly, with regard to artisans, Megasthenes informs us that he who caused an artisan to lose his eye or his hand was punished with death.

A severe penance is ordained for the man who attempts suicide, and the relations of a suicide are prohibited from performing funeral rites for him (*Vasishtha*, XXIII, 14, &c.).

Such was the Criminal Law of the Hindus over two thousand years ago. We now turn to the more complicated subject of Civil Law, which may be conveniently treated under five heads, viz., (1) Law of Agriculture and Pasture, (2) Law of Property, (3) Usury Laws, (4) the all-important Law of Inheritance, and (5) the Law of Partition. We begin with the Law of Agriculture and Pasture:—

"1. If a person who has taken a lease of land does not exert himself, and hence the land bears no crop, he shall, if he be rich, be made to pay the value of the crop that ought to have been grown.

"2. A servant in tillage who abandons his work shall be flogged.

"3. The same punishment shall be awarded to a herdsman who leaves his work.

"4. And the flock entrusted to him shall be taken away.

"5. If cattle, leaving their stable, eat crops, the owner of the crops may make them lean (by impounding them); but shall not exceed.

"6. If a herdsman who has taken cattle under his care, allows them to perish or loses them, he shall replace them to the owners.

"7. If (the king's forester) sees cattle that have been sent into the forest through negligence, he shall lead them back to the village and make them over to the owners" (*Ápastamba*, II, 11, 28).

Again, Gautama says:—

"19. If damage is done by cattle, the responsibility falls on the owner.

"20. But if the cattle were attended by a herdsman, it falls on the latter.

"21. If the damage was done in an unenclosed field near the road, the responsibility falls on the herdsman and on the owner of the field" (*Gautama*, XII).

As in the present day, unenclosed fields were used as common property for grazing cattle and for obtaining firewood.

"He may take, as his own, grass for a cow, and fuel

for his fire, as well as the flowers of creepers and trees, and their fruit if they be unenclosed" (*Gautama*, XII, 28).

Some equitable provisions are laid down by Vasishtha about the right of way, and about the evidence necessary in disputes about immovable property.

"10. It is declared in the Smriti that there are three kinds of proof which give a title to property, viz., documents, witnesses, and possession; thereby an owner may recover property which formerly belonged to him.

"11. From fields through which there is a right of way, a space sufficient for the road must be set apart, likewise a space for turning a cart.

"12. Near new-built houses and other things of the same description, there shall be a passage three feet broad.

"13. In a dispute about a house or a field, reliance must be placed on the depositions of neighbours.

"14. If the statements of the neighbours disagree, documents may be taken as proof.

"15. If conflicting documents are produced, reliance must be placed on the statements of aged inhabitants of the village or town, and on those of guilds and corporations of artisans or traders" (*Vasishtha*, XVI).

And this brings us to the Law of Property. Property is divided into eight classes, thus:—

"16. Now they quote also the following verse: 'Property inherited from a father, a thing bought, a pledge, property given to a wife after marriage by her husband's family, a gift, property obtained for performing a sacrifice, the property of re-united co-partners, and wages as the eighth.'

"17. Whatever belonging to these eight kinds of property has been enjoyed by another person for ten years continuously is lost to the owner.

"18. They quote also a verse on the other side: 'A pledge, a boundary, and the property of minors, an (open) deposit, a sealed deposit, women, the property of a king, and the wealth of a Srotriya, are not lost by being enjoyed by others.'

"19. Property entirely given up by its owner goes to the king" (*Vasishtha*, XVI).

Gautama has similar rules :—

"37. The property of a person who is neither an idiot nor a minor, having been used by strangers before his eyes for ten years, belongs to him who uses it.

"38. But not if it is used by Srotriyas, ascetics, or royal officials.

"39. Animals, land, and females are not lost to the owner by another's possession" (*Gautama*, XII).

Women and females in the above extracts mean female slaves. With regard to minors, widows, &c., there are provisions to the effect that the king shall administer their property and shall restore it in the case of a minor when he comes of age (*Vasishtha*, XVI, 8 and 9).

We next turn to the important Usury Laws of Ancient India, and many of our readers will admit that they compare not unfavourably with usury laws which prevailed in Europe only a few centuries ago.

"Hear the interest for a money-lender declared by the words of Vasishtha: Five *Mâshâs* for twenty (*Kârshâpanas*) may be taken every month; thus the law is not violated" (*Vasishtha*, II, 51).

Similarly Gautama declares (XII, 29):—

"The legal interest for money lent is at the rate of five *Mâshâs* a month for twenty (*Kârshâpanas*)."

The commentator Hara Datta reckons 20 mâshâs to the kârshâpana, so that the rate of interest comes to $1\frac{1}{4}$ per cent. per month, or 15 per cent. per annum. Krishna Pandita correctly states that this rate of interest applies to loans for which security is given. Manu specially mentions (VIII, 140) that this rate is prescribed by Vasishtha. Gautama says that after the principal has been doubled, interest ceases, and when the object pledged is an object used by the creditor, the money lent bears no interest at all (XII, 31 and 32).

Other articles might be lent at a much higher percentage of interest, apparently when no security was given.

"44. Gold may be lent, taking double its value on repayment, and grain trebling the original price.

"45. The case of flavouring substances has been explained by the rule regarding grain.

"46. As well as the case of flowers, roots, and fruit.

"47. He may lend what is sold by weight, taking eight times the original value on repayment."

Similarly Gautama says:—

"The interest on products of animals, on wool, on the produce of a field, and on beasts of burden, shall not increase more than five-fold the value of the object lent" (*Gautama*, XII, 36).

Thus apart from the loan of money on security, articles and products were lent, apparently without security, at an enormous rate of interest. In the former case the interest was only 15 per cent., and the principal could only be doubled; in the latter case it could increase six or eight-fold.

Gautama names no less than six different forms of interest, viz., compound interest, periodical interest, stipulated interest, corporal interest, daily interest, and the use of a pledge (XII, 34 and 35). He lays down that the heirs shall pay the debts of a deceased person, but provides that money due by a surety, a commercial debt, a fee due to the parents of the bride, immoral debts, and fines shall not devolve on the sons of the debtor (XII, 40 and 41).

And this brings us to the most important portion of the Civil Law, viz., the Law of Inheritance.

To leave male issue was considered a religious duty by the ancient Hindus, and in the absence of a legitimate son, therefore, other kinds of sons seem to have been recognised in ancient times.

In the following passage Gautama indicates the different kinds of sons who were considered by him to be heirs, and those who were not heirs, but only members of the family :—

"32. A legitimate son (*Aurasa*), a son begotten on the wife (*Kshetraja*), an adopted son (*Datta*), a son made (*Kritrima*), a son born secretly (*Gûdhaja*), and a son abandoned (*Apaviddha*), inherit the estate.

"33. The son of an unmarried damsel (*Kânîna*), the son of a pregnant bride (*Sahodha*), the son of a twice-married woman (*Paunarbhava*), the son of an appointed daughter (*Putrikâputra*), a son self-given (*Svayam-datta*), and a son bought (*Krîta*), belong to the family" (XXVIII).

Baudhâyana and Vasishtha lived long after Gautama, and their opinions varied from that of Gautama as well as from each other in some respects.

"14. One must know a son begotten by the husband himself on a wedded wife of equal caste to be a legitimate son of the body (*Aurasa*). . . .

"15. The male child born of a daughter after an agreement has been made is the son of an appointed daughter (*Putrikâputra*). . . .

"17. He who is begotten by another man on the wife of a deceased man, of a eunuch, or of one diseased, after permission, is called the son begotten on a wife (*Kshetraja*).

"20. He is called an adopted son (*Datta*) who, being given by his father and his mother, or by either of the two, is received in the place of a child.

"21. He is called a son made (*Kritrima*) whom a man himself makes his son with the (adoptee's) consent only, and who belongs to the same caste.

"22. He is called a son born secretly (*Gûdhaja*) who is secretly born in the house, and whose origin is afterwards recognised.

"23. He is called a son cast off (*Apaviddha*) who,

being cast off by his father and his mother, or by either, is received in the place of a child.

"24. If anybody approaches an unmarried girl without the permission (of her father or guardian), the son born by such a woman is called the son of an unmarried damsel (*Kânîna*).

"25. If one marries either knowingly or unknowingly a pregnant bride, the child which is born of her is called a son taken with the bride (*Sahodha*).

"26. He is called a son bought (*Krîta*) who, being purchased from his father and his mother, or from either of them, is received in the place of a child.

"27. He is called the son of a twice-married woman (*Paunarbhava*) who is born of a remarried female, *i.e.*, of one who, having left an impotent man, has taken a second husband.

"28. He is called a self-given son (*Svayamdatta*) who, abandoned by his father and his mother, gives himself to a stranger.

"29. He who is begotten by a man of the first twice-born caste, on a female of the Sûdra caste, is called a *Nishâda*.

"30. He who is begotten by the same parents through lust is called a *Pârasava*. . . ." (*Baudhâyana*, II, 2, 3).

Baudhâyana then quotes verses which declare that of the fourteen kinds of sons enumerated above, the first-named seven, *i.e.*, the Aurasa, the Putrikâputra, the Kshetraja, the Datta, the Kritrima, the Gûdhaja, and the Apaviddha, were entitled to share the inheritance. The next six, *i.e.*, the Kânîna, the Sahodha, the Krîta, the Paunarbhava, the Svayamdatta, and the Nishâda, were considered members of the family. The Pârasava was not even considered a member of the family.

Vasishtha enumerates twelve kinds of sons like Gautama.

"12. Twelve kinds of sons only are noticed by the ancients.

"13. The first is begotten by the husband himself on his legally married wife (*Aurasa*).

"14. The second is the son begotten on a wife (or widow—*Kshetraja*), duly authorised thereto on the failure of the first kind of sons.

"15. The third is an appointed daughter (*Putrikâ-putra*).

"16. It is declared in the Veda, 'a maiden who has no brothers comes back to the male ancestors (of her own family); *returning she becomes their son*.'*

"17. With reference to this, a verse (to be spoken by the father when appointing his daughter), 'I shall give thee a brotherless damsel, decked with ornaments, the son whom she may bear, shall be my son.'

"18. The fourth is the son of a remarried widow (*Paunarbhava*).

"19. She is called remarried (*Punarbhû*) who, leaving the husband of her youth, and having lived with others, re-enters his family.

"20. And she is called remarried who, *leaving an impotent, outcast, or mad husband, or after the death of her husband, takes another lord.*†

"21. The fifth is the son of an unmarried damsel (*Kânîna*).

"24. A male child secretly born in the house is the sixth (*Gûdhaja*).

"25. They declare that *these six are heirs and kinsmen*, preservers from a great danger.

* "The curious fact that Vasishtha here calls the appointed daughter a son may perhaps be explained by a custom which, though rarely practised, still occurs in Kashmir, and by which a brotherless maiden is given a male name. A historical instance of this kind is mentioned in the Râjataranginî, where it is stated that Kalyânadevî, princess of Gauda and wife of King Jayâpîda, was called by her father Kalyânamalla."—*Dr. Bühler.*

† The circumstances which allowed the second marriage of a woman have been enumerated in this verse. They are insanity, impotency, loss of caste, or death of her husband. The son of a woman thus remarried a second time is allowed by Vasishtha to inherit.

"26. Now among those sons *who are not heirs but kinsmen*, the first is he who is received with a pregnant bride (*Sahodha*).

"28. The second is the adopted son (*Datta*).

"30. The son bought (*Krîta*) is the third.

"33. The fourth is the son self-given (*Svayamdatta*).

"36. The son cast off is the fifth (*Apaviddha*).

"38. They declare that the son of a woman of the Sûdra caste (*Nishâda*) is the sixth. . . ." (*Vasishtha*, XVII).

The last-named six kinds of sons cannot inherit according to Vasishtha, but he quotes a verse that they shall be allowed "to take the heritage of him who has no heir belonging to the first-mentioned six classes."

The rules of Gautama, Vasishtha, and Baudhâyana may be thus shown in parallel columns :—

	GAUTAMA.	VASISHTHA.	BAUDHÂYANA.
Kinsmen and heirs.	1. Aurasa.	1. Aurasa.	1. Aurasa.
	2. Kshetraja.	2. Kshetraja.	2. Putrikâputra.
	3. Datta.	3. Putrikâputra.	3. Kshetraja.
	4. Kritrima.	4. Paunarbhava.	4. Datta.
	5. Gûdhaja.	5. Kânîna.	5. Kritrima.
	6. Apaviddha.	6. Gûdhaja.	6. Gûdhaja.
			7. Apaviddha.
Kinsmen not heirs.	7. Kânîna.	7. Sahodha.	8. Kânîna.
	8. Sahodha.	8. Datta.	9. Sahodha.
	9. Paunarbhava.	9. Krîta.	10. Krîta.
	10. Putrikâputra.	10. Svayamdatta.	11. Paunarbhava.
	11. Svayamdatta.	11. Apaviddha.	12. Svayamdatta.
	12. Krîta.	12. Nishâda.	13. Nishâda.
Neither kinsmen nor heirs.	,, ,,	,, ,,	14. Pârasava.

But a reaction appears to have set in early against the recognition of sons legitimate and illegitimate,—even to escape the torments of hell after death! Âpastamba, who lived a century or more after Baudhâyana, protests against the recognition of heirs and sons of various kinds, and explains away ancient customs by stating that what had been allowed in ancient times could not be permitted among the sinful men of the present time.

"1. Sons begotten by a man who approaches in the proper season a woman of equal caste, who has not belonged to another man, and who has been married legally, have a right to follow the occupations (of their castes).

"2. And to inherit the estate.

"8. Transgression of the law and violence are found among the ancients.

"9. They committed no sin on account of the greatness of their lustre.

"10. A man of later times who, seeing their deeds, follows them, falls.

"11. The gift (or acceptance of a child) and the right to sell (or buy) a child are not recognised" (*Âpastamba*, II, 6., 13).

Elsewhere Âpastamba says:—

"2. (A husband) shall not make over his (wife), who occupies the position of a 'gentilis,' to others than to his 'gentiles' in order to cause children to be begot for himself.

"3. For they declare that a bride is given to the family.

"4. That is (at present) forbidden on account of the weakness of men's senses.

"5. The hand of a 'gentilis' is considered in law to be that of a stranger, as well as that of any other person except the husband.

"6. If the marriage vow is transgressed, both husband and wife certainly go to hell" (*Âpastamba*, II, 10, 27).

Thus Âpastamba makes a clear sweep not only of Niyoga or appointment of a wife to raise issue, but also of the adoption or the buying of a son. Modern Hindus recognise no kinds of sons except legitimate sons, and sons adopted in the absence of legitimate issue.

Lastly, we come to the subject of the Law of Partition. There is the same dissimilarity of opinion in respect of the partition of property among brothers. The law of primogeniture never obtained in India, but so long as the joint family system remained in vogue, the property of the father was inherited by the eldest son, who supported the rest as a father. It would seem, however, that to live in a joint family under the eldest brother was never the universal custom in India, and even Gautama, the earliest of the Sûtrakâras whose works are extant, considers a partition among brothers preferable, for "in partition there is an increase of spiritual merit" (XXVIII, 4).

According to Gautama, the eldest son gets as an additional share a twentieth part of the estate, some animals, and a carriage; the middlemost sons gets some poor animals, and the youngest get sheep, grain, utensils, a house, a cart, and some animals; and then the remaining property is equally divided. Or he would allow the eldest two shares, and the remaining sons one share each; or he would allow them each to take one kind of property by choice according to seniority; or the special shares may be adjusted according to their mothers (XXVIII, 5–17).

Vasishtha allows the eldest brother to take a double share and a little of the kine and horses; he allows the youngest to take the goats, sheep, and house; while the middlemost gets utensils and furniture. And if a Brâhman has sons by Brâhman, Kshatriya, and Vaisya wives, the first gets three shares, the second two shares, and the third, *i.e.*, the son by the Vaisya wife, gets one share (XVII, 42–50).

Baudhâyana allows all the children to take equal shares, or the eldest son to take one tenth in excess. Where there are sons born of wives of different castes, the sons will take four, three, two and one shares, according to the order of the castes (II, 2, 3, 2–10).

Âpastamba differs in this respect also from his predecessors, and protests against the unequal division of property. He quotes the opinion about giving a preference to the eldest son, examines the texts on which the opinion is based, argues that the texts make a statement of facts and is not a rule, and therefore declares the preference of the eldest son to be forbidden. All sons who are virtuous inherit, but he who spends money unrighteously shall be disinherited, though he be the eldest son (II, 6, 14, 1–15).

The separate property of a wife, *i.e.*, her nuptial presents and ornaments, were inherited by her daughters (*Gautama*, XXVIII, 24; *Vasishtha*, XVII, 46; *Baudhâyana*, II, 2, 3, 43).

Such were the laws of the Rationalistic Age. They show unmistakably the vast distance of time between this and the Epic Age, and show also the culture, the training, and the practical method of dealing with intricate subjects which were the peculiar features of the Rationalistic Period. Everything that was confused during the Epic Period was brought to order and subjected to a severe classification; everything that was discursive was condensed; everything that was vague and uncertain was dealt with in a practical manner. Criminal offences and civil cases were no longer dealt with according to the vague and varying opinions and feelings of learned men and priests; those opinions were arranged, condensed, and codified into bodies of laws which learned men were called upon to administer. The caste-rules, which were still pliable in the Epic Period, were made more rigid, more in accordance with the inviolable codified rules of the Rationalistic Period; and the whole social system of the Hindus underwent a similar rigid treatment. We will dwell on these two subjects in the next two chapters, and will then proceed to show how Science and Philosophy also underwent the same logical treatment.

CHAPTER V.

CASTE.

IN trying to reduce the caste-system into a code of rigid rules, the Sûtrakâras of the period met with an initial difficulty. They firmly believed that there were originally but four castes among men, viz., Brâhmans, Kshatriyas, Vaisyas, and Sûdras;—but they actually found around them various other castes, formed by tribes of non-Aryans, who had gradually entered into the Hindu fold, and formed low Hindu castes. Whence these new castes? What was their origin? Believing that all mankind was originally divided only into four castes, the Sûtrakâras tried to evolve the new castes from the four parent castes. The strange fiction was then conceived that the new castes were formed by inter-marriages among the parent castes! We may imagine a dogmatic Greek priest of the fifth century declaring that the Huns were descended from a Roman patrician who married a Parthian maiden; or we may conceive a monk of the thirteenth century declaring that the Moguls were descended from a German baron who married a Chinese maiden. Such wild theories would be accepted in an ignorant age, but would be forgotten with the progress of knowledge. But in India, where popular knowledge has become gradually restricted, such theories have been scrupulously adhered to by all later writers, and obtain credence in India to the present day!

Vasishtha says:—

"1. They declare that the offspring of a Sûdra

and of a female of the Brâhman caste, becomes a Chandâla.

"2. That of a Sûdra and of a female of the Kshatriya caste, a Vaina.

"3. That of a Sûdra and of a female of the Vaisya caste, an Antyâvasâyin.

"4. They declare that the son begotten by a Vaisya on a female of the Brâhman caste becomes a Râmaka.

"5. The son begotten by the same on a female of the Kshatriya caste, a Paulkasa.

"6. They declare that the son begotten by a Kshatriya on a female of the Brâhman caste becomes a Sûta.

"8. Children begotten by Brâhmans, Kshatriyas, and Vaisyas on females of the next lower, second lower, and third lower castes become respectively Ambashthas, Ugras, and Nishâdas.

"9. The son of a Brâhman and of a Sûdra woman is a Pârasava" (*Vasishtha*, XVIII).

Baudhâyana is somewhat different.

"3. A Brâhman begets on a female of the Kshatriya caste a Brâhman, on a female of the Vaisya caste an Ambashtha, on a female of the Sûdra caste a Nishâda.

"4. According to some, a Pârasava.

"5. A Kshatriya begets on a female of the Vaisya caste a Kshatriya, on a female of the Sûdra caste an Ugra.

"6. A Vaisya begets on a female of the Sûdra caste a Rathakâra.

"7. A Sûdra begets on a female of the Vaisya caste a Mâgadha, on a female of the Kshatriya caste a Kshattri, but on a female of the Brâhman caste a Chandâla.

"8. A Vaisya begets on a female of the Kshatriya caste an Âyogava, on a female of the Brâhman caste a Sûta."

And so a Svapâka has an Ugra father and a Kshattri mother; a Vaina has a Vaidehaka father and an Ambashtha mother; a Paulkasa has a Nishâda father and a

Sûdra mother; a Kukkutaka has a Sûdra father and a Nishâda mother; and "the wise declare those sprung by an intermixture of the castes to be Vrâtyas" (*Baudhâyana*, I, 9, 17).

Gautama's enumeration is comprehensive as well as brief, and we will give it below:—

"16. Children born in the regular order of the wives of the next, second, or third lower castes become Savarnas, *i.e.*, of equal caste, Ambashthas, Ugras, Nishâdas, Daushyantas, and Pârasavas.

"17. Children born in the inverted order (of wives of higher castes) become Sûtas, Mâgadhas, Âyogavas, Kshattris, Vaidehakas, or Chandâlas.

"18. Some declare that a woman of the Brâhman caste has borne successively to husbands of the four castes sons who are Brâhmans, Sûtas, Mâgadhas, or Chandâlas;

"19. And that a woman of the Kshatriya caste has borne to the same Murdhâvasiktas, Kshatriyas, Dhîvaras, Paulkasas.

"20. Further, a woman of the Vaisya caste has borne to the same Bhrigyakanthas, Mâhishyas, Vaisyas, and Vaidehas;

"21. And a woman of the Sûdra caste to the same Pârasavas, Yavanas, Karanas, and Sûdras" (*Gautama*, IV).

Here we have an authoritative statement which may well stagger the most faithful believer! Mâgadhas and Vaidehas who were different races, Chandâlas and Paulkasas who were undoubtedly non-Aryan tribes, and even Yavanas who were Bactrian Greeks and foreigners, were all treated by the same general and rigid law which recognised no exception, and were all declared to be descended from the four parent castes! And as the Hindus came to know other foreign nations later on, the elastic theory was stretched, and Manu derived those nations too from the same Hindu parent castes!

It is remarkable, however, that the castes or races

named above, of whom such a strange origin has been expounded, were nearly all aboriginal tribes or foreigners, or Aryans who had incurred odium by their partiality for scepticism and Buddhism. We do not find names of profession-castes, answering to the Kâyasthas, the Vaidyas, the goldsmiths, the blacksmiths, the potters, the weavers, and other artisans of Modern India. How were these professions classed in Ancient India, if they were not classed as separate castes? The reply is plain, that the great and yet undivided Vaisya caste of the Rationalistic Period still embraced all those different professions which in modern times have been divided and disunited into castes.* The Aryan Vaisyas followed different trades and professions in Ancient India without forming separate castes; they were scribes and physicians, goldsmiths and blacksmiths, potters and weavers, while still belonging to the same common Vaisya caste. Thus the great body of the Aryan population was still united, and was still entitled to religious knowledge and learning.

The study of the Veda, the performance of sacrifices, and the gift of alms are prescribed for all twice-born men, *i.e.*, for Brâhmans, Kshatriyas, and Vaisyas. The special and additional occupations of the Brâhman were the performance of sacrifice for others, and the receiving of alms, and agriculture and trade were also allowed to him *provided he did not work himself* (*Gautama*, X, 5).

* One instance will suffice. The Vaidyas or physician caste of Bengal were unknown in the Rationalistic Period, but later tradition has applied to them the same fiction that was developed in the Rationalistic Period, and the Vaidyas are said to have descended from the union of men and women of different castes. And yet common sense would suggest that they are the descendants of a section of the Aryan people,—the Vaisyas,—who specially applied themselves to one particular science as soon as the science was sufficiently developed to call for special application, and thus in course of time formed a hereditary caste. This view receives a curious confirmation from the name which the Bengal Vaidyas still bear. All Vaidyas are Guptas (Sena Guptas, Dâsa Guptas, &c.). Now there are passages in the Sûtra literature which clearly lay down that all Brâhmans are Sarmans, all Kshatriyas are Barmans, and *all Vaisyas are Guptas*. We will quote such a passage in the next chapter.

The abuses begotten of the privileges of caste had already commenced as early as the Rationalistic Period, and Brâhmans, relieved of manual labour, had already commenced to feed on the resources of the industrious classes, without acquiring that learning which would alone justify their exemption from labour. Vasishtha felt the abuse and the injustice keenly, and protested against idlers being supported and fed, in language which could only be indited when Hinduism was still a living nation's religion.

"1. (Brâhmans) who neither study nor teach the Veda nor keep sacred fires *become equal to Sûdras.*

"4. The king shall punish that village where Brâhmans, unobservant of their sacred duties and ignorant of the Veda, subsist by begging, *for it feeds robbers.*

"6. The sin that *dunces, perplexed by ignorance,* and unacquainted with the sacred law, declare to be duty, shall fall, increased a hundred-fold, on those who propound it.

"11. An elephant made of wood, an antelope made of leather, and a Brâhman ignorant of the Veda, those three *have nothing but the name of their kind.*

"12. Those kingdoms where ignorant men eat the food of the learned will be visited by drought; or some other *great evil will befall them*" (*Vasishtha,* III).

The additional occupations of the Kshatriya were to govern and fight and make conquests, to learn the management of chariots and the use of the bow, and to stand firm in battle and not to turn back (*Gautama,* X, 15 and 16). The special occupations of the Vaisya were trade, agriculture, tending cattle, lending money, and labour for gain (*Gautama,* X, 49). Sûdras were to serve the other three castes, but were also allowed to labour for gain (*Gautama,* X, 42); and there can be no doubt they traded and earned money by independent work to a large extent in the Rationalistic Period as in all succeeding periods. Religious knowledge was, however, forbidden to Sûdras.

"To see ourselves as others see us" is always a gain, and we will therefore now examine how the caste-system was regarded by foreigners. It is quite evident that the seven castes spoken of by Megasthenes are virtually the four castes spoken of above. His philosophers and councillors were the Brâhmans, those who engaged themselves in religious study, and those who took employment under the State respectively. His husbandmen, shepherds, and artisans were the Vaisyas and Sûdras, who engaged themselves in cultivation, in pasture, and in manufacture. And his soldiers were the Kshatriyas; while his overseers were only special servants, spies of the king.

Megasthenes further subdivides the philosophers into Brâhmans or householders, and Srâmans or ascetics. Of the former he says that "the children are under the care of one person after another, and as they advance in age, each succeeding master is more accomplished than his predecessor. The philosophers have their abode in a grove in front of the city within a moderate-sized enclosure. They live in a simple style, and lie on beds of rushes or (deer) skins. They abstain from animal food and sensual pleasures, and spend their time listening to religious discourse and in imparting their knowledge to such as will listen to them. . . . After living in this manner for seven and thirty years each individual retires to his own property, where he lives for the rest of his days in ease and security. They then array themselves in fine muslin, and wear a few trinkets of gold on their fingers and in their ears. They eat flesh, but not that of animals employed in labour. They abstain from hot and highly seasoned food. They marry as many wives as they please, with a view to having numerous children, for by having many wives, greater advantages are enjoyed, and since they have no slaves, they have more need to have children around them to attend to their wants."

Of the Srâmans or ascetics, Megasthenes tells us that "they live in the wood, where they subsist on leaves of trees and wild fruits, and wear garments made from the bark of trees. . . . They communicate with the kings, who consult them by messengers, regarding the causes of things, and who through them worship and supplicate the deity." Some of them practised medicines, and Megasthenes writes: "By their knowledge of pharmacy they can make marriages fruitful, and determine the sex of the offspring. They effect cures rather by regulating diet than by the use of medicines. The remedies most esteemed are ointments and plasters." We learn from this account, as we learn from other sources, that sects of ascetics subsisting on roots and wild fruits, lived in Ancient India, and bore the name of Srâmanas, before and after the time of Gautama Buddha. And when that great reformer preached a holy life and retirement from the world, as the essence of his religion, his followers, who retired from the world, were called Sâkyaputrîya Srâmans,—or ascetics who followed the Sâkya,—to distinguish them from other sects of ascetics.

Elsewhere Megasthenes says of the Philosopher-caste that they, "being exempted from all public duties, are neither the masters nor the servants of others. They are however engaged by private persons to offer the sacrifices due in lifetime, and to celebrate the obsequies of the dead. . . . They forewarn assembled multitudes about droughts and wet weather, and also about propitious winds and diseases." We have thus a brief but intelligent sketch, from the hand of an impartial foreigner, of the life which the Brâhmans lived in the Rationalistic Period. They gave religious instruction to the young, they presided at sacrifices and funeral ceremonies, they advised villagers and cultivators about weather and harvests, and they also prescribed medicines for various diseases. Kings looked up to them for advice in emergencies, and the class of Brâhmans whom Megasthenes considers a separate caste and calls councillors, also advised the king in state affairs, were entrusted with the treasury, and were the judges in civil and criminal cases. The educated classes looked up to the Brâhmans for priestly advice and assistance at large sacrifices, while the humble cultivators consulted the wise men about the prospects of the year. With the gradual decline of the nation the caste so universally honoured gradually came to abuse its privileges, and tried to strengthen by superstition that pre-eminence which was first acquired by sanctity and knowledge.

Of the military class or the Kshatriya caste Megasthenes gives a very brief sketch. The soldiers were organised and equipped for war, but in times of peace gave themselves up to idleness and amusements.

"The entire force, men-at-arms, war-horses, war-elephants, and all are maintained at the king's expense." It was the duty of the overseers to inquire into all that went on in the kingdom and report them to the king.

Of the husbandmen, shepherds, and artisans, who obviously were the Vaisya and Sûdra castes, Megasthenes gives us a more interesting and life-like sketch. Being exempted from fighting and other public services, the husbandmen "devote the whole of their time to tillage; *nor would an enemy, coming upon a husbandman at work on his land, do him any harm,* for men of this class, being regarded as public benefactors, are protected from all injury. The land thus remaining unravaged, and producing heavy crops, supplies the inhabitants with all that is requisite to make life very enjoyable. . . . They pay a land tribute to the king, because all India is the property of the crown, and no private person is permitted to own land. Besides the land tribute, they pay into the royal treasury a fourth part of the produce of the soil." *

"The shepherds neither settle in towns nor in villages, but live in tents.† By hunting and trapping they clear

* The usual land tax in India was one-sixth of the produce in the Hindu times.

† This description must refer to some tribes of aborigines who were scarcely yet completely Hinduised.

the country of noxious birds and wild beasts. Of the artisans some are armourers, while others make the implements which husbandmen and others find useful in their different callings. This class is not only exempted from paying taxes, but even receives maintenance from the royal exchequer."

CHAPTER VI.

SOCIAL LIFE.

IT is in the Sûtras that we first find mention of the different forms of marriage with which we are familiar from the later metrical codes of law. Vasishtha mentions only six forms, viz.:—

Brâhma marriage; the father pours out a libation of water and gives his daughter to a suitor, a student.

Daiva marriage; the father decks his daughter with ornaments and gives her to an officiating priest, when sacrifice is being performed.

Ârsha marriage; the father gives his daughter for a cow or a bull.

Gândharva marriage; the lover takes and weds a loving damsel.

Kshâtra (or *Râkshasa*) marriage; the bridegroom forcibly takes a damsel, destroying her relatives by strength of arms.

Mânusha (or *Âsura*) marriage; the suitor purchases a damsel from her father.

Âpastamba, too, recognises only these six forms of marriage, but calls the Kshâtra marriage by the name Râkshasa, and the Mânusha marriage by the name Âsura. Âpastamba further mentions the first three forms only, viz., the Brâhma, the Daiva, and the Ârsha, as praise worthy.

The older writers Gautama and Baudhâyana, however, prescribe eight forms of marriage, adding to the above six forms one rite, Prâjâpatya, which was considered praiseworthy, and another form, *Paisâcha*, which was sinful. In the Prâjâpatya form the father simply gave away his daughter to the suitor, saying, "Fulfil ye the law conjointly." The Paisâcha form was simply a form of rape, when a man embraced a woman deprived of consciousness.

Marriages among kinsfolk were rigorously prohibited in the Rationalistic Period. Vasishtha prohibits marriage between a man and a woman of the same *Gotra* or *Pravara*, or who are related within four degrees on the mother's side, or within six degrees on the father's side (VIII, 1 and 2). Âpastamba prohibits marriage between men and women of the same *Gotra*, or who are related (within six degrees) on the mother's or (father's) side II, 5, 11, 15 and 16). But Baudhâyana allows a man to marry the daughter of a maternal uncle or a paternal aunt (I, 1, 2, 4).

The marriage of girls at a tender age was not yet prevalent in the Rationalistic Period. Vasishtha says:—

"67. A maiden who has attained puberty *shall wait for three years.*

"68. After three years, she may take a husband of equal caste" (XVII).

In contradiction, however, to the above, there is a passage, immediately after, recommending the marriage of girls while they are yet children. The passage appears to be an interpolation.

The marriage of widows, which was a prevalent custom in the Vedic and Epic Periods, continued to prevail in the Rationalistic Period, but except in the case of child-widows, was not looked upon with favour. The son of a widow married again was, as will appear from passages quoted in the previous chapter, often classed with adopted sons, or sons by an appointed wife or daughter.

Such are the rules laid down in the Dharma Sûtras for marriage. Marriage marks the entrance to a new stage of life, viz., that of a *Householder*; before marriage, a young man is only a *Student.* It would be interesting to briefly review the rules laid down in the Sûtras regarding the conduct of a student and that of a householder, respectively.

The first great event in a boy's life seems to have been his initiation as a student. A Brâhman boy was initiated between 8 and 16, a Kshatriya between 11 and 22, and a Vaisya between 12 and 24. The initiated boy then lived as a religious student in the house of his teacher for 12, 24, 36, or 48 years, according as he wished to master one, two, three, or the four Vedas. During this period of his life he avoided all spiced food, perfumes, and articles of luxury; he tied his hair in a knot, he bore a staff and a girdle, and a cloth of flax or hemp, or even only a skin. Avoiding all places of amusement and of pleasure, restraining his senses, modest and humble, the young student went out every morning with his staff to beg for food from charitable householders in the neighbouring villages, and all that he obtained in the course of the day he placed before his teacher, and he only tasted food after his teacher had done with his meals. He went to the forest to fetch fuel, and evening and morning he fetched water for household use. Every morning he swept and cleaned the altar, kindled the fire, and placed the sacred fuel on it; and every evening he washed his teacher's feet and rubbed him and put him to bed, before he retired to rest. Such was the humble and simple life which ancient Hindu students led, when they devoted all the energies of their mind to the acquisition of the sacred learning of their forefathers.

Instruction, it is needless to repeat, was imparted by rote. The student respectfully held the hand of his teacher, and fixed his mind on the teacher and said, "Venerable sir, recite," and the Sâvitrî (the well-known Gâyatrî verse of the Rig Veda) was recited, and learnt as the introduction to the learning of the Vedas (*Gautama*, I, 55, 56). And from day to day new lessons were recited and learnt, the student dividing his day's work between minding his lessons and minding the household work of his teacher.

When after years of study, often under different teachers, the student at last returned to his home, he made a handsome gift to his instructors, married, and settled down as a householder or *snâtaka, i.e.*, a man who has bathed after his studentship is over. The Sûtrakâras are never tired with impressing on householders the paramount duty of courtesy and hospitality towards guests, for the reception of guests is an everlasting sacrifice offered by the householder to God (*Âpastamba*, II, 3, 7, 1).

Besides the order of the student and that of the householder, there were two other orders of life, viz., those of the *Ascetic* (Bhikshu), and that of the *Hermit* (Vaikhânasa). We learn from later Sanscrit literature that a typical or perfect life was the life of a man who belonged to these four orders in the successive periods of his life. Âpastamba, too, who is one of the latest of the Sûtrakâras, says that "if he lives in all these four (orders of life) . . . he will obtain salvation" (II, 9, 21, 2). But this was not the original idea, and in early times a man might have chosen to spend the whole of his life in one of these four orders. Thus Vasishtha says that a man after completing his education may, according to his choice, embrace one of the four orders for the rest of his life (VII, 3), and Baudhâyana too quotes a rule that a man on finishing his education may be an ascetic at once (II, 10, 17, 2). It is needless for our purpose to dwell on rules laid down for an ascetic and a hermit respectively. It will suffice to state that an ascetic shaved his head, had no property or home, practised austerities, fasted or lived on alms, wore a single garment or a skin, slept on the bare ground, wandered about from place to place, discontinued the performance of all religious ceremonies, but never discontinued the study of the Veda or the contemplation of the Universal Soul (*Vasishtha*, X). A hermit, on the other hand, though dwelling in woods, living on roots and fruits, and leading a chaste life, kindled the sacred fire and offered the morning and evening libations (*Vasishtha*, IX).

We now return to the householders, who form the best of the four orders. For the householders, and not hermits and ascetics, formed the nation, and "as rivers, both great and small, find a resting place in the ocean, even so men of all orders find protection with householders" (*Vasishtha*, VIII, 15).

No less than forty sacraments have been prescribed for the householder (*Gautama*, VIII, 14–20), and an account of these sacraments will give us a glimpse into the religious and domestic life of the ancient Hindu.

Domestic ceremonies.—(1) Garbhâdhâna (ceremony to cause conception); (2) Pumsavana (ceremony to cause the birth of a male child); (3) Sîmantonnayana (arranging the hair of the pregnant wife); (4) Jâtakarman (ceremony on birth of a child); (5) naming the child; (6) the first feeding; (7) the tonsure of the head; (8) the initiation; (9 to 12) the four vows for the study of the Veda; (13) the bath or completion of studentship; (14) marriage, or, as it is called, the taking a helpmate for the performance of religious duties; and (15 to 19) the five sacrifices to gods, manes, men, spirits, and to Brahman or God.

Grihya rites, also called *Pâkayajnas.*—(1) Astakâ, or rites performed in winter; (2) Pârvana, or new and full moon rites; (3) Srâddha, or sacrifices to departed ancestors; (4) Srâvanî, a rite performed in the Srâvana month; (5) Âgrahâyanî, performed in the Agrahâyana month; (6) Chaitrî, performed in the month of Chaitra; and (7) Âsvayugî, performed in the month of Âsvina.

Srauta rites.—These are again divided into two classes, viz., *Haviryajna*, performed with offerings of rice, milk, butter, meat, &c.; and the *Somayajna*, performed with libations of the Soma-juice.

The Haviryajnas are—(1) Agnyâdhâna, (2) Agnihotra, (3) Darsapûrnamâsa, (4) Âgrayana, (5) Châturmâsya, (6) Nirûdhapasubandha, and (7) Sautrâmanî.

The Somayajnas are (1) Agnishtoma, (2) Atyagnishtoma, (3) Ukthya, (4) Shodasin, (5) Vâjapeya, (6) Atirâtra, and (7) Âptoryâma.

Such were the forty sacraments prescribed for householders;—but far above the performance of these sacrifices was esteemed the possession of virtue and goodness, which alone led to heaven. Gautama says:—

"He who is sanctified by these forty sacraments, but whose soul is destitute of the eight good qualities, will not be united with Brahman, nor does he reach His heaven.

"But he, forsooth, who is sanctified by a few only of these forty sacraments, and whose soul is endowed with the excellent qualities, will be united with Brahman and will dwell in His heaven" (VIII, 24 and 25).

Similarly Vasishtha says:—

"The Vedas do not purify him who is deficient in good conduct, though he may have learnt them all, together with the six Angas; the sacred texts depart from such a man, even as birds when full fledged leave their nests.

"As the beauty of a wife causes no joy to a blind man, even so all the four Vedas, together with the six Angas and sacrifices, bring no blessing to him who is deficient in good conduct.

"The several texts do not save from sin the deceitful man who behaves deceitfully. But that Veda, two syllables of which are studied with due observances of rules of conduct, purifies, just as the clouds in the month of Âsvina" (VI, 3-5).

We will now say a few words about the forty sacraments, or rather with regard to those of them which illustrate Hindu life. They include, as stated above, Domestic ceremonies, Grihya rites, and Srauta rites. The Srauta rites are described in detail in the Yajur Veda and the Brâhmanas, and also in a condensed form in the Srauta Sûtras, as we have stated before. These rites have been briefly described in our account of the Epic Age, and throw little light on the manners and life of the people, and are therefore not of very much importance for our historical purpose. The Domestic ceremonies and Grihya rites, on the other hand, give us glimpses which are of inestimable value into the manners of the ancient Hindus, and indeed give us a perfect picture of the life that they lived and the habits and customs they followed.

We will first treat of the Domestic ceremonies, and afterwards speak of the Grihya religious rites. The most important of the Domestic ceremonies are Marriage, Ceremonies performed during pregnancy of wife, Birth of child, Annaprâsana or the first feeding of a child, Tonsure, Initiation, and Return from School on the completion of education. As we read accounts of these domestic ceremonies, we think we survey the whole life of our ancient ancestors;—and the ceremonies are all the more interesting to us, because we continue to practise many of them to the present day, after a lapse of over two thousand years.

Marriage.—The bridegroom sends messengers to the house of the girl's father, reciting verse X, 85, 23, of the Rig Veda, which we have translated before. If the proposal pleases both parties, the promise of marriage is ratified, and both parties touch a full vessel into which flowers, fried grain, barley, and gold have been put, and recite a formula. The bridegroom then performs a sacrifice. On the appointed day, the bride's relations wash her with water fragrant with the choicest fruits and scents, make her put on a newly dyed garment, and cause her to sit down by a fire while the family

Âchârya performs a sacrifice. The bridegroom, who has also bathed and gone through auspicious ceremonies, "is escorted by happy young women who are not widows to the girl's house" (*Sânkhâyâna.*)

The actual marriage ceremony varied in detail in different localities, but agreed in the essential points. "Various indeed are the customs of the different countries, and the customs of the different villages. . . . What however is commonly accepted, that we shall state" (*Âsvalâyana*). The bridegroom holds the bride by the hand, and leads her three times round a fire, reciting some verses, as, "Come, let us marry. Let us beget offspring. Loving, bright, with genial mind, may we live a hundred autumns." Each time he makes her tread a millstone, saying, "Like a stone be firm." The bride's brother or guardian fills her hands with Âjya or fried grain, and she sacrifices it to the fire. The bridegroom then causes the bride to step forward seven steps, reciting suitable words. The going round the fire, treading the stone, sacrificing the fried grain, and stepping forward seven steps, constituted the principal forms of the marriage ceremony. "And she should dwell that night in the house of an old Brâhman woman whose husband is alive, and whose children are alive. When she sees the Polar star, the star of Arundhatî, and the Seven Rishis (Ursa Major), let her break the silence, and say, May my husband live, and I get offspring" (*Âsvalâyana*). Sânkhâyana says, "Let them sit silent, when the sun has set, until the Polar star appears. He shows her the star with the words, 'Firm be thou, thriving with me.' Let her say, 'I see the Polar star; may I obtain offspring.' Through a period of three nights let them refrain from conjugal intercourse."

Pregnancy.—Various were the rites performed during the pregnancy of a wife. In the first place, there was the Garbhâdhâna rite, which was supposed to secure conception. The *Pumsavana* rite was supposed to determine the male sex of the child, and the *Garbharakshana* secured the child in the womb from dangers. The *Sîmantonnayana*, performed according to Âsvalâyana in the fourth month, and according to Sânkhâyana in the seventh month of pregnancy, is a more interesting ceremony. Gobhila says it may be performed in the fourth, sixth, or eighth month, and it consisted in the husband affectionately parting his wife's hair, with certain rites.

Birth of child.—The rites performed on this occasion are called *Jâtakarman* or birth ceremony, *Medhâjananam* or the production of intelligence, and *Âyushya* or rite for prolonging life. On this occasion the father gives the child a secret name,—of an even number of syllables if the child is male, and an uneven number if it is female, and only the father and mother know that name. On the tenth day, when the mother gets up from childbed, a name for common use is given to the child. "The name of a Brâhman should end in Sarman (*e.g.*, Vishnu Sarman), that of a Kshatriya in Varman (*e.g.*, Lakshmî Varman), that of a Vaisya in Gupta (*e.g.*, Chandra Gupta)" (*Pâraskara*, I, 17, 4).

First feeding of the child with solid food.—This is the well-known *Annaprâsana* ceremony. The child seems to have been allowed a greater variety of food in the olden days than in the present time. "Goat's flesh, if he is desirous of nourishment; flesh of partridge, if desirous of holy lustre; boiled rice with ghee, if desirous of splendour" (*Âsvalâyana and Sânkhâyana*). "Flesh of that bird called Bhâradvâjî, if he wishes fluency of speech; fish, if swiftness was desired, &c., &c." (*Pâraskara*).

Tonsure of the child's head, called *Chûdâ Karana*.—This was performed when the child was one year old according to Sânkhâyana and Pâraskara, or when the child was in his third year according to Âsvalâyana and Gobhila. The child's head was shaved with a razor with certain mantras (without mantras in the case of a girl), and some hair was left and arranged according to the custom of the family.

Initiation or *Upanayana.*—This was an important ceremony, and was performed when a boy was made over by his father or guardian to the teacher for education. The age of initiation, as we have seen before, varied in the case of Brâhmans, Kshatriyas, and Vaisyas, and the sacred thread was worn on this occasion by all the three castes.

A garment, a girdle, and a staff of appropriate materials were then assumed by the student, and he approached the teacher.

"He (the teacher) fills the two hollows of his own and the student's joined hands with water, and then says to him (*i.e.*, to the student), 'What is thy name?'

"'I am N. N., sir,' says the other.

"'Descending from the same Rishis,' says the teacher.

"'Descending from the same Rishis, sir,' says the other.

"'Declare that thou art a student, sir.'

"'I am a student, sir,' says the other.

"With the words 'Bhûr Bhuvah Svah,' the teacher sprinkles thrice with his joined hands water on the joined hands of the student.

"And seizing the student's hands with his own hands, holding the right uppermost, he murmurs:—

"By the impulse of the god Savitri, with the arms of the two Asvins, with Pûshan's hands, I initiate thee, N. N."

Such was the ceremony of the *Upanayana* in ancient times, the initiation into the life of a student, the commencement of the study of the Veda. How has the *Upanayana* custom degenerated in modern times! It no longer means the study of the Veda, which is now forgotten, nor the performance of sacrifices, which have now fallen into disuse. It now means the habitual assumption of a meaningless thread, which was neither meaningless nor habitually worn in ancient days; and modern Brâhmans claim a monopoly of the sacrificial thread, which the ancient Brâhmans used to wear along with Kshatriyas and Vaisyas, who all sacrificed and learnt the Veda. Thus national degeneracy has converted significant rites into meaningless forms, all tending to the enforced ignorance of the people, and to the exclusive privileges of priests.

Return from school. — The student, after he had finished his education, returned to his home, and if he had no ancestral house to go to, had to build a house. This, too, was accompanied by a ceremony and by the utterance of the hymns of the Rig Veda (VII, 54, 55) to Vâstospati, the lord of dwelling-houses, as well as to other divinities. Then followed marriage, and the setting up of fires,—the Agnyâdhâna—which is a Srauta rite, and which has been described in Chapter VIII. of the last Book. The student is now changed into a householder, and has other and graver duties to perform.

Such were the most important Domestic ceremonies in which the ancient Hindus rejoiced. We will now give a brief account of the Grihya rites.

The most important of the Grihya rites was the *Srâddha* or monthly offering to the departed fathers, and the feeding of Brâhmans. "Brâhmans who are endowed with learning, moral character, and correct conduct," were invited, and sat down "as representatives of the fathers" to whom the oblations were offered. The sacrificer then offered the Arghya water to the fathers with the words, "Father, this is thy Arghya; Grandfather, this is thy Arghya; Great-grandfather, this is thy Arghya." Gifts of perfumes, garlands, incense, lights, and clothes were then offered to the Brâhmans. With the permission of the Brâhmans, food of the *Sthâlîpâka* prepared for the *Pindapitriyajna* was smeared with ghee and sacrificed in the fire, or in the hands of the Brâhmans, together with other food. And when the sacrificer saw that the

Brâhmans were satiated, he recited the verse (Rig Veda, I, 82, 2), "They have eaten, they have enjoyed themselves" (*Âsvalâyana*).

Pârvana.—This was the rite observed on the new and full moon days, and consisted in fasting as well as in offering cooked oblations to the deities of those days, with appropriate mantras. Orthodox Hindus still make it a point to fast on these days.

Srâvanî.—This was a rite observed on the full moon day of the month of Srâvana in the rainy season, and the idea was to propitiate serpents, which multiply in India in the rains. The words uttered were sufficiently grotesque.

The propitiation of serpents as such has nearly disappeared from the upper classes of the people of India, and they will have some difficulty in recognising the rite performed at the *Râkî Pûrnimâ* as a survival of the *Srâvani* rite of the Rationalistic Period. The *Râkî* string bracelet which friends distribute to friends, and sisters affectionately send to their brothers, is a bracelet which is intended to save them from any harm or evil proceeding from serpents.*

Asvayugî.—This was a rite performed on the full moon day of Âsvayuga or Âsvina month.

"1. On the full moon day of Âsvayuga a milk-rice oblation to Indra.

"2. Having sacrificed Âjya with the words, 'To the two Asvins, svâhâ! To the two Âsvayuga, svâhâ! To the full moon of Âsvayuga, svâhâ! To the autumn, svâhâ! To Prajâpati, svâhâ! To the tawny one, svâhâ!'

"3. He shall sacrifice a mixture of curds and butter with this hymn, 'The cows come hither' (Rig Veda, VI, 28), verse by verse.

* A new and aboriginal goddess, the *Manasâ*, is now worshipped in Bengal to save men from snake-bite, and the story of her admission into the Hindu Pantheon is dimly seen in the popular tale of *Manasâr Bhâsân*.

"4. That night they let the calves join their mothers.

"5. Then feeding of the Brâhmans."

This is all the account which Sânkhâyana gives of this rite, and it is impossible not to suspect from the above account that the rite is essentially agricultural. This suspicion is confirmed when Pâraskara tells us that the above rite was to be followed by a sacrifice to Sîtâ, *the goddess of the field furrow*.

"In whose substance dwells the prosperity of all Vedic and worldly works, *Indra's wife Sîtâ*, I invoke. May she not abandon me in whatever work I do. Svâhâ!

"Her, who, rich in horses, rich in cows, rich in delight, indefatigably supports living beings, *Urvarâ* (*the fertile*), *who is wreathed with threshing floors*, I invoke at this sacrifice, the firm one. May she not abandon me. Svâhâ!" (II, 17, 9).

The worship of Sîtâ or the furrow goddess, following the Âsvajugî rite, her description as the wife of Indra the rain-giver, and as Urvarâ or the fertile, wreathed with threshing floors, all suggest that the Âsvajugî rite was an agricultural rite of thanksgiving on the reaping of the crop which was harvested in Âsvina. And if this rite of agricultural thanksgiving was already somewhat obscure in the Rationalistic Period, how has that rite been further obscured in the *Kojâgara Lakshmî Pujâ* of modern India.

Lakshmî is a young goddess who was unknown in the Rationalistic Period, but is now the most cherished deity in the Hindu Pantheon. Sîtâ is now remembered only as the heroine of the Râmâyana, and as a pattern of female virtue and female self-abnegation, but Lakshmî has taken her place as the goddess of crops and of rice.

We have seen that the Kojâgara Lakshmi Pûjâ is the modern form of the ancient Âsvajugî rite. Still more recent than the Lakshmî Pûjâ is the worship of Durgâ, which has in Bengal assumed wonderful dimensions within recent times, owing no doubt to the gladness of the harvest season. How has the petty harvest festival, —the milk-rice oblation to Indra and his consort Sîtâ,— developed in modern times!

Âgrahâyanî.—This rite was performed on the full moon day of Agrahâyana month. This particular night was considered to be the consort of the year, or the image of the year, and adoration was offered to the year, to Samvatsara, Parivatsara, Idâvatsara, Idvatsara, and to Vatsara, which terms designate the different years of the quinquennial period of Yuga (*Pâraskara*, III, 2, 2).

Ashtakâ.—So called because they were rites which were performed on the *eighth* day of the three or four successive dark fortnights after the full moon of Agrahâyana. Oblations were made with vegetables, flesh, and cakes respectively. Gobhila quotes different opinions as to the object of these oblations, and says they may be for the gratification of Agni, or of the Fathers, or of Prajâpati, or of the Season gods, or of all the gods (*Gobhila*, III, 2, 3). The intelligent reader will hardly fail to perceive, however, that the rites were suggested by the winter season, which is an enjoyable season in India, when the Aman rice is harvested and wheat and barley thrive, and when cakes and flesh and vegetables are not only acceptable to the "season gods," but are also highly gratifying to men! And the Hindu reader will, no doubt, at once perceive that a survival of this ancient rite still exists in Bengal in the *Pausha Pârvana*, when, after the Aman has been harvested, our ladies delight in the preparation of delicious cakes of various kinds, to the infinite joy of the young and old alike!

Chaitrî, the last rite in the year, was performed on the full moon day of Chaitra. Indra and Agni and Rudra and the Nakshatras or constellations were propitiated.

Such were the Domestic ceremonies and Grihya rites in which Hindu ladies delighted in ancient times. And if some of these rites have since lost their original significance, and have even been replaced by modern forms, we can nevertheless trace most of them in the rites that we practise to this day, after a lapse of two thousand years and more. The conservative spirit of the Hindus and their loyalty to the past are pre-eminently conspicuous in their adherence to ancient ceremonies, which were generally conceived in a pure and healthy spirit. And the healthy joyousness which attended ancient Hindu celebrations has certainly lost nothing in the course of many centuries of foreign subjection and national decline.

CHAPTER VII.

GEOMETRY AND GRAMMAR.

WE have seen before that it was in the Rationalistic Age that all the religious rules and laws of the previous ages received a philosophical treatment, and were condensed, arranged, and codified. It was in this period that the contents of the verbose and somewhat chaotic Brâhmanas were brought into order, that civil and criminal laws and the law of inheritance were codified, that the caste rules and social laws were rigidly fixed, and the duties of men, both as citizens and as members of a family, defined. And it can well be imagined, therefore, that science and philosophy received a high degree of development in this age, and some departments of inquiry and thought received their last development in India in this period.

We do not know what progress was made in this period in Astronomy. No Sûtra work on Astronomy has come down to us, and there can be little doubt that the astronomical works of the Rationalistic Period have long since been replaced by the later and completer works of the Puranic Period,—by the works of Âryabhatta and Varâhamihira, of Brahmagupta and Bhâskarâchârya. But there is one branch of mathematics which was carried to a high degree of excellence in the Rationalistic Period. Dr. Thibaut has deserved the thanks of all Oriental scholars by publishing the fact that Geometry, as a science, was first studied in India. The Greeks of a later age cultivated the science with greater success, but it should never be forgotten that the world owes its first lessons in Geometry not to Greece, but to India.

Geometry, like Astronomy, owes its origin in India to religion, and Grammar and Philosophy too were similarly inspired by religion. As Dr. Thibaut remarks : "The want of some rule by which to fix the right time for the sacrifices gave the first impulse to astronomical observations; urged by this want, the priest remained watching night after night the advance of the moon through the circle of the Nakshatras, and day after day the alternate progress of the sun towards the north and the south. The laws of phonetics were investigated, because the wrath of the gods followed the wrong pronunciation of a single letter of the sacrificial formulas; grammar and etymology had the task of securing the right understanding of the holy texts. The close connection of philosophy and theology,—so close that it is often impossible to decide where the one ends and the other begins,—is too well known to require any comment." And the learned Doctor then lays down the principle, which should never be overlooked by Indian historians, that whatever science "is closely connected with the Ancient Indian Religion must be considered as having sprung up among the Indians themselves," and not borrowed from other nations.*

Geometry was developed in India from the rules for the construction of altars. The Black Yajur Veda (V, 4, 11) enumerates the different shapes in which altars could be constructed, and Baudhâyana and Âpastamba furnish us with full particulars about the shape of these *chitis* and the bricks which had to be employed for their construction. (1) The Chaturasra Syena is a falcon-shaped altar built of square bricks, and is the most ancient. (2) The Syena Vakrapakshavyastapuchchha is an altar of the shape of a falcon with curved wings and outspread tail. (3) The Kankachit is a heron-shaped altar with two feet, and (4) the Alajachit is very similar

* Journal Asiatic Society, Bengal, 1875, p. 227.

to it. (5) The Praugachit is of the shape of the forepart of the poles of a chariot, an equilateral triangle, and (6) the Ubhayatah Praugachit is of the form of two such triangles joined with their bases. Then follow (7) the Ratha Chakrachit and (8) the Sâraratha Chakrachit of the shape of wheels, without and with spokes. (9) The Chaturasradronachit and (10) the Parimandaladronachit are of the shape of a drona or vessel, square or circular. (11) The Parichâyyachit is also of a wheel-shape, and (12) the Samûhyachit has likewise a circular shape. (13) The Smasânachit is a sloping quadrilateral altar wider at one base than at the other, and higher at the wider end. The last chiti mentioned is the Kurma or tortoise, which may be either (14) Vakrânga, curved, or (15) angular, or (16) Parimandala, circular.

The area of the earliest Chaturasra Syena was to be 7½ square purushas, which means 7½ squares, the side of each square being equal to a purusha, *i.e.*, the height of a man with uplifted arms. When any other shape of altar was required, *the size or area did not change*, so that a wheel, an equilateral triangle, or a tortoise had to be constructed,—all of the area of 7½ purushas. Then again at the second construction of the altar one square purusha had to be added to the area, and at the third construction two square purushas had to be added, *without changing the shape or the relative proportions of the figure.* All this could not be done without a considerable knowledge of Geometry, and the science of Geometry was thus invented. As Dr. Thibaut says, "squares had to be found which would be equal to two or more given squares; or equal to the difference of two given squares; oblongs had to be turned into squares and squares into oblongs; triangles had to be constructed equal to given squares or oblongs; and so on. The last task, and not the least, was that of finding a circle, the area of which might equal as closely as possibly that of a given square."

The result of these operations was the compilation of

a series of geometrical rules which are contained in the Sulva Sûtras, which form a portion of the Kalpa Sûtras, as we have stated before. These Sulva Sûtras date from the eighth century before Christ. The geometrical theorem that the square of the hypotenuse is equal to the squares of the other two sides of a rectangular triangle is ascribed by the Greeks to Pythagoras; but it was known in India at least two centuries before, and Pythagoras undoubtedly learnt this rule from India. The proposition referred to above is contained in two rules, viz., (1) The square of the diagonal of a square is twice as large as that square, and (2) The square of the diagonal of an oblong is equal to the square of both its sides.

Our limits forbid us to follow Dr. Thibaut's remarks contained in his most valuable and instructive paper, and all we can do is to briefly mention a few of the most important results achieved in the Sulva Sûtras. One remarkable result was to find the value of a diagonal in number in relation to the side of the square. The rule laid down is, "Increase the measure by its third part, and this third by its own fourth, less the thirty-fourth part of that fourth." In other words, if 1 represents the side, the diagonal will be $1 + \frac{1}{3} + \frac{1}{3 \times 4} - \frac{1}{3 \times 4 \times 34} = 1.4142156$. The real value of the diagonal is, we know, $\sqrt{2} = 1 \cdot 414213 \ldots$ and we see, therefore, that the rule given in the Sulva Sûtras is correct up to five places of the decimal.

Rules were framed for the formation of squares of three, four, five, or any times the area of a given square; for combining two squares of different sizes; for deducting one square from another; for turning an oblong into a square or a square into an oblong; for turning a square into a circle or a circle into a square. As an example, we will quote the rule of describing a circle equal to a given square.

The rule is this: "If you wish to turn a square into a circle, draw half of the cord stretched in the diagonal from the centre towards the Prâchî line (*i.e.*, the line due east); describe the circle, together with the third part of that piece of the cord which will lie outside the square."

The rule may be thus illustrated:—

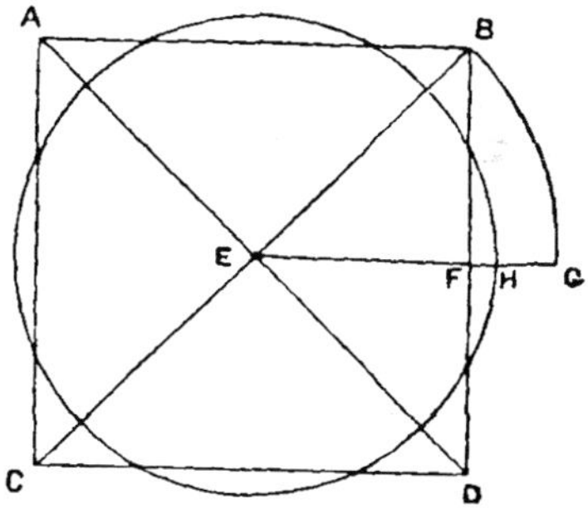

E B is half of the cord of the square A B C D stretched in the diagonal C B. Keep the point E fixed, and draw the cord towards the Prâchî or eastern line E F. A part of the cord, *i.e.*, F G, will lie outside the square. Take a third part of it, F H, together with the part inside, E F, and describe a circle with the radius E H.

It is needless to add that the result is only approximately correct.

Similarly: "If you wish to turn a circle into a square, divide the diameter into eight parts, and again one of these eight parts into twenty-nine parts; of these twenty-nine parts remove twenty-eight, and moreover the sixth part (of the one left part) less the eighth part (of the sixth part)."

The meaning of the rule is this:—

$$\frac{7}{8} + \frac{1}{8 \times 29} - \frac{1}{8 \times 29 \times 6} + \frac{1}{8 \times 29 \times 6 \times 8} \text{ of the}$$

diameter of a circle is the side of a square, the area of which is equal to the area of the circle.

Geometry is a lost science in India; for as soon as it was found that geometrical truths could be represented by algebra and arithmetic, Geometry gradually fell out of use. And the practical necessity for geometrical studies no longer existed in India when the Hindus began to worship images in the Puranic Age, and the setting up of sacred fires in the worshipper's house was discontinued, and the construction of altars was forgotten.

While the Greeks soon left the Hindus far behind in Geometry, they could never rival their Asiatic brethren in the science of Numbers. The world owes the Decimal Notation to the Hindus, and Arithmetic as a practical science would have been impossible without the Decimal Notation. The Arabs first learnt that notation from the Hindus and introduced it into Europe. The ancient Greeks and Romans were ignorant of it, and consequently never made much progress in the numerical science.

There is yet another science in which the Hindus were the first in the field, and achieved results in the Rationalistic Period which have never since been surpassed in the world. Professor Max Müller says that the Hindus and the Greeks are the only nations who developed the science of Grammar; but the achievements of the Greeks in Grammar are poor indeed compared with the marvellous work of Pânini,—the greatest Grammarian that the world has ever seen. We will not enter into the controversy on the age of Pânini. Professor Max Müller calls him the contemporary of Kâtyâyana, and gives the fourth century before Christ as his probable date, while Dr. Goldstücker maintains that the Grammarian lived in the ninth or tenth century before Christ. Our own opinion is that he lived long before Katyâyana, and before the rise of Buddhism, and that the eighth century before Christ is not an improbable date. He undoubtedly belongs to the Rationalistic Period, the period when every department of learning received a philosophical treatment. But being born in the extreme west of India, he may not have been acquainted with, or may not have recognised, the Brâhmanas and

Upanishads, which, as we have seen before, were mostly produced among the nations of the Gangetic valley, who were widely separated by their learning, their customs, and even their form of religion from the Punjab Hindus.

It would be foreign to our purpose to attempt even a brief review of Pânini's system of Grammar. The great discovery has been made in Europe in the present century that the tens of thousands of words in a language can be resolved to a small number of roots. This discovery was made in India three thousand years ago, before the time of Pânini, and the great Grammarian resolves the Sanscrit language of his time to its simple roots.

It was the knowledge of Sanscrit which enabled European scholars in the present century to discover the Science of Language; and Bopp and Grimm, and a host of other learned scholars, have resolved the Aryan languages to their original roots, as Pânini resolved the Sanscrit language to its roots in the dawn of Aryan history, when Athens and Rome were unknown!

CHAPTER VIII.

SÂNKHYA AND YOGA.

BUT the glory of the Rationalistic Period consists in the philosophy of Kapila and the religion of Buddha. Kapila and Buddha worked to some extent on the same lines. They both started with the great object of affording humanity a relief from the suffering which is the lot of all living beings. They both rejected with evident scorn the remedies which the Vedic rites pretended to offer, and called those rites impure, because connected with the slaughter of living beings. They both declared knowledge and meditation to be the means of salvation (see Sânkhya Kârikâ, 1 and 2). They both adopted the doctrine of transmigration from the Upanishads (Sânkhya Kârikâ, 45), and declared that pious acts lead to higher states of life. And lastly, they both aimed at Nirvâna (Sânkhya Kârikâ, 67), and the creed of the philosopher as well as of the reformer is agnostic.

But here the parallel ends. Kapila, who probably lived a century before Buddha, started the system of philosophy, but meant it only as philosophy. He addressed himself to high thinkers and to speculative scholars. His philosophy knows nothing of sympathy with mankind in general, he did not go to the masses, he founded no society or class. Buddha came after him, and was probably born in the very town sanctified by the memory of the great philosopher.* Certain it is that

* Buddha was born in Kapilavastu, which, according to the Pali Dâtha Vansa, was built by the sons of Ikshvâku, by the permission of the sage Kapila.

he was well versed in the philosophy of Kapila, and obtained his principal tenets from that source. But he possessed, what his predecessor did not possess, a living, all-embracing sympathy, a feeling for the poor, a tear for the bereaved and the sufferer. This was the secret of Buddha's great success. For philosophy is barren if it is not true to its name, if it does not seek earnestly, and in a loving spirit, the good of fellow-creatures, if it does not look with equal eye on the rich and the poor, on the Brâhman and the Sûdra. And the Sûdra and the poor came to Buddha one by one for his loving sympathy and meek beneficence. Good men admired his high-souled piety, just men yielded to his theory of the equality of men, and all the world admired his pure system of morality. The tide of the new religion rolled onwards, and swept away in its course the inequality of laws and the inequality of castes. Three centuries after his death, the Emperor of Pâtaliputra, who ruled over the whole of Northern India, accepted the poor man's religion, and proclaimed it as the religion of all India. And a living nation accepted the faith of the equality of men, such as the Hindus have never done again since they have ceased to be a living nation.

These matters, however, will be treated in future chapters, and we return therefore to the philosophy of Kapila,—"the first recorded system of philosophy" in the world, "the earliest attempt on record to give an answer from reason alone, to the mysterious questions which arise in every thoughtful mind about the origin of the world, the nature and relations of man and his future destiny." *

The *Sânkhya Pravachana* or *Sânkhya Sûtra* is ascribed to Kapila himself, but has probably been compiled or recast at a more recent age. An excellent edition of the work, with commentaries and translation, has been published by Dr. Ballantyne. The *Sânkhya Sâra* is composed by

* Davies's *Hindu Philosophy*.

Vijnâna Bhikshu, the commentator of Sânkhya Pravachana. And lastly, the *Sânkhya Kârikâ* is an ancient and concise treatise on the subject in only seventy-two distichs, composed by Isvara Krishna, and commented on by Guadapada and Vâchaspati. This small but excellent treatise has been translated into Latin by Lassen, into German by Windischmann and Lorinser, into French by Pantier and St. Hilaire, and into English by Colebrooke and Wilson, and recently by Davies. This small treatise will be our guide, specially as we have Mr. Davies's valuable notes to help us. We have only to add that it is impossible to give our readers the barest skeleton of Sânkhya Philosophy in a few pages, and that all we can do here is to notice a few essential principles of the system.

To relieve mankind from the three kinds of pain, viz., (1) bodily and mental, (2) natural and extrinsic, (3) divine or supernatural, is the object of Kapila's philosophy. Vedic rites are inefficacious, because they are impure, and are tainted with the slaughter of living beings; the complete and final emancipation of the soul is secured by knowledge alone.

Nature and Soul are eternal and self-existent. From nature (*Prakriti*) is produced the *intellect*, the *consciousness*, the five *subtle elements*, the five *grosser elements*, the five *senses of perception*, the five *organs* of *action*, and the *mind*. Soul (*Purusha*) produces nothing, but is only linked with Nature, with the corporeal body, until its final emancipation. Kapila does not accept the orthodox opinion of the Upanishads that all Souls are portions of the Universal Soul. He asserts that each Soul is separate, and has a separate existence after its emancipation from the bonds of Nature.

It will be seen that according to Kapila everything except *Purusha*, or soul, is derived from *Prakriti*, or primordial matter, and is therefore material. Not only the elements and the senses and the organs of action, but the mind, the consciousness, and the intellect are results of matter, of "mind stuff," as European philosophers call it. Kapila only differs from modern materialistic philosophers in asserting that there is a soul, independent of matter and eternal, though for a time linked with matter.

It is necessary to clearly understand the distinctions between the senses, the organs, the mind, the consciousness, the intellect, the elements, and the soul, in order to grasp the mental philosophy of Kapila.

The five senses simply observe, *i.e.*, receive impressions; the five organs of action, the voice, hands, feet, &c., act according to their functions (S. K. 28). The mind (*manas*) is not what is implied by the English word, but is only a sense organ (S. K. 27); it is the *sensorium commune*, it simply arranges the impressions and presents them to consciousness. Consciousness (S. K. 24) individualises those impressions as "mine." And the intellect distinguishes and discriminates (S. K. 23), and forms them into ideas. It will thus be seen that the distinctions made between the senses, the *manas*, the consciousness, and the intellect are real distinctions in the functions of the mind. In the language of European philosophy, *manas* receives the sensations and makes them actual perceptions; consciousness individualises them as "mine," and intellect turns individualised perceptions into "concepts or judgments," in the language of Sir W. Hamilton.

Hindu commentators love to describe this mental operation in a poetic garb. "As the headmen of the village," says Vâchaspati, "collect the taxes from the villagers and pay them to the governor of the district, as the local governor pays the amount to the minister, and the minister receives it for the use of the king, so the *manas*, having received ideas from the external organs, transfers them to consciousness, and consciousness delivers them to the intellect, the general superintendent, who takes charge of them for the use of the sovereign, Soul." Such metaphorical descriptions should not disguise from us the strictly scientific nature of the distinctions made,—

distinctions which are recognised by European philosophers as well as by Hindu thinkers. "Sensation proper," says Morell in his Elements of Psychology, "is not purely a passive state, but implies a certain amount of mental activity." A clock, for instance, may strike within our hearing, and yet we may be perfectly unconscious of the fact if we are absent-minded, *i.e.*, if our mind is not sufficiently active to catch the sensation; and this mental activity, which has no special name in European philosophy, is the *manas* of Kapila.

It shows no ordinary philosophic acumen in Kapila to have declared, at a time when the functions of the brain were still imperfectly understood, that the *manas*, the consciousness or *ahankâra*, and even the intellect or *buddhi*, were material in their origin. More than this, Kapila declares that the elements proceed from consciousness. Kapila herein seems to anticipate the philosophy of Berkeley and Hume, that objects are but permanent possibilities of sensations; and he agrees with Kant that we have no knowledge of an external world except as by the actions of our faculties it is represented to the soul, and take as granted the objective reality of our sense perceptions.

It will be observed that Kapila is not content with enumerating the five gross elements, ether, air, earth, fire, and water, but adds the five subtler principles, sound, tangibleness, odour, visibility, and taste. What are we to understand by the statement that these subtle principles have an independent existence? "The doctrine of Kapila seems to be, that in hearing, the ear has a relation not only to the ether, but to the subtler principle which underlies it, a dim apprehension of the truth that hearing depends not only on some channel of communication between the ear and the source of sound, but on some modification of the material element through which the sound is conducted." *

* Davies, p. 72.

Kapila recognises only three kinds of evidence, viz., Perception, Inference, and Testimony (S. K. 4). The Nyâya or Logical school recognises four, — dividing Kapila's Perception into *Anumâna* or perception, and *Upamâna* or analogy. The Vedantic school adds a fifth, which is called *Arthâpatti*, an informal kind of presumption: "Devadatta does not eat by day and yet is fat; it is presumed, therefore, that he eats by night."

Kapila will admit nothing which cannot be known by his three kinds of evidence. He rejects all inner ideas. And as neither Perception, nor Inference, nor reliable Testimony, presents to him the idea of an external Author of all things, the Supreme Deity is not admitted by him as knowable by his philosophy.

Kapila, however, believes in causation; *sat—kâryam—asat—akâranât;* what exists must have been caused, as there can be no existence without cause (S. K. 9). He also appeals to the observation of mankind that cause and effect imply each other, and ends by stating that an effect is identical with cause.

The three *gunas*, or constituent elements of nature, *sattva* (goodness), *rajas* (passion), and *tamas* (darkness), form an important part of all Hindu philosophy, and find a place in Kapila's (S. K. 11). The *gunas* are only a hypothesis which accounts for the manifest differences in the conditions of all formal existences.

Kapila argues the production of all formal existences from *Prakriti* or Nature on five different grounds (S. K. 15). Firstly, specific objects are finite in their nature and must have cause. Secondly, different things have common properties and must be different species of the same primary genus. Thirdly, all things are in a constant state of progression, and show an active energy of evolution which must have been derived from a primary source. Fourthly, the existing world is an effect, and there must be a primary cause. And fifthly, there is an undividedness, a real unity in the whole universe, which argues a common origin. On these grounds Kapila argues that all formal existences have been produced from *Prakriti* or primordial matter.

All except *Purusha* or Soul. And his reasons for the separate existence of soul also deserve mention. The first is the celebrated argument of design, but Kapila uses it differently from modern theologians. Matter has been apparently collected and arranged with a design, but this proves, according to Kapila, not a Designer, but the existence of soul, for which the things must have been arranged (S. K. 17). As a bed, argues Gaudapada, which is an assemblage of bedding, props, cotton, coverlet, and pillows, is for another's use, not its own, even so this world, which is an assemblage of the five elements, is for the use of the soul. Secondly, Matter furnishes materials for pleasure and pain; hence sentient nature, which feels pleasure and pain, must be different from it. Thirdly, there must be a superintending force. Fourthly, there must be a nature that enjoys. And the fifth argument is Plato's argument that the yearning for a higher life points to the possibility of gaining it. These are Kapila's arguments for the existence of soul independent of matter, but he will not believe in one soul, but asserts and gives reasons for believing that the souls of different beings are different, not one (S. K. 18). Here he goes counter to the Upanishads and to the Vedantic school, which is based on the Upanishads.

The vital actions of living systems are ascribed to certain subtle forces, and are generally described in Hindu philosophy as the five vital "airs." It was these subtle forces which were supposed to cause respiration, exertion, digestion, the circulation of blood, and the sensibility of the skin.

We have already said that Kapila borrowed the doctrine of transmigration of souls from the Upanishads. And having borrowed this idea, he had to suit it to his own system of philosophy. The soul, according to

Kapila, is so passive that the individuality of a man is scarcely stamped on it. The intellect, the consciousness, and the *manas*, all belong to the material part of a man. Hence Kapila was constrained by his own rigid reasoning to assume that something more than the soul migrated, that a subtle body, consisting of the intellect, the consciousness, and the *manas* and the subtle principles, migrated with the soul (S. K. 39 and 40). And this idea of a subtle body, the *linga sarîra*, runs through the whole of Hindu philosophy, and Manu says (XII, 16) that a subtle body envelops the souls of the wicked, that they may suffer the torments of hell. The religious systems of all nations furnish something analogous to this idea, and the notion of a *linga sarira* is accepted by the Hindus as the doctrine of the resurrection of the body is accepted by all Christian nations. This *linga sarîra* forms the personality of an individual, and ascends to a higher region or descends to a lower with the soul, according to the virtues or vices committed in this life (S. K. 44). The different regions are (1) that of Pisâchas, (2) that of Râkshasas, (3) that of Yakshas, (4) that of Gandharvas, (5) that of Indra (sun), (6) that of Soma (moon), (7) that of the Prajâpatis, the abode of the Fathers and Rishis, and (8) that of Brahmâ, the highest heaven. Besides these eight superior orders of beings, there are five inferior orders: (1) domestic quadrupeds, (2) wild quadrupeds, (3) birds, (4) reptiles, fishes, and insects, and (5) vegetables and inorganic bodies. Man stands alone between the eight superior orders and the five inferior orders (S. K. 53). The quality of *sattva* prevails in the superior orders, of *rajas* in man, and of *tamas* in the lower orders (S. K. 54). A man, according to his actions, may descend or ascend to a lower or higher order, or be born again as man of some caste or other. When the soul is finally rid of the *linga sarîra*, it is finally emancipated.

It is the knowledge which the soul acquires through

its union with nature that leads to its final emancipation. "As a dancer having exhibited herself on the stage ceases to dance, so does nature cease when she has made herself manifest to soul" (S. K. 59).

Even after the soul has obtained complete knowledge, it resides for a time in the body, "as a potter's wheel continues to revolve from the force of the previous impulse." This is the *Nirvâna* of Buddha, a state of quietude, when perfect knowledge has been gained, when all passions have been restrained, all desires have been checked, and the enlightened soul awaits its final emancipation. That separation of soul and matter comes at last. Nature ceases to act, as her purpose has been accomplished, and the soul obtains an abstraction from matter, and both continue to exist eternally isolated from each other, and independent (S. K. 68).

Such is the barest outline of Sânkhya Philosophy. The latest German philosophy, the system of Schopenhauer (1819) and Von Hartmann (1869), is "a reproduction of the philosophic system of Kapila in its materialistic part, presented in a more elaborate form, but on the same fundamental lines. In this respect the human intellect has gone over the same ground that it occupied more than two thousand years ago; but on a more important question it has taken a step in retreat. Kapila recognised fully the existence of a soul in man, forming indeed his proper nature,—the absolute ego of Fichte,—distinct from matter and immortal; but our latest philosophy, both here and in Germany, can see in man only a highly developed physical organisation. 'All external things,' says Kapila, 'were formed that the soul might know itself and be free.' 'The study of psychology is vain,' says Schopenhauer, 'for there is no Psyche.'" *

The great want of Kapila's philosophy as a creed for the people was its agnosticism,—and the Yoga system of philosophy sought to remove this want. It is ascribed

* Davies, Preface to Hindu Philosophy.

to Patanjali, who, according to Dr. Goldstücker, lived in the second century before Christ. All that we know of the life and history of Patanjali is that his mother was called Gonikâ, as he himself tells us, and that he resided for a certain time in Kashmîra, a circumstance which may have led to his great grammatical commentary having been preserved by the kings of that country. Patanjali calls himself Gonardiya, or a native of Gonarda, a place in the eastern part of India.

We have seen before that Kâtyâyana attacked Pânini's grammar about the fourth century B.C., and Patanjali's greatest work was his Mahâbhâsya or Great Commentary, in which he defended Pânini, and left a monument of his profound erudition. The Yoga system of philosophy is also ascribed to him, and it is quite reasonable to suppose that the great defender of Pânini also sought to popularise Kapila among his countrymen by adding to his cold and agnostic philosophy the doctrine of faith in a Supreme Deity, as well as some mystic practices and meditation by which final emancipation (it was believed) could be obtained.

The work ascribed to Patanjali—the *Yoga Sûtra*—has been edited and translated into English by Dr. Rajendra Lala Mitra, who also gives a brief abstract of its contents in his preface. As a system of philosophy the Yoga has no value by the side of the Sânkhya, and our account of it will therefore be brief. And the learned translator of the Yoga Sûtra will be our guide in our brief account of the system.

The Yoga Sûtra comprises 194 aphorisms, divided into four chapters. The first chapter is called *Samâdhi Pâda*, and contains 51 aphorisms treating of the nature of meditation. The second chapter consists of 55 aphorisms, and is called *Sâdhana Pâda*, and treats of the practices and exercises required in meditation. The third chapter is called *Vibhûti Pâda*, and treats in 55 aphorisms of the occult powers which may be acquired. The fourth chapter is called *Kaivalya Pâda*, and treats in 33 aphorisms of the isolation and detachment of the soul from all worldly ties, which is the ultimate object of meditation.

In the first chapter *Yoga* is derived from *Yuj*, "to join" or "to meditate," and this meditation is possible only by the suppression of the functions of the mind. By constant exercise and by dispassion the functions of the mind may be suppressed, and Yoga, conscious or unconscious, may be attained. The latter form of Yoga is higher than the former, and is devoid even of deliberation or joy, egoism or the exercise of reason.

Devotion to God hastens the attainment of this coveted state of mind. The conception of God or Îsvara is that of a Soul untouched by affliction, works, deserts, and desires. In Him "the seed of the Omniscient attains infinity," and He "is the instructor of even all early ones, for He is not limited by time" (*Yoga Sûtra*, I, 25 and 26). The sacred syllable *om* indicates the Deity.

Disease, doubt, worldly-mindedness, &c., are obstacles to the attainment of Yoga, but these may be overcome by concentration of the mind, by benevolence, by indifference to happiness or misery, and even by the regulation of the breath. The chapter ends with a description of various kinds of Yoga.

The second chapter details the exercises necessary for the performance of the Yoga. Asceticism, the muttering of a mantra, and devotion to God, are the earliest exercises. These overcome all afflictions like ignorance, egoism, desire, and aversion or ardent desire to live. These are the motives to work, and works must bear their fruits in subsequent births. We shall see hereafter that this is the Buddhist theory of *Karma*, about which so much has been written. The object of Yoga is to devise means to abstain from works, and so preclude future births.

We have then the Sânkhya definition of the soul and

the intellect; knowledge finally severs the connection between the two, and thenceforward the soul is free, and an end is put to future births and suffering. Knowledge passes through seven stages before it is perfect, and eight means (which remind one of the eight-fold path of the Buddhists) are prescribed, by which this perfect knowledge can be obtained. The first way is abstaining from evil actions, slaughter, falsehood, theft, incontinence, and avarice; and the second consists of an obligation to perform certain acts, purification, contentment, penance, study, and devotion to God. These two means are prescribed for all, householders and ascetics alike. Then come the duties special to Yogins. The third is assuming special postures for meditation; the fourth is regulation of the breath; the fifth is the abstraction of the organs from their natural functions; and the sixth, seventh and eighth are steadfastness (*Dhâranâ*), contemplation (*Dhyâna*), and meditation (*Samâdhi*), which three are the essential constituents of Yoga itself. When these three are united, *Samyama* follows, and results in the acquisition of occult powers.

The occult powers, or *Siddhis*, described in the third chapter are indeed wonderful! One may know the past and the future, make himself invisible to men, observe the details of what is passing in distant regions or in the stars and planets, converse with spirits, travel in the air or through water, and acquire various superhuman powers! The noble philosophy of Kapila was trailed through dirt and mire as soon as it was blended with popular superstitions!

But these occult powers are not the final objects which a Yogin seeks. The ultimate isolation of the soul is the final object of the Yogin, and this is discussed in the fourth and last chapter. We come back now to the theory that all works, all sensations and impressions on the mind, bear their fruit in future births. A discussion ensues regarding the nature of sensations and perceptions, of the intellect and the soul, and the distinctions are much the same as in Sânkhya philosophy. Having explained these distinctions, Patanjali concludes by saying that perfect knowledge sweeps away all residue of former works (IV, 28–30), and the moment at last arrives when the three qualities become defunct, and the soul abides solely in its own essence. This emancipation of the soul is the object of Yoga (IV, 33), it is absolute and eternal, and the soul which has attained it remains free for evermore.

It will thus be seen that as a system of philosophy Yoga is valueless; all its fundamental maxims about the soul and intellect and sensations, about the transmigration of souls and their eternity and final emancipation by knowledge, are those of Sânkhya Philosophy. In fact, Patanjali tried to blend the idea of a Supreme Deity with the philosophy of Kapila; but unfortunately he also mixed up with it much of the superstition and the mystic practices of the age! Or rather we are inclined to hold that the great Grammarian founded a pure theistic system of philosophy, which has since been mixed up with much of popular superstitions and mystic rites, and the result is the Yoga Sûtra as we find it now. In still later times the philosophy of the Yoga system has been completely lost sight of, and the system has degenerated into cruel and indecent Tântrika rites, or into the impostures and superstitions of the so-called Yogins of the present day.

CHAPTER IX.

NYÂYA AND VAISESIKA.

GAUTAMA* is the Aristotle of India, and his system of Nyâya is the Hindu Logic. His date is unknown, and he is said to have married Ahalyâ. He lived no doubt in the Rationalistic Period, but probably a century after Kapila. The *Nyâya Sûtra*, which is ascribed to him, is divided into five books, each divided into two "days" or diurnal lessons, and these are again divided into articles, and each article consists of a number of Sûtras. Nyâya is still a favourite study in India, and we have seen students from Kashmir and Rajputana and Northern India attending the celebrated Nyâya schools in Navadvîpa in Bengal, living in the houses of their teachers, and pursuing their studies for years together, in the very same way in which students among the Magadhas and Angas and Kosalas and Videhas pursued their studies when Gautama, the logician, lived and taught! Everything else has changed in India, but ancient traditional learning is still handed down in *tols* from generation to generation in the same ancient method. The spirit of the time, however, has told on these time-honoured institutions; the mass of students turn away from these secluded seats of learning to schools and universities; the founders of *tols* get scarcely enough to live upon, and travel from place to place to seek the bounty of well-

* One must be careful to distinguish Gautama the earliest Sûtrakâra from Gautama the Logician. And we have a third Gautama still,—the founder of Buddhism.

disposed men; and the number of students is getting fewer year by year. Nevertheless, with their wonderful loyalty to the past, Hindu pandits and Hindu students still adhere to this ancient system of teaching, of which we have given a brief account before from the Dharma Sûtras; and it is to be hoped this relic of the past will yet survive modern changes and innovations.

The Nyâya system starts with the subjects to be discussed. These are (1) *Pramâna*, proof, and (2) *Prameya*, or the thing to be proved. These are the principal subjects, while there are fourteen subsidiary subjects, viz., (3) Doubt, (4) Motive, (5) Instance or Example, (6) Determined truth, (7) Argument or Syllogism, (8) Confutation, (9) Ascertainment, (10) Controversy, (11) Jangling, (12) Objection, (13) Fallacy, (14) Perversion, (15) Futility, and (16) Controversy.

Proof, as we have said before, is of four kinds: Perception, Inference, Analogy, and Verbal Testimony. Cause (*Kârana*) is that which necessarily precedes an effect, which could not be without the cause; and effect (*Kârya*) is that which necessarily ensues and otherwise could not be. For the relation of cause and effect, the connections might be twofold,—simple conjunction (*Sanjoga*), and constant relation (*Samavâya*). Hence cause may be of three kinds: (1) Immediate and direct, as the yarn is of cloth; (2) Mediate or indirect, as the weaving is of cloth; and (3) Instrumental, as the loom is of cloth.

The things to be proved, the objects of knowledge, are (1) Soul, (2) Body, (3) the Senses, (4) the Objects of Sense, (5) Intellect, (6) *Manas*, (7) Production, (8) Fault, (9) Transmigration, (10) Fruit or Retribution, (11) Pain, (12) Emancipation.

The soul is different in each person, and is separate from the body and the senses, and is the seat of knowledge. Each individual soul is infinite and eternal, and transmigrates according to the works performed in life.

So far we see an agreement with Kapila's philosophy. But the Nyâya adds that the Supreme Soul is one, the seat of eternal knowledge, and the maker or former of all things. The body is earthly, the five external senses are also material, and the *manas* is the organ of the senses. The reader will mark here how far the Nyâya system, and indeed every system of Hindu Philosophy, is indebted to Sânkhya Philosophy, which may justly be called the basis of Hindu Philosophy.

Intellect is two-fold, including *memory* and *concept*. A concept is true if derived from clear proof, and is wrong if not derived from proof. Similarly, memory may be right or wrong. The objects of sense are odour, taste, colour, touch, and sound.

Production or action is the cause of virtue or vice, of merit or demerit; and the only motive to action, as we are told by European philosophers also, is the desire to attain pleasure or to avoid pain.

Transmigration is the passing of the soul to successive bodies. Pain is the primary evil, and there are twenty-one varieties of evil which are causes of pain. The soul attains its emancipation by knowledge and not by action.

The speciality of Nyâya is its development of inference by the construction of a true syllogism, and, as Mr. Davies states, "the right methods of reasoning have been discussed with as much subtlety as by any of the Western logicians." We quote below an instance of Hindu syllogism :—

1. The hill is fiery.
2. For it smokes.
3. Whatever smokes is fiery, as a kitchen.
4. The hill is smoking.
5. Therefore it is fiery.

The Hindu syllogism therefore consists of five parts, which are called (1) the proposition (*pratijnâ*), (2) the reason (*hetu* or *apadesa*), (3) the instance (*udâharana* or *nidarsana*), (4) the application of the reason (*upanaya*), and (5) the conclusion (*nigamana*). If the first two or the last two parts be omitted, it becomes a perfect syllogism of Aristotle. The question therefore arises, Is this coincidence purely accidental, or did one nation get some hint from another? Comparing dates, we are disposed to say of this as of many other sciences, The Hindus invented logic, the Greeks perfected it.

Among the many technical terms in use in Hindu logic, *Vyâpti* and *Upâdhi* are the most important. *Vyâpti* means invariable concomitance,—the connection in the major premiss of Aristotle's syllogism. "Whatever smokes is fiery,"—this invariable concomitance is *Vyâpti*. As Sankara Misra argues, "It is not merely a relation of co-extension. Nor is it the relation of totality. For if you say that invariable concomitance is the connection of the middle term with the whole of the major term, such connection does not exist in the case of smoke (for smoke does not always exist where there is fire). We proceed then to state that invariable concomitance is a connection requiring no qualifying term or limitation. It is an extensiveness co-extensive with the predicate. In other words, invariable concomitance is invariable co-inherence of the predicate." *

On the other hand, the qualifying term or limitation is called *Upâdhi*. Fire always underlies smoke, but smoke does not invariably accompany fire. The proposition, therefore, that smoke accompanies fire requires a qualifying condition,—a limitation,—an *Upâdhi*, viz., that there must be moist fuel.

Logic is a favourite study with learned Hindus, and neither the Ancient Greeks, nor the Mediæval Arabs, nor the European schoolmen of the Middle Ages displayed more acuteness and subtlety in reasoning, or more rigid and scientific strictness in their discussions, than is witnessed in the numerous works of the Hindus on Logic.

* Gough's Translation. Quoted in Monier Williams' *Indian Wisdom*, p. 73.

Kanâda's atomic philosophy is supplementary to Gautama's logic, as the Yoga is supplementary to the Sânkhya, and therefore need not detain us long. The cardinal principle of Kanâda is that all material substances are aggregates of atoms. The atoms are eternal, the aggregates only are perishable by disintegration.

The mote which is visible in the sunbeam is the smallest perceptible object. But being a substance and an effect, it must be composed of what is less than itself;—the ultimate atom only is not a compound, but is simple.

The first compound is of two atoms; the next consists of three double atoms, and so on. The mote visible in the sunbeam is thus a compound of six atoms. In this way two earthly atoms acting under an unseen law, *adrishta*, (and not under the will of God, which is unknown in Kanâda's philosophy), constitute a double atom of earth; three binary atoms constitute a tertiary atom; four tertiary atoms make a quarternary atom; and so on to gross, grosser, and grossest masses of earth. In this manner the great earth is produced, the great water is thus produced from aqueous atoms, great light from luminous atoms, and great air from aërial atoms.

Kanâda recognises seven categories of objects (*padârtha*), viz., (1) Substances, (2) Quality, (3) Action, (4) Community, (5) Particularity, (6) Coherence, and (7) Non-existence.

Under the first of these categories, the nine substances of Kanâda are (1) Earth, (2) Water, (3) Light, and (4) Air, all eternal in atoms, but transient and perishable in aggregates. Next is (5) *Âkâsa* or Ether, which transmits sound, and which has no atoms, but is infinite, one, and eternal. (6) Time and (7) Space similarly are not material, and therefore are not compounded of atoms. They are infinite, one, and eternal. The last two in the category are (8) Soul, and (9) *Manas* or the Internal Organ. *Light and heat are considered as only different forms of the same essential substance.* Âkâsa or ether conveys sound; and Manas or the internal organ is supposed to be extremely small, like an atom.

The second category, Quality, embraces seventeen varieties or qualities of the nine substances enumerated above. The qualities are colour, savour, odour, tangibility, number, extension, individuality, conjunction, disjunction, priority, posteriority, intellections, pleasure, pain, desire, aversion, and volition.

The third category, Action, is divided into five kinds, upward and downward movement, contraction, dilation, and general motion.

The fourth category, Community, is the source of our notion of genus. It denotes qualities common to many objects, and also denotes species. These genera and species have a real and objective existence according to Kanâda, but not according to the Bauddhas, who affirm that individuals only have existence, and that abstractions are unreal conceptions. "It is the quarrel revived in the Realist and Nominalist theories of the mediæval schoolmen." *

The fifth category, Particularity, denotes simple objects, devoid of community. They are soul, mind, time, place, the ethereal element, and atoms.

The sixth category, Coherence (the *samavâya* of Gautama's philosophy), is connection between things which must be connected so long as they exist, as yarn and cloth.

The seventh category, Non-existence, is either universal or mutual.

It will be seen from the above brief account that the Vaisesika system of Kanâda, in so far as it is an original system, is physics more than philosophy. It was the first attempt made in India to inquire into the laws of matter and force, of combination and disintegration.

* Davies, p. 131.

In every system of Hindu Philosophy (except Vedântism) matter is supposed to be eternal, and distinct from soul. The Vedântists alone regard matter as the manifestation of the One Supreme Soul who comprises and is himself *all.* Of this system we will speak in the next chapter.

CHAPTER X.

PÛRVA MÎMÂNSÂ AND VEDÂNTA.

WE now come to the last two systems of the philosophy of the Hindus, the Pûrva Mîmânsâ of Jaimini and the Uttara Mîmânsâ of Bâdarâyana Vyâsa. To the historian of India they are of the utmost importance and value. For the Mîmânsâ schools represent the conservative phase of the Hindu mind at a time when philosophers and laymen were alike drifting towards agnostic and heterodox opinions. Sânkhya philosophy led away hosts of thinking men from the teachings of the Upanishads on the Universal Soul; and the Buddhist religion was embraced by many of the lower classes as a relief from caste inequalities and elaborate Vedic rites. Against this general movement of the day the Mîmânsâ schools made a stand. The Pûrva Mîmânsâ insisted on those Vedic rites and practices which modern philosophers had come to regard as useless or even as unholy; and the Uttara Mîmânsâ proclaimed the doctrine of the Universal Soul which the Upanishads had taught before, and which continues to be the cardinal doctrine of Hinduism to this day.

The controversy, or rather the division in opinion, went on for centuries, but orthodoxy prevailed in India in the end. The great Kumârila Bhatta, who lived in the seventh century after Christ, wrote his celebrated Vârtika or commentary on the Pûrva Mîmânsâ Sûtras, and was the most redoubted champion of Hinduism, and the most uncompromising opponent of Buddhism. He not only vindicated the ancient rites of the Vedas, he not only proclaimed against the heterodox opinions of the Buddhists, but he denied them any consideration even when they happened to agree with the Veda.

The Uttara Mîmânsâ too had its champion,—and a greater man than Kumârila rose, two centuries later, in the celebrated Sankarâchârya. Sankara's great commentary is known as the Sârîraka Mîmânsâ Bhâsya. He was born in 788 A.D., and therefore wrote and preached in the first half of the ninth century.

Thus both Kumârila and Sankarâchârya belong to the Puranic Period, but they finally secured the triumph of that orthodox philosophy which was based on the Brâhmanas and Upanishads. The history of philosophy in India is the history of the Hindu mind; and an account of the systems of philosophy which took their rise in the Rationalistic Period would not be intelligible, unless we indicated, however briefly, the bearings of these systems on the later history of the nation.

The Sûtras of the Pûrva Mîmânsâ are ascribed to Jaimini, and are divided into twelve lectures and subdivided into sixty chapters. The Sûtras have an old commentary by Sabara Svâmî Bhatta. Kumârila Bhatta came later on the stage, and his commentary, as we have stated before, marks a new epoch in the history of this school, and has been respected by a host of succeeding commentators.

Jaimini's Sûtras, as stated before, are divided into twelve lectures. The first lecture treats of the authority of enjoined duty. The varieties of duty, supplemental duties, and the purpose of the performance of duties are treated in the second, third, and fourth chapters. The order of their performance is considered in the fifth, and the qualification for their performance is treated in the sixth. This completes the first half of the Sûtras.

The subject of indirect precept is treated in chapters seven and eight. Inferable changes are discussed in the ninth, and exceptions in the tenth chapter. Efficacy is considered in the eleventh chapter, and the work closes with a discussion of co-ordinate effect in the twelfth chapter.

These are the principal topics of the Pûrva Mîmânsâ Sûtras, but a great many other matters are introduced, which are very interesting.

In the very first lecture we are told that the Vedas are *eternal and revealed.* They had no human origin, because no human author is remembered. This eternal and superhuman Veda consists of two parts, *Mantra* and *Brâhmana.* Mantras are distinguished under three designations, viz., (1) those in metre are Rik, (2) those chanted are Sâman, and (3) the rest are Yajush. Generally, a Mantra is a prayer or invocation; a Brâhmana is a precept directing religious observances, and the Brâhmanas include the Upanishads.

After the Veda, which is *Sruti,* comes the *Smriti,* or works *composed by holy personages,* and possessing authority as grounded on the Veda. *Smriti* includes the *Dharmasâstras* (the Dharma Sûtras of the Rationalistic Period), comprising the institutes of civil and religious law.

Besides the Dharma Sûtras, we are told of the *Kalpa Sûtras,* also composed by authors conversant with the Veda. The Kalpa Sûtras are not a part of the Veda, and have no authority except as is derived from the Veda. The reader will mark the broad line of demarcation which ancient Hindus have drawn between the Brâhmana literature, which is considered revealed and eternal, and the Sûtra literature, which is ascribed to human authors, and has no independent authority. The priority of the Brâhmana literature may fairly be inferred from this.

Sacrifice (*Yâga*) is the act of religion most inculcated in the Veda, and consequently most discussed in the Mîmânsâ. Three ceremonies are mentioned as types of the rest: they are the setting up of the sacrificial fire, the presenting of an oblation, and the preparation of the Soma. Various curious questions are raised and discussed and answered with regard to sacrifices. One very remarkabe example will suffice.

At certain sacrifices the votary is told to bestow all his property on the officiating priests. The question is raised whether a king should give up all lands, including pasture lands, highways, and the sites of lakes and ponds. The answer is that *a king has not property in the land*, and cannot bestow it. His kingly power is for the government of the realm, but the right of property is not thereby vested in him, else he would have property in house and lands appertaining to his subjects. The lands of a kingdom cannot be given away by a king, but a house or field acquired by purchase, &c., may be given away.

Similarly, the question of self-immolation on fire, the question of performing sacrifices to injure others, and various similar questions are discussed with considerable acumen and closeness of reasoning. As Colebrook remarks, the logic of the Mîmânsâ is the logic of the law. "Each case is examined and determined upon general principles, and from the cases decided the principles may be collected. A well-ordered arrangement of them would constitute the philosophy of the law; and this is in truth what has been attempted in the Mîmânsâ."

To return to the subject of sacrifices, which is the all-pervading subject of the Pûrva Mîmânsâ, we are told that the full complement of persons officiating at a great ceremony is seventeen, viz., the sacrificer and sixteen priests. On occasions of less solemnity four priests only are engaged.

The number of victims varies according to the nature of the sacrifice. At an *Asvamedha* sacrifice there must be not fewer than 609 victims of all kinds, tame and wild, terrestrial and aquatic, walking, flying, swimming, and creeping things!

The cardinal idea of the Mîmânsâ is to teach man his

Duty. Jaimini commences his Mîmânsâ with the enunciation of Duty, the only topic he has to propound. "Now then," he begins, "the study of Duty is to be commenced. Duty is a purpose which is inculcated by a command. Its reason must be inquired." But his idea of Duty is extremely limited, it consists in the proper performance of Vedic rites and practices. Pûrva Mîmânsâ Philosophy is therefore merely a philosophy of Vedic rites.

In his anxiety to insist on ancient Vedic rites and practices, Jaimini has forgotten to speak of Vedic faith and belief! As Dr. Banerjea says in his Dialogues on Hindu Philosophy, Jaimini "urges the consideration of *Duty* without caring for any to whom it may be *due*." While insisting on the eternity of the Veda, as Sabda or the Word, he has made no mention "of any co-eternal Intelligence uttering or revealing it." While enjoining the performance of the sacrifices inculcated in the Brâhmanas, he has nothing to say of the Universal Soul of the Upanishads. The philosophy of Jaimini has, therefore, although orthodox, been stigmatised as agnostic, and even Sankarâchârya admits that God is not deducible from this philosophy.

A supplementary system of philosophy was therefore called for, and the Uttara Mîmânsâ or Vedânta supplied this want. It is the Vedânta which tells us of the Supreme Being, the Universal Soul, the Pervading Breath, as the Pûrva Mîmânsâ speaks of rights and sacrifices. The Vedânta is the direct outcome of the Upanishads, as the Pûrva Mîmânsâ is the outcome of the Brâhmanas. The very first aphorism of the Vedânta substitutes Brahman or God for Dharma or Duty. The two schools of Mîmânsâ taken together represent orthodox Vedic Hinduism,—Hinduism in rites and observances, and Hinduism in its belief. The two schools taken together are an answer to Buddhist heretics who ignored Vedic rites and ignored a Supreme Being. The two schools together are an answer to the agnostic Sânkhya system of philosophy, and to other systems which proclaim matter eternal. The two schools together form the basis of true Hinduism.

The Sârîraka Mîmânsâ Sûtra or Brahma Sûtra is attributed to Bâdarâyana Vyâsa. It refers to the doctrines of Kapila, and the Yoga of Patanjali; and also to the Atomic theory of Kanâda, which is itself a sequel to the Nyâya of Gautama. There is reference also to Jaimini, and to the sects of Jainas, Bauddhas, and Pâsupatas; and altogether the Brahma Sûtra is undoubtedly the latest of the six schools of philosophy, and could not have been compiled very long before the Christian Era.

The Vedânta adopts the syllogism of Nyâya, with the obvious improvement of reducing its five members into three, as in the syllogism of Aristotle. Colebrooke thinks this improvement was borrowed from the Greeks, which is very likely.

Bâdarâyana's Brahma Sûtra is divided into four lectures, and each lecture is subdivided into four chapters. Anything like a complete analysis of this work is impossible within our limits, and we must therefore glean a few leading tenets from Colebrooke's excellent analysis, to which we refer those of our readers who wish to have an adequate idea of the subject.

The Uttara Mîmânsâ opens precisely as the Pûrva Mîmânsâ, announcing its purport in the very same terms, only substituting Brahman or God for Dharma or Duty. The author then confutes the Sânkhya doctrine of Nature being the material cause of the universe, and declares a Sentient Rational Being to be the first Cause. That Supreme Being is the material as well as the efficient cause of the universe. To Him meditation should be directed, and on Him the thoughts are to be fixed for obtaining final emancipation.

The second lecture continues the confutation of Kapila's Sânkhya philosophy, as well as of Patanjali's Yoga philosophy and Kanâda's Atomic theory. All the universe is rigidly assigned to Brahman, who is the Cause and the

Effect. The distinction between cause and effect, and between different effects, does not invalidate the unity of the whole. "The sea is one and not other than its waters; yet waves, foam, spray, drops, froth, and other modifications of it, differ from each other" (II, 1, 5). "As milk changes into curd, and water to ice, so is Brahman variously transformed" (II, 1, 8).

Then follows a confutation of the doctrines of the Sânkhyas, the Vaisesikas, the Bauddhas, the Jainas, the Pâsupatas, and the Pâncharâtras.

The soul is active, not passive as the Sânkhyas maintain. Its activity is, however, adventitious. As the carpenter, having tools in hand, toils and suffers, and laying them aside, rests and is easy, so the soul in conjunction with the senses and organs is active, and quitting them, reposes (II, 3, 15). The soul is a portion of the Supreme Ruler, as a spark is of fire (II, 3, 17). As the sun's image reflected on water is tremulous, quaking with the undulations of the pool, without however affecting the images on other sheets of water, or the solar orb itself, so the sufferings of one individual affect not another, nor the Supreme Ruler. The corporeal organs and the vital actions are all modifications of Brahman.

The third lecture treats of transmigration of souls, of the attainment of knowledge, of final emancipation, and of the attributes of the Supreme Being. The soul transmigrates, invested with a subtle frame, passing from one state to another. Departing from one body, it experiences the recompense of its works, and returns to occupy a new body with the resulting influence of its former deeds. Evil doers suffer in seven appointed regions of retribution.

The Supreme Being is impassable, unaffected by worldly modifications, as the clear crystal, seemingly coloured by the hibiscus flower, is really pellucid. He is pure Sense, Intellect, Thought.

"Like the sun and other luminaries, seemingly multiplied by reflection though really single, and like space apparently subdivided in vessels containing it within limits, the Supreme Light is without difference or distinction." "There is none other but He" (III, 2). The reader will perceive that the Vedânta philosophy is a direct and legitimate result of the Upanishads, and the idea of Unity is carried to its extreme limit in the Vedânta as in the Upanishads.

The last half of this lecture relates to devout exercises and pious meditation, which are necessary for the reception of divine knowledge.

The fourth and last lecture relates to the fruit of pious meditations properly conducted, and the attainment of divine knowledge. So soon as that knowledge is attained, past sins are annulled and future sins are precluded. In like manner the effects of merit and virtue are also annulled. And "having annulled by fruition other works which had begun to have effect, having enjoyed the recompense and suffered the pains of good and bad actions, the possessor of divine knowledge, on the demise of the body, proceeds to a reunion with Brahman" (IV, 1, 14). This, as we know, is the Final Beatitude of the Upanishads.

There are two other less perfect forms of emancipation. One of them qualifies the soul for reception at Brahman's abode, but not for immediate reunion and identity with his being. The other is still less perfect, and is called *Jîvan-mukti*, which can be acquired in lifetime by Yogins, and enables them to perform supernatural acts, as evoking the shades of forefathers, assuming different bodies, going immediately to any place at pleasure, &c. This is only a repetition of superstition of the Yoga philosophy, described in a previous chapter.

The attributes of God, according to the Vedânta philosophy, have thus been recapitulated by Colebrooke: "God is the omniscient and omnipotent cause of the existence, continuance, and dissolution of the universe. Creation is an act of His will. He is both efficient and material cause of the world, creator and nature, framer and frame, doer and deed. At the consummation of all things, all are resolved into Him. . . . The Supreme Being is one, sole existent, secondless, entire, without parts, sempiternal, infinite, ineffable, invariable, ruler of all, universal soul, truth, wisdom, intelligence, happiness."*

Such are the six systems of philosophy which were developed in India in the Rationalistic Period; such are the answers which Hindu philosophers have given to the questions which were started in the Upanishads, to questions which rise in the mind of every reflective man, but which it is not given to him to answer completely, —What is God, and What is man?

For the rest, the Rationalistic Period is rich in results of which every Hindu may be proud. It was probably in this period that the great Epics of India received their epic form. It was in this period that the infant sciences of Geometry and of Grammar were developed by the Hindus. It was in this period that the first recorded systems of Mental Philosophy and of Logic were conceived and perfected. It was in this period that Civil and Criminal Laws were codified and treated on a scientific basis. It was at the close of this period that the whole of Northern India was first brought under one great and able ruler, and that an excellent and enlightened system of administration was finally perfected. And, lastly, it was in this period that the great saint and reformer Gautama Buddha proclaimed that religion of equality and brotherhood of man which is at the present day the living faith of one-third of the human race. To the story of that great revolution we now turn.

* The Philosophy of the Hindus (*Vedânta*).

CHAPTER XI.

BUDDHIST SACRED LITERATURE.

IN the sixth century before Christ, India witnessed the commencement of a great revolution. Her ancient religion, which the Hindu Aryans had practised and proclaimed for fourteen centuries, had degenerated into forms. The gods of the Rig Veda, whom the ancient Rishiṣ had invoked and worshipped lovingly and fervently, had come to be regarded as so many names; and Indra and Ushas raised no distinct ideas and no grateful emotions. The simple libations of the Soma-juice, or offerings of milk, corn, or flesh, which the Rishis of old had offered with a fervent heart to their gods, had developed into cumbrous ceremonials, elaborate rites, unmeaning forms. The descendants or successors of those Rishis had now stepped forth as a powerful and hereditary caste, and claimed the right to perform elaborate religious rites and utter sacred prayers for the people. The people were taught to believe that they earned merit by having these rites performed and prayers uttered by hired priests. The religious instinct, the grateful emotions which had inspired the composers of the Vedic hymns, were dead; vast ceremonials, dead forms, remained.

A reaction had taken place. About the eleventh century before Christ, *i.e.*, five centuries before the time of which we are now speaking, earnest and thoughtful

Hindus had ventured to go beyond the wearisome rituals of the Brâhmana literature, and had inquired into the mysteries of the soul and its Creator. The composers of the Upanishads had dared to conceive the bold idea that all animate and inanimate nature proceeded from One Universal Deity, and were portions of One Pervading Soul. Inquiries were made into the mysteries of death and the future world, conjectures were made about the transmigration of souls, and doctrines were started containing in a crude form the salient principles of later Hindu philosophy.

But few could devote their lives to these abstruse speculations, and the abstruse philosophy which they led to. The mass of the Aryan householders,—Brâhmans, Kshatriyas, and Vaisyas,—contented themselves with performing the rites, unintelligible to them, which the Brâhmanas had laid down and the Sûtras had condensed. The rules of social and domestic life were similarly condensed for the people in the Sûtras, and all the learning and science known to the age were also codified in the Sûtra form.

Such was the state of things in India in the sixth century before Christ. Religion in its true sense had been replaced by forms. Excellent social and moral rules were disfigured by the unhealthy distinctions of caste, by exclusive privileges for Brâhmans, by cruel laws for Sûdras. Such exclusive caste privileges did not help to improve the Brâhmans themselves. As a community they became grasping and covetous, ignorant and pretentious, until Brâhman Sûtrakâras themselves had to censure the abuse in the strongest terms. For the Sûdras, who had come under the shelter of the Aryan religion, there was no religious instruction, no religious observance, no social respect. Despised and degraded in the community in which they lived, they sighed for a change. And the invidious distinction became unbearable as they increased in number, pursued various useful industries, owned lands and villages, and gained in influence and power. Thus society was still held in the cast-iron mould which it had long outgrown; and the social, religious, and legal literature of the day still proclaimed and upheld the cruel injustice against the Sûdra long after the Sûdra had become civilised and industrious, and a worthy member of society.

To an earnest and inquisitive mind, to a sympathetic and benevolent soul, there was something anomalous in all this. Gautama of the Sâkya race was versed in the Hindu learning and religion of the age, but he pondered and asked if what he had learnt could be efficacious or true. His righteous soul rebelled against the unrighteous distinctions between man and man; and his benevolent heart hankered for a means to help the humble, the oppressed, and the lowly. The dead ceremonials and rites which householders practised appeared as vain and fruitless to him as the penances and mortifications which hermits voluntarily underwent in forests. The beauty of a holy life, of a sinless benevolent career, flashed before his mind's eye as the perfection of human destiny, as the heaven on earth; and, with the earnest conviction of a prophet and a reformer, he proclaimed this as the essence of religion. His world-embracing sympathy led him to proclaim this method of self-culture and holy living to suffering humanity, and he invited the poor and the lowly to end their sufferings by cultivating virtue, by eschewing passions and evil desires, and by spreading brotherly love and universal peace. The Brâhman and the Sûdra, the high and the low, were the same in his eyes,—all could equally effect their salvation by a holy life, and he invited all to embrace his catholic religion of love. Mankind responded to the touching appeal, and Buddhism in the course of a few centuries became the prevailing faith, not of a sect or a country, but of the continent of Asia.*

Nevertheless, it would be historically wrong to suppose that Gautama Buddha consciously set himself up as the founder of a new religion. On the contrary, he believed to the last that he was proclaiming only the ancient and pure form of religion which had prevailed among the Hindus, among Brâhmans, Srâmans, and others, but which had been corrupted at a later day. As a matter of fact, Hinduism recognised wandering bodies of ascetics who renounced the world, performed no Vedic rites, and passed their days in contemplation (see *ante*, Chap. VI.). Such bodies were known as Bhikshus in the Hindu law-books, and were generally known as Srâmans. Gautama founded only one sect of Srâmans among many sects which then existed, and his sect was known as that of the Sâkyaputrîya Srâmans, to distinguish them from others. He taught them relinquishment of the world, a holy life, and pious meditation, such as all sects of Srâmans recommended and practised.

What then is the distinguishing feature in Buddha's life-work which has made his tenets a religion,—and the religion of a third of the human race?

Gautama's holy and pious life, his world-embracing

* The figures given below will show approximately the proportion of Buddhists to the world's population :—

Jews	7,000,000
Christians	328,000,000
Hindus	160,000,000
Musalmans	155,000,000
Buddhists	500,000,000
Not included in the above	100,000,000
Population of the world	1,250,000,000

Between the fifth and tenth centuries after Christ more than one-half of the human race were Buddhists.

sympathy, his unsurpassed moral precepts, his gentle and beautiful character, stamped themselves on his teachings, which were not altogether new, gathered round him the meek and the lowly, the gentlest and the best of the Aryans, struck kings on their thrones and peasants in their cottages, and united sects and castes together as in a communion of love! And the sacred recollections of his life and doings remained after he had passed away, and held together the community which cherished his teachings, and in course of time gave those teachings the character of a distinct and noble religion.

Inspired by his love of purity, and a holy, gentle life, Gautama eschewed the rites of the Vedas and the penances of ascetics alike; he insisted only on self-culture, on benevolence, on pious resignation. He knew of no caste-distinction among his Bhikshus; he recognised no meritorious ceremonials and no meritorious penances except the practice of virtue. This is what has made Buddhism a living and life-giving religion, when so many rival forms of asceticism have withered and died away.

It will be our endeavour to indicate the salient features of the Buddhist religion, and its far-reaching consequences on the history of India. Fortunately, we have no reason to complain of want of materials.

Indeed, so much has been written about Buddhism in recent years that it is almost difficult to imagine that Buddhist literature and religion were almost an unknown subject half a century ago. The distinguished missionary, Dr. Marshman, who lived and wrote in India for many years, could give no better account of Buddha in 1824 than that his worship was probably connected with the Egyptian Apis! And theories more wild and more imaginary were seriously recorded by other scholars.

Happily those days are past. Earnest inquirers and scholars have collected Oriental manuscripts and works in different Buddhist countries, have studied, published, and translated many of them, and have thus formed a generally accurate idea of the religion as it was first preached by Gautama, and as it was subsequently modified in different times among different nations. It is not our purpose to record here a history of the researches into Buddhism during the last half-century, but a few facts are so interesting that they cannot be passed over.

Mr. Hodgson was the English resident of Nepal from 1833 to 1843, and he was the first to collect original manuscripts on which a sober account of the religion could be based. He sent 85 bundles to the Asiatic Society of Bengal, 85 to the Royal Asiatic Society of London, 30 to the India Office Library, 7 to the Bodleian Library of Oxford, and 174 to the Société Asiatique in Paris, or to M. Burnouf personally. Mr. Hodgson also gave some account of these works and of the Buddhist religion in his essays.

The genius of Eugene Burnouf breathed life into these dead manuscripts, and his "Introduction to the History of Indian Buddhism," published in 1844, was the first rational, scientific, and comprehensive account of the Buddhist religion. The fame of the eminent scholar and the great ability and philosophical acumen with which he treated the subject attracted the attention of learned Europe to this wonderful religion, and the inquiry which Burnouf started has continued to the present day, and has been fruitful of great results.

What Hodgson did in Nepal, Alexander Csoma Korosi, a Hungarian scholar, did in Thibet. The annals of literary inquiry and research have few more wonderful stories to tell than that of the single-minded devotion of this simple Hungarian. He early made up his mind to devote himself to the study of Eastern languages, and he set forth from Bucharest in 1820, without friends or money, and travelled on foot or by water on a raft till he came to Bagdad. He pushed on to Teheran, and thence started again with a caravan and came by

Khorasan to Bokhara. In 1822 he came to Kabul and thence to Lahore, and from Lahore he travelled through Kashmir to Ladak, where he finally settled. He sojourned and travelled long in these parts, and in 1831 he was at Simla "dressed in a coarse blue cloth loose gown, extending to his heels, and a small cloth cap of the same material. He wore a grizzly beard, shunned the society of Europeans, and passed his whole time in study." * In 1832 he came to Calcutta, where he was kindly received by Dr. Wilson and Mr. James Prinsep, and resided many years. In 1842 he left Calcutta again to go to Thibet, but died of fever on his way, at Darjeeling. The Asiatic Society of Bengal has raised a monument on his grave in Darjeeling. The present writer had the mournful satisfaction of paying a visit to this grave, not many months ago.

About his work on Thibetan Buddhist books, we find all necessary information in Vol. XX. of the Asiatic Researches. Since Csoma's time other scholars have laboured in the same field of Thibetan Buddhist literature, and have added to our knowledge of the subject.

To the Rev. Samuel Beal is due the credit of procuring a complete collection of Chinese works on Buddhism. A request was made to this effect to the Japanese ambassador who visited England, and the ambassador at once acceded to the request, and on his return to Tokio ordered the entire collection known as "The Sacred Teaching of the Three Treasures" to be sent to England. The collection contains over 2000 volumes, and represents the entire series of sacred books taken during successive centuries from India to China, as also works and commentaries of native Chinese priests.

Buddhism and Buddhist scriptures were carried to Ceylon in the reign of Asoka the Great, about 242 B.C., and the whole of the Buddhist scriptures, the "Three

* Quoted in Beal's *Buddhism in China*, from Ralston's *Thibetan Tales*.

Baskets," exist to this day in Ceylon, as we will see further on, in the Pâli language, and in almost the identical shape in which they were taken there over two thousand years ago. A number of eminent scholars, Turnour, Fausböll, Oldenberg, Childers, Spence Hardy, Rhys Davids, Max Müller, Weber, and others, have worked on these materials, and much of the Pâli scriptures has been published, and the most important portions of them have been translated.

Burma too has contributed to our knowledge of Buddhism, and a great deal of information on Burmese Buddhism is embodied in Bigandet's life of the Gaudama, first published in 1868. All countries near and around India have furnished us with valuable records and contributions towards a scholarlike knowledge of this great religion. India alone,—the home of that religion,—the country where it flourished more or less for nearly fifteen centuries,—has kept no memorials worth the name of that noble faith! So complete has been the destruction of Buddhism, Buddhist monasteries, and Buddhist records in India!

Thanks to the researches of the scholars whom we have named above, the English-reading public have sufficient materials before them now for studying the developments of Buddhism in the different countries of the world,—in China, Japan, and Thibet, in Burma and Ceylon. English readers can thus study the progress of the religion in its various phases, at different ages, and among different conditions of life and civilisation.

The historian of India must, however, forego that pleasant and most interesting task. The developments which Buddhism received in China, and Thibet, and Burma, have no direct bearing on Indian history. It is his duty, therefore, to select from the materials before him those works only which illustrate the history of *Early Buddhism in India*. It is necessary for him to go to the fountain source of the information which is available, and to place his reliance on those works specially which illustrate the rise of Buddhism in India in the Rationalistic Period.

The forms of Buddhism prevailing in Nepal and Thibet, China and Japan, are called Northern Buddhism, while the forms prevailing in Ceylon and Burma are called Southern Buddhism. The Northern Buddhists furnish us with scanty materials directly illustrating the religion in its earliest form in India. For the Northern nations embraced Buddhism some centuries after the Christian Era, and the works which they then obtained from India do not represent the earliest form of Indian Buddhism. The Lalita Vistâra, a most important work of the Northern Buddhists, is only a gorgeous poem; it is no more a biography of Gautama than the Paradise Lost is a biography of Jesus. It was composed probably in Nepal in the second or third or fourth century after Christ, although it contains passages,—the Gathas,—which are of a very much older date. In China, Buddhism was introduced from the first century after Christ, but did not become the state religion until the fourth century, and the works on Buddhism which were then carried by Chinese pilgrims from India from century to century, and translated into the Chinese language, do not illustrate the earliest phase of Buddhism in India. Buddhism spread in Japan in the fifth century, and in Thibet in the seventh century after Christ. Thibet has drifted far away from primitive Buddhism in India, and has adopted forms and ceremonies which were unknown to Gautama and his followers.

On the other hand, the Southern Buddhists furnish us with the most valuable materials for our purpose. The sacred books of the Southern Buddhists are known by the inclusive name of the Three Pitakas; and there is evidence to show that these Pitakas, now extant in Ceylon, are substantially identical with the canon as settled in the Council of Patna about 242 B.C.

The date of Buddha's death was for a long time believed to be 543 B.C.; but many facts ascertained within the last thirty years lead to the conclusion that the great reformer was born about 557 B.C., and died in 477 B.C. A Council of 500 monks was held in Râjagriha, the capital of Magadha, immediately after his death, and they chanted the sacred laws together to fix them on their memory. A hundred years later, *i.e.*, in 377 B.C., a second Council was held in Vesâli, mainly for the discussion and settlement of ten questions on which difference of opinion had arisen. A hundred and thirty-five years after this, the great Asoka, king of the Magadhas, held a third Council in Patna about 242 B.C., to finally settle the religious works or Pitakas.

It is well known that Asoka was a most zealous Buddhist, and sent missionaries to foreign countries, and even to Syria, Macedon, and Egypt, to preach the religion. He sent his own son Mahinda to Tissa, the king of Ceylon, about 242 B.C., and Mahinda took with him a number of Buddhist monks, and thus conveyed to Ceylon the Pitakas as just settled in the Council of Patna.* It is needless to say that Tissa, the king of Ceylon, was glad to embrace the religion which Asoka recommended and his son preached, and thus Ceylon embraced Buddhism in the third century B.C. About a hundred and fifty years after this these Pitakas were formally reduced to writing, and thus we have the most authentic account of the earliest form of Buddhism in Magadha in the Pâli Pitakas of Ceylon.

These facts will show that the Three Pitakas of the Southern Buddhists can claim a date anterior to 242 B.C. For no work which could not claim a respectable antiquity was included as canon by the Council of Patna. Indeed,

* Dîpavansa, XII. According to this historical epic of Ceylon, Mahinda, was the son of Asoka (born when Asoka was a sub-king at Ujjayinî under his father, who was king at Magadha), by the daughter of the Sethi or banker of Vidisâ (*Dipavansa*, VI, 15 and 16).

there is internal evidence in the Vinaya Pitaka to lead to the supposition that the main portions of that Pitaka were settled before the Vesâli Council, *i.e.*, before 377 B.C. For in the main portions of the Vinaya Pitaka there is no mention of the discussion on the ten questions alluded to above,—questions which were "as important for the history of Buddhism as the Arian controversy for that of Christianity," and which agitated the whole of the Buddhist world to its very centre. The inference is irresistible that the main portion of the Vinaya Pitaka is anterior to the date of the Council, *i.e.*, anterior to 377 B.C.

We have thus found in the Scriptures of the Southern Buddhists reliable materials for the history of India for the centuries immediately after the time of Gautama Buddha. For the contents of the Three Pitakas were composed, settled, and arranged in India during the hundred or two hundred years after the death of Gautama, just as the four Christian Gospels were composed and settled within a century or two after the death of Jesus. Hence the Three Pitakas illustrate the manners and life of the Hindus and the history of Hindu kingdoms in the Gangetic valley. And, lastly, they give us a more consistent and a less exaggerated account of the life and work and teachings of Buddha himself than anything which the Northern Buddhists can supply us with. Both as an index to the Hindu civilisation of the period, and as an account of Gautama's life and work, the Three Pitakas will be our guide. It is to these Pâli works that "we must go in preference to all other sources if we desire to know whether any information is obtainable regarding Buddha and his life." *

The Three Pitakas are known, as the Sutta Pitaka, the Vinaya Pitaka, and the Abhidhamma Pitaka. The works comprised in the Sutta Pitaka profess to record the sayings and doings of Gautama Buddha himself. Guatama

* Oldenberg's *Buddha* (translation), p. 75.

himself is the actor and the speaker in the earliest works of this Pitaka, and his doctrines are conveyed in his own words. Occasionally one of his disciples is the instructor, and there are short introductions to indicate where and when Gautama or his disciple spoke. But all through the Sutta Pitaka, Gautama's doctrines and moral precepts are preserved, professedly in Gautama's own words.

The Vinaya Pitaka contain very minute rules, often on the most trivial subjects, for the conduct of monks and nuns,—the Bhikkhus and the Bhikkhunîs who had embraced the holy order. Gautama respected the lay disciple (Upâsaka), but he held that to embrace the Holy Order was a quicker path to salvation. As the number of Bhikkhus and Bhikkhunîs multiplied, it was necessary to fix elaborate rules, often on very minute subjects, for their proper conduct and behaviour in the Vihâra or monastery. As Gautama lived for nearly half a century after he had proclaimed his religion, there can be no doubt that he himself settled many of these rules. At the same time, it is equally certain that many of the minute rules grew up after his death, but they are all attributed in the Vinaya Pitaka to the direct order of the Blessed One himself.

And lastly, the Abhidamma Pitaka contains disquisitions on various subjects, on the conditions of life in different worlds, on personal qualities, on the elements, on the causes of existence, &c. We now subjoin a list of works contained in the Three Pitakas :—

I. *Sutta Pitaka.*

1. Dîgha Nikâya or long treatises, being a collection of 34 Suttas.
2. Majjhima Nikâya or middling treatises, a collection of 152 Suttas of moderate size.
3. Samyutta Nikâya, or the connected treatises.

4. Anguttara Nikâya, treatises in divisions the length of which increases by one.

5. Khuddaka Nikâya or short treatises. It contains 15 works which should be mentioned in detail: *—

(1) Khuddaka Pâtha or short passages.

(2) Dhammapada, an excellent collection of Moral Precepts.

(3) Udâna, 82 short lyrics supposed to have been uttered by Gautama at different periods under strong emotion.

(4) Itivuttika, 110 sayings of Buddha.

(5) Sutta Nipâta, 70 didactic poems.

(6) Vimâna Vatthu, stories of celestial mansions.

(7) Peta Vatthu on departed spirits.

(8) Thera Gâthâ, stanzas of monks.

(9) Therî Gâthâ, stanzas of nuns.

(10) Jâtaka, 550 stories of former births.

(11) Niddesa, explanations on the Sutta Nipâta (No. 5) by Sâriputta.

(12) Patisambhidâ, on intuitive insight.

(13) Apadâna, legends about Arhats or Saints.

(14) Buddha Vansa. Lives of 24 preceding Buddhas, and of Gautama, the historical Buddha.

(15) Chariyâ Pitaka, Gautama's virtuous acts in former births.

II. *Vinaya Pitaka.*

1. Vibhanga. Doctors Oldenberg and Rhys Davids consider it as only an extended reading of the Pâtimokkha, *i.e.*, as the Pâtimokkha with notes and commentary included. The Pâtimokkha is a formular of sins and their punishments recited every new moon and full moon day, and the members of the order who have committed any such sin are supposed to confess it and are disburdened of it.

* The fifteen works composing the fifth Nikâya are by some classed in the Abhidhamma, and not in the Sutta Pitaka.

2. Khandakas, *i.e.*, the Mahâvagga and the Chullavagga.

3. Parivâra Pâtha, admittedly an appendix and a later résumé of the preceding portions of the Vinaya Pitaka.*

III. *Abhidamma Pitaka.*

1. Dhamma Sangani. Conditions of life in different worlds.
2. Vibhanga, 18 books of disquisitions.
3. Kathâ Vatthu, 1000 subjects for controversy.
4. Puggala Pannatti. On Personal Qualities.
5. Dhâtu Kathâ. On the elements.
6. Yamaka, *i.e.*, pairs, *i.e.*, on apparent contradictions or contrasts.
7. Patthâna. On the causes of existence.

Such are the contents of the Three Pitakas which have preserved to us the most reliable materials that are available for the history of Buddha's life and work, and the history of Buddhist India. Although writing was known when the Three Pitakas were settled and compiled, yet for hundreds of years they were preserved solely by memory, even as the Vedas in India were preserved by memory.

"The text of the Three Pitakas and the commentary too thereon.

"The wise Bhikkhus of former time had handed down by word of mouth."†

And it was in the first century before Christ, about 88 B.C., that the sacred works were at last recorded into writing, as we have seen before.

It is well known that Gautama, disregarding the precedent set by all classical writers and thinkers in India, preached his doctrine and morality to the people of India

* But compiled by the time of Asoka and carried to Ceylon by his son Mahinda according to the Dîpavansa, VII, 42. The works learnt and carried to Ceylon by Mahinda are thus described :—The five Nikâyas (Sutta Pitaka), the seven sections (Abhidhamma), the two Vibhangas, the Parivâra, and the Khandaka (Vinaya).

† Dîpavansa, XX, 20, 21.

in the language of the people, not in Sanscrit. It is said in the Chullavagga (V, 33, 1), that "There were two brothers, Bhikkhus, by name Yamelu and Tekula, Brâhmans by birth, excelling in speech, excelling in pronunciation." And they went up to Gautama and said, "At the present time, Lord, Bhikkhus differing in name, differing in lineage, differing in birth, differing in family, have gone forth. These corrupt the word of the Buddhas by their own dialect. Let us, Lord, put the word of the Buddhas into Sanscrit verse (Chhandaso âropema)."

But Gautama would have none of this;—he worked for the humble and the lowly, his message was for the people, and he wished it to be conveyed to them in their own tongue. "You are not, O Bhikkhus, to put the word of the Buddhas into (Sanscrit) verse. . . . I allow you, O Bhikkhus, to learn the word of the Buddhas *each in his own dialect.*"

Generally we can apply to the Three Pitakas the remarks which Doctors Rhys Davids and Oldenberg make in respect of the Vinaya Pitaka. "The text, as it lies before us, stands so well against all proofs, whether we compare its different parts, one with another, or with the little that is yet known of its Northern counterparts, that we are justified in regarding these Pâli books as in fact the authentic mirror of the old Mâgadhî text as fixed in the central schools of the most ancient Buddhist Church. That text in the dialect of Magadha may have been lost to us once for all; and we can scarcely hope, unless some isolated sentences may hereafter be found, preserved here and there in inscriptions, that this loss will ever be even partially made good. But we may well be thankful that the faithful zeal and industry of these old monks has preserved for us a translation, in a dialect so nearly allied to the original, and in so perfect and trustworthy a state as the Pâli version of the Vinaya still undoubtedly presents."*

* Vinaya Texts (translation), Part I., Introduction, xxxvi.

CHAPTER XII.

LIFE OF GAUTAMA BUDDHA.

IN the sixth century before Christ, the kingdom of Magadha was rising to power and greatness. The kingdom, corresponding to modern South Behar, extended to the south of the Ganges, and on either side of the Son river. To the north of the Ganges it had a powerful rival in the haughty confederation of the Lichchavis. Râjagriha, to the south of the Ganges, was the capital of Bimbisâra, king of the Magadhas; and Vaisâli, to the north of the Ganges, was the capital of the Lichchavis. To the east lay the kingdom of Anga or East Behar, which is spoken of in connection with Magadha, and Champâ was the capital of Anga. Far to the north-west lay the ancient kingdom of the Kosalas, and its capital had been removed from Ayodhyâ or Sâketa further northwards to the flourishing town of Srâvasti, where Prasenajit reigned at the time of which we are speaking. The equally ancient country of the Kâsîs, lying to the south, seemed to be at this time subject to the king of Srâvasti, and a viceroy of Prasenajit ruled at Benares.

A little to the east of the Kosala kingdom, two kindred clans, the Sâkyas and the Koliyans, lived on the opposite banks of the small stream Rohinî, and enjoyed a sort of precarious independence, more through the jealousies of the rival kings of Magadha and Kosala than by their own power. Kapilavastu was the capital of the Sâkyas, who were then living in peace with the Koliyans, and

Suddhodana, chief of the Sâkyas, had married two daughters of the chief of the Koliyans.

Neither queen bore any child to Suddhodana for many years, and the hope of leaving an heir to the principality of the Sâkyas was well-nigh abandoned. At last, however, the elder queen promised her husband an heir, and, according to ancient custom, left for her father's house in order to be confined. But before she reached the place she was confined, in the pleasant grove of Lumbinî, of a son. The mother and the child were carried back to Kapilavastu, where the former died seven days after, leaving the child to be nursed by his step-mother and aunt, the younger queen.

The birth of Gautama is naturally the subject of many legends which have a most remarkable resemblance with the legends about the birth of Jesus Christ. One of them may be quoted here. The Rishi Asita saw the gods delighted, and

"Seeing the gods with pleased minds, delighted, and showing his respect, he said this on that occasion: 'Why is the assembly of the gods so exceedingly pleased, why do they take their clothes and wave them?'. . .

"The Bodhisatta, the excellent pearl, the incomparable, is born for the good and for a blessing in the world of men, in the town of the Sâkyas in the country of Lumbinî. Therefore, we are glad and exceedingly pleased."

Having obtained this reply, the Rishi went to Suddhodana's palace and asked, "Where is this prince? I wish to see him."

"Then the Sâkyas showed to Asita the child, the prince, who was like shining gold, manufactured by a very skilful smith in the mouth of a forge, and beaming in glory and beautiful." And the Rishi foretold that the boy would reach the summit of enlightenment, and would establish righteousness, and that his religion would be widely spread (*Nâlaka Sutta*).

The boy was named Siddhârtha, but Gautama was his

family name. He belonged to the Sâkya tribe, and is therefore often called Sâkya Sinha; and when he had proclaimed and preached a reformed religion, he was called Buddha, or the "awakened" or "enlightened."

Little is known of the early life of young Gautama, except that he was married to his cousin Subhadhrâ or Yasodharâ, daughter of the chief of Koli, about the age of eighteen. It is said that Gautama neglected the manly exercises which all Kshatriyas of his age delighted in, and that his relations complained of this. A day was accordingly fixed for the trial of his skill, and the young prince of the Sâkyas is said to have proved his superiority to his kinsmen.

Ten years after his marriage, Gautama resolved to quit his home and his wife for the study of philosophy and religion. The story which is told of the young prince abandoning his home and his position is well known. He must have for a long time pondered deeply and sorrowfully on the sins and sufferings of humanity, he must have been struck with the vanity of wealth and position. In the midst of his prosperity, position, and wealth, he felt a secret yearning after something higher, which neither wealth nor position could satisfy; and a strong, irresistible desire to seek for a remedy for the sufferings of men arose in his heart even in the midst of the luxuries and comforts of his palace-home. It is said that the sight of a decrepit old man, of a sick man, of a decaying corpse, and of a dignified hermit led him to form his resolution to quit his home. The story has little foundation in truth, and only represents in a concrete shape the thoughts that arose in his mind with regard to the woes of a worldly life, and the holy calm of a retired life.

At this time a son was born unto him. It is said that the news was announced to him in a garden on the riverside, and the pensive young man only exclaimed, "This is a new and strong tie I shall have to break." The news gladdened the heart of the Sâkyas, and Kapilavastu resounded with notes of joy at the birth of an heir to the throne. A perfect ovation awaited Gautama on his return to that town, and among the deafening cheers which arose, Gautama heard a young girl say, "Happy the father, happy the mother, happy the wife of such a son and husband." Gautama understood the word "happy" in the sense of "emancipated" from sins and new births, and he took off his necklace of pearls and sent it to the girl. The girl believed the young prince was enamoured of her, and little knew the thoughts which were struggling within him.

That night he repaired to the threshold of his wife's chamber, and there—by the light of the flickering lamp—he gazed on a scene of perfect bliss. His young wife lay surrounded by flowers, and with one hand on the infant's head. A yearning arose in his heart to take the babe in his arms for the last time before relinquishing all earthly bliss. But this he might not do. The mother might be awakened, and the importunities of the fond and loving soul might unnerve his heart and shake his resolution. Silently he tore himself away from that blissful sight—that nest of all his joy and love and affection. In that one eventful moment, in the silent darkness of that night, he renounced for ever his wealth and position and power, his proud rank and his princely fame, and more than all this, the affections of a happy home, the love of a young wife and of a tender infant now lying unconscious in sleep. He renounced all this, and rode away to become a poor student and a homeless wanderer. His faithful servant Channa asked to be allowed to stay with him and become an ascetic, but Gautama sent him back, and repaired alone to Râjagriha.

Râjagriha, as we have stated before, was the capital of Bimbisâra, king of the Magadhas, and was situated in a valley surrounded by five hills. Some Brâhman ascetics lived in the caves of these hills, sufficiently far from the town for studies and contemplation, and yet sufficiently near to obtain supplies. Gautama attached himself first to one Alâra, and then to another Udraka, and learnt from them all that Hindu philosophers had to teach.

Not satisfied with this learning, Gautama wished to see if penances would bring superhuman insight and power as they were reputed to do. He retired therefore into the jungles of Uruvelâ, near the site of the present temple of Buddha Gayâ, and for six years, attended by five disciples, he gave himself up to the severest penances and self-mortification. His fame spread all round, for the ignorant and the superstitious always admire self-inflicted pain; but Gautama did not obtain what he sought. At last one day he fell down from sheer weakness, and his disciples thought he was dead. But he recovered, and despairing of deriving any profit from penance, he abandoned it. His disciples, who did not understand his object, lost all respect for him when he gave up his penances; they left him alone and went away to Benares.

Left alone in the world, Gautama wandered towards the banks of the Niranjarâ, received his morning meal from the hands of Sujâtâ, a villager's daughter, and sat himself down under the famous Bo-tree or the tree of wisdom. Many are the legends told of Mâra, the evil spirit, who tempted him on this occasion, legends which have a curious resemblance with the legends of the temptation of Jesus Christ. For a long time he sat in contemplation, and the scenes of his past life came thronging into his mind. The learning he had acquired had produced no results, the penances he had undergone were vain, his disciples had left him alone in the world. Would he now return to his happy home, to the arms of his loving, widowed wife, to his little child now a sweet boy of six years, to his affectionate father and his loyal people? This was possible; but where would be the satisfaction? What would become of the mission to which he had devoted himself? Long he sat in contemplation and in doubt, until the doubts cleared away like mists in the morning, and the daylight of truth flashed before his eyes. What was this truth which learning did not teach and penances did not impart? He had made no new discovery, he had acquired no new knowledge, but his pious nature and his benevolent heart told him that a holy life and an all-embracing love were the panacea to all evils. Self-culture and universal love,—this was his discovery,—this is the essence of Buddhism.

The conflict in Gautama's mind, which thus subsided in calm, is described in Buddhist writings by marvellous incidents. Clouds and darkness prevailed, the earth and oceans quaked, rivers flowed back to their sources, and peaks of lofty mountains rolled down. Dr. Rhys Davids justly states that these legends have a deep meaning, and are "the first half-inarticulate efforts the Indian mind had made to describe the feelings of a strong man torn by contending passions." *

Gautama's old teacher Alâra was dead, and he went therefore to Benares to proclaim the truth to his five former disciples. On the way he met a man of the name of Upaka, belonging to the Âjîvaka sect of ascetics, who, looking at the composed and happy expression on Gautama's face, asked, "Your countenance, friend, is serene; your complexion is pure and bright. In whose name, friend, have you retired from the world? Who is your teacher? What doctrine do you profess?" To this Gautama replied that he had no teacher, that he had obtained Nirvâna by the extinction of all passions, and added, "I go to the city of the Kâsîs to beat the drum of the immortal in the darkness of the world." Upaka did not understand him, and replied after a little conversation,

* *Buddhism.*—Dr. Rhys Davids quotes a passage from Milton's Paradise Regained, describing a similar disturbance of the elements on the occasion of Christ's Temptation.

"It may be so, friend," shook his head, took another road, and went away (*Mahâvagga*, I, 6).

At Benares Gautama entered the Deer Park (Migadâya) in the cool of the evening and met his former disciples. And he explained to them his new tenets.

"There are two extremes, O Bhikkhus, which the man who has given up the world ought not to follow,—the habitual practice, on the one hand, of those things whose attraction depends upon the passions, and specially of sensuality, a low and pagan way, unworthy, unprofitable, and fit only for the worldly minded;—and the habitual practice, on the other hand, of asceticism, which is painful, unworthy, and unprofitable.

"There is a middle path, O Bhikkhus, avoiding these two extremes, discovered by the Tathâgata (Buddha), a path which opens the eyes and bestows understanding, which leads to peace of mind, to the higher wisdom, to full enlightenment, to Nirvâna!"

And then he explained to them the four truths concerning suffering, the cause of suffering, the destruction of suffering, and the way which leads to such destruction of suffering. And the way was described to be eightfold, and consisted in correct beliefs, aims, speech and actions, in correct living and endeavour, mindfulness and meditation.* And this doctrine, Gautama rightly said, "was not, O Bhikkhus, among the doctrines handed down." "In Benares, in the hermitage of Migadâya, the Supreme Wheel of the Empire of Truth has been set rolling by the Blessed One,—that wheel which not by any Sâman or Brâhman, not by any god, not by any Brahmâ or Mâra, not by any one in the universe, can ever be turned back" (*Dhamma Chakka Ppavattana Sutta; Anguttara Nikaya*).

* We shall have to dwell hereafter on these four truths and the eightfold path which are the cardinal principles of Buddhism. The above extracts will show that they were also the principles which Gautama proclaimed to the world at the very outset of his career.

It is needless to say that the five former disciples were soon converted, and were the first members of the Order.

Yasa, son of the rich Sethi (banker) of Benares, was his first lay disciple, and the story of the conversion of this young man, nurtured in the lap of luxury and wealth, is worth repeating. "He had three palaces, one for winter, one for summer, one for the rainy season." One night he awoke from sleep and found the female musicians still sleeping in the room with their dress and hair and musical instruments in disorder. The young man, who had apparently been satiated with a life of luxury, became disgusted with what he saw, and in a moment of deep thoughtfulness said: "Alas! what distress; alas! what danger!" And he left the house and went out.

It was dawn, and Gautama was walking up and down in the open air, and heard the perplexed and sorrowful young man exclaiming, "Alas! what distress; alas! what danger!" The sage replied, "Here is no distress, Yasa, here is no danger. Come here, Yasa, sit down; I will teach you the truth." And Yasa heard the truth from the lips of the saintly instructor.

Yasa's father and mother and wife missed him, and they all came to Gautama and listened to the holy truth. And they soon became lay disciples (*Mahâvagga*, I, 7 and 8).

Within five months after his arrival at Benares Gautama had sixty followers. And now he called them together and dismissed them in different directions to preach the truth for the salvation of mankind. "Go ye now, O Bhikkhus, and wander, for the gain of the many, for the welfare of the many, out of compassion for the world, for the good, for the gain, for the welfare of gods and men. *Let not two of you go the same way.* Preach, O Bikkhus, the doctrine which is glorious in the beginning, glorious in the middle, glorious in the end, in the spirit, and in the letter; proclaim a *consummate, perfect, and pure life of holiness*" (*Mahâvagga*, I, II, I). No missionaries of later days have evinced a holier zeal to proclaim the truth to the ends of the earth than the followers of Gautama, acting on the sacred mandate quoted above. Gautama himself went to Uruvelâ, and Yasa remained in Benares.

At Uruvelâ, Gautama achieved distinguished success by converting three brothers named Kâsyapa, who worshipped fire in the Vedic form, and had high reputation as hermits and philosophers. The eldest brother Uruvelâ Kâsyapa and his pupils "flung their hair, their braids, their provisions, and the things for the *agnihotra* sacrifice into the river," and received the Pabbâjja and Upasampadâ ordination from the Blessed One. His brothers, who lived by the Nadî (River Niranjarâ) and at Gayâ, soon followed the example (*Mahâvagga*, I, 15–20).

The conversion of the Kâsyapas created a sensation, and Gautama with his new disciples and a thousand followers walked towards Râjagriha, the capital of Magadha. News of the new prophet soon reached the king, and Seniya Bimbisâra, surrounded by numbers of Brâhmans and Vaisyas, went to visit Gautama. Seeing the distinguished Uruvelâ Kâsyapa there, the king could not make out if that great Brâhman had converted Gautama, or if Gautama had converted the Brâhman. Gautama understood the king's perplexity, and in order to enlighten him, asked Kâsyapa, "What knowledge have you gained, O inhabitant of Uruvelâ, that has induced you, who were renowned for your penances, to forsake your sacred fire." Kâsyapa replied that he had "seen the state of peace," and "took no more delight in sacrifices and offerings." The king was struck and pleased, and, with his numerous attendants, declared himself an adherent of Gautama, and invited him to take his meal with him the next day.

The solitary wanderer accordingly went, an honoured guest, to the palace of the king, and the entire population of the capital of Magadha turned out to see the great preacher of the religion of love, who had suddenly appeared in the land. The king then assigned a bamboo grove (Veluvana) close by for the residence of Gautama and his followers, and there Gautama rested for some time. Shortly after Gautama obtained two renowned converts, Sârîputra and Moggallâna (*Mahâvagga*, I, 22–24).

The daily life of Gautama has been well described by Dr. Oldenberg. "He, as well as his disciples, rises early, when the light of dawn appears in the sky, and spends the early moments in spiritual exercises or in converse with his disciples, and then he proceeds with his companions towards the town. In the days when his reputation stood at its highest point, and his name was named throughout India among the foremost names, one might day by day see that man before whom kings bowed themselves, alms-bowl in hand, through streets and alleys, from house to house, and without uttering any request, with downcast look, stand silently waiting until a morsel of food was thrown into his bowl."

Such was the manner in which the greatest man of his age begged his food, day by day, from house to house, and preached his religion of love to men and to women. For women were Gautama's listeners as well as men. "The seclusion of women from the outer world, which later custom has enjoined, was quite unheard of in ancient India; women took their share in the intellectual life of the people, and the most delicate and tenderest of the epic poems of the Indians show us how well they could understand and appreciate true womanhood." *

The fame of Gautama had now travelled to his native town, and his old father expressed a desire to see him once before he died. Gautama accordingly went to Kapilavastu, but, according to custom, remained in the grove outside the town. His father and relations came to see him there; and the next day Gautama himself

* Oldenberg's *Buddha* (translation), pp. 149 and 164.

went into the town, begging alms from the people who once adored him as their beloved prince and master! The story goes on to say that the king rebuked Gautama for this act, but Gautama replied, it was the custom of his race. "But," retorted the king, "we are descended from an illustrious race of warriors, and not one of them has ever begged his bread." "You and your family," answered Gautama, "may claim descent from kings, my descent is from the prophets (Buddhas) of old."

The king took his son into the palace, where all the members of the family came to greet him except his wife. The deserted Yasodharâ, with a wife's grief and a wife's pride, exclaimed, "If I am of any value in his eyes, he will himself come; I can welcome him better here." Gautama understood this and went to her, with only two disciples with him. And when Yasodharâ saw her lord and prince enter,—a recluse with shaven head and yellow robes,—her heart failed her, she flung herself to the ground, held his feet, and burst into tears. Then, remembering the impassable gulf between them, she rose and stood aside. She listened to his new doctrines, and when, subsequently, Gautama was induced to establish an order of female mendicants,—Bhikkhunîs,—Yasodharâ became one of the first Buddhist nuns. At the time of which we are now speaking, Yasodharâ remained in her house, but Râhula, Gautama's son, was converted.

Gautama's father was much aggrieved at this, and asked Gautama to establish a rule that no one should be admitted to the Order without his parents' consent. Gautama consented to this, and made a rule accordingly (*Jâtaka*, 87–90; *Mahâvagga*, I, 54).

On his way back to Râjagriha, Gautama stopped for some time at Anupiyâ, "a town belonging to the Mallas." And while he was stopping here, he made many converts both from the Koliyan and from the Sâkya tribe, some of whom deserve special mention. Anuruddha, the Sâkya, went to his mother and asked to be allowed to go into the houseless state. His mother did not know how to stop him, and so told him, "If, beloved Anuruddha, Bhaddiya, the Sâkya Râja, will renounce the world, thou also mayest go forth into the houseless state."

Anuruddha accordingly went to Bhaddiya, and it was decided that they would embrace the Order in seven days. "So Bhaddiya the Sâkya Râja, and Anuruddha and Ânanda and Bhagu and Kimbila and Devadatta, just as they had so often previously gone out to the pleasure ground with fourfold array, even so did they now go out with fourfold array, and Upâli the barber went with them, making seven in all.

"And when they had gone some distance, they sent their retinue back and crossed over to the neighbouring district, and took off their fine things, and wrapped them in their robes and made a bundle of them, and said to Upâli the barber, 'Do you now, Upâli, turn back. These things will be sufficient for you to live upon.'" But Upâli was of a different mind, and so all the seven went to Gautama and became converts. And when Bhaddya had retired into solitude he exclaimed over and over, "O happiness! O happiness!" and on being asked the cause said—

"Formerly, Lord, when I was a king, I had a guard completely provided both within and without my private apartments, both within and without the town, and within the borders of my country. Yet though, Lord, I was thus guarded and protected I was fearful, anxious, distrustful, and alarmed. But now, Lord, even when in the forest, at the foot of a tree, in solitude, I am without fear or anxiety, trustful, and not alarmed; I dwell at ease, subdued, secure, with mind as peaceful as an antelope" (*Chullavagga*, VII, 1).

We have narrated the above story because some of the converts, spoken of here, rose to distinction. Ânanda became the most intimate friend of Gautama, and after his death led a band of 500 monks in chanting the

Dharma in the Council of Râjagriha. Upâli, though a barber by birth, became an eminent member of the Holy Order, and was recognised as an authority in matters connected with Vinaya. It is a striking proof how completely the caste-system was ignored in the Holy Order established by Gautama. Anuruddha lived to become the greatest master of Abhidamma or metaphysics. Devadatta became subsequently the rival and opponent of Gautama, and is even said to have advised Ajâtasatru, the prince of Magadha, to kill his father Bimbisâra, and then attempted to kill Gautama himself (*Chullavagga*, VII, 2–4). All these charges, however, which are heaped on Devadatta, who was a rival of Gautama, should not be accepted.

After spending his second *vassa* or rainy season in Râjagriha, Gautama repaired to Srâvasti, the capital of the Kosalas, where, as we have seen before, Prasenajit reigned as king. A wood called Jetavana was presented to the Buddhists, and Gautama often repaired and preached there. Gautama's instructions were always delivered orally, and preserved in the memory of the people, like all the ancient books of India, although writing was known in his time.*

The third *vassa* was also passed in Râjagriha, and in the fourth year from the date of his proclaiming his creed Gautama crossed the Ganges, went to Vaisâli, and stopped in the Mahâvana grove. Thence he is said to have made a miraculous journey to settle a dispute between the Sâkyas and the Koliyans about the water of the boundary river Rohinî. In the following year he again repaired to Kapilavastu, and was present at the death of his father, then ninety-seven years old.

His widowed step-mother Prajâpati Gautamî, and his

* "Brief written communications, brief written notifications, appear to have been common in India even at that time (*i.e.*, Gautama Buddha's time): books were not written, but learnt by rote and taught from memory." —Oldenberg's *Buddha* (translation), p. 177.

no less widowed wife Yasodharâ, had now no ties to bind them to the world, and insisted on joining the Order established by Gautama. The sage had not yet admitted women to the Order, and was reluctant to do so. But his mother was inexorable and followed him to Vaisâli, and begged to be admitted.

Ânanda pleaded her cause, but Gautama still replied, "Enough, Ânanda! Let it not please thee that women should be allowed to do so." But Ânanda persisted, and asked—

"Are women, Lord, capable—when they have gone forth from the household life and entered the homeless state, under the doctrine and discipline proclaimed by the Blessed One,—are they capable of realising the fruit of conversion or of the second path, or of Arhatship?"

There could be only one reply to this. Honour to women has ever been a part of religion in India, and salvation and heaven are not barred to the female sex by the Hindu religion. "They are capable, Ânanda," replied the sage. And Prajâpati and the other ladies were admitted to the Order as Bhikkhunîs under some rules making them strictly subordinate to the Bhikkhus (*Chullavagga*, X, 1). After this Gautama retired to Kosambî near Prayâga.

In the sixth year, after spending the rains at Kosambî, Gautama returned to Râjagriha, and Kshemâ, the queen of Bimbisâra, was admitted to the Order. In the same year Gautama is said to have performed some miracles at Srâvasti, and went to heaven to teach Dharma to his mother, who had died seven days after his birth.

In the eleventh year Gautama converted the Brâhman Bhâradvâja by the parable of the sower, which deserves to be quoted.

Kâsî Bhâradvâja's five hundred ploughs were tied in the sowing season. He went to the place where his men were distributing food to the poor, and he saw Gautama standing there to get alms. On this he said:—

"I, O Saman, both plough and sow, and having ploughed and sown, I eat; thou also, O Sâman, shouldst plough and sow, and having ploughed and sown, thou shouldst eat."

"I also, O Brâhman, both plough and sow, and having ploughed and sown, I eat." So said Bhagavat.

"Yet we do not see the yoke or the plough, or the ploughshare, or the goad, or the oxen of the venerable Gautama."

Bhagavat answered,—"Faith is the seed, penance the rain, understanding my yoke and plough, modesty the pole of the plough, mind the tie, thoughtfulness my ploughshare and goad. . . .

"Exertion is my beast of burden; carrying me to Nibbâna, he goes without turning back to the place where, having gone, one does not grieve."

The Brâhman was abashed, and after further instructions joined the order (*Sutta Nipâta; Kâsî Bhâradvâja Sutta*).

In the next year he undertook the longest journey he had ever made, and went to Mantala and returned by Benares, and then preached the famous Mahâ Râhula Sutta to his son Râhula, then eighteen years old. Two years after, Râhula, being twenty, was formally admitted in the Order, and the Râhula Sutta was preached.

In the following year, *i.e.*, in the fifteenth year from the date of his proclaiming his creed, he visited Kapilavastu again, and addressed a discourse to his cousin Mâhânâma, who had succeeded Bhadraka, the successor of Suddhodana, as the king of the Sâkyas. Gautama's father-in-law, Suprabuddha, king of Koli, publicly abused Gautama for deserting Yasodharâ, but is said to have been swallowed up by the earth shortly after.

In the seventeenth year he delivered a discourse on the death of Srîmatî, a courtesan; in the next year he comforted a weaver who had accidentally killed his daughter; in the following year he released a deer caught in a snare and converted the angry hunter who had wanted to shoot him; and in the twentieth year he similarly converted the famous robber Angulimâla of the Chaliya forest.

For twenty-five years more Gautama wandered through the Gangetic valley, preached benevolence and a holy life to the poor and the lowly, made converts among the high and the low, the rich and the poor, and proclaimed his law through the length and breadth of the land. His pure life of benevolence and his pure religion of love were widely known and universally respected by his followers and the orthodox Hindus alike; nations and their kings honoured the doctrines of the saintly reformer whose acts were those of kindness and benevolence; and when Gautama died at the advanced age of eighty, Buddhism was already a power in the land, which "not by any Sâman or Brâhman, not by any god, not by any Brahmâ or Mâra, not by any one in the universe, could ever be turned back."

Gautama lived forty-five years from the date of his proclaiming his new religion; and accepting the year 477 B.C. as the year of his death, the mains facts of his life may be thus arranged:—

Born near Kapilavastu	557 B.C.
His marriage with Yasodharâ	538 "
He left his home, wife, and infant	528 "
He became enlightened at Buddha Gayâ, and proclaimed his religion at Benares	522 "
He revisited his home	521 "
His father Suddhodana died, and his step-mother and wife joined the Order	517 "
His son Râhula joined the Order	508 "
Yasodharâ's father died	507 "
Gautama died	477 "

Happily we have a fairly complete account of the events immediately before his death in the *Mahâparinibbâna Sutta* in the *Dîgha Nikâya*, and to these facts we now turn.

Gautama was now eighty years of age, and the generation among whom he had worked in his youth had passed away. Most of those men whom he had known in his early days were dead, and the aged saint preached to sons and grandsons the same holy law which he had proclaimed to their sires and grandsires before. Many of his intimate friends were dead, but the faithful Ânanda still accompanied him like his shadow, and ministered to his wants. The old king of Râjagriha was no more; his warlike and ambitious son Ajâtasatru had ascended the throne of Magadha,—it is said by murdering his father,—and was now maturing schemes of conquest. It was no part of Ajâtasatru's policy to offend so popular and widely respected a person as Gautama, and, outwardly at least, Ajâtasatru honoured the reformer.

The powerful Vajjian clans who occupied the plains on the northern shore of the Ganges, opposite to Magadha, first attracted Ajâtasatru's attention. They were a Turanian tribe who had entered into India through the northern mountains, and had established a republican form of government in the very centre of Hindu civilisation, and were threatening the conquest of all Magadha. They were probably the same Yu-Chi tribe* who conquered Kashmîra and Western India four or five centuries later, and became, under Kanishka, the most powerful supporters of Buddhism.

Ajâtasatru Videhiputra † said to himself, "I will root out these Vajjians, mighty and powerful though they be. I will destroy these Vajjians, I will bring these Vajjians to utter ruin."

Gautama was then residing in the Vulture's Peak

* See Beal's *Buddhism in China*, p. 43.

† This appellation shows that the king's mother was a lady of the ancient Videha tribe. Persons were frequently called in those days by their mother's name; and Upatissa, the distinguished disciple of Gautama, was always better known as Sāriputra.

(Gridhrakûta), a cave on the side of the loftiest of the five hills overlooking the beautiful valley of Râjagriha. Ajâtasatru, who was not without some kind of superstitious faith in prophecies, sent his prime minister Vassakâra to Gautama to inquire how his expedition against the Vajjians would end. Gautama was no respecter of kings, and replied that so long as the Vajjians remained united in their adherence to their ancient customs "we expect them not to decline, but to prosper."

From the Vulture's Peak Gautama wandered to neighbouring places, — to Ambalathikâ, to Nâlanda, and to Pâtaligrâma, the site of the future capital of Magadha, Pâtaliputra. At the time of Gautama it was an insignificant grâma or village, but Sunîdha and Vassakâra, the chief ministers of Magadha, were building a fortress at Pâtaligâma to repel the Vajjians. Such was the origin of the town which became the capital of Chandragupta and Asoka, and was the metropolis of India for nearly a thousand years, and which is still one of the largest cities in India. Gautama is said to have prophesied the greatness of the place and said to Ânanda: "And among famous places of residence and haunts of busy men, this will become the chief, the city of Pâtaliputra, a centre for the interchange of all kinds of wares."

Vassakâra and Sunîdha, the ministers of Ajâtasatru, invited Gautama there and fed him with sweet dishes of boiled rice and cakes, and after this Gautama left the place, and is said to have crossed the Ganges, which was then brimful and overflowing, by a miracle,—passing over the water without a boat or a raft.

He then went to Kotigrâma, and then to Nâdika, where he rested in the "brickhall," which was a resting-place for travellers. There Gautama taught Ânanda the pregnant lesson that each disciple could ascertain for himself if he had attained salvation. If he was conscious, if he felt within himself, that he had faith in the Buddha, that he had faith in Dharma, that he had faith in the Order;

then he was saved. Buddha, Dharma, and Sangha became the Trinity or the Buddhists.

From Nâdika, Gautama came to Vaisâli, the capital of the powerful confederacy of the Lichchavis to the north of the Ganges. Ambapâli, a courtesan, heard that the saint was stopping in her mango grove and came and invited him to a meal, and Gautama accepted the invitation.

"Now the Lichchavis of Vaisâli heard that the Blessed One had arrived at Vaisâli and was staying at Ambapâli's grove. And ordering a number of magnificent carriages to be made ready, they mounted one of them and proceeded with their train to Vaisâli. Some of them were dark, dark in colour, and wearing dark clothes and ornaments; some of them were fair, fair in colour and wearing light clothes and ornaments; some of them were red, ruddy in colour, and wearing red clothes and ornaments; some of them were white, pale in colour, and wearing white clothes and ornaments.

"And Ambapâli drove against the young Lichchavis, axle to axle, wheel to wheel, and yoke to yoke; and the Lichchavis said to Ambapâli the courtesan, How is it, Ambapâli, that thou drivest up against us thus?

"My Lords, I have just invited the Blessed One and his brethren for their morrow's meal, said she.

"Ambapâli, give us this meal for a hundred thousand, said they.

"My Lords, were you to offer all Vaisâli with its subject territory, I would not give up so honourable a feast.

"Then the Lichchavis cast up their hands exclaiming, 'We are outdone by this mango-girl,* we are outreached by this mango-girl,' and they went on to Ambapâlikâ's grove."

There they saw Gautama and invited him to a meal on the morrow, but Gautama replied, "O Lichchavis, I have promised to dine to-morrow with Ambapâli the

* *Ambapâlikâ* means the grower of mangoes.

courtesan." And Ambapâli fed Gautama and his brethren with sweet rice and cakes, and "waited upon them till they refused any more." And then she was edified and instructed, and said, "Lord, I present this mansion to the Order of mendicants, of which Buddha is the chief," and the gift was accepted.*

From Ambapâli's grove, Gautama went to Beluva. He felt his end approaching, and said to the faithful Ânanda, "I am now grown old and full of years, my journey is drawing to its close, I have reached the sum of my days, I am turning eighty years of age. . . . Therefore, O Ânanda! be ye lamps unto yourselves. Be ye a refuge to yourselves. Betake yourselves to no external refuge. Hold fast to the truth as a lamp. Hold fast as a refuge to the truth."

In Châpâla Chetiya, Gautama delivered a discourse in which he enumerated four classes of men, viz., the Nobles, the Brâhmans, the Householders, and the Sâmans;—and four classes of angels, viz., the Angels, the Great Thirty-three,† Mâra,‡ and Brahmâ.§

At Kûtagâra, Gautama once more proclaimed to his followers the substance and essence of his religion, and enjoined upon them to practise it, to meditate upon it, and to spread it abroad, "in order that pure religion may last long and be perpetuated, in order that it may continue to be for the good and the happiness of the great multitudes."

Having paid his last visit to Vaisâli, Gautama then

* Bishop Bigandet says: "In recording the conversion of a courtesan like Apapâlikâ, her liberality and gifts to Buddha and his disciples, and the preference designedly given to her over princes and nobles, who, humanly speaking, seemed in every respect better entitled to attentions,—one is almost reminded of the conversion of 'a woman that was a sinner,' mentioned in the Gospels."—*Life or Legend of Gaudama.*

† Vedic gods reduced to the position of beneficent spirits.

‡ The tempter or evil spirit. "Mâra est le demon de l'amour, du péché, et de la mort; ce la tentateur et l'ennemi de Buddha."—*Burnouf.*

§ The Universal Being of the Upanishads reduced to the position of a beneficent spirit.

wandered through villages, Bhandagrâma, Hastigrâma, Ambagrâma, Jambugrâma, and Bhoganagara, and then went to Pâvâ. There, Chunda, a goldsmith and ironsmith, invited him to a meal, and gave him sweet rice and cakes and a quantity of dried boar's flesh. Gautama never refused the poor man's offering, but the boar's flesh did not agree with him. "Now when the Blessed One had eaten the food prepared by Chunda, the worker in metal, there fell upon him a dire sickness, the disease of dysentery, and sharp pain came upon him even unto death. But the Blessed One, mindful and self-possessed, bore it without complaint."

On his way from Pâvâ to Kusinagara, Gautama converted a low-caste man Pukkusa. At Kusinagara, eighty miles due east from Kapilavastu, Gautama felt that his death was nigh. With that loving anxiety which had characterised all his life, he tried on the eve of his death to impress on his followers that Chunda was not to blame for the food he had supplied, but that the humble smith's act, kindly meant, would redound to length of life, to good birth, and to good fortune.

It is said that just before his death the trees were in bloom out of season, and sprinkled flowers on him; that heavenly flowers and sandalwood powder descended on him, and that music and heavenly songs were wafted from the sky. But the great apostle of holy life said, "It is not thus, Ânanda, that the Tathâgata (Buddha) is rightly honoured, reverenced, venerated, held sacred, or revered. But the brother or the sister, the devout man or the devout woman, who continually fulfils all the greater and the lesser duties, who is correct in life, walking according to precepts,—it is he who rightly honours, reverences, venerates, holds sacred, and reveres the Tathâgata with the worthiest homage." Who is not reminded by these noble precepts of the holy precept in the Bible so happily rendered into verse by a Christian poet?—

"But Thou hast said, the flesh of goat,
The blood of ram, I would not prize,
A contrite heart, an humble thought,
Are My accepted sacrifice."

On the night of Gautama's death, Subhadra, a Brâhman philosopher of Kusinagara, came to ask some questions, but Ânanda, fearing that this might be wearisome to the dying sage, would not admit him. Gautama, however, had overheard their conversation, and he would not turn back a man who had come for instruction. He ordered the Brâhman to be admitted, and with his dying breath explained to him the principles of his religion. Subhadra was the last disciple whom Gautama converted, and shortly after, at the last watch of the night, the great sage departed this life,—with the exhortation to his brother men still on his lips,—"Decay is inherent in all component things; work out your salvation with diligence."

The body of Gautama was cremated by the Mallas of Kusinagara who surrounded his bones "in their council-hall with a lattice-work of spears and with a rampart of bows; and there, for seven days, they paid honour and reverence and respect and homage to them with dance and song and music, and with garlands and perfumes."

It is said that the remains of Gautama were divided into eight portions. Ajâtasatru of Magadha obtained one portion, and erected a mound over it at Râjagriha. The Lichchavis of Vaisâli obtained another portion, and erected a mound at that town. Similarly the Sâkyas of Kapilavastu, the Bulis of Allakappa, the Koliyas of Râmagrâma, the Mallas of Pâvâ, the Mallas of Kusinagara, and a Brâhman Vethadîpaka obtained portions of the relics and erected mounds over them. The Moriyans of Pipphalivana made a mound over the embers, and the Brâhman Dona made a mound over the vessel in which the body had been burnt.

CHAPTER XIII.

DOCTRINES OF GAUTAMA BUDDHA.

IT is not possible that we should, within the limits of a single chapter, give our readers anything like a complete summary of the doctrines of a religion which now forms the subject of so much elaborate and learned inquiry by so many distinguished and able scholars. Our attempt will rather be to give here the substance of the great lessons and ideas which Gautama preached and inculcated to his countrymen.

Buddhism is, in its essence, a system of self-culture and self-restraint. Doctrines and beliefs are of secondary importance in this system ; the effort to end human suffering by living a holy life, free from passions and desires, is the cardinal idea with which Gautama was impressed on the day on which he was "enlightened" under the Bo-tree in Buddha Gayâ, and it was the central idea which he preached to the last day of his life.

When he went from Buddha Gayâ to Benares, and first preached his religion to his five old disciples, he explained to them the Four Truths and the Eightfold Path, which form the essence of Buddhism.

"This, O Bhikkhus, is the *Noble Truth of Suffering.* Birth is suffering, decay is suffering, illness is suffering, death is suffering. Presence of objects we hate is suffering, not to obtain what we desire is suffering. Briefly, the fivefold clinging to existence (*i.e.*, clinging to the five elements) is suffering.

"This, O Bhikkhus, is the *Noble Truth of the Cause*

of Suffering. Thirst, that leads to re-birth accompanied by pleasure and lust, finding its delight here and there. (This thirst is threefold), viz., thirst for pleasure, thirst for existence, thirst for prosperity.

"This, O Bhikkhus, is the *Noble Truth of the Cessation of Suffering.* It ceases with the complete cessation of thirst,—a cessation which consists in the absence of every passion, with the abandoning of this thirst, with the doing away with it, with the deliverance from it, with the destruction of desire.

"This, O Bhikkhus, is the *Noble Truth of the Path* which leads to the cessation of suffering. That holy Eightfold Path, viz.—

Right Belief,
Right Aspiration,
Right Speech,
Right Conduct,
Right Means of Livelihood,
Right Exertion,
Right Mindfulness,
Right Meditation" (*Mahâvagga*, I, 6).

The substance of this teaching is that life is suffering, the thirst for life and its pleasures is the cause of suffering, the extinction of that thirst is the cessation of suffering, and that such extinction can be brought about by a holy life. It is impossible to convey in a few words all that is implied by the eight maxims into which a holy life has been analysed, but to Buddhists, trained in the traditions of their religion, these maxims speak volumes. Correct views and beliefs must be learnt and entertained; high aims and aspirations must always remain present before the mind's eye; truthfulness and gentleness must characterise every word that is uttered; uprightness and absolute integrity must mark the conduct. A livelihood must be sought and adhered to which does no harm to living and sentient things; there must be a lifelong perseverance in doing good, in acts of kindness, gentleness, and beneficence; the mind, the intellect must be active and watchful; a calm and tranquil meditation shall fill the life with peace. This is the Eightfold Path for conquering desires and passions and thirst for life. A more beautiful picture of life was never conceived by poet or visionary; and a more perfect system of self-culture was never proclaimed by philosopher or saint.

The idea of self-culture was no doubt developed during the long course of meditation and practical good work in which Gautama passed his life. On the eve of his death he called together his brethren, and appears to have recapitulated the entire system of self-culture under seven heads, and these are known as the Seven Jewels of the Buddhist Law.

"Which, then, O brethren, are the truths which, when I had perceived, I made known to you; which when you have mastered, it behoves you to practise, meditate upon, and spread abroad, in order that pure religion may last long and be perpetuated, in order that it may continue to be for the good and the happiness of the great multitudes, out of pity for the world, to the good and the gain and the weal of gods and men?

"They are these:—

The four earnest meditations,
The fourfold great struggle against sin,
The four roads to saintship,
The five moral powers,
The five organs of spiritual sense,
The seven kinds of wisdom, and
The Noble Eightfold Path" (*Mahâparinibbâna Sutta*, III, 65).

Here, again, it is impossible to convey in a few words any adequate conception of all that is implied by these rules of discipline; a volume could be written on this most edifying subject.

The four earnest meditations alluded to are the meditations on the body, the sensations, the ideas, and the reason. The fourfold struggle against sin is the struggle to prevent sinfulness, the struggle to put away sinful states which have arisen, the struggle to produce goodness, and the struggle to increase goodness. The fourfold struggle comprehends in fact a life-long, earnest, unceasing endeavour on the part of the sinner towards more and more of goodness and virtue. The fourfold roads to saintship are the four means,—the will, the exertion, the preparation, the investigation,—by which Iddhi is acquired. In later Buddhism, Iddhi means supernatural powers, but what Gautama meant was probably the influence and power which the mind by long training and exercise can acquire over the body. The five moral powers, and the five organs of spiritual sense, are Faith, Energy, Thought, Contemplation, and Wisdom; and the seven kinds of wisdom are Energy, Thought, Contemplation, Investigation, Joy, Repose, Serenity. The Eightfold Path has already been described.

It is by such prolonged self-culture, by the breaking of the ten fetters, doubt, sensuality, &c., that one can at last obtain NIRVÂNA.

"There is no suffering for him who has finished his journey and abandoned grief, who has freed himself on all sides, and thrown off all fetters.

"They depart with their thoughts well collected, they are not happy within abode; like swans who have left their lake, they leave their house and home.

"Tranquil is his thought, tranquil are his word and deed, who has been freed by true knowledge, who has become a tranquil man" (*Dhammapada*, 90, 91, 96).

It was generally believed that "Nirvâna" implied final extinction or death; and Professor Max Müller was the first to point out, what most scholars have now accepted, that Nirvâna does not mean death, but only the extinction of that sinful condition of the mind, that thirst for life and its pleasures, which brings on new births. What Gautama meant by Nirvâna is attainable in life; it is what he attained in life; it is the sinless calm state of mind, the freedom from desires and passions, the perfect peace, goodness and wisdom, which continuous self-culture can procure for man. As Rhys Davids puts it, "the Buddhist heaven is not death, and it is not on death, but on a virtuous life here and now, that the Pitakas lavish those terms of ecstatic description which they apply to Arhatship, the goal of the excellent way, and to Nirvâna as one aspect of it."

But is there no future bliss, no future heaven beyond "the virtuous life here and now" for those who have attained Nirvâna? This was a question which often puzzled Buddhists, and they often pressed their great Master for a categorical answer.

On this point Gautama's replies are uncertain; nor does he ever appear to have inspired in his followers any hopes of heaven, beyond Nirvâna, which is the Buddhist's heaven and salvation.

Malûkyaputta pressed this question on Gautama, and desired to know definitely if the perfect Buddha did or did not live beyond the death. Gautama inquired, "Have I said, Come, Malûkyaputta, and be my disciple; I shall teach thee whether the world is everlasting or not everlasting?" "That thou hast not said, sire," replied Malûkyaputta. "Then," said Gautama, "do not press the inquiry." If a man, struck by a poisoned arrow, says to his physician, "I shall not allow my wound to be treated until I know who the man is by whom I have been wounded, whether he is a Kshatriya, a Brahmân, a Vaisya, or a Sûdra,"—what would be the end of him? He would die of his wound. And so would the man perish who did not strive after enlightenment and a holy life, because he did know what lay beyond. "Therefore, Malûkyaputta, whatsoever has not been revealed by me, let that remain unrevealed, and what has been revealed, let it be revealed" (*Chûla-Malukya-Ovâda, Majjhima Nikâya*).

In the same manner we are told that King Prasenajit

of Kosala, during a journey between his two chief towns, Sâketa and Srâvasti, fell in with the nun Khemâ, renowned for her wisdom. The king paid his respects to her, and asked: "Venerable lady, does the Perfect One exist after death?" She replied: "The Exalted One, O great King, has not declared that the Perfect One exists after death." "Then does the Perfect One not exist after death, Venerable lady?" inquired the king. But Khemâ still replied: "This also, O great King, the Exalted One has not declared, that the Perfect One does not exist after death" (*Samyutta Nikâya*).

These extracts will show that Gautama's religion does not look beyond the Nirvâna.* Gautama's aim was clear and well-defined; he invited all men, by a strict self-culture, to end their sufferings, to avoid future states of suffering, to attain in this world to a state of holy bliss and perfect sinlessness, which is Nirvâna.

If a man does not attain to this state of Nirvâna in life, he is liable to future births. Gautama did not believe in the existence of a soul; but, nevertheless, the theory of transmigration of souls was too deeply implanted in the Hindu mind to be eradicated, and Gautama therefore adhered to the theory of transmigration without accepting the theory of soul. But if there is no soul, what is it that undergoes transmigration? The reply is given in the Buddhist doctrine of KARMA.

The doctrine is, that "Karma," or the "doing" of a man cannot die, but must necessarily lead to its legitimate result. And when a living being dies, a new being is produced according to the Karma of the being that is dead. Thus, though the pious Buddhist does not believe in a soul, he believes that his state of life is determined by his Karma in a previous birth. And Buddhist writers

* See the question fully and elaborately discussed by Dr. Oldenberg in his work on *Buddha, his Life, his Doctrine, his Order*. The learned scholar has based his opinion on a careful examination of the entire body of the Buddhist canon.

are fond of comparing the relation of one life to the next, as that of the flame of a lamp to the flame of another lighted by it. And if the innocent man suffers in this world, he argues, "It is the result of my own work, why should I complain?" But wherein is the identity of the man who suffers with the man who is dead, if there is no soul? The Buddhist answers: "In that which alone remains when a man dies and is dissolved into atoms—in his action, thought and speech, in his Karma, which cannot die."

The reasoning seems to us like arguing in a circle, but nevertheless there is one aspect of the theory the correctness of which will be admitted by modern social philosophers. The Buddhist believes, as well as the modern philosopher, that each generation is the heir to the consequences of the virtues and sins of the preceding generation, and that, in this sense, a nation reaps as it sows. "The Buddhist saint does not mar the purity of his self-denial by lusting after positive happiness which he himself shall enjoy hereafter. *His* consciousness will cease to feel, but his virtue will live and work out its full effect in the decrease of the sum of the misery of sentient beings." *

But the theory of transmigration was not the only doctrine which Gautama accepted from ancient Hinduism and adopted in a modified form into his own religion. The whole of the Hindoo Pantheon of the day was similarly accepted, and similarly modified to suit his cardinal idea, the supreme efficacy of a holy life. The thirty-three gods of the Rig Veda were recognised, but they were not supreme. Brahmâ, the Supreme Deity of the Upanishads, was recognised, but was not supreme. For they too were struggling through repeated births, to attain to that holy life, that Nirvâna, which alone was supreme. Never was there such a daring attempt made by man to elevate holiness and purity above the super-

* Rhys David's *Buddhism*, p. 104.

natural and the celestial; to raise goodness,—attainable by man,—above the gods and the unknown powers of the universe!

It is necessary, however, to remark that it is doubtful whether Gautama himself recognised the Hindu Pantheon. It is not impossible that the Devas and Gandharvas and Brahmâ lingered in the traditional language of the people who had adopted Buddhism.

With regard to the Caste-system, Gautama respected a Brâhman as he respected a Buddhist Srâman, but he respected him for his virtue and learning, not for his caste, which he in his soul ignored. When two Brâhman youths, Vasishtha and Bhâradvâja, began to quarrel on the question, "How does one become a Brâhman?" and came to Gautama for his opinion, Gautama delivered to them a discourse in which he emphatically ignored caste, and held that a man's distinguishing mark was his work, not his birth. "The grass and the trees," he said, "the worms, moths, and ants, the quadrupeds, snakes, fishes, and birds are all divided into species which are known by their distinguishing marks. Man, too, has his distinguishing mark, and that is his profession.

"For whoever amongst men lives by cow-keeping, know this, O Vasishtha, he is a husbandman, not a Brâhman.

"And whoever amongst men lives by different mechanical arts . . . is an artisan, not a Brâhman.

"And whoever amongst men lives by trade . . . is a merchant, not a Brâhman.

"And whoever amongst men lives by serving others . . . is a servant, not a Brâhman.

"And whoever amongst men lives by theft . . . is a thief, not a Brâhman.

"And whoever amongst men lives by archery . . . is a soldier, not a Brâhman.

"And whoever amongst men lives by performing household ceremonials . . . is a sacrificer, not a Brâhman.

"And whoever amongst men possesses villages . . . is a king, not a Brâhman.

"And I do not call one a Brâhman on account of his birth, or of his origin from a particular mother,—he may be called Bhûpati, and he may be wealthy,—but the one who is possessed of nothing and seizes upon nothing, him I call a Brâhman. . . .

"The man who is free from anger, endowed with holy works, virtuous, without desire, subdued, and wearing his last body, him I call a Brâhman.

"The man who like water on a lotus leaf, or a mustard seed on the point of a needle, does not cling to sensual pleasures, him I call a Brâhman" (*Vâsettha Sutta*).

Similarly in the Assalâyana Sutta of the Majjhima Nikâya we are told that a distinguished Brâhman scholar, Assalâyana, came to controvert Gautama's opinion that all castes were equally pure. Gautama, who could meet a logician with his own weapons, asked if the wives of Brâhmans were not subject to all the disabilities of child-birth like other women. "Yes," replied Assalâyana. "Were there not differences in colour among the people of adjacent countries like Bactria and Afghanistan," asked Gautama, "and yet could not slaves become masters, and masters slaves, in those countries?" "Yes," replied Assalâyana. "Then," asked Gautama, "if a Brâhman is a murderer, a thief, a libertine, a liar, a slanderer, violent or frivolous in speech, covetous, malevolent, given to false doctrine, will he not after death be born to misery and woe, like any other caste?" "Yes," said Assalâyana, and he also admitted that good works would lead to heaven irrespective of caste. Gautama proceeded further to argue that when a mare was united with an ass, the offspring was a mule, but the offspring of a Kshatriya united to a Brâhman resembled its parents, and the obvious conclusion, therefore, was that there was really no difference between a Brâhman and a Kshatriya! By such arguments Gautama drove the truth home to the young logician's mind, and he "sat there silent, awkward, distressed, looking downwards, reflecting, not able to answer,"—and then became a disciple of Gautama.

At another time Gautama explained to his followers, "As the great streams, O disciples, however many they may be,—the Gangâ, Yamunâ, Asirâvatî, Sarabhû, and Mahî,—when they reach the great ocean lose their old name and their old descent, and bear only one name,—the great ocean,"—so also do Brâhmans, Kshatriyas, Vaisyas, and Sûdras lose their distinctions when they join the Order. And we know that this theory was consistently carried out in practice, and Upâli, a barber, as we have seen before, joined the Order and became one of the most revered and learned of Buddhist monks. A touching story is also told in the *Theragâthâ*, which enables us to comprehend how Buddhism came like a salvation to the humble and the lowly in India, and how they eagerly embraced it as a refuge from caste-injustice. Sunîta the thera or elder says, "I have come of a humble family, I was poor and needy. The work which I performed was lowly,—sweeping the withered flowers. I was despised of men, looked down upon and lightly esteemed. With submissive mien I showed respect to many. Then I beheld Buddha with his band of monks as he passed, the great hero, into the most important town of Magadha. Then I cast away my burden and ran to bow myself in reverence before him. From pity for me he halted, that highest among men. Then I bowed myself at the master's feet, stepped up to him and begged him, the highest among all beings, to accept me as a monk. Then said unto me the gracious master, 'Come hither, O monk'—that was the initiation I received." And the passage concludes with the lesson which Gautama had so often preached, "By holy zeal and chaste living, by restraint and self-repression, thereby a man becomes a Brâhman: that is the highest Brâhmanhood."

Who can read this touching story of humble Sunîta's

conversion without realising the loving spirit of equality which was the soul of early Buddhism, and which ensured its success? The great teacher who regarded nor wealth, nor rank, nor caste, came to the poor and the despised as well as to the rich and the noble, and welcomed them to effect their own salvation by a pure life and unstained conduct. A virtuous life opened the path to the highest honour to the low-born and the high-born alike,—no distinction was known or recognised in the Holy Order. Thousands of men and women responded to this loving and rational appeal, and merged their caste inequalities in a common love for their teacher and a common emulation of his virtues. And within three centuries from the date when Gautama proclaimed his message of equality and of love in Benares, the religion of equality and of love was the state religion of India. Caste was unknown within the Holy Order, and lost its sting among laymen outside the Order; for it was open to the lowest born among them to embrace the Order and thus win the highest honour.

"393. A man does not become a Brâhman by his platted hair, by his family, or by birth; in whom there is truth and righteousness, he is blessed, he is a Brâhman.

"394. What is the use of platted hair, O fool! What of the raiment of goat skins? Within thee there is ravening, but the outside thou makest clean.*

"422. Him I call, indeed, a Brâhman, the manly, the noble, the hero, the great sage, the conqueror, the impassible, the accomplished, the awakened.

"141. Not nakedness, not platted hair, not dirt, not fasting or lying on earth, nor rubbing with dust, nor sitting motionless, can purify a mortal who has not overcome desires" † (*Dhammapada*).

* Compare Matthew xxiii. 27, Luke xi. 39.

† Professor Max Müller has the following interesting note to the above verse :—

"Walking naked and the other things mentioned in our verse, are out-

It is a mistake to suppose that Gautama positively enjoined on all to retire from the world and to embrace the Holy Order. To conquer the yearning for life and its pleasures was the cardinal aim of the reformer, and he assigned no peculiar virtue to an outward act of renouncement of the world. But, nevertheless, as it is difficult to conquer that thirst so long as one is actually living in the midst of his family and enjoying the pleasures of life, Gautama recommended the life of a Bhikkhu as the more efficacious means for securing the great end. And so thousands retired from the world and became Bhikkhus, and thus the Buddhist Monastic system was formed; probably the first organised Monastic system in the world.

It is not necessary to narrate here the rules of the Buddhist Monastic system, as they do not come in among the essential doctrines of the religion. We will only quote here a beautiful Sûtra, giving a supposed conversation between Gautama and a herdsman relating to the comparative virtues of worldly life and a religious life:—

1. "I have boiled my rice, I have milked my cows,"—so said the herdsman Dhaniya,—"I am living together with my fellows near the banks of the Mahî river. My house is covered, the fire is kindled: therefore, if thou like, rain, O Sky!"

"2. I am free from anger, free from stubbornness,"—so said Bhagavat,—"I am abiding for one night near the

ward signs of saintly life, and these Buddha rejects because they do not calm the passions. Nakedness he seems to have rejected on other grounds, if we may judge from Sumâgadhâ Avadâna. A number of naked friars were assembled in the house of the daughter of Anâtha Pindika. She called her daughter-in-law Sumâgadhâ, and said, 'Go and see those highly respectable persons.' Sumâgadhâ, expecting to see some of the saints like Sâriputra, Maudgalâyana, and others, ran out full of joy. But when she saw these friars, with their hair like pigeon-wings covered by nothing but dirt, offensive, and looking like demons, she became sad. 'Why are you sad?' said her mother-in-law. Sumâgadhâ replied, 'O mother, if these are saints, what must sinners be like?'"

banks of the Mahî river. My house is uncovered, the fire (of passions) is extinguished: therefore, if thou like, rain, O Sky!"

3. "Gadflies are not to be found with me,"—so said the herdsman Dhaniya,—"in meadows abounding with grass the cows are roaming, and they can endure the rain when it comes: therefore, if thou like, rain, O Sky!"

4. "By me is made a well-constructed raft,"—so said Bhagavat,—"I have passed over (to Nirvâna). I have reached the further bank, having overcome the torrent (of passions); there is no further use for a raft: therefore, if thou like, rain, O Sky!"

5. "My wife is obedient, not wanton,"—so said the herdsman Dhaniya,—"for a long time she has been living together with me. She is winning, and I hear nothing wicked of her: therefore, if thou like, rain, O Sky!"

6. "My mind is obedient and freed,"—so said Bhagavat,—"it has for a long time been highly cultivated and well subdued. There is no longer anything wicked in me: therefore, if thou like, rain, O Sky!"

7. "I support myself by my own earnings,"—so said the herdsman Dhaniya,—"and my children are about me healthy. I hear nothing wicked of them: therefore, if thou like, rain, O Sky!"

8. "I am no one's servant,"—so said Bhagavat,—"with what I have gained, I wander about in all the world. There is no need for me to serve: therefore, if thou like, rain, O Sky!"

9. "I have cows, I have calves,"—so said Dhaniya,—"I have cows in calf and heifers. And I have also a bull as lord over the cows; therefore, if thou like, rain, O Sky!"

10. "I have no cows; I have no calves,"—so said Bhagavat,—"I have no cows in calf and no heifers. And I have no bull as a lord over the cows: therefore, if thou like, rain, O Sky!"

11. "The stakes are driven in, and cannot be shaken,"

—so said the herdsman Dhaniya,—"the ropes are made of munga grass, new and well made, the cows will not be able to break them: therefore, if thou like, rain, O Sky!"

12. "Having, like a bull, rent the bonds; having, like an elephant, broken through the galuchchhi creeper, I shall not again enter into a womb: therefore, if thou like, rain, O Sky!"

Then at once a shower poured down, filling both sea and land. Hearing the sky raining, Dhaniya spoke thus:—

13. "No small gain indeed to us, since we have seen Bhagavat. We take refuge in thee, O thou endowed with the eye of wisdom! Be thou our master, O great Muni!" (*Dhaniyasutta*).*

These are the leading doctrines of Gautama's religion, and a brief recapitulation of them will probably be useful to our readers. We have explained that Buddhism is in its essence a system of self-culture,—an effort towards a holy life on this earth, and nothing more. We have seen that Gautama preached the *Four truths* that life was suffering, the thirst after life was the cause of suffering, the conquering of that thirst was the cessation of suffering, and the path of self-culture was the means of conquering the thirst after life. Placing a holy life and sinless peace as the ideal of his religion and as the highest aim of human destiny, Gautama carefully elaborated a system of self-culture, a method of self-restraint in thought, word, and speech, which he called the *Noble Eightfold Path*, or which is known as the *Seven Jewels of the Law.*

And that holy peace, that sinless, tranquil life which is the object of so much self-restraint and self-culture, is attainable in this earth; it is the Buddhist's heaven, it is *Nirvâna.* Gautama's religion offers no glowing rewards in a world to come; virtue is its own reward;

* Compare the parable in St. Luke xii. 16.

a virtuous life is the Buddhist's final aim; a virtuous peace on earth is the Buddhist's Nirvâna.

We have seen that Gautama nevertheless adopted the Hindu idea of transmigration in a modified form into his own religion. If Nirvâna is not attained in life, the *Karma* or actions of a living being lead to their legitimate results in re-births, until the discipline is complete and Nirvâna is attained.

In the same manner Gautama adopted or permitted the adoption of the popular belief in the *Hindu Pantheon*,—the thirty-three gods of the Rig Veda, and Brahmâ, and the Gandharvas. All these beings, all living creatures in the universe, are struggling through repeated births in various spheres to attain that Nirvâna which is the supreme aim and destiny and salvation of all.

But there were doctrines and customs of Hinduism which he could not accept. The caste-system he eschewed, asceticism and penances he disapproved, the Vedic rites he declared to be fruitless. In place of such rites, he enjoined a benevolent life and the conquest of all passions and desires; and he recommended a retirement from the world as the most efficacious means for securing this end. The recommendation was followed, and led to the *Buddhist Monastic system*.

The great distinguishing feature of Buddhism, then, is that it is a training towards a virtuous and holy life on this earth, and takes little thought of rewards and punishments. It appeals to the most disinterested feelings in man's nature, sets before him virtue as its own reward, and enjoins a life-long endeavour towards its attainment. It knows of no higher aim among gods or men than the attainment of a tranquil, sinless life; it speaks of no other salvation than virtuous peace, it knows of no other heaven than holiness. "It swept away from the field of its vision the whole of the great soul-theory which had hitherto so completely filled and dominated the minds of the superstitious and of the thoughtful alike. For the first time in the history of the world, it proclaimed a salvation which each man could gain for himself, and by himself, in this world, during this life, without any, the least, reference to God or to gods, either great or small." *

On the other hand, this very feature of Buddhism is the subject of charges frequently brought against the religion. It is urged that it is an agnostic religion, that it knows of no God, no soul, no future world for those who have attained salvation. Dr. Rhys Davids points out, however, that agnostic philosophy has come, not once or twice, but repeatedly to the forefront when theology has failed to offer satisfactory replies to inquiries after the unknown, and men have sought for new solutions to old questions. "It is their place in the progress of thought that helps us to understand how it is that there is so much in common between the agnostic philosophers of India, the stoics of Greece and Rome, and some of the newest schools in France, in Germany, and among ourselves." †

* Rhys Davids, Hibbert Lectures, 1881.

† Buddhist Suttas, p. 145.

CHAPTER XIV.

MORAL PRECEPTS OF GAUTAMA BUDDHA.

A RELIGION, the great aim of which is the teaching of holy living in this world, must necessarily be rich in moral precepts, and such precepts are the peculiar beauty of Buddhism, for which the religion is held in honour all over the civilised world. It will be our pleasant task in this chapter to glean some of these graceful precepts, which will give our readers some idea of the essence of Gautama's moral teachings.

Gautama prescribed for lay disciples five prohibitory rules or Commandments, which were, no doubt, suggested by the five *Mahâpâtakas* or heinous crimes of the Hindu law books, referred to before.

"18. A householder's work, I will also tell you, how a Sâvaka is to act to be a good one; for that complete Bhikkhu Dhamma cannot be carried out by one who is taken up by worldly occupations.

"19. Let him not kill or cause to be killed any living being, nor let him approve of others killing, after having refrained from hurting all creatures, both those that are strong and those that tremble in the world.

"20. Then let the Sâvaka abstain from taking anything in any place that has not been given to him, knowing it to belong to another; let him not cause any one to take, nor approve of those that take. Let him avoid all theft.

"21. Let the wise man avoid an unchaste life as a burning heap of coals; not being able to live a life of chastity, let him not transgress with another man's wife.

"22. Let no one speak falsely to another in the hall of justice, or in the hall of the assembly; let him not cause any one to speak falsely, nor approve of those that speak falsely. Let him avoid all untruth.

"23. Let the householder, who approves of this Dhamma, not give himself to intoxicating drinks; let him not cause others to drink, nor approve of those that drink, knowing it to end in madness."—*Dhâmmika Sutta, Sutta Nipâta.*

These five precepts, which are known as the Five Commandments, or the five rules of conduct (Pancha Sila), are binding on all Buddhists, laymen, and Bhikkhus. They are recapitulated thus:—

"25. Let not one kill any living being.
Let not one take what is not given to him.
Let not one speak falsely.
Let not one drink intoxicating drinks.
Let not one have unchaste sexual intercourse."

(*Ibid.*)

Three other rules are laid down which are not considered obligatory, but which are recommended to austere and pious lay disciples. They are—

"25, 26. Let him not at night eat untimely food.
Let him not wear wreaths or use perfumes.
Let him lie on a bed spread on the earth."

(*Ibid.*)

The austere and pious householder is recommended to take a vow of all these eight precepts, which are known as the Eight Commandments, or the eight rules of conduct (Ashtânga Sîla).

To these eight rules two more are added, and they are: To abstain from dancing, music, singing, and stage plays; and, To abstain from the use of gold and silver. These Ten Commandments (Dasa Sîla) are binding on Bhikkhus, as the Five Commandments are binding on all laymen.

To honour one's father and mother, and to follow an

honourable trade, though not included in the Commandments, are duties enjoined in the same Sutta on all householders.

"Let him dutifully maintain his parents, and practise an honourable trade. The householder who observes this strenuously goes to the gods Sayampabhas (*Sanscrit* Svayambhû)."

A more exhaustive category of the duties of the householder is given in the well-known *Sigâlovâda Sutta*, common both to the Northern and the Southern Buddhists, and which has been more than once translated into European languages. The enumeration of the duties gives us so clear an insight into the state of Hindu society and into the ideal of Hindu social life, that we feel no hesitation in quoting it:—

1. *Parents and Children.*

Parents should—

1. Restrain their children from vice.
2. Train them in virtue.
3. Have them taught in arts or sciences.
4. Provide them with suitable wives or husbands.
5. Give them their inheritance.

The child should say—

1. I will support them who supported me.
2. I will perform family duties incumbent on them.
3. I will guard their property.
4. I will make myself worthy to be their heir.
5. When they are gone, I will honour their memory.

2. *Pupils and Teachers.*

The pupil should honour his teachers—

1. By rising in their presence.
2. By ministering to them.
3. By obeying them.
4. By supplying their wants.
5. By attention to instruction.

The teacher should show his affection to his pupils—

1. By training them in all that is good.
2. By teaching them to hold knowledge fast.
3. By instruction in science and lore.
4. By speaking well of them to their friends and companions.
5. By guarding them from danger.

3. *Husband and Wife.*

The husband should cherish his wife—

1. By treating her with respect.
2. By treating her with kindness.
3. By being faithful to her.
4. By causing her to be honoured by others.
5. By giving her suitable ornaments and clothes.

The wife should show her affection for her husband—

1. She orders her household aright.
2. She is hospitable to kinsmen and friends.
3. She is a chaste wife.
4. She is a thrifty housekeeper.
5. She shows skill and diligence in all she has to do.

4. *Friends and Companions.*

The honourable man should minister to his friends—

1. By giving presents.
2. By courteous speech.
3. By promoting their interest.
4. By treating them as his equals.
5. By sharing with them his prosperity.

They should show their attention to him—

1. By watching over him when he is off his guard.
2. By guarding his property when he is careless.
3. By offering him a refuge in danger.
4. By adhering to him in misfortune.
5. By showing kindness to his family.

5. *Masters and Servants.*

The master should provide for the welfare of his dependents—

1. By apportioning work to them according to their strength.
2. By supplying suitable food and wages.
3. By tending them in sickness.
4. By sharing with them unusual delicacies.
5. By now and then granting them holidays.

They should show their attachment to him as follows:—

1. They rise before him.
2. They retire later to rest.
3. They are content with what is given them.
4. They work cheerfully and thoroughly.
5. They speak well of him.

6. *Laymen and those devoted to religion.*

The honourable man ministers to Bhikkhus and Brâhmans—

1. By affection in act.
2. By affection in words.
3. By affection on thoughts.
4. By giving them a ready welcome.
5. By supplying their temporal wants.

They should show their affection to him—

1. By dissuading him from vice.
2. By exhorting him to virtue.
3. By feeling kindly towards him.
4. By instructing him in religion.
5. By clearing up his doubts and pointing the way to heaven.

What glimpses of pure Hindu life, of pleasant domestic and social feelings and duties, do we obtain from the above categories! The anxious care of parents to give children education and moral teaching and earthly comforts; the dutiful desire of children to support and respect their parents and honour their memory when dead; the respectful behaviour of the pupil towards the teacher, and the teacher's anxious care and affection for the pupil; the respect, the kindness, the honourable and affectionate treatment which the Hindu religion has ever enjoined on husbands towards their wives, and the faithfulness and scrupulous attention to domestic duties for which Hindu wives have always been known; the kindly relations between friends and friends, between masters and servants, between laymen and spiritual instructors: these are among the noblest lessons that the Hindu religion has taught, and these are among the noblest traditions which Hindu literature has handed down for thousands of years. Buddhism accepted this noble heritage from the ancient Hindus, and embalmed it in its sacred literature.

We turn now from Gautama's categories of duties to those precepts and benevolent maxims to which Buddhism mainly owes its deserved fame in the modern world. Gautama's religion was a religion of benevolence and love; and five centuries before Jesus Christ was born, the Hindu teacher had declared—

"5. Hatred does not cease by hatred at any time, hatred ceases by love: this is its nature."

"197. Let us live happily, not hating those who hate us. Among men who hate us, let us live free from hatred."

"223. Let one overcome anger by love, let him overcome evil by good. Let him overcome the greedy by liberality, the liar by truth" (*Dhammapada*).

Parables were told to impress this great lesson on the followers of the gentle and pure-souled Gautama, and we will here narrate one of these parables as briefly as we can. Trying to heal contentions and differences among his followers, Gautama said:—

"In former times, O Bhikkhus, there lived at Benares a king of the Kâsîs, Brahmadatta by name, wealthy, rich in treasures, rich in revenues, and rich in troops and vehicles, the lord over a great realm, with full treasuries and storehouses. And there was also a king of the Kosalas, Dîghîti by name, not wealthy, poor in treasures, poor in revenues, poor in troops and vehicles, the lord over a small realm, with empty treasuries and storehouses."

As often happens, the rich king robbed the weak one of his realm and treasures, and Dîghîti with his queen fled to Benares, and dwelt there in a potter's house in the guise of an ascetic. There the exiled queen gave birth to a child who was called Dîghâvu, and in course of time the boy reached his years of discretion.

In the meantime King Brahmadatta heard that his former rival was living in the town in disguise with his wife, and he ordered them to be brought before him, and had them cruelly executed.

Their son Dîghâvu was then living outside Benares, but happened to come to the town at the time of his father's execution. The dying king looked at his son, and with more than human forgiveness left his last injunctions on his son. "*Not by hatred, my dear Dîghâvu, is hatred appeased. By love, my dear Dîghâvu, hatred is appeased.*"

And young Dîghâvu, O Bhikkhus! went to the forest; there he cried and wept to his heart's content. He then returned to the town, after having formed his resolutions, and took employment under an elephant trainer in the royal stables.

Early in the dawn he arose and sang in a beautiful voice and played upon the lute. And the voice was so beautiful that the king inquired who it was that had risen so early and had sung in the elephant stables in so beautiful a voice. And the young boy was taken to the king, pleased him, and was employed as his attendant.

And it so happened that on one occasion the king went out to hunt, taking young Dîghâvu with him. Dîghâvu's secret resentment was burning within him, and he so drove the royal chariot, that the hosts went one way, and the king's chariot went another way.

At last the king felt tired and lay down, laying his head on the lap of young Dîghâvu, and as he was tired, he fell asleep in a moment.

"And young Dîghâvu thought, O Bhikkhus, 'This king Brahamadatta, of Kâsî, has done much harm to us. By him we have been robbed of our troops and vehicles, our realm, our treasuries, and storehouses. And he has killed my father and mother. Now the time has come to me to satisfy my hatred,'—and he unsheathed his sword."

But with the recollection of his father, the last words of his dying parent came to the recollection of the vengeful prince. "*Not by hatred, my dear Dîghâvu, is hatred appeased. By love, my dear Dîghâvu, hatred is appeased.*" It would not become me to transgress my father's word, said the prince, and he put up his sword.

The king dreamt a frightful dream, and arose terrified and alarmed. Dîghâvu told him the whole truth. The king was astonished, and exclaimed, "Grant me my life, my dear Dîghâvu! Grant me my life, my dear Dîghâvu!" The noble young prince forgave his father's murder in carrying out his father's injunction, and granted Brahmadatta his life. And Brahmadatta gave him back his father's troops and vehicles, his realm, his treasures and storehouses, and he gave him his daughter.

"Now, O Bhikkhus, if such is the forbearance and mildness of kings who wield the sceptre and bear the sword, so much more, O Bhikkhus, must you so let your light shine before the world, that you, having embraced the religious life according to so well-taught a doctrine and a discipline, are seen to be forbearing and mild" (*Mahâvagga*, X, 2).

But not only forbearance and mildness, but the virtue of good acts is repeatedly and impressively enjoined by Gautama on his followers.

"51. Like a beautiful flower, full of colour, but without

scent, are the fine and fruitless words of him who does not act accordingly."

"183. Not to commit sin, to do good, and to purify one's mind, this is the teaching of the Buddhas."

"200. In like manner his good works receive him who has done good and who has gone from this world to the other—as kinsmen receive a friend on his return."

"260. A man is not an elder, because his head is grey. His age may be ripe, but he is called old in vain."

"261. He in whom there is truth, virtue, love, restraint, moderation, he who is free from impurity and is wise, he is called an elder" (*Dhammapada*).

And Gautama told the parable of Mâtanga, the Chandâla, who reached the highest fame, mounted the vehicle of gods, and went to the Brahmâ world by good deeds. Therefore,

"Not by birth does one become an outcast, not by birth does one become a Brâhman. By deeds one becomes an outcast, by deeds one becomes a Brâhman" (*Vasala Sutta, Sutta Nipâta*, 27).

And again in the *Âmagandha Sutta* of the *Sutta Nîpâta*, Gautama explains to a Brâhman, Kâsyapa by name, that destroying life, killing, cutting, binding, stealing, lying, fraud, and adultery; backbiting, treachery, and cruelty; intoxication, deceit, and pride and a bad mind and wicked deeds are what defile a man. Neither abstinence from fish or flesh, nor nakedness, nor tonsure, nor matted hair, nor dirt, nor rough garment, nor sacrifices to the fire, nor penances, nor hymns, nor oblations, nor sacrifices can purify him.

The whole of the *Dhammapada* is a string of 423 moral precepts which for their beauty and moral worth are unsurpassed by any similar collection of precepts made in any age or country. And a good-sized volume might be compiled from the legends and maxims, the parables and precepts which are interspersed throughout the Buddhist Sacred Scriptures. We will close this chapter with only a few more extracts:—

"129. All men tremble at punishment, all men fear death. Remember that you are like unto them, and do not kill, nor cause slaughter.

"130. All men tremble at punishment, all men love life. Remember that you are like unto them, and do not kill nor cause slaughter."

"252. The fault of others is easily perceived, but that of oneself is difficult to perceive; a man winnows his neighbour's faults like chaff, but his own fault he hides, as a cheat hides the bad die from the gambler" (*Dhammapada*).

"This is called progress in the discipline of the Noble One, if one sees his sin in its sinfulness, and duly makes amends for it, and refrains from it in future" (*Mahâvagga*, IX, 1, 9).

"Thus he lives as a binder together of those who are divided, an encourager of those who are friends, a peacemaker, a lover of peace, impassioned for peace, a speaker of works that make for peace" (*Tevijja Sutta*, II, 5).

Who is not struck by the remarkable coincidence of these noble precepts with those preached five hundred years after in Palestine by the gentle and pure-souled Jesus Christ? But the relations between Buddhist and Christian ethics and moral precepts will be discussed in the following chapter.

CHAPTER XV.

HISTORY OF BUDDHISM.

WE are told in the *Chullavagga*, XI, that, on the death of Gautama, the venerable Mahâkâsyapa proposed, "Let us chant together the Dhamma and the Vinaya." The proposal was accepted, and 499 Arhats were selected for the purpose; and Ânanda, the faithful friend and follower of Gautama, completed the number 500.

"And so the Thera Bhikkhus went up to Râjagriha to chant together the Dhamma and the Vinaya." Upâli, who was a barber before, was questioned as the great authority on Vinaya, and Ânanda, the friend of Gautama, was questioned as the authority on Dhamma (Sutta).

This was the Council of Râjagriha held in the year of Gautama's death, 477 B.C., to settle the sacred text and fix it on the memory by chanting it together.

A century after the death of Gautama the Bhikkhus of Vaisâli (Vajjians), promulgated at Vaisâli ten theses, which permitted among other things the use of unfermented toddy, and the receipt of gold and silver by Bhikkhus or monks.

Yasa, the son of Kakandaka, a venerable Bhikkhu, protested against these licenses, and invited venerable teachers to a great Buddhist Council at Vaisâli. He "sent messengers to the Bhikkhus of the western country, and of Avanti, and of the southern country, saying, 'Let your reverences come! We must take in charge this legal question before what is not Dhamma is spread abroad and what is Dhamma is put aside; before what is not Vinaya is spread abroad and what is Vinaya is put aside.'"

In the meantime the Bhikkhus of Vaisâli heard that Yasa was obtaining support from the Bhikkhus of the Western Provinces, and they too sought for support from the East. Indeed the difference was between the Eastern Buddhists of Vaisâli, and the Western Buddhists of the provinces along the higher course of the Ganges, and also of Malwa and the Deccan. The Eastern opinions were started by the Vajjians of Vaisâli, and if the Vajjians be the same as the Turanian Yu-Chi tribe, as has been supposed by Beal, the dispute was mainly between Turanian Buddhists and Hindu Buddhists. We shall see further on that the Eastern opinions were subsequently upheld by the Buddhists of the Northern school, and that the Turanian nations of the world, the Chinese, the Japanese and the Thibetans belong to this Northern school.

The proceedings in the Council are interesting. The Sangha met at Vaisâli, and after much talk—

"The venerable Revata laid a resolution before the Sangha: 'Let the venerable Sangha hear me. Whilst we are discussing this legal question, there is both much pointless talking, and no sense is clear in any single speech. If it seem meet to the Sangha, let the Sangha settle this question by referring it to a jury.'"

And he proposed four Bhikkhus from the East and four Bhikkhus from the West to form the jury. The resolution was put to the vote and carried unanimously that these eight should form a jury.

The ten questions were then put one by one to the jury, and the jury disallowed all the ten licenses for which the Vaisâli Bhikkhus had contended, except only the sixth license, which, it was declared, was allowable in certain cases, and not in other cases.

At this rehearsal, seven hundred Bhikkhus took part,

and this was called the Council of Vaisâli, and was held in 377 B.C.

It must not be supposed, however, this settlement of the ten questions was finally accepted by all parties. The older and more influential members of the order decided the questions, but the majority was against them, and they seceded in large numbers from the bosom of the orthodox church. And the Northern Buddhists are the successors of these seceders. Hence the stream of Buddhism flows in two different channels, known as the Northern Buddhism of Nepal, Thibet, and China, and the Southern Buddhism of Ceylon, Burma, and Siam.

It has been well observed that new religious systems, however noble in their intrinsic worth, depend much on external circumstances for their acceptance by mankind. The Christian religion, which made little progress during the first few centuries, was then embraced by Constantine when Roman sway and Roman culture were predominant in Europe, and thus made an easy and rapid progress in the western world. The religion of Muhammad was proclaimed when the Arabians had no rivals to oppose them in the world, when the Roman power had declined, and the Feudal power had not been developed in Europe. In India the ancient Hindu religion had spread with the conquests of the Aryans issuing from the Punjab and subjugating the whole of India. In the same way the religion of Buddha, which made no distinction between the Brâhman and the low-born, found acceptance in the non-Aryan kingdom of Magadha more than in older Aryan provinces. And when Magadha became the supreme power in India in the third century before Christ, Buddhism was accepted as a state religion for India.

The Sisunâga dynasty, to which Bimbisâra and Ajâtasatru belonged, came to an end about 370 B.C., and Nanda, born of a Sudra woman, ascended the throne, and he and his eight sons ruled for about fifty years. A defeated rebel under the last of the Nandas escaped from Magadha about 325 B.C., and met Alexander the Great on the banks of the Sutlej. After Alexander's departure, Chandragupta gathered round him the hardy warriors of the west, and, about 320 B.C., succeeded in having the last Nanda killed, and ascended the throne of Magadha.

Neither Chandragupta nor his son Bindusâra was a Buddhist. But Bindusâra's successor, who ascended the throne about 260 B.C., embraced the popular religion, and became its most powerful promulgator all over India, and beyond India. Asoka's name is honoured from the Volga to Japan, and from Siberia to Ceylon, and "if a man's fame can be measured by the number of hearts who revere his memory, by the number of lips who have mentioned and still mention him with honour, Asoka is more famous than Charlemagne or Cæsar." * Asoka extended his empire all over Northern India, and his inscriptions have been found at Delhi and Allahabad, near Peshawar and in Gujrat, in Orissa, and even in Mysore.

He held the third Council at Patna about the eighteenth year of his reign, *i.e.*, about 242 B.C. One thousand elders attended the Council which lasted for nine months, under the presidency of Tissa son of Moggali. And the sacred texts were once more chanted and settled.

After the close of the Council, Asoka sent missionaries, as we are told in the *Dîpavansa* and the *Mahâvansa*, to Kashmir and Gândhâra, to Mahîsa (near modern Mysore), to Vanavâso (probably Rajputana), to Aparantaka (West Punjab), to Mahârattha, to Yonaloka (Bactria and Greek kingdoms), to Himavanta (central Himâlayas), to Subannabhûmi (probably Burma), and to Lankâ (Ceylon). The edicts of Asoka also inform us that his orders were carried out in Chola (Madras country), Pândya (Madura),

* Kopen, quoted in Rhys Davids' *Buddhism*, p. 222.

Satyapura (Satpura range), Kerala (Travancore), Ceylon, and the land of the Greek king Antiochus of Syria. And in another edict he tells us that he sent embassies to five Greek kingdoms, viz., Syria, Egypt, Macedon, Epiros, and Cyrene.

We have seen before that Asoka sent his own son to Ceylon, and Mahinda soon converted the king and spread Buddhism in Ceylon. The scenes of Mahinda's labours are still visible in Ceylon. Eight miles from the ruined city of Anurâdhapura is the hill of Mihintale, where the Ceylonese king built a monastery for the Indian monks. "Here on the precipitous western side of the hill, under a large mass of granite rock, at a spot which, completely shut out from the world, affords a magnificent view of the plains below, he (Mahinda) had his study hollowed out and steps cut in the rock, over which alone it could be reached. There also the stone couch which was carved out of the solid rock still exists, with holes, either for curtain rods, or for a protecting balustrade beside it. The great rock effectually protects the cave from the heat of the sun, in whose warm light the broad valley below lies basking. Not a sound reaches it from the plain, now one far-reaching forest, then full of busy homesteads. . . . I shall not easily forget the day when I first entered that lonely, cool, and quiet chamber, so simple and yet so beautiful, where more than 2000 years ago the Great Teacher of Ceylon had sat and thought and worked through the long years of his peaceful and useful life." *

After the death of King Tissa, and of Mahinda, Ceylon was twice overrun and conquered by Dravidian conquerors, who were finally expelled by Watta Gâmini about 88 B.C. And it was then that the Three Pitakas, which had been so long preserved by word of mouth, are said to have been reduced to writing, "seeing the destruction of men," as the Dîpavansa has it.

* Rhys Davids' *Buddhism*, pp. 230, 231.

Buddhagosha was the great commentator of Buddhist sacred works, the Sâyanâchârya of Buddhism. He was a Brâhman of Magadha, and went to Ceylon and wrote the great commentaries for which he is known. He then went to Burma about 450 A.D., and introduced Buddhism into that country.

Buddhism was introduced in Siam in 638 A.D. Java seems to have received Buddhist missionaries about the same time, and Buddhism seems to have spread thence to Sumatra. All these countries belonged to the Southern Buddhist school.

With regard to Northern Buddhism, we know that it was the prevailing faith in the north-west of India before the commencement of the Christian Era. Pushpa Mitra, king of Kashmir, persecuted the Buddhists early in the second century B.C., and Pushpa Mitra's son Agni Mitra met the Greeks on the banks of the Ganges. The Greeks under Menander were victorious, and about 150 B.C. extended their conquests as far as the Ganges. But the victory of the Greeks was no loss to Buddhism, and Nâgasena, a renowned Buddhist teacher of the time, had religious controversies with the Greek king, which have been preserved to us in a most interesting Pâli work.

In the first century after Christ the Yu-Chis under Kanishka conquered Kashmir. Kanishka's vast empire extended over Kabul, over Yarkand and Khokan, over Kashmir and Rajputana, and over the whole of the Punjab, to Gujrat and Sind in the south, and to Agra in the east. He was a zealous Buddhist of the Northern school, and held a Council of 500 monks. If this Council had settled the text as the Council of Asoka at Patna had done, we should now have had in our possession the settled scriptures of Northern Buddhism as we have the Three Pitakas of the South. But Kanishka's Council satisfied itself with writing three commentaries only, and Northern Buddhism therefore has drifted more and more from the original religion, and assumed different forms in different countries. It is necessary to add that Kanishka's Council is unknown to the Southern Buddhists, as Asoka's Council is unknown to the Northern Buddhists. Asvaghosa, who has written a life of Buddha for the Northern Buddhists, lived in Kanishka's court. It is supposed that the Christian apostle St. Thomas visited Western India about this time, and died a martyr. The king Gondophares of the Christian legend is supposed to be Kanishka of Kandahar.

As early as the second century B.C., Buddhist books were taken to the Emperor of China, probably from Kashmir. Another emperor, in 62 A.D., procured more Buddhist works, and Buddhism spread rapidly from that date until it became the state religion in the fourth century.

From China Buddhism spread to Korea in 372 A.D., and thence to Japan in 552 A.D. Kochin-China, Formosa, Mongolia, and other places received Buddhism from China in the fourth and fifth centuries; while from Kabul the religion travelled to Yashkand, Balk, Bokhara, and other places.

Buddhism must have penetrated into Nepal early, but the kingdom became Buddhist in the sixth century, and the first Buddhist king of Thibet sent for scriptures from India in 632 A.D.

We have now narrated the history of the spread of Buddhism in the Southern countries, as well as among the nations of the North and East. And it remains for us only to ascertain the result of the missions which Asoka sent to the West, *i.e.*, to Egypt and Palestine. And this brings us face to face with one of the most interesting questions in the history of modern civilisation and religion.

The remarkable resemblance between the legends, traditions, forms, institutions, and moral precepts of Christianity and those of Buddhism has struck every candid inquirer. A few instances only are cited below.

The myths connected with the birth of Buddha are strangely similar to those relating to the birth of Jesus. In both the cases there was a divine annunciation, both to the father and to the mother of the child, and both the children were miraculously born, or virgin-born. "By the consent of the king," says the Lalita Vistâra, "the queen was permitted to lead the life of a maiden, and not of a wife, for the space of thirty-two months." We are not aware, however, that this myth is to be found in the older Pâli records of the southern Buddhists.

As in the case of Jesus, a star presided at the birth of Gautama, and the star was Pushya, identified by Colebrooke with δ of cancer. Asita, the Simeon of Buddhist story, came to Gautama's father and wished to see the divine child. The child was shown, and the saint foretold that the boy would establish righteousness, and his religion would be widely spread (*Nalaka Sutta.*)

We do not attach much importance to the good omens which are said to have hailed the auspicious event in the one case as in the other. At Buddha's birth "the blind received their sight as if from very longing to behold his glory; the deaf heard the noise; the dumb spake one with another; the crooked became straight; the lame walked; all prisoners were freed from bonds and chains."* Such happy events are narrated by the followers of all religions as attending on the birth of their Great Masters.

We have commented before on the close and remarkable resemblance between the temptation of Gautama and the temptation of Jesus. The story of the temptation is told in a poetic garb in the Lalita Vistâra, but even as told in the southern records, it has a curious resemblance with the Biblical story.

Like Jesus, Gautama had twelve disciples. "Only in my religion," said he shortly before his death, "can be found the twelve great disciples who practise the highest virtues, and excite the world to free itself from its

* Rhys Davids' *Birth Stories*, p. 64.

torments."* And the same missionary spirit impelled the preacher of Kapilavastu and the preacher of Bethlehem. "Let not two of you go the same way," said Gautama. "Preach, O Bhikkhus, the doctrine which is glorious" (*Mahâvagga*, I, 11, 1).

Baptism is common to Buddhism and to Christianity, and indeed John the Baptist adopted the rite of baptism from the Essenes, who admittedly represented the Buddhist movement in Palestine, before the birth of Christ, as we shall see later on. When Jesus was a young preacher in Galilee, the fame of John the Baptist reached him. Jesus went to John and lived with him, and no doubt learnt from John many of the precepts and teachings of the Essenes, and adopted the rite of baptism which John had practised so long. Baptism has since been accepted as a fundamental rite in Christendom. A Christian acknowledges the Father, the Son, and the Holy Ghost at baptism, as a Buddhist, after *abhisheka*, acknowledges Buddha, Dharma, and Sangha.

We pass by the subject of miracles, which are said to have been performed both by Gautama and by Jesus. And we also pass by Gautama's parables, of which we have said something in a previous chapter, and which have such a remarkable resemblance with Christian parables. Renan, who is so unwilling to admit Buddhist influence on the development of the Christian faith, nevertheless states that there was nothing in Judaism which could have furnished Jesus with a model for the parable style. On the other hand, "we find in the Buddhist books parables of exactly the same tone and the same character as the Gospel parables." †

It is when we turn to monastic forms, rites, and ceremonies, that we are struck with the most remarkable resemblance, a resemblance about which Dr. Rhys Davids states, "If all this be chance, it is a most

* Bigandet, p. 301.

† Life of Jesus (translation), p. 136.

stupendous miracle of concidence; it is in fact ten thousand miracles." *

A Roman Catholic missionary, Abbé Huc, was much struck by what he saw in Thibet. "The crosier, the mitre, the dalmatic, the cope or pluvial, which the grand llamas wear on a journey, or when they perform some ceremony outside the temple, the service with a double choir, psalmody, exorcisms, the censer swinging on five chains and contrived to be opened or shut at will, benediction by the llamas with the right hand extended over the heads of the faithful, the chaplet, sacerdotal celibacy, lenten retirements from the world, the worship of saints, fasts, processions, litanies, holy water, these are the points of contact between the Buddhists and ourselves." Mr. Arthur Lillie, from whose book the above passage is quoted, remarks, "The good Abbè has by no means exhausted the list, and might have added confessions, tonsure, relic worship, the use of flowers, lights and images before shrines and altars, the sign of the cross, the Trinity in Unity, the worship of the Queen of Heaven, the use of religious books in a tongue unknown to the bulk of the worshippers, the aureole or nimbus, the crown of saints and Buddhas, wings to angels, penance, flagellations, the flabellum or fan, popes, cardinals, bishops, abbots, presbyters, deacons, the various architectural details of the Christian temple." †

It is not possible for us to go into the details of all these rites and ceremonies, or to point out how the whole fabric and structure of the Roman Catholic system seems like a copy of the Buddhist system. So strong is the resemblance, that the first Christian missionaries who travelled in Thibet believed and recorded their impression that the Buddhist Church had borrowed their rites and forms from the Roman Catholic Church. It is well known, however, that the Buddhists excavated many

* Hibbert Lectures, 1881, p. 93.

† Buddhism in Christendom, p. 202.

of their great church edifices in India before Jesus Christ was born; that a vast monastery, a wealthy church, and a learned university flourished in Nâlanda near Patna, before similar church edifices and monasteries were seen in Europe; and that as Buddhism declined in India, gorgeous Buddhist rites, ceremonials, and institutions were copied from Nâlanda and other places by the Buddhists of Nepal and Thibet, before Europe had yet recovered from the invasions of barbarous races, or had developed her Feudal civilisation or Feudal church system. It is clear, therefore, that the entire structure of church government and church institutions—in so far as there is resemblance between the two systems—was borrowed from the East by the West, not from the West by the East.

But we are not concerned here with the later forms and institutions of the Buddhist Church. The glory of Buddhism consists not in the pompous eeremonials which were witnessed in Nâlanda and Thibet, and which were reproduced after several centuries in Rome, but in the moral precepts of surpassing beauty which were preached in Benares and Râjagriha by Gautama himself, and were repeated after five centuries in Jerusalem. "Never has any one," says M. Renan, "so much as He (Jesus) made the interests of humanity predominate in His life over the littlenesses of self-love. . . . There never was a man, Sâkya Muni, perhaps, excepted, who has to this degree trampled under foot family, the joys of this world, and all temporal care." To do good unto those who smite you, to love those who hate and persecute you, and to relinquish the world for righteousness,—these were the cardinal teachings of Gautama and of Jesus. Was this similarity in precepts merely accidental?

In order to enable our readers to form an opinion on this great question, we will refer them to a few historic facts. We know from the edicts of Asoka that he sent Buddhist missionaries to work in Egypt and in Syria, and these missionaries settled in those countries and formed large and influential Buddhist communities. The Therapeuts of Alexandria and the Essenes of Palestine who were so well known to the Greek world were in fact communities of Buddhist Bhikkhus, practising Buddhist rites, preaching Buddhist doctrines and precepts, and spreading the teachings of Gautama Buddha in the West. Christian thinkers like Dean Mansel. and Dean Milman, and philosophers like Schelling and Schopenhauer alike admit that the Therapeuts and the Essenes sprang from the Buddhist missionaries who came from India.

The communities lived and continued their work. Three centuries after the time of Asoka,—and at the time when Jesus Christ lived and preached,—the Essenes were so well known, and so influential, that the celebrated Pliny wrote of them.

Pliny flourished between 23 and 79 A.D., and thus describes the Essenes:—"On the western shore (of the Dead Sea), but distant from the sea far enough to escape its noxious breezes, dwelt the Essenes. They are an hermit clan, one marvellous beyond all others in the whole world, without any women, with sexual intercourse entirely given up, without money; and the associates of palm-trees. Daily is the throng of those who crowd about them renewed, men resorting to them in numbers, driven through weariness of existence and the surges of ill fortune in their manner of life. Thus it is that through thousands of ages, incredible to relate, their society, in which no one is born, lives on perennial" (*Hist. Nat.*, V, 17).

This is a most remarkable piece of evidence. It is the evidence of an impartial and cultured Roman, describing the progress which Eastern ideas and institutions had made in Palestine at the time of Jesus Christ. We see in the passage given above the result which Buddhist missionaries had achieved in Palestine in three centuries from the time of Asoka. They had founded a sect there answering to the Buddhists of India, and the sect followed the same practices, engaged themselves in the same speculations, and lived the same abstemious and celibate life as the Indian Buddhists. The heritage of Gautama's moral precepts was not lost on them; they revered it and repeated it, and spread it among the pious and thoughtful among the Jews.

We are content to leave the matter here. We have shown that Buddhism was preached in Syria in the third century B.C. We have shown that Buddhism was received in Palestine, and that Buddhists under different names lived in Palestine when Christ was born, and were preaching Gautama's doctrines and moral precepts in Palestine. We have shown that Christ came in contact with their rites and teachings through John, as well as through various other channels probably. And, lastly, we have shown the remarkable resemblance between Christian moral precepts and Buddhist precepts in sentiment and in language, between Christian resignation of the world and Buddhist resignation, between Christian and Buddhist rites and legends and forms. Is this coincidence fortuitous? Let each reader form his own opinion on the subject.

Some writers go so far as to maintain that early Christianity was Essenism, *i.e.*, Buddhism as it prevailed in Palestine. We do not agree in this opinion. Christianity in doctrinal matters is little indebted to Buddhism,—Christ having adopted the national Monotheistic faith of the Jews, as Gautama had adopted the national beliefs of the Hindus in Transmigration and Final Beatitude. Christianity as an ethical and moral advance on the religions of antiquity is indebted to Buddhism, as preached in Palestine by the Essenes when Jesus was born.

CHAPTER XVI.

HISTORY OF JAINAISM.

THE Jaina religion has long been considered as an offshoot from the religion proclaimed by Gautama Buddha. Houen Tsang, who travelled in India in the seventh century after Christ, viewed it in this light; and all that we have hitherto known of the tenets of Jainaism justified this supposition.

Both Lassen and Weber denied, and with very good reasons, the independent origin of the Jaina religion, and both the scholars maintained that the Jainas were seceders from Buddhism, and had branched off from the Buddhists, and formed a sect of their own. The scriptures of the Jainas were not reduced to writing till the fifth century A.D., and Barth held very plausibly that the traditions of the Jainas as to the origin of their religion were formed of vague recollections of the Buddhist tradition. Jaina architecture in India, too, is of comparatively recent date, and, as we shall see in a subsequent chapter, may be said to have commenced centuries after Buddhist architecture had declined and disappeared in India.

Doctors Bühler and Jacobi, however, have recently discovered facts on the basis of which they contend that Jainaism had its commencement at about the same time as the religion of Gautama, and that the two religions flowed in parallel streams for long centuries, until Buddhism declined, while Jainaism still continues to be a living religion in some parts of India. We will place before our readers the facts and traditions on which this opinion is based.

The Jainas, both Svetâmbaras (with white clothing), and Digambaras (without clothing), allege that Mahâvîra, the founder of the religion, was the son of Siddhârtha of Kundagrâma, and belonged to the clan of Jnâtrika Kshatriyas. We know that Gautama Buddha, when travelling in Kotigrâma, was visited by the courtesan Ambapâli and the Lichchavis. This Kotigrâma is identified with Kundagrâma of the Jainas, and the Nâtikas spoken of in the Buddhist Scriptures are identified with the Jnâtrika Kshatriyas. Further, Mahâvîra's mother Trisaâ is said to have been the sister of Kataka, king of Vaisâli, whose daughter was married to the renowned Bimbisâra, king of Magadha.

Mahâvîra, at first called Vardhamâna or Jnâtriputra, was like his father a Kâsyapa. At the age of twenty-eight he entered into the Holy Order, and after twelve years of self-mortification, became a Kevalin or Jina, Tîrthakara or Mahâvîra, *i.e.*, a saint and prophet. During the last thirty years of his life he organised his Order of ascetics. He was thus a rival of Gautama Buddha, and is mentioned in Buddhist writings under the name of Nâtaputra as the head of the Niganthas (Nirgranthas, without clothing), already a numerous sect in Vaisâli. Mahâvîra died at Pâpâ.

The Jaina tradition goes on to say that in the second century after Mahâvîra's death there was a famine in Magadha. The renowned Chandragupta was then the sovereign of Magadha. Bhadrabâhu, with a portion of his Jaina followers, left Magadha under pressure of the famine and went to Karnâta. During his absence, the Jainas of Magadha settled their scriptures, consisting of the eleven Angas and the fourteen Puvvas, which latter are sometimes called the twelfth Anga. On the return of peace and plenty, the exiled Jainas returned to Magadha; but within these years a difference in custom had arisen between those who had stayed in Magadha, and those who had gone to Karnâta. The former had assumed a white dress, and the latter adhered to the old rule of absolute nakedness. The former were thus called Svetâmbras, the latter were called Digambaras. The scriptures which had been settled by the former were not accepted by the latter, and for the Digambaras therefore there are no Angas. The final division between the two sects is said to have taken place in 79 or 82 A.D.

In course of time the scriptures of the Svetâmbaras fell into disorder, and were in danger of becoming extinct. It was necessary to record them into writing, and this was done at the Council of Vallabhi (in Gujrat) in 454 or 467 A.D. The operations of the Council resulted in the redaction of the Jaina canon, in the form in which we find it at the present day.*

Besides these facts and traditions, inscriptions have been discovered on the pedestals of Jaina statues at Mathura which, according to Dr. Bühler (who first discovered this evidence), proves that the Svetâmbara sect existed in the first century A.D. The inscriptions are dated according to the era of Kanishka, king of Kashmir, *i.e.*, the Saka Era, 78 A.D. One of the inscriptions, dated 9 of the Era (and therefore corresponding to 87 A.D.), states that the statue was erected by a Jaina lay-woman Vikatâ.

Such is the substance of the evidence on which it is contended that the Jaina religion is coeval with Buddhism, and not an offshoot from that religion. From the mention of "Nâtaputra" and of the "Nirgranthas" in the Buddhist Scriptures, it is reasonable to suppose that the Jaina sect of unclad ascetics had its origin too about the same time. Indeed, we have repeatedly stated before that various sects of ascetics lived in India at the time when Gautama Buddha lived and taught and

* Dr. Hœrnle's Introduction to his translation of the Uvâsagadasâo.

led *his* sect of ascetics. What we find it difficult to accept is that the Jaina religion, as we have it now, was professed by the Nirgranthas of the sixth century B.C. The story that the Jaina canon was settled in a Council in Magadha at the time of Chandragupta is probably a pure myth; and even if that story was true, the canon settled in the third century B.C. would be very different from the canon recorded in the fifth century A.D. For there can be little doubt that the early tenets of the first Nirgranthas have long since been modified, and completely transformed; and that the more cultured section of that body, who adopted a white garment, continuously borrowed their maxims and precepts, their rules and customs, their legends and traditions from Buddhism, which was the prevailing religion of India after the third century B.C. Thus the Jainas drifted more and more towards Buddhism for long centuries, until they had adopted the substance of the Buddhist religion as their own, and very little of the early tenets of the unclad Nirgranthas was left. It was then,—in the fifth century A.D.,—that their scriptures were recorded, and it is no wonder that those scriptures appear like a copy of the Buddhist Scriptures recorded *six centuries before*. Admitting, then, the independent origin of the Nirgranthas in the sixth century B.C., we hardly think Houen Tsang was very far wrong, when he described the Jaina religion, as he saw it in the seventh century (and as we see it in the present day), to be an offshoot from Buddhism.

Among the other sects of ascetics which flourished side by side with the Buddhists and the Nirgranthas in the sixth century B.C., the Âjîvakas founded by Gosâla were the best known in their day. Asoka names them in his inscriptions, along with the Brâhmans and Nirgranthas. Gosâla was therefore a rival of Buddha and Mahâvîra; but his sect has now ceased to exist.

It follows from what has been stated before, that the religious tenets of the Jainas differ but slightly from that of the Buddhists. Like the Buddhists, the Jainas have their Monastic Order, and they refrain from killing animals, and praise retirement from the world. In some respects they even go further than the Buddhists, and maintain that not only animals and plants, but the smallest particles of the elements, fire, air, earth, and water, are endowed with life or jîva. For the rest, the Jainas, like the Buddhists, reject the Veda, they accept the tenets of *Karma* and of *Nirvâna*, and believe in the transmigration of souls. They also believe in 25 Tîrthakaras, as the early Buddhists believed in 24 Buddhas who had risen before Gautama Buddha.

The sacred books or Âgamas of the Jainas consist of seven divisions, among which the Angas form the first and most important division. The Angas are eleven in number, of which the Âchârânga Sûtra, setting forth the rules of conduct of Jaina monks, has been translated by Dr. Jacobi, and the Upâsakadasâh, setting forth the rules of conduct of Jaina laymen, has been translated by Dr. Hœrnle.

We will now present our readers with some extracts relating to the life of Mahâvîra from the Âchârânga Sûtra. Hermann Jacobi, the learned translator of the work, assigns to it the third or fourth century B.C., but from the verbose and artificial language of the work, many readers will be inclined to assign to it a date as many centuries after Christ. The entire work reads like a very distant and very perverted imitation of the simple Buddhist accounts of the life of Gautama.

"When the Kshatriyânî Trisalâ, having seen these fourteen illustrious great dreams, awoke, she was glad, pleased and joyful, ... rose from her couch and descended from the footstool. Neither hasty nor trembling, with a quick and even gait like that of a royal swan, she went to the couch of the Kshatriya Siddhârtha. There she awakened the Kshatriya Siddhârtha, addressing him with kind, pleasing, amiable, tender, illustrious, beautiful, lucky, blest, auspicious, fortunate, heart-going, heart-easing, well-measured, sweet and soft words . . . . 'O beloved of the gods, I was just now on my couch . . . . and awoke after having seen the fourteen dreams, to wit, an elephant, &c. What, to be sure, O my Lord, will be the happy result portended by these fourteen illustrious great dreams?' . . . . He grasped the meaning of those dreams with his own innate intelligence and intuition, which were preceded by reflection, and addressing the Kshatriyâni Trisalâ with kind, pleasing, &c., words, spoke thus: 'O beloved of the gods, you have seen illustrious dreams, &c. . . . . you will give birth to a lovely, handsome boy, who will be the ensign of our family, the lamp of our family, the crown of our family, the frontal ornament of our family, the maker of our family's glory, the sun of our family, the stay of our family, the maker of our family's joy and fame, the tree of our family, the exalter of our family.' . . . .

"Surrounded by many chieftains, satraps, kings, princes, knights, sheriffs, heads of families, ministers, chief ministers, astrologers, counsellors, servants, dancing masters, citizens, traders, merchants, foremen of guilds, generals, leaders of caravans, messengers, and frontier-guards, he—the lord and chief of men, a bull and a lion among men, shining with excellent lustre and glory, lovely to behold, like the moon emerging from a great white cloud in the midst of the flock of the planets and of brilliant stars and asterisms—left the bathing-house, entered the exterior hall of audience, and sat down on his throne with the face towards the east . . . . 'Quickly, O beloved of the gods, call the interpreters of dreams who well know the science of prognostics with its eight branches, and are well versed in many sciences besides!' . . . . When the interpreters of dreams had heard and perceived this news from the Kshatriya Siddhârtha, they—glad, pleased, and joyful, &c.—fixed the dreams in their minds, entered upon considering them, and conversed together. . . . .

"In that night in which the venerable ascetic Mahâvîra

was born, there was a divine lustre originated by many descending and ascending gods and goddesses, and in the universe, resplendent with one light, the conflux of gods occasioned great confusion and noise. . . . Before the venerable ascetic Mahâvîra had adopted the life of a householder (*i.e.* before his marriage), he possessed supreme, unlimited, unimpeded knowledge and intuition. The venerable ascetic Mahâvîra perceived with this his supreme unlimited knowledge and intuition that the time for his Renunciation had come. He left his silver, he left his gold, he left his riches, corn, majesty, and kingdom, his army, grain, treasure, storehouse, town, seraglio, and subjects; he quitted and rejected his real, valuable property, such as riches, gold, precious stones, jewels, pearls, conches, stones, corals, rubies, &c.; he distributed presents through proper persons. He distributed presents among indigent persons. . . . The venerable ascetic Mahâvîra for a year and a month wore clothes; after that time he walked about naked, and accepted the alms in the hollow of his hand. For more than twelve years the venerable ascetic Mahâvîra neglected his body and abandoned the care of it; he with equanimity bore, underwent, and suffered all pleasant or unpleasant occurrences arising from divine powers, men, or animals. . . . During the thirteenth year, in the second month of summer, in the fourth fortnight, the light (fortnight) of Vaisâkha, on its tenth day, when the shadow had turned towards the east and the first wake was over, on the day called Suvrata, in the Muhûrta called Vijaya, outside of the town Jrimbhikagrâma on the bank of the river Rijupâlikâ, not far from an old temple, in the field of the householder Sâmâga, under a sal tree, when the moon was in conjunction with the asterism Uttaraphalgunî (the Venerable One) in a squatting position with joined heels exposing himself to the heat of the sun, after fasting two and a half days without drinking water, being engaged in deep meditation, reached the highest knowledge and intuition, called

Kevala, which is infinite, supreme, unobstructed, unimpeded, complete, and full. . . .

"In that period, in that age, the venerable ascetic Mahâvîra stayed the first rainy season in Asthikagrâma, three rainy seasons in Champâ and Prishtichampâ, twelve in Vaisâli and Vanijagrâma, fourteen in Râjagriha and the suburb of Nâlanda, six in Mithilâ, two in Bhadrikâ, one in Alabhikâ, one in Panitabhûmi, one in Srâvasti, one in the town of Pâpâ, in king Hastipâla's office of the writers: that was his very last rainy season. In the fourth month of that rainy season, in the seventh fortnight, in the dark (fortnight) of Kârtika, on its fifteenth day, in the last night, in the town of Pâpâ, in king Hastipâla's office of the writers, the venerable ascetic Mahâvîra died, went off, quitted the world, cut asunder the ties of birth, old age, and death; became a Siddha, a Buddha, a Mukta, a maker of the end (to all misery), finally liberated, freed from all pains."

The Upâsakadasâh, as its name indicates, details the duties of Jaina laymen in ten lectures. The first lecture details the vows and observances that must regulate a layman's conduct; the next four lectures detail various kinds of temptations arising from external persecutions; the sixth lecture treats of temptations from internal doubts, and specially from the antagonism of other religions, like that of the Âjîvakas founded by Gosâla; the seventh shows the superiority of the Jaina religion; the eighth dwells on the temptations to sensual enjoyments; and the ninth and tenth give examples of a quiet and peaceful career of a faithful Jaina layman.

We are unable to make room for extracts from Dr. Hœrnle's translation of this work, but we will glean some facts from the portion which treats of Ânanda's conversion, which will be interesting, as detailing many articles of luxury in which a Hindu householder indulged in the olden times. Ânanda does not become a monk, but only becomes a Jaina layman, and he therefore takes the five lesser vows, *anu-vratâni*, in contrast with the *mahâ-vratâni* of monks, as also the disciplinary vows.

Ânanda renounces all gross ill-usage of living beings, all gross lying, and all gross theft. He contents himself with one wife, saying, "excepting with one woman, Sivanandâ my wife, I renounce every other kind of sexual intercourse." He limits himself to the possession of a *treasure* of four kror measures of gold deposited in a safe place, of a *capital* of four kror measures of gold put out on interest, and of a well-stocked *estate* of the value of four kror measures of gold. Similarly he limits himself to the possession of four herds, each consisting of ten thousand head of cattle; to the possession of 500 ploughs and land at the rate of 100 *nivartanas* for each plough; to the possession of five hundred carts for foreign traffic, and five hundred carts for home traffic; and lastly, to the possession of four boats for foreign traffic and four boats for home use. The above enumeration gives us a very fair idea of a Hindu capitalist, land-owner, money-lender, and merchant of olden days,—a Seth, such as Jains have always been in India. We now turn to the articles of household use and luxury.

Ânanda limits himself to one kind of red-tinted bathing towel, to one kind of green stick for tooth-cleaning, to one kind of fruit, the milky pulp of Âmalaka, to two kinds of oil as unguents, to one kind of scented powder, to eight *gharas* of washing water, to one kind of clothes, viz., "a pair of cotton clothes;" to perfumes made of aloes, saffron, sandal, and similar substances, to one kind of flower, the white lotus, to two kinds of ornaments, viz., ear-pendants and a finger-ring engraved with his name, and to certain kinds of incense.

With regard to food, he limits himself in his use of beverages to a decoction of pulses or rice, and in the use of pastry to such as are fried in clarified butter or turned in sugar. He confines himself to boiled rice of the cultivated varieties, to *dâl* made of *kalai*, *mug*, or *mâs*, to clarified butter produced from cows' milk in autumn, to certain kinds of curry, to one kind of liquor made from *pâlangâ*, to plain relishes or sauces, to rain water as drinking water, and lastly, to betel with its five spices. Many of our readers will be inclined to think that our friend Ânanda with his broad acres and large trade, and with the articles of use and luxury left to him, was not so badly off after all.

END OF VOL. I.